ALWAYS FIGHTING IRISH

PLAYERS, COACHES, AND FANS SHARE THEIR PASSION FOR NOTRE DAME FOOTBALL

JOHN HEISLER & TIM PRISTER
FOREWORD BY REGGIE BROOKS

TRIUMPH
BOOKS

This book is available in quantity at special discounts for your group or organization. For further information, contact:

Triumph Books LLC
814 North Franklin Street
Chicago, Illinois 60610
(312) 337-0747
www.triumphbooks.com

Printed in the U.S.A.
ISBN 978-1-60078-754-6
Design and editorial production by Prologue Publishing Services LLC
All photos courtesy of Notre Dame Archives unless otherwise indicated

*To Roger Valdiserri and Bill Callahan, two pillars
of the sports information/media relations business—
they knew what quality writing was all about*

CONTENTS

FOREWORD

WE SPENT 13 HOURS driving through the night in the van. The whole time I was thinking, *Where are we going?*

I was 16 years old and a junior at Booker T. Washington High School in Tulsa, Oklahoma. Before we got in the van, I had played a high school football game under the lights that Friday night. I went home, took a quick shower, and then my parents, aunt, uncle, and I hit the road, heading northeast more than 700 miles.

I had no idea what Notre Dame football was about until they started recruiting my older brother, Tony. I thought Notre Dame was in France. I didn't even think it was in the United States. I just remember seeing the Golden Dome in commercials.

But now, after that 13-hour trip, we were driving down Notre Dame Avenue on Saturday morning. I was going to see my brother play for the Irish, and now I saw the Golden Dome in person. It was a game day at home against that West Coast rival, the Trojans of USC. The leaves were turning as they do in autumn. Thousands of people were walking around the campus. I had been to campuses at Oklahoma State and Oklahoma and Tulsa, but there was a distinct difference coming here.

I don't want to say "magical" because that is a cliché, but there was something different, something awe-inspiring. Years later, Coach Lou Holtz captured what I had experienced that morning: "If you have never been a part of Notre Dame and are asked to explain it, you can't. There are no words to describe what we have here. But once you've been a part of the Notre Dame family, no explanation is necessary."

That day, Notre Dame came into the game with a 4–1 record, and USC was 4–2. The Trojans scored early, but the Fighting Irish unleashed a dominant ground attack, tallying 351 yards. My brother, a freshman, had four carries for 12 yards and a catch for two. USC scored a meaningless touchdown late in the game, and Notre Dame won 26–15. It marked the fourth consecutive victory the Irish posted against USC.

I grew up going to see Oklahoma play Oklahoma State. I had witnessed editions of the Red River Rivalry between Texas and Oklahoma. Those rivalries are intense. But seeing Notre Dame–USC was off the charts. That was the deal, and it just stuck with me. The excitement and the intensity of that game were something I had never seen before. It was just awesome. To have the opportunity to be part of that always stuck with me as I finished my high school years.

It is common for football players to talk about how much we value the bond we have with the teammates with whom we line up, the guys who were at our side when we went into battle. My time at Notre Dame is no different. Well, I guess there might be one difference in the bond players of my era shared, and it is initially summed up in three words: *Lou Holtz practices.* They were intense...and I mean *intense.*

The best examples were set by my teammates in the backfield. On any given practice during my time, I was competing with Ricky Watters, Jerome Bettis, Rodney Culver, Anthony Johnson, and my brother Tony. Those guys taught me how to practice and to practice with a purpose every day. You had to step up and bring your A game or you needed to go home. I didn't necessarily enjoy practice, but I hated losing more—so pushing through practice was a requisite action.

Later I would find that these grueling sessions weren't unique to my era, but they were unique to winning. When I talk to guys who played for Ara Parseghian and guys who played for Frank Leahy, intense practices are a common denominator. They all talk about how critical it was to do the little things in practice. Practice under Coach Holtz—and from what I gather, from Ara's era and during Leahy's time—made the games feel as if they were a break. I've heard players like Ross Browner and Johnny Lujack talk about the rigorous nature of practice. We all felt we were so well prepared that losing just wasn't a possibility—and that stemmed from how we were drilled before game day. When we got to the game, we knew we were ready.

There's another common denominator you hear when you talk to players from the Holtz, Parseghian, and Leahy eras—a love for one another. This commitment to one another is built on the practice field, in the classroom, and in sharing the Notre Dame experience. It's not easy to be a football player at Notre Dame. Some people might believe it's a perfect world. It's not. If you want to take the easy road out, Notre Dame is definitely not the place for you. It's not easy. If you're not dealing with something challenging, it's not going to make you any better. And you know if you made it through Notre Dame, you accomplished something. All of us had the privilege of sharing that road together, and along that path our love grew for each other.

That's the thing that really got me: if you want to be great, if you're committed to working hard, then Notre Dame is where you want to be. That is the tone of success on this campus. You can turn a tape recorder on and talk to 20 different guys from different decades, and you will hear that very same message.

In my junior year we lost three games, and there was talk of our maybe not going to a bowl game. Some suggested we didn't deserve to go. That resonated with the team. You lose some games, and how do you rebound from those losses? Sometimes you can lose your way and lose your focus. How do you recover from that? We found our answer at the Sugar Bowl. Some others might remember this game as the "Cheerios Bowl." No matter what you call it, 18th-ranked Notre Dame ran all over third-ranked Florida in a 39–28 victory.

Our last home game in 1992 against Penn State has been dubbed the "Snow Bowl." On fourth down and with less than 30 seconds to go, Rick Mirer connected with Jerome Bettis on a touchdown pass to pull us to within one at 16–15. We had used our typical two-point conversion play on the touchdown, so now we had to call something different. Rick dropped back and looked left. Then he rolled to his right. Penn State defenders were closing in on him. He pumped the ball once and then threw a wobbling ball to the back corner of the end zone where I was streaking across the field. I caught it as I fell to the ground and slid. We won the game, and it was a mob scene. I almost got trampled to death.

A lot of people remember the touchdown run I had against Michigan where I was spun around and knocked out as I entered the end zone. I don't. Hanging in my office is a painting of me crossing the goal line. But it's a play I don't even remember. After the game, reporters asked me, "What happened? Take us through that play." There was no way I could recount it. Now, when people ask, I tell them, "From what I saw on the replay, that's a pretty good run." But in the moments following the game, I had no clue. I saw the hit coming, but that is the last thing I recall. I was knocked out for a few seconds in the end zone. All I remember is the smelling salts and thinking, *Wow, what happened?*

Those may be considered my "big" moments at Notre Dame. But I don't see it that way. I just enjoyed playing with my teammates. Again, that bond was always the biggest thrill for me and it still is today.

This program has endured through the years. The game of football has evolved and changed multiple times as Knute Rockne, Leahy, Parseghian, Dan Devine, and Holtz have shepherded the Fighting Irish flock. Through it all, from the invention of the forward pass to speeches about winning one for the Gipper to battles with Army in New York City to legendary tales about chicken soup, there are a few things that remain constant. To be successful at Notre Dame you play for your teammates, you develop a demanding work ethic, and you practice hard—all of that transcends time. I'm just a thread in time that can hopefully connect Notre Dame's past to a bright future.

—Reggie Brooks
Notre Dame, Indiana
May 5, 2012

INTRODUCTION

THE VENERABLE SPORTS print offering *Sporting News* celebrated its 125th birthday in November 2011 with a special commemorative issue that featured the best of just about everything in athletics from 1886 to 2011.

On page 122, the headline read, "Three Reasons South Bend Is Our Best College Football City."

Sporting News college football staff writer Matt Hayes then went on to detail why South Bend and, in effect, the University of Notre Dame earned the No. 1 nod:

- There's nothing like the campus.
- The history and tradition are unmatched.
- The future is always bright.

Dig down into the second point, and here's what else Hayes offered:

> Where do we begin? Knute Rockne or Lou Holtz? The Four Horsemen or Joe Montana? Maybe it's safe to begin with 11 national championships, seven Heisman Trophy winners, and 99 All-Americans. The second-highest winning percentage in college football history and the third-most wins and fewest losses all-time. Twelve undefeated seasons.... Maybe the most telling number of all is 50: the number of players

and coaches Notre Dame has in the College Football Hall of Fame, more than any other school. "We've had some lean years lately," says Notre Dame legend Paul Hornung. "But that doesn't diminish the history that was built by all those players and teams of the past."

So, as Notre Dame celebrates 125 years of football in 2012 (first game in 1887), it's worth noting that a good reason for its prominence in ratings like that conducted by *Sporting News* comes from the sheer longevity of the Irish success over the decades.

Three national titles in the 1920s under Rockne. Four more in the 1940s under Frank Leahy. Two more in the 1960s and 1970s with Ara Parseghian—then another under Dan Devine in 1977 and one more in '88 with Holtz.

Sprinkled in between are dozens of All-Americans and major award-winners. The Irish produced Heisman winners in the decades of the 1940s, 1950s, 1960s, and 1980s.

Plus, Notre Dame has never been short on the little bits of color and pageantry that make the college game so appealing—"Win One for the Gipper," *Rudy*, and "Play Like A Champion Today."

Notre Dame athletics director and vice president Jack Swarbrick likes to use the 1913 Notre Dame–Army game as a history primer when it comes to Irish football. In his estimation, that one game maybe did more than any other single football contest to set the stage for what Notre Dame has been all about on the gridiron.

It included Notre Dame making its longest road trip yet to play one of the established powers of the day. And winning. It's probably no accident that Rockne had a hand in that victory—and lots of others in the nearly two decades that he played a major role in Notre Dame fortunes as both a coach and player.

If that victory at West Point set the table for what was to come, it's still worth considering all the many things that needed to fall into place for the Notre Dame program to achieve the long-term success it has enjoyed.

What if those individuals running the Western Conference (later to become the Big Ten) hadn't rebuffed Notre Dame and its interest in joining that conference? Notre Dame's resulting long-term independence might never have enabled the Irish to build their reputation by playing from coast to coast and border to border.

What if Rockne's family hadn't opted for Chicago as its destination on its trip from Norway? Maybe young Knute would have played end somewhere else other than South Bend.

What if Rockne hadn't spied a youthful George Gipp on campus and convinced him to give football a try? Gipp instead today might reside in Cooperstown in the Baseball Hall of Fame.

What if veteran sportswriter Grantland Rice had received a different assignment that Saturday in October 1924? Maybe the Four Horsemen would never have been baptized.

What if the wives of Rockne and USC coach Howard Jones had never made acquaintance on that train and then never convinced their husbands of the worth of a Notre Dame–Southern California football game? We might never have been treated to the glorious moments that Irish-USC series has provided.

What if Rockne's teams had never enjoyed the successes they did? That surely proved a factor in Rockne being able to convince the Notre Dame administration that a structure like Notre Dame Stadium made sense.

What if Rockne had never boarded that plane in Kansas City that fell to the earth in Bazaar, Kansas? No matter what else he might have gone on to accomplish, it's hard to imagine he could be any more revered today than he is.

What if Leahy had decided, after two landmark seasons at Boston College, to remain at Chestnut Hill? The sheer volume of talent on campus might still have been so overwhelming that the Irish in the late 1940s might still have found ways to win Saturday after Saturday.

What if Louisville product Hornung had listened to his mother and stayed home and attended Kentucky instead of coming to Notre Dame? Irish fans might have missed watching one of the more multitalented players in Notre Dame history.

What if Parseghian, a Presbyterian whose Northwestern teams had their way with the Irish six straight years, had decided he had a good thing going in Evanston?

What if quarterback Joe Theismann had been adamant about telling Notre Dame sports information director Roger Valdiserri that his name was really pronounced THEESE-mun?

What if Montana had accepted a basketball scholarship from North Carolina State?

What if Holtz hadn't had the foresight to include a clause in his coaching contract at Minnesota that enabled him to leave if the Notre Dame job became available?

What if administrators from Notre Dame and NBC Sports hadn't been able to handcraft an agreement for the network to carry Irish home games starting in 1991?

Maybe one or more of those decisions going the other way might have impacted Notre Dame football fortunes to some extent. However, the lengthy laundry list of blue-chip players and coaches who have performed so admirably over time (it's almost an exact century since that 1913 win over Army that Swarbrick cites) suggests that not much about the game in South Bend is an accident.

All things considered, even as the players and coaches come and go, not much has changed about Notre Dame football.

The Irish still play in essentially the same facility they did 80 years ago—even if an extra 20,000 seats joined the manifest in 1997.

The same white end zone stripes and the same devotion to avoiding corporate logos and signage have enabled Notre Dame Stadium to maintain its simple look.

The Irish still play games from coast to coast and recruit players from Texas to Minnesota, from Seattle to West Palm Beach.

They still enjoy a widespread rabid fandom—with a relatively small (but geographically spread) alumni base supplemented by an even more vociferous subway alumni faction.

They still enjoy substantial exposure—not much that takes place at Notre Dame goes unnoticed.

And they still, maybe better than ever, graduate just about everyone who comes to campus to take part in athletics of any sort. That's always counted at Notre Dame.

So, whether you're a died-in-the-wool Irish fanatic—or simply a casual college football observer—sit back and enjoy the ride.

Always Fighting Irish is designed to take you through the names and seasons and traditions and championships.

When Theismann talked about bottling the Notre Dame spirit, he knew enough about marketing to suggest it could fetch a pretty price on the exchange.

And that indomitable spirit hasn't faded, as Irish players and coaches and teams through the years continue their assignments to wake up the echoes and shake down the thunder.

chapter 1

THE TRADITIONS OF NOTRE DAME: PLAYING LIKE A CHAMPION FOR 125 YEARS

EVERY SCHOOL THAT PLAYS football boasts the normal trappings—the game itself, the band and cheerleaders, the tailgating, and the usual spots for pregame and postgame (and Friday night) revelry. At Notre Dame, you'll find a few items you don't see every day—and they're particular parts of the fabric of football on the Irish campus. Check these out—in fact, you can go to see and touch most of these for yourself:

1. PLAY LIKE A CHAMPION TODAY

It's just a simple wooden sign, painted gold and blue and mounted on a cream-colored brick wall at the foot of a stairwell in Notre Dame Stadium. Yet, the "Play Like A Champion Today" sign, found outside Notre Dame's locker room, is one of the most recognizable in the world.

While no one knows the exact origin of the slogan, the sign that currently hangs in Notre Dame Stadium came courtesy of former Irish coach Lou Holtz. "I read a lot of books about the history of Notre Dame and its football program," Holtz explains.

"I forget which book I was looking at—it had an old picture in it that showed the slogan 'Play Like a Champion Today.' I said, 'That is really appropriate; it used to be at Notre Dame and we needed to use it again.' So, I had that sign made up."

Irish players began hitting the sign before every game, creating a ritual that developed into a tradition. Holtz even used a copy of the sign when traveling to road contests to help motivate the team.

The slogan caught fire not long after NBC Sports began televising Irish home games in 1991, when broadcast producers stuck a camera above the door leading to the stairs down to the Notre Dame Stadium tunnel. The camera pointed toward the "Play Like a Champion Today" sign, so viewers would watch the Irish hit the sign as they passed it either coming or going to the locker room.

The person responsible for the look of the sign is Laurie Wenger, a longtime sign painter at the Joyce Center. Now retired, she created the graphic look and color scheme that became as recognizable as the phrase itself—and the University allowed her to maintain the rights to the phrase. Stop by the bookstore and you'll find more than your share of products bearing the familiar phrase—and loyal fans have been know to create their own one-off phrases that say, "(Fill in the blank) Like A Champion Today."

Mention "Play Like A Champion Today" to almost anyone who follows collegiate sports—and the connection to Notre Dame is almost instantaneous.

2. Touchdown Jesus

The 132-foot-high stone mosaic on the south side of the Hesburgh Library was patterned after Millard Sheet's painting, "The Word of Life," with Christ as teacher surrounded by his apostles and an assembly of saints and scholars who have contributed to knowledge through the ages. A gift of Mr. and Mrs. Howard Phalin, the mural contains 80 different types of stone material from 16 countries, plus 171 finishes during the fabrication stage and 5,714 individual pieces. The mural of Christ with upraised hands—which is visible from inside parts of Notre Dame Stadium—often is referred to as "Touchdown Jesus." Since the expansion of Notre Dame Stadium in 1997 added additional height to the facility, the mosaic isn't as easily visible from locales inside the Irish arena. Still, it remains difficult to miss since the library is located directly north of Notre Dame Stadium.

3. WE'RE NO. 1 MOSES

Crafted by Josef Turkalj—a protégé of Notre Dame's famed artist-in-residence Ivan Mestrovic—this bronze sculpture is located on the west side of Hesburgh Library. Known to many as "We're No. 1 Moses," the sculpture depicts Moses in flowing robes at the foot of Mt. Sinai as he chastises the Israelites who have fallen into idolatry in his absence. His right hand is extended heavenward as he declares there is but one God (creating the reference to "We're No. 1") while his left hand grasps the stone tablets upon which God has inscribed the Ten Commandments, with the right knee bent as his foot crushes the head of the golden calf idol. Leave it to Notre Dame fans and students to create a football connection to a religious sculpture.

4. FAIR-CATCH CORBY

A campus sculpture placed in front of Corby Hall in 1911 depicts Chaplain William J. Corby, C.S.C., with his right arm raised in the act of giving absolution to the Irish Brigade before its members went into action on the three-day Battle of Gettysburg (July 2, 1863). A duplicate sculpture that honors his long service to the Union cause was dedicated on the battlefield in 1910. Corby served as Notre Dame's president from 1866 to 1872 and again from 1887 to 1891. His campus sculpture also is known to the Notre Dame football faithful as "Fair-Catch Corby."

5. NOTRE DAME STADIUM

Any list of iconic sporting facilities generally includes a handful of usual suspects, most of them with great history—Yankee Stadium, Madison Square Garden, Lambeau Field, Wimbledon, the Augusta National Golf Club (home of the Masters). Include a college football stop and it's hard to ignore Notre Dame Stadium. Around since 1930 and designed by Notre Dame Hall of Fame coach Knute Rockne (he modeled it to some extent after Michigan Stadium in Ann Arbor), it hasn't changed all that much over the years. In fact, when the 1997 expansion added about 20,000 new seats, part of the charm of the construction plan became the intent to build the areas holding the new seats on the outside of the original structure—then marrying the old and new portions together. That meant that the vast majority of the original stadium walls could still be preserved in the lower concourses of the facility. Even in the home locker room area (that doubled in size from the original space) for the Notre Dame team, original bricks were preserved, re-gilded, and then reused to maintain the look and feel of the old stadium. A new shower and restroom area was constructed—yet the original sections remained intact. And nothing has really changed at all as far as the stairs down to the tunnel and field level—with the "Play Like a Champion Today" sign appearing the same as ever at the bottom of that stairwell. That sign remains probably the most photographed aspect of Notre Dame Stadium. Access to Notre Dame Stadium has increased in recent years, with the north tunnel entrance available on home football Fridays for fans to walk down to the edge of the field. Old-school Irish fans like the fact that not much has changed over the years as far as the look of the inner bowl itself. No logos have appeared on the field, with plain diagonal stripes gracing the two end zones. The lone corporate identifications are signage acknowledging NBC Sports and IMG as Notre Dame's television and radio partners for football. Notre Dame Stadium remains one of the few Football Bowl Subdivision facilities without video boards (there are message boards at both ends that are part of the scoreboards).

6. PEP RALLIES

For years the old Notre Dame Fieldhouse in the middle of campus played host to Irish football pep rallies—with the Irish squad seated in the balcony. Later those events moved to Stepan Center when that geodesic-domed building came online in the 1960s. But that was back when pep rallies essentially were campus-only events. Thanks to expanded interest during the Gerry Faust and Lou Holtz eras, Irish fans at large began to show a keen interest in attending these Friday night events, and the fire marshals determined that the events had outgrown the Stepan space. For a while rallies played festival style in the north dome of the Joyce Center, then eventually settled for some years into the arena in the Joyce Center's south dome (now Purcell Pavilion).

A few rallies on especially big weekends have switched to Notre Dame Stadium, and most recently Irish Green has become the more consistent locale for outdoor rallies—as ticketing and seating challenges indoors prompted a need for more flexibility and capacity for fans. Another change in recent years has been the inclusion of the traditional Dillon Hall rally (formerly a Thursday night tradition prior to the first Notre Dame home game) as the Friday site on the initial home weekend.

Content for the rallies generally has included remarks from a combination of players and coaches, plus involvement from the

Band of the Fighting Irish and cheerleaders. Over the years all kinds of names have been celebrity guest speakers—from former Irish football greats to Regis Philbin to Wayne Gretzky and Jon Bon Jovi and many more. National championship teams returning for reunions often have been feted, as well.

One of the more memorable rallies took place outdoors prior to the 1988 Notre Dame–Miami game—in a makeshift area near Grace and Flanner Halls on the north end of campus. At that event, Irish coach Lou Holtz in some form promised an Irish win—leading him to later opine that "you should never be held responsible for anything said at a pep rally."

Plans for rallies remain a work in progress. However, it's safe to say Notre Dame is the only school in the country that for years has held a pep rally on the Friday night prior to every single home game.

In recent years Notre Dame students have planned campus rallies prior to a few select road games—and the Notre Dame Alumni Association often plans rallies at its designated hotels for road games.

The biggest lure for the Irish rallies? Special guests generally have not been announced in advance, so there's always been some level of curiosity as to exactly who would appear at a particular rally and exactly what would be said.

7. VICTORY MARCH

The most recognizable collegiate fight song in the nation, the "Notre Dame Victory March" was written in the early 1900s by two brothers who both qualified as University of Notre Dame graduates. Michael Shea, a 1905 graduate, composed the music while his brother, John Shea, who earned degrees in 1906 and 1908, provided the corresponding lyrics. The song was copyrighted in 1908 and a piano version, complete with lyrics, was published that year. Michael, who became a priest in Ossining,

New York, collaborated on the project with John, who lived in Holyoke, Massachusetts. Michael Shea was pastor of St. Augustine's Church in Ossining until his death in 1938. John Shea, a baseball monogram winner at Notre Dame, became a Massachusetts state senator and lived in Holyoke until his death in 1965.

The song's public debut came in the winter of 1908, when Michael played it on the organ of the Second Congregational Church in Holyoke. The "Notre Dame Victory March" later was presented by the Shea brothers to the University, and it first appeared under the copyright of the University of Notre Dame in 1928. The copyright was assigned to the publishing company of Edwin H. Morris, and the copyright for the beginning of the song still is in effect. The more well-known second verse, which begins with the words "Cheer, cheer for Old Notre Dame," is considered part of public domain in the United States (for both the music and lyrics)—but the second verse remains protected in all territories outside of the country.

Notre Dame's fight song first was performed at Notre Dame on Easter in 1909 in the rotunda of the Main Administration Building. The Notre Dame band, under the direction of Prof. Clarence Peterson, performed the "Victory March" as part of its traditional Easter morning concert. It was first heard at a Notre Dame athletic event 10 years later. In 1969, as college football celebrated its centennial, the "Notre Dame Victory March" was honored as the "greatest of all fight songs."

> *Rally sons of Notre Dame*
> *Sing her glory and sound her fame,*
> *Raise her Gold and Blue*
> *And cheer with voices true:*
> *Rah, rah, for Notre Dame.*

We will fight in ev'ry game,
Strong of heart and true to her name.
We will ne'er forget her
And will cheer her ever Loyal to Notre Dame.

Cheer, cheer for old Notre Dame,
Wake up the echoes cheering her name.
Send a volley cheer on high,
Shake down the thunder from the sky.

What though the odds be great or small
Old Notre Dame will win over all,
While her loyal sons are marching
Onward to victory.

The original lyrics, written when all athletes at Notre Dame were male, refer to "sons," but in recognition of the fact that the "Victory March" is now played for athletic teams composed of men and women, many modify the words accordingly. The "Victory March" earned a No. 1 ranking in ratings compiled in 1998 in a book, "College Fight Songs: An Annotated Anthology." The "Victory March" was also the No. 1–ranked fight song in a survey in 1990 by Bill Studwell, a librarian at Northern Illinois University.

"Cheer, cheer for old Notre Dame," indeed.

8. ALMA MATER

The University of Notre Dame alma mater, "Notre Dame Our Mother," dovetails with the opening of Notre Dame Stadium in 1930 since it was composed for the dedication of that facility by Joseph Casasanta, a 1923 Notre Dame graduate. Rev. Charles

O'Donnell, C.S.C., then president of the University, wrote the lyrics. The alma mater historically has been played at the end of football games and pep rallies and other University events. Notre Dame students often join arms and shoulders and sway as they sing. Former Irish football coach Charlie Weis began a recent tradition of Irish players facing the Notre Dame student section and joining in the singing of the alma mater at the conclusion of home football games before they head into the locker room.

> *Notre Dame, our Mother*
> *Tender, strong and true*
> *Proudly in the heavens*
> *Gleam thy gold and blue*
> *Glory's mantle cloaks thee*
> *Golden is thy fame*
> *And our hearts forever*
> *Praise thee Notre Dame*
> *And our hearts forever*
> *Love thee Notre Dame!*

9. YOUR OWN PERFECT FOOTBALL WEEKEND AT NOTRE DAME

You may have read a version of this in United Airlines' *Hemisphere* magazine (the "Three Perfect Days" feature). Or you may have seen a similar version in another airline or travel magazine.

But, with apologies to all of the above—not to mention in deference to all the changes the Notre Dame campus and the Michiana area have seen in recent years, and to Gridiron Graffiti, Notre Dame's own printed list of weekend events—here's a guide to the perfect football weekend with the Irish (more apologies up front for any personal biases and any and all the worthy additions we've left out):

Thursday

3:47 PM—If you planned it right and had the time and the cash, you've spent the last three days in Chicago. Either way, you've just arrived in South Bend on the South Shore, taking a leisurely train ride through the Indiana countryside.

4:32 PM—Check in at your on-campus home, the Morris Inn (go north on Notre Dame Avenue and it's on your left). Can't beat the convenience.

5:45 PM—Stop by the LaBar Practice Complex and check out the final tune-up practice session by Brian Kelly and his charges. Catch Kelly's final words to the media post-practice so you can namedrop at dinner. You also may spy any number of former Irish players who drop by practice to maintain connections.

7:12 PM—For something different, try a half-hour drive east and a little north on Route 12 in Michigan through the country to the shores of Lake Michigan. Try dinner at Casey's in downtown New Buffalo or cruise up Red Arrow Highway to Union Pier and hit (a personal favorite) the Red Arrow Roadhouse (try the Roadhouse Mudd Pie I or II for dessert).

11:08 PM—Consider a late nightcap at Corby's, near downtown South Bend at the corner of LaSalle and Niles. You have to go there, if only because *Rudy* was filmed there.

Friday

7:19 AM—Venture northeast to Granger to a relatively new place called the Uptown Kitchen for breakfast (stuffed French toast earns good reviews). It's a hip place by any standards. If you slept in, it's open for lunch and dinner, too.

8:43 AM—Barely time for nine holes at the Warren Golf Course on the north edge of campus. Open since 1999, it's a Ben Crenshaw-designed layout that already has had a handful of its tees adjusted to make the course longer and eligible for NCAA consideration.

10:35 AM—If golf isn't your thing, leave your buddies at the Warren and venture over to Notre Dame Stadium. You can wander down the north tunnel—festooned with Notre Dame national championship banners—and go all the way down to field level. Bring your camera or cell phone to authenticate.

12:01 PM—The Notre Dame Football Live luncheon at the Joyce Center fieldhouse (north dome) is a great football forum because you can hear live interviews with Irish head coach Brian Kelly and his players and assistant coaches in a Jay Leno–style, host-behind-the-desk format. Plus, host Jack Nolan is as tied in with Irish athletics as anyone.

2:03 PM—You wouldn't be here on one of these weekends if you didn't like football, so head on down to the College Football Hall of Fame in downtown South Bend. You can while away a couple of hours and soak in all the gridiron history you can ever hope to handle. While you're downtown, don't miss the South Bend Chocolate Café for double-dipped chocolate peanuts.

4:20 PM—Before the crowds get too large, wander to the Hammes Notre Dame Bookstore (it only looks like a Barnes & Noble). You'll find all the Adidas and other Irish gear you could expect.

6:00 PM—Head over to the pep rally, wherever the location (Irish Green, Purcell Pavilion, or others to be determined). You may catch a guest speaker such as Joe Theismann, Rocket Ismail, Regis Philbin, Tim Brown, or some other noted name connected with Irish football.

7:25 PM—Catch a period or two of Notre Dame hockey (assuming it's October or November), assuming you can find a ticket in the state-of-the-art Compton Family Ice Arena. If not hockey, it's likely Irish teams in soccer or volleyball are playing on campus on a home football Friday night.

8:21 PM—You're hungry again, so try one of Michiana's traditional favorites: LaSalle Grill (downtown), the Carriage House (way west of town and now with outdoor seating options), the intimate Main Street Grille in downtown Mishawaka, or even Ruth's Chris Steak House.

11:00 PM—No way you can pass on a stop at any place called the Linebacker Lounge. Catch the outdoor music offerings at Eddy Street Commons, complete with stops at O'Rourke's, Brothers, and The Mark.

Midnight—Check out the Notre Dame drum line on the steps of the Main Building (the Golden Dome).

Saturday

10:16 AM—Find your parking spot in the Stadium lot just south of Notre Dame Stadium. If breakfast is your option, try Legends or Greenfields Café at the Hesburgh Center. If lunch is the alternative, wander the campus and you'll find all sorts of ready-made grills manned by various clubs and residence halls.

2:00 PM—Head over to Bond Hall on campus where the Band of the Fighting Irish does its pregame show.

3:43 PM—Kickoff for today's game at Notre Dame Stadium.

7:05 PM—Stick around for the post-game playing of the Alma Mater, with the Notre Dame players arm in arm in front of the student sections.

7:32 PM—Tailgate until your stomach can't handle any more of anything. The better the weather, the longer the tailgating will last (especially after an Irish victory).

Sunday

8:20 AM—If there's room left (in your stomach), one last meal at Nick's Patio over on Ironwood. There's breakfast 24 hours a day,

and you may even run into some late-night revelers who haven't been to bed yet (that's a good sign—it probably signifies an Irish win).
9:53 AM—Back on the South Shore for points west.

Anyone who has been a student at Notre Dame or otherwise spent any amount of time in the South Bend area has a mental listing of favorite haunts, maybe a few from way back when. Any list from decades back or of more recent vintage is bound to include at least a few of these:

- Five Points—Corby's, Nicky's, Bridget's, the Commons, Louie's, Franky's, The Library and the rest of the mainly student bars have been gone for some years, so this one-time favorite intersection for thirsty students is now barely recognizable.
- Rocco's—This South Bend Avenue staple (corner of North Saint Louis) hasn't changed a bit, same pizza, same pasta and salad, all since its 1951 opening. The wall décor features mostly photos of guests, mainly of them connected with Notre Dame athletics or sports in general. This is an unabashed Italian joint.
- Maury's Pat's Pub—Located in an old-school Mishawaka neighborhood, Maury's (formerly known as Pat's) is more of an alumni and Irish fan haunt. Don't go unless you're jazzed about hearing the "Victory March" played (more than once).
- The Linebacker—This stop for beverages located just southeast of campus has been around forever; the sign out front alone is legendary. It has gone back and forth between a student hangout and a local tavern, but there's no shortage of business there on a football weekend.

- Parisi's—Just down the street from the Linebacker, Parisi's offers another Italian option in view of the Golden Dome. Now with outdoor seating available in arm weather, it remains a favorite of Dick Vitale and Digger Phelps among others.
- Eddy Street Commons—With Notre Dame long lacking a real campus-town area, Eddy Street Commons has filled that void in the last few years. There's fast food, but there's also The Mark and O'Rourke's and Brothers—and football Friday nights feature live bands set up in the middle of Eddy Street.

Apologies once again to those who didn't find their favorite spot included.

10. MEDIA COVERAGE

In 1973 you could plunk down $9 for a three-month mail subscription to the *South Bend Tribune*.

Off to college out of state? There was no other way to follow Notre Dame football fortunes on a daily basis.

Hard to believe, isn't it? These days you are absolutely inundated with options when it comes to Brian Kelly and his squad.

In the absence of video boards in Notre Dame Stadium, you may be watching replays on gamedays as part of the live NBC Sports feed on your iPhone. In fact, University officials made sure the campus had enough back-end technology to support the concept.

Think how far we've come.

In 1973 there was the *South Bend Tribune*, three live football games that season on ABC-TV (two national, one regional), Sunday morning television replays by the C.D. Chesley Company, and live radio on the Mutual Broadcasting Company.

There was Joe Doyle, Van Patrick, Lindsey Nelson, Al Wester, Paul Hornung.

That was it. Seriously. No Internet. No tabloids.

Athletic communication with media covering the Irish back then moved at such a caterpillar pace that the favored mode was the then-state-of-the-art Xerox telecopier that required six minutes to transmit a single page of copy via a telephone line. Imagine how much time would be spent monitoring that device when the Irish media relations staff would send eight or 10 pages of a press release and statistics to a newspaper?

No e-mail.

No NBC. No ESPN. No CBS College Sports.

No *Blue & Gold Illustrated*. No *Irish Sports Report*. No *Irish Eyes*.

None of the multiple Web sites that now cover Notre Dame football all-year around.

No Sirius or XM. No *Mike & Mike in the Morning* on ESPN Radio. Very few of the dozens of other local, regional and national talk-radio sports shows.

No access to every newspaper and essentially any other print publication via the Internet.

No Hulu. No Kindle. No Nook.

No chat rooms anywhere in sight. No bloggers.

No Lou Holtz (he was coaching at North Carolina State). No Mark May (he was 13 years old).

Seriously, how did anyone ever keep up with Notre Dame football back then without Twitter?

Back in 1973, sports media relations were heavily print-focused.

Press guides (until 1966 the Notre Dame football guide was known as the "dope book"). Press releases that went via traditional mail (there was no Fed-Ex or other express mail service). Printed game programs.

Now, the immediacy of our need for information is so acute that printed pieces are all but obsolete. Why wait for the morning paper to show up in your driveway, when the same information could be found on various Web sites hours earlier?

Media guides, long the staple of sports information offices, are going the way of the dinosaur, if they are being printed at all. They are now more likely to be found in a digital, online format. The Notre Dame print version must be in black and white, based on NCAA regulations, but the online version on und.com is in full color and is easily accessible in nifty page-turning format by Issuu software.

Meanwhile the social media revolution rolls on. A YouTube video (oh, by the way, there was no YouTube in 1973, either) on "socialnomics" from a few years back contained some startling statistics:

- One of every eight couples married in the United States in 2009 met via social media.
- It took radio 38 years to achieve 50 million users. It took Facebook less than nine months to reach 100 million. If Facebook were a country, it would be the fourth largest in the world (China, India, United States).
- Ashton Kutcher and Ellen DeGeneres have more Twitter followers than the entire populations of Ireland, Norway, and Panama.
- Seventy percent of 18-to-34-year-olds have watched television on the Web.
- Twenty-five percent of Americans in the past month (this was 2009, remember) say they've watched at least one short video *on their phone.*

What this also means is that no student-athlete anywhere, not just at Notre Dame, has a shred of privacy remaining in his or her life. College athletes are subject to social media coverage and criticism of every single solitary second of their behavior.

Meanwhile, 24 of the 25 largest newspapers in the country have experienced record declines in circulation.

That's partly because that mail subscription to the *South Bend Tribune* became extinct some time ago. You can find all you can handle between the *Tribune* Web site, the *ISR* site, not to mention the dozens of other options.

As the saying goes, we no longer search for the news about Notre Dame football—the Notre Dame football news finds us.

If you're an Irish fan, consider yourself lucky.

11. FRIDAY KICKOFF LUNCHEONS

These events began as Monday noon functions in the Ara Parseghian years in the Athletic and Convocation Center Monogram Room—with Ara commenting over 16-millimeter film highlights of the previous Saturday's game for the benefit of mostly local businessmen. Like pep rallies, these events seemingly blew up in terms of interest in the Gerry Faust and Lou Holtz years. Holtz, in particular, had a gift for entertaining with a sense of humor with a microphone in front of him—and even fans who knew nothing about football would walk away from luncheons repeating memorable Holtz lines. Truth be told, Holtz's abilities as both an after-dinner-style speaker and a standup comic haven't made it easy for future Irish coaches to match his entertainment value.

Like pep rallies, the luncheons required more space and in the 1980s moved into the north dome of the Joyce Center. The same lengthy list of special guests has included all sorts of individuals connected with Notre Dame football or college football in general. In recent years, local media personalities including Bob Nagle and Jack Nolan have served as hosts most of the time—working from behind a desk, talk-show-host style. The current Irish head coach always makes an appearance, and Notre Dame players and assistant coaches generally are part of the program, as well.

The weekly luncheons began as Notre Dame Quarterback Club functions when the club began in 1971 with its 200 charter members. These days as many as 2,000 fans may attend luncheons in the north dome of the Joyce Center.

12. Helmet Painting

The Golden Dome, which tops the Notre Dame's Administration Building, for years has been replicated in the gold helmets worn by the Irish football team. The paint for the helmets for decades was mixed on campus by student managers and featured actual gold dust bought from the O'Brien Paint Company. The dust then was mixed with lacquer and lacquer thinner and applied to the helmet of each player dressing for Saturday's game on Friday nights before home games or on Thursday nights if the game was on the road. The helmet-painting process that normally took place in the concourses on the north end of Notre Dame Stadium became something of a spectator sport for Irish fans for a while, in part because the process was featured in the movie *Rudy*.

The 2011 season provided a new day for Notre Dame helmets. As the old, metal helmets became obsolete—and newer molded plastic helmets provided greater comfort and safety—a move to find a way to better match the true Notre Dame gold color ensued. The result went on display beginning with the 2011 Notre Dame-USC prime-time game at Notre Dame Stadium, courtesy of Hydro Graphics Inc. The tradition of having 23.9 karat gold in the helmet continues. Actual gold flakes, collected when the Golden Dome was re-gilded, are still included in the painting process by Hydro Graphics Inc. The end result is a gold helmet that is closer to the color of the Golden Dome than helmets Notre Dame had worn previously—and provides that color on a consistent basis from week to week and year to year. Notre Dame director of athletics Jack Swarbrick had been frustrated with the color of the helmets over the last couple of seasons and charged Notre Dame football head equipment manager Ryan Grooms with the challenge of getting it right.

There were actually five different shades of gold applied to Notre Dame football helmets during the 2010 season in an attempt to get the color correct. After an exhaustive search and creation process (more than 12 versions), HydroGraphics was able to deliver the final product that Irish fans saw beginning on that Saturday night.

After exhausting many options, the Notre Dame football equipment staff had to decide between continuing the tradition of painting helmets and having a subpar helmet or altering the painting process to obtain a superior product. Student managers are still involved with the maintenance of the helmet each game week, including inspection, removal of scuff marks and cleaning. The new paint process is so detailed it is unable to be duplicated by Notre Dame, so it is impossible to be applied each week.

The 2011 season also featured several other helmet versions—the first with green shamrocks on the side (similar to the early 1960s Notre Dame helmet look) based on the throwback uniforms both Notre Dame and Michigan wore in their "Under The Lights" matchup at Michigan Stadium, then the second featuring a larger, brighter shamrock to go with the green jerseys worn by the Irish in their off-site home contest against Maryland at FedEx Field in Landover, Maryland. Expect uniform and helmet variations in future Notre Dame off-site home contests.

13. KNUTE ROCKNE'S GRAVE

If you haven't been to Highland Cemetery on the west side of South Bend, it's worth a stop if only to locate the gravesite of former Irish coaching legend Knute Rockne. You'll need to stop at the cemetery offices and ask for a map because the grave isn't easy to locate. Don't be surprised to find a variety of items around the grave stone left behind by Irish fans—cigars, empty whiskey bottles, notes, and photos and other Irish football ephemera.

14. LEPRECHAUN (AND IRISH TERRIERS)

The mascot of the Notre Dame football team during the 1930s through the 1950s actually became a succession of Irish terrier dogs. The first, named Brick Top Shaun-Rhu, was donated by Cleveland native Charles Otis and was presented to Notre Dame coach Knute Rockne the week of the 1930 Notre Dame–Pennsylvania game. There was a companion mascot named Pat in the 1950s along with several female terriers—but most of Notre Dame's terrier mascots were known as Clashmore Mike. Football game programs in the 1930s and 1940s included a regular "column" from Clashmore Mike, who also was the subject of a 1949 book entitled *Mascot Mike of Notre Dame*. The feisty terrier appeared on the cover of the 1963 Notre Dame Football *Dope Book* alongside head coach Hugh Devore and captain Bob Lehman. Two years later, the leprechaun—which is consistent with the Notre Dame athletic teams' nickname of the Fighting Irish—was registered as an official University mark, with the leprechaun mascot going on to be a regular part of the gameday atmosphere alongside the Notre Dame cheerleaders. Each year male students at Notre Dame are given the opportunity to try out to be the leprechaun. Traditionally a gold squad and a blue squad cheerleader are chosen, and the blue squad leprechaun graduates to the gold squad position. The gold squad leprechaun is the mascot fans see leading the team on to the field each football Saturday and dancing a jig on the sidelines.

15. George Gipp/"Win One for the Gipper"

Sporting News more than a decade back released a list of Top 10 Moments in college football (print edition of November 13, 1999). The No. 3 moment was the legend of former Notre Dame all-star George Gipp and the famous deathbed speech made by Gipp to coach Knute Rockne. The magazine's account: "'The day before he died (in 1920), George Gipp asked me to wait until the situation seemed hopeless...then ask a Notre Dame team to beat Army for him,' said Rockne in 1928. 'This is the day and you are that team.' The Irish beat unbeaten Army 12–6." The "Win One for the Gipper" phrase has lived through the ages—in great part because it came back to life when Ronald Reagan, who played Gipp in the 1940 movie "Knute Rockne All-American," was elected President of the United States. In fact, when a commemorative stamp of Rockne was issued by the U.S. Postal Service (former Irish basketball coach Digger Phelps helped with that as a member of the Postal Service's Citizens' Stamp Advisory Committee) and it was dedicated on the Notre Dame campus (March 9, 1988), Reagan returned to Notre Dame for the ceremonies, as did actor Pat O'Brien, who played Rockne in the movie. In the midst of the ceremonies at the Joyce Center, Reagan grabbed a football, tossed it into the crowd—and it was caught by none other than Tim Brown, Notre Dame's 1987 Heisman Trophy winner. The stamp honored the 100th anniversary of Rockne's birth, with Rockne qualifying as the first athletic coach at any level to featured on a U.S. stamp.

16. BAND OF THE FIGHTING IRISH

Notre Dame's marching band, appropriately called The Band of the Fighting Irish, is the oldest university band in continual existence and has been on hand for every home game since football started at Notre Dame in 1887. Notre Dame's band, born in 1845, celebrated its 150th season in 1995 and held a reunion at the Northwestern game that year. The band was among the first in the nation to include pageantry, precision drill, and now-famous picture formations. It first accepted women from neighboring Saint Mary's College in 1970 before Notre Dame became coeducational in 1972. The band was declared a "landmark of American Music" in 1976 by the National Music Council. Current director of bands Ken Dye holds degrees from the University of Houston, Long Beach State, and USC. He previously directed bands at Rice and Houston and arranged music performed at the 2000 Olympic Games in Sydney, Australia.

The Notre Dame band in 2011 was awarded the Sudler Trophy. This trophy, dating back to 1982, is presented by the John Philip Sousa Foundation and recognizes "collegiate marching bands of particular excellence that have made outstanding contributions to the American way of life." The award is considered the Heisman Trophy for college bands and recognized Notre Dame's contributions to college bands over a number of years. It is the only nationally recognized award for college marching bands. Past winners of the Sudler Trophy included the University of Michigan, Michigan State University, University of Kansas, University of Texas at Austin, Florida A&M University, UCLA, and several others. The trophy consists of a marble base with a bronze drum major astride a football stadium. The award is produced by Dieges and Clust, who also make the Heisman Trophy.

The Band of the Fighting Irish has performed at every Notre Dame home football game in history. *Photo courtesy of Mike Bennett/Lighthouse Imaging*

17. WALK FROM THE BASILICA TO NOTRE DAME STADIUM

Not so long ago, Notre Dame football players spent their Saturday mornings of home football weekends in relative obscurity. For years they spent Friday nights at Moreau Seminary on the north edge of campus—then later moved to the Holiday Inn in Plymouth, Indiana, for Friday evenings. They'd take part in a pregame meal on campus and a pregame Mass, held for many years in the Pangborn Hall chapel (the residence hall where longtime Notre Dame athletic chaplain Father Jim Riehle resided). Eventually pregame Mass moved to the Basilica of the Sacred Heart—and suddenly the game-day movements of the Irish players became far more public.

Irish fans soon came to know exactly when the Notre Dame players would make their walk as a group from the Basilica to Notre Dame Stadium about two hours before kickoff—and they would line the path where the players walked, shouting all sorts of encouragement. The crowds grew as the years went by, and the pregame walk seemed to become a "must-see" part of the game-day routine for many Notre Dame fans.

The Irish in 2011 made a slight adjustment to their route—leaving the Basilica by bus and returning through the parking lots for brief, final meetings at the Guglielmino Athletic Complex. Then, the Notre Dame team left the Gug, walked mostly west to the Hesburgh Library, then turned left and walked directly south down the library quad to the north end of Notre Dame Stadium.

18. Sculptures at Notre Dame Stadium Gates

First came Frank Leahy. The Leahy's Lads group of former players from the ultra-productive Leahy years in the 1940s and 1950s made fundraising for scholarships at Notre Dame a major priority of their work. Along the way came a sculpture of Leahy that was erected on the east side of Notre Dame Stadium in 1997. Eventually the Notre Dame Monogram Club professed an interest in adding sculptures of Notre Dame's other national-title-winning head coaches—and so one by one additional sculptures arrived on the scene (several of them originally placed inside Notre Dame Stadium).

The final puzzle piece came to fruition in 2011 when a sculpture of former Irish coach Dan Devine, a member of the College Football Hall of Fame and coach of the 1977 Irish national championship team, was dedicated October 7 (the day before Notre Dame's home football game against Air Force). The dedication took place at Notre Dame Stadium's Gate A, which in 2010 was designated the Dan Devine gate when the sculptures of Knute Rockne (north tunnel), Ara Parseghian (Gate B), Leahy (Gate C) and Lou Holtz (Gate D) were re-located outside the stadium walls. Rockne (sculpture erected in 2009), Parseghian (2007), Leahy, Holtz (2008), and Devine are the five former Irish football coaches—all of them Hall of Fame inductees—who have won one or more national titles at Notre Dame.

Notre Dame graduate Jerry McKenna created all five sculptures around Notre Dame Stadium. He also created the Moose Krause sculpture east of Notre Dame Stadium, the Knute Rockne sculpture in 2005 at the College Football Hall of Fame in downtown South Bend, Indiana (with an identical version in Voss, Norway, where Rockne was born), and the miniature Four Horsemen sculpture in the lobby of the Guglielmino Athletic Complex.

19. GREEN JERSEYS

If you're not a dyed-in-the-wool Notre Dame fan and you're confused about the Irish uniform colors, there's no reason for alarm. Although Notre Dame's official colors for athletics long have been listed as gold and blue, the color of the Irish home football jersey has switched back and forth between blue and green for decades. The origin of school colors can be traced back to the founding of the University. At that time in 1842, Notre Dame's original school colors were yellow and blue; yellow symbolized the light and blue the truth. However, sometime after the Golden Dome and Statue

In recent years Irish teams have worn green jerseys at their off-site home game each season. *Photo courtesy of Mike Bennett/Lighthouse Imaging*

of Mary atop the Main Administration Building were gilded, gold and blue became the official colors of the University.

Back in the 1920s during the Knute Rockne days, the Notre Dame varsity generally wore blue—while the freshman squad wore green. But, on several occasions the varsity team did wear green—simply for purposes of distinction when the Irish opponent also came out in blue. Games against Navy, for example, in the late 1920s featured green-clad Notre Dame teams to avoid confusion with the Navy's blue uniforms. Rockne didn't mind using the color change as a psychological ploy. When Notre Dame faced Navy in Baltimore in 1927, the Irish head coach started his second-string reserves. Navy retaliated by scoring a touchdown in the first five minutes of the game. But, just as the Midshipmen scored, reported George Trevor in the *New York Sun*, Rockne made his move: "Instantaneously the Notre Dame regulars yanked off their blue outer sweaters and like a horde of green Gila monsters darted onto the field. From that moment on Notre Dame held the initiative, imposed its collective will upon the Navy." The Irish came from behind to win that one 19–6—then did the same thing the following year in Chicago's Soldier Field, this time beating Navy 7–0. The 1928 edition of the *Scholastic Football Review* included this description: "Mr. K.K. Rockne may, or may not, be a psychologist. But, he did array his Fighting Irish in bright green jerseys for their battle with the United States Naval Academy. Mr. Rockne evidently surmised that garbing a band of native and adopted Irish in their native color is somewhat akin to showing a bull the Russian flag."

The green jerseys remained prominent throughout the Frank Leahy years—particularly so in September 1947 when Heisman Trophy winner Johnny Lujack graced the cover of *Life* magazine clad in green. Several of Joe Kuharich's squads wore green with UCLA-style shoulder stripes and shamrocks on the helmets. Even Hugh Devore's 1963 team—after wearing navy blue all season—switched to green in the finale against Syracuse. The Irish returned to the standard navy blue worn throughout the Ara Parseghian years and an early portion of the Dan Devine era. The Irish had worn navy blue all during Parseghian's 11 seasons and through the first two-and-a-half years of the Devine era—but they stayed with the green after the landmark victory over USC in 1977, when the Irish warmed up in blue then donned green jerseys just prior to kickoff.

When Gerry Faust took over in 1981, Notre Dame went to royal blue jerseys with three one-inch stripes on the sleeves, two gold surrounding one white. But the stripes were eliminated on the 1984 tops, which didn't feature any trim or feathering other than the white numbers on the navy blue shirts. However, Faust made use of the green jersey on two occasions. He outfitted his Irish in green in a 27–6 win over USC in 1983—six years to the day after Devine first went to the green in a win over those same Trojans. The Irish also wore green during the second half of the 37–3 win over USC in 1985.

Lou Holtz's only change beginning in 1986 involved adding the interlocked Notre Dame logo to the shoulder of the jerseys and to the left front side of the pants. For the first time during Holtz's tenure as head coach, the Irish used green as part of their uniform in the 1992 Sugar Bowl as they donned white jerseys with green numbers and green socks. The last time the Irish had worn their road white jerseys with green numbers was in the Superdome in Notre Dame's loss to Georgia in the Sugar Bowl 17–10 exactly 11 years earlier. Notre Dame again wore green jerseys in a 41–24 loss to Colorado in the 1995 Fiesta Bowl and donned the green against Georgia Tech in the 1999 Gator Bowl—a 35–28 loss. Most recently, the Irish have utilized green jerseys in 2009, 2010, and 2011 in their off-site home games against Washington State, Army, and Maryland, respectively. Here's when you've seen Notre Dame wear green since that 1977 game versus USC:

- 1977: USC (Irish won 49–19 and stayed in green through end of the 1980 season)
- 1983: USC (Irish won 27–6 after halftime switch)

- 1985: USC (Irish won 37–3 after halftime switch)
- 1992: Sugar Bowl vs. Florida (Irish won 39–28 in white jerseys with green numbers)
- 1995: Fiesta Bowl vs. Colorado (Irish lost 41–24)
- 1999: Gator Bowl vs. Georgia Tech (Irish lost 35–28)
- 2002: Boston College (Irish lost 14–7)
- 2005: USC (Irish lost 34–31)
- 2006: Army (Irish won 41–9)
- 2007: USC (Irish lost 38–0)
- 2009: Washington State in San Antonio (Irish won 40–14)
- 2010: Army at Yankee Stadium (Irish won 27–3)
- 2011: Michigan (Irish lost 35–31 in uniforms from the 1960s—white jerseys with green stripes and green socks)
- 2011: USC at Notre Dame Stadium (Irish lost 31–17)
- 2011: Maryland at FedEx Field (Irish won 45–21)

20. Sgt. Tim McCarthy

Since 1960, Irish football fans have grown silent for a moment during the fourth quarter of every Notre Dame home game as they strain to hear Sergeant Tim McCarthy, now retired from the Indiana State Police (since 1978) and as Porter (Indiana) County sheriff (1979–1987). McCarthy has found that the atrocious pun is the best way to get the crowd's attention for the serious message of auto safety. Some of his best groaners: "Drive like a musician: C Sharp or B Flat," and, "Those who have one for the road may have a policeman as a chaser." His messages are all typed on three-by-five-inch index cards. McCarthy in recent years has made appearances at pep rallies and other Notre Dame events. In fact, his recorded messages have been played the last few years at Irish games in San Antonio (2009), Yankee Stadium (2010), and FedEx Field (2011). McCarthy and current Irish football public-address announcer Mike Collins recently collaborated on a book (*May I Have Your Attention Please...*) that chronicled McCarthy's contributions. He's a recipient of an honorary monogram from the Notre Dame Monogram Club. These are the sayings McCarthy lists as his favorites:

— The automobile replaced the horse...but the driver should stay on the wagon.
— Drive when you're stoned...and you may hit rock bottom.
— Drive like a musician...C Sharp or B Flat.
— You may be at the end of your rope...if you tie one on.
— Drive like a happy doctor...have a lot of patience.
— If you horse around in traffic...you may get saddled with a ticket.
— Safe drivers get the cheers...by avoiding the booze.
— Drinking drivers are not very funny...but they can still crack you up.
— Don't short-change yourself...by driving without any sense.
— Don't let your day go down the drain...by forgetting today's safety plug.
— With all the rainfall today...we do not need a drip behind the wheel.

21. LINDSEY NELSON

You may find your fair share of Notre Dame fans who have never been to Notre Dame Stadium and maybe have never seen the Irish play in person—other than on Sunday mornings on the Notre Dame football television replays shows produced by C.D. Chesley Company. And the connection is Lindsey Nelson, who did play-by-play on all those Notre Dame games for at least a generation of Irish fans from 1967–1979. Nelson worked with Paul Hornung and others on those games. Since the edited shows did not include every play or drive, Nelson became famous for his phrase: "and now we move to further action in the third period..."

22. IRISH GUARD

As the Notre Dame band enters Notre Dame Stadium for its pregame salute, it is led by the drum major, who is closely followed by the famous Irish Guard. Each Guard member is dressed in an Irish kilt and will tower more than eight feet tall when wearing his or her bearskin shako. The guardsmen are skilled marchers who are chosen for this honor on the basis of marching ability, appearance, and spirit. The late John Fyfe, originally from Glasgow, Scotland, served as the longstanding adviser to the Irish Guard. The uniform of the Guard is patterned after the traditional Irish kilt. According to Seumas Uah Urthuile, an Irish historian, laws were introduced in Ireland about 1000 AD concerning the use of colors in clothing in order to distinguish between various occupations, military rank, and the various stages of the social and political spectrum. The Irish Guard's colors are significant to Notre Dame and utilize the "Notre Dame plaid." The blue and gold represent the school colors intermixed with green for the Irish. The doublets are papal red. Molly Kinder in 2000 became the first female member of the Guard.

23. THE SHIRT

For the 23rd consecutive year in 2012, Notre Dame student activities and student government are sponsoring a T-shirt that benefits scholarship funds, student groups, and service projects. Over the first 22 years, the venture earned well over $3 million in net profit for worthy causes and serves the dual purpose of promoting spirit and raising funds. The 2006 shirt was the most successful to date, with more than 155,000 sold and more than $650,000 in net profits. Some of the proceeds support students and employees who have incurred catastrophic accidents, and profits also benefit endowment funds, while other monies are given to support service projects for student organizations on campus. Each year the shirt is a new color (generally a shade of blue, green, or gold) and features a motto. Notre Dame students and fans at each home game of the football season traditionally wear the short-sleeve T. In recent years the new version of the shirt has been unveiled on the weekend of Notre Dame's final spring football game.

24. AT THE MOVIES

Notre Dame football has been the subject of a number of motion pictures over the years. *Knute Rockne All-American* starred Pat O'Brien as the legendary coach—while future President of the United States Ronald Reagan played the role of George Gipp— with the film making its debut in 1940. In 1997 Librarian of Congress James Billington designated *Knute Rockne All-American* as part of the National Film Registry, qualifying the film as an "irreplaceable part of America's cinematic heritage." An earlier movie, *The Spirit of Notre Dame*, released in 1931, starred Lew Ayres and told the story of two fictional freshman Notre Dame football players. The picture featured a number of Notre Dame players in cameo roles and was reviewed as "the best college picture since the coming of the talkies." The most recent movie involving Notre Dame football was the 1993 picture *Rudy*, the story of Daniel "Rudy" Ruettiger, who earned a spot on the Irish squad as a walk-on and later played 27 seconds against Georgia Tech in 1975 in his last game as a senior.

For years, *Knute Rockne All-American* was required viewing for incoming Notre Dame students during freshman orientation. And, if you're any sort of film buff, you'll be intrigued with some

Many current Irish fans who have never been to the Notre Dame campus identify with the university via the version presented in the movie *Rudy*.

of the famous names that came to be a part of that cinematic venture (courtesy of Cappy Gagnon):

— Two of the producers of the movie were Hollywood giants Jack Warner and Hal Wallis.
— George Reeves, who was also in *Gone with the Wind* and *From Here to Eternity* and would later star in the television series *Superman*, played a Notre Dame football player who was distraught after the death of Rockne (Reeves was not listed in the credits).

— Nick Lukats, Notre Dame's starting left halfback in 1933, played QB Harry Stuhldreher of the 1924 Four Horsemen team. Nick was also listed in the credits as a "technical advisor," as was longtime Notre Dame employee Art Haley.

— Johnny Sheffield played the young Knute Rockne. Sheffield went on to play "Boy," son of Tarzan, and also "Bomba," in a bunch of vine-swinging movies.

— Dickie Jones, who later went on to a long television and movie career, mostly in westerns, played a young boy football player. He was Jock Mahoney's sidekick in the television series *The Range Rider.*

— Brian Keith had a long and distinguished career as an actor, perhaps best known as the father on the television series *Family Affair.* He played an uncredited role as a student at the train station. Back in Rockne's days, the students would meet the victorious team as it returned to South Bend by train.

— There were several real college football coaches in the movie playing themselves: Bill Spaulding, Howard Jones, Pop Warner, and Amos Alonzo Stagg.

— William Hopper also had an uncredited role in the movie as a New York reporter. He was best known as private investigator Paul Drake on *Perry Mason.* Hopper also had a baseball connection: his father was DeWolf Hopper, who first performed *Casey at the Bat* in 1888 and did it more than 10,000 times after that. His mother was famed Hollywood gossip columnist Hedda Hopper.

There were several other actors with bit parts and uncredited roles in *Knute Rockne All-American* who had long acting careers. The next time you watch the movie, see if you can identify some of these performers.

25. STREAKS

If football isn't enough all by itself at Notre Dame, Irish fans in all sports like it when they break someone else's winning streak or otherwise establish a streak of their own. So, in that light, we present our own list of Notre Dame football streaks for your pregame entertainment:

226: Consecutive pass attempts without an interception, by Brady Quinn in 2006 (Michigan State through Army).

225: Consecutive games sold out in Notre Dame Stadium (through end of 2011 season).

136: Consecutive PATs, by Craig Hentrich, 1989–1992.

131: Consecutive Irish home games televised nationally from Notre Dame Stadium by NBC Sports (through end of 2011 season).

93: Consecutive home games without defeat, 1905–1928 (90 wins, three ties).

52: Consecutive seasons of providing late-in-the-game Notre Dame Stadium safety message, by Tim McCarthy, retired Indiana State Police sergeant (through the end of 2011).

50: Consecutive starts by Irish offensive tackle Sam Young (2006–2009).

47: Consecutive pass attempts in one game without an interception, by Brady Quinn versus BYU in 2004.

47: Longest opponent winning streak ended, by Notre Dame against Oklahoma in 1957 (still the NCAA record).

43: Consecutive wins by any team over a major opponent in an uninterrupted current series, by Notre Dame over Navy, 1964–2006.

42: Consecutive winning seasons, from 1889–1932 (no teams in 1890–1891). That was an all-time NCAA record, since tied by Nebraska (1962–2003) and surpassed by Penn State (1939–1987).

40: Consecutive wins at home, 1907–1918.

39: Consecutive games without defeat, 1946–1950 (37 wins, two ties).

28: Consecutive wins in Notre Dame Stadium, 1942–1950.

23: Consecutive victories, 1988–1989.

23: Consecutive quarters opponents held without a touchdown, in 1980 (Army through Air Force).

23: Consecutive field goals connected on by Irish kicker David Ruffer (last five of 2009 season, first 18 of 2010 season).

19: Consecutive weeks as No. 1 team in Associated Press poll, by Notre Dame, 1988–1989 (was the NCAA record, since surpassed by Miami, 2001–2002, and by USC, 2003–2005).

18: Consecutive years in which Notre Dame had at least one consensus All-American, from 1964 through 1981. That streak began with John Huarte and Jack Snow in 1964 and went through Bob Crable in 1981.

17: Consecutive Notre Dame games with an Irish field goal, 2001–2002.

17: Career games with at least 100 receiving yards, by Michael Floyd in 2008–2011.

14: Consecutive pass completions in a game, Ron Powlus vs. Michigan State in 1997 and Brady Quinn vs. Ohio State (Fiesta Bowl) in 2006.

12: Consecutive career field goals made between 40 and 49 yards, by John Carney in 1984–1985 (also an NCAA record).

10: Consecutive years that Notre Dame had at least one College Football Hall of Fame selection, from 1970 through

1979. That accounted for the inductions of Don Miller, Red Salmon, Heisman Trophy winner Angelo Bertelli, Ray Eichenlaub, Heisman winner Leon Hart, Marchy Schwartz, Hunk Anderson, Clipper Smith, Creighton Miller, Ziggy Czarobski, Nordy Hoffmann, and Heisman winner John Lattner.

9: Consecutive years in which Notre Dame played in a traditional January 1 bowl game, starting with the 1987 season and going through the 1995 campaign (three Cottons, three Oranges, two Fiestas, one Sugar). The Irish won five of those, with all nine of them under head coach Lou Holtz.

9: Consecutive shutouts, in 1903 (one 0–0 tie).

8: Consecutive defeats, in 1960.

8: Consecutive rushing attempts by same player, by five Irish (Mark Green vs. Boston College in 1987, Phil Carter vs. Air Force in 1980, Larry Conjar vs. Army in 1965, Neil Worden vs. Oklahoma in 1952, James Aldridge vs. Navy in 2006).

6: Consecutive games rushing for at least 100 yards, by Lee Becton in 1993.

chapter 2

125 FIRSTS IN NOTRE DAME FOOTBALL HISTORY

IN ANOTHER BOW TO 125 years of football at the University of Notre Dame (1887–2012), here's a list of firsts through that first century and another 25 years:

1. 1887—1st game in history: against Michigan on the Notre Dame campus
2. 1887—1st game at which the Band of the Fighting Irish performed: Michigan
3. 1888—1st win in Notre Dame history: 20–0 over Harvard Prep School of Chicago
4. 1889—1st time team played a road game: at Northwestern
5. 1894—1st team to play with benefit of a head coach: J.L. Morrison
6. 1899—1st time Notre Dame team was referred to as Fighting Irish: Northwestern
7. 1903—1st All-American: fullback Louis "Red" Salmon, a third-team pick by *Collier's* (Walter Camp team)
8. 1908—1st time "Notre Dame Victory March" was copyrighted and played in public

9. 1908—1st time Notre Dame scored through the air: on TD pass from Don Hamilton to Fay Wood against Franklin

10. 1911—1st time a Notre Dame player scored at least 35 points in a game: 37 by Art Smith vs. Loyola (Chicago)

11. 1911—1st time the sculpture could be viewed in front of Corby Hall depicting Chaplain William J. Corby, C.S.C., with his right arm raised in the act of giving absolution to the Irish Brigade before they went into action on the three-day Battle of Gettysburg (July 2, 1863); Corby was Notre Dame's president from 1866–1872 and again from 1887–1891 and his campus statue came to known as "Fair-Catch Corby."

12. 1913—1st first-team All-American: quarterback Gus Dorais by Frank Menke Syndicate and International News Service

13. 1913—1st time team played Army at West Point

14. 1913—1st year the university designated a director of athletics: Jesse Harper (he also served as head football coach)

15. 1917—1st consensus All-American: center Frank Rydzewski

16. 1919—1st time Notre Dame was listed as national champion: by Parke H. Davis Ratings

17. 1920—1st first-team Walter Camp All-America selection: George Gipp

18. 1921—1st time Irish won 10 games in a season: 10–1–0

19. 1921—1st time a Notre Dame player scored at least 10 TDs in a season: John Mohardt with 12

20. 1921—1st time Notre Dame held an opponent without a first down in a game: Michigan State

21. 1921—1st game in which team wore green jerseys: Navy
22. 1922—1st time team played at home in front of capacity crowd: 22,000 at Cartier Field for Homecoming against Indiana
23. 1922—1st time a Notre Dame game was broadcast on radio (by WSBT in South Bend): Indiana
24. 1924—1st time team played in a postseason bowl game: Rose Bowl against Stanford
25. 1924—1st time Notre Dame listed as consensus national champion
26. 1926—1st Associated Press first-team All-American: center Art Boeringer
27. 1926—1st time Notre Dame played USC
28. 1926—1st time a Notre Dame player returned two punts for TDs in a game: Vince McNally vs. Beloit
29. 1927—1st time Irish played Navy in what remains longest the continuous intersectional rivalry in college football
30. 1929—1st unanimous All-American: quarterback Frank Carideo
31. 1929—1st time an Irish player returned an interception 100 yards for a TD: Jack Elder vs. Army
32. 1929—1st year Notre Dame played a final spring football game, then known as the Old-Timers Game pitting the current squad versus former players
33. 1930—1st game in Notre Dame Stadium: SMU
34. 1930—1st time a Notre Dame player returned a kickoff 100 yards for a TD: Joe Savoldi vs. SMU
35. 1930—1st year an Irish terrier dog made its appearance as the Notre Dame mascot
36. 1931—1st capacity crowd in Notre Dame Stadium: 50,731 for USC game

37. 1931—1ˢᵗ year the movie *The Spirit of Notre Dame* made its debut with Lew Ayres starring in the fictional story of two Notre Dame freshman football players

38. 1934—1ˢᵗ participants in College All-Star Game in Chicago against NFL champions: Tom Gorman, Ed Krause, and Nick Lukats

39. 1936—1ˢᵗ game against a No. 1–ranked opponent: Northwestern (Notre Dame won 26–6)

40. 1936—1ˢᵗ time Irish were ranked in the AP poll coming into a game: No. 7 vs. Pittsburgh

41. 1936—1ˢᵗ time an Irish player was a first-round selection in the NFL Draft: Bill Shakespeare by Pittsburgh

42. 1938—1ˢᵗ time Irish were ranked No. 1 in AP poll coming into a game: Northwestern

43. 1940—1ˢᵗ year the movie *Knute Rockne All-American* made its debut with Ronald Reagan playing the role of George Gipp

44. 1941—1ˢᵗ national Coach of the Year selection: Frank Leahy by American Football Coaches Association

45. 1941—1ˢᵗ time an Irish player threw for at least 1,000 yards in a season: Angelo Bertelli with 1,027

46. 1943—1ˢᵗ of seven Heisman Trophy wins: Angelo Bertelli

47. 1943—1ˢᵗ time Irish finished first in final AP poll

48. 1943—1ˢᵗ time an Irish player led the nation in rushing: Creighton Miller with 911

49. 1943—1ˢᵗ time a Notre Dame team played in an Associated Press No. 1–vs.–No. 2 matchup: the No. 1 Irish did it twice that year, against No. 2 Michigan and No. 2 Iowa Pre-Flight

50. 1944—1ˢᵗ time a Notre Dame player was first player picked in NFL Draft: Angelo Bertelli by Boston

51. 1946—1st time Irish led the nation in scoring defense: 2.7

52. 1950—1st time a Notre Dame graduating class went through four years without seeing its football team lose a game: The Irish from 1946–1949 finished a combined 36–0–2, won three national titles, and had two Heisman Trophy winners

53. 1951—1st inductees into College Football Hall of Fame: Knute Rockne, George Gipp, Elmer Layden

54. 1952—1st Academic All-American: halfback Joe Heap

54. 1952—1st time a Notre Dame game was nationally televised on ABC Sports: Oklahoma

55. 1957—1st time the longest win streak in college football history, 47 games by Oklahoma, came to an end at the hands of Notre Dame in a 7–0 Irish victory in Norman

56. 1959—1st time Irish uniforms feature UCLA stripes on shoulders and shamrocks on helmets, under new coach Joe Kuharich

57. 1960—1st year Indiana State Police Sergeant Tim McCarthy delivered his safety messages over the pubic-address system at Irish home games

58. 1961—1st time Notre Dame won a game as time expired: 17–15 vs. Syracuse

59. 1963—1st time an Irish player made 100 tackles in a season: Bill Pfeiffer with 101

60. 1964—1st time Irish averaged more than 200 yards passing per game: 210.5

61. 1964—1st time a Notre Dame player led the nation in interceptions: Tony Carey with eight

62. 1964—1st time an Irish player recorded at least 1,000 receiving yards in a season: Jack Snow with 1,114

63. 1964—1ˢᵗ year a Notre Dame head coach won the Paul "Bear" Bryant and Eddie Robinson awards as national coach of the year: Ara Parseghian

64. 1965—1ˢᵗ time an Irish player led the nation in punt return yards: Nick Rassas with 459

65. 1965—1ˢᵗ year the leprechaun was registered as an official university mark

66. 1966—1ˢᵗ Notre Dame recipient of National Football Foundation post-graduate scholarship: linebacker Jim Lynch

67. 1966—1ˢᵗ time Irish finished first in final UPI poll

68. 1966—1ˢᵗ time Irish led the nation in scoring: 36.2

69. 1966—1ˢᵗ time an Irish player made at least 100 tackles in two straight seasons: Jim Lynch with 106 after 108 in 1965

70. 1967—1ˢᵗ Notre Dame recipient of NCAA post-graduate scholarship: offensive tackle Fred Schnurr

71. 1967—1ˢᵗ time former Irish players played in the Super Bowl: Paul Hornung and Red Mack for Green Bay

72. 1968—1ˢᵗ year Mutual Broadcasting System (later Westwood One) began radio broadcasts of Notre Dame games

73. 1968—1ˢᵗ time Notre Dame averaged more than 500 yards per game of total offense: 504.4

74. 1968—1ˢᵗ year Notre Dame played the Blue-Gold final spring game as an intrasquad contest

75. 1969—1ˢᵗ time a Notre Dame bowl game was nationally televised by CBS Sports: Cotton Bowl vs. Texas in first Irish bowl game in 45 years

76. 1970—1ˢᵗ time a Notre Dame player threw for at least 500 yards in a game: Joe Theismann with 526 vs. USC

77. 1972—1st time female students from Notre Dame represented the University as cheerleaders (previous female cheerleaders had come from Saint Mary's College)

78. 1973—1st time Notre Dame averaged more than 350 rushing yards per game: 350.2

79. 1974—1st time Irish led the nation in rushing defense: 102.8

80. 1976—1st time an Irish player rushed for at least 1,000 yards in a season: Al Hunter with 1,058

81. 1976—1st time an Irish player kicked a field goal of at least 50 yards: Dave Reeve 53 vs. Pittsburgh

82. 1978—1st time Notre Dame played the most difficult schedule in the nation, as rated by NCAA (.709)

83. 1979—1st time the Irish played outside the United States: Mirage Bowl in Tokyo against Miami

84. 1979—1st time an Irish player scored at least 100 points in a season: Vagas Ferguson with 102

85. 1979—1st time a Notre Dame player rushed for at least 1,000 yards in successive seasons: Vagas Ferguson with 1,457 after 1,192 in 1978

86. 1980—1st time an Irish player rushed 40 times in a game: Phil Carter vs. Michigan State (254 yards)

87. 1981—1st time an Irish player made at least 100 tackles in three straight seasons: Bob Crable with 167, after 154 in 1980 and 187 in 1979

88. 1982—1st night game at Notre Dame Stadium: Michigan

89. 1982—1st year Notre Dame won the Academic Achievement Award from College Football Association: 83.8 percent

90. 1985—1st time an Irish player rushed for at least 1,000 yards in three straight seasons: Allen Pinkett with 1,100, after 1,105 in 1984 and 1,394 in 1983

91. 1986—1ˢᵗ time an Irish player kicked at least 20 field goals in a season: John Carney with 21

92. 1987—1ˢᵗ season Irish made use of Loftus Center indoor practice facility

93. 1988—1ˢᵗ time Irish won seven games in a season in Notre Dame Stadium

94. 1989—1ˢᵗ time Irish played seven ranked opponents (AP) in a season

95. 1988—1ˢᵗ time an Irish player led the nation in kickoff returns: Raghib Ismail at 36.1

96. 1990—1ˢᵗ Notre Dame selection to Academic All-America Hall of Fame: Joe Theismann

97. 1990—1ˢᵗ time Notre Dame kicked five field goals in a game: Miami

98. 1991—1ˢᵗ game televised as part of university contract with NBC Sports: Indiana

99. 1991—1ˢᵗ time an Irish player rushed for 20 TDs in a season: Jerome Bettis with 20

100. 1992—1ˢᵗ time Notre Dame played in a Bowl Coalition game: Cotton Bowl vs. Texas A&M

101. 1993—1ˢᵗ year the movie *Rudy* made its debut in the story of former Irish football walk-on Daniel Ruettiger

102. 1995—1ˢᵗ year the College Football Hall of Fame opened in downtown South Bend

103. 1996—1ˢᵗ time Irish played an overtime game: Air Force (lost 20–17)

104. 1996—1ˢᵗ time Notre Dame returned five punts for TDs in a season

105. 1997—1ˢᵗ game in expanded Notre Dame Stadium: Georgia Tech

106. 1997—1ˢᵗ time the Frank Leahy sculpture appeared just east of Notre Dame Stadium
107. 1997—1ˢᵗ time an Irish team played a game without a turnover or a penalty: LSU
108. 1997—1ˢᵗ season in which Notre Dame Stadium utilized permanent lights
109. 2000—1ˢᵗ time Irish won an overtime game: 34–31 vs. Air Force
110. 2000—1ˢᵗ season Notre Dame played in a Bowl Championship Series game: Fiesta Bowl vs. Oregon State
111. 2005—1ˢᵗ time an Irish player threw for at least 30 TD passes: Brady Quinn with 32
112. 2005—1ˢᵗ time Notre Dame threw six TD passes in a game: BYU
113. 2005—1ˢᵗ time an Irish player caught four TD passes in a game: Maurice Stovall vs. BYU
114. 2005—1ˢᵗ year the Guglielmino Center opened to house the Notre Dame football offices
115. 2005—1ˢᵗ time Notre Dame produced a 3,000-yard passer (Brady Quinn with 3,919), a 1,000-yard rusher (Darius Walker with 1,196), and two 1,000-yard receivers (Jeff Samardzija with 1,249 and Maurice Stovall with 1,149) in a single season
116. 2006—1ˢᵗ time an Irish receiver totaled at least 1,000 receiving yards two seasons in a row: Jeff Samardzija with 1,017 after 1,249 in 2005
117. 2008—1ˢᵗ time the Irish led the nation in kickoff-return defense: 16.47
118. 2009—1ˢᵗ time Notre Dame played an "off-site" home game: in San Antonio against Washington State

119. 2010—1ˢᵗ time a football game took place at the new Yankee Stadium—with the Irish defeating Army

120. 2010—1ˢᵗ time a Notre Dame head coach won a bowl game in his first season on the Irish sideline: Brian Kelly and Sun Bowl win over Miami

121. 2010—1ˢᵗ time a Notre Dame player attended law school while also competing regularly for the Irish: offensive lineman Chris Stewart

122. 2010—1ˢᵗ time a Notre Dame kicker converted 18 straight field-goal attempts to begin a season: David Ruffer

123. 2011—1ˢᵗ time an Irish receiver ever caught 100 passes in a single season: Michael Floyd with exactly 100

124. 2011—1ˢᵗ time an Irish team wore shamrocks on its helmets since 1963: Irish and Michigan wore throwback uniforms in Ann Arbor in first home night game in Michigan football history

125. 2011—1ˢᵗ night game in Notre Dame Stadium in 21 years: Notre Dame vs. USC

chapter 3

THE RIVALRIES: ANY AND ALL FOR THE IRISH

IF YOU WANT TO engage in a debate to single out Notre Dame's biggest football rival, pull up a chair. This could take awhile.

Though Notre Dame generally has dominated the Navy series—including an NCAA-record 43-game win streak from 1964 to 2006—the Irish-Midshipmen matchup still qualifies as the longest continuous intersectional rivalry in the country (continuous since 1927).

Notre Dame's annual outing game with USC has probably won its share of national headlines, mainly because there have been so many games where one or both teams were contending for national honors. It doesn't hurt that the game goes back to Knute Rockne and Howard Jones—and that the first two Midwest versions of the rivalry lured more than 100,000 fans each to Chicago's Soldier Field.

Michigan State and Purdue have been long-time Big Ten Conference opponents—and Northwestern isn't far behind in longevity. Michigan and Penn State are more recent opponents, but both those series have produced superb football. The same could be said for the Irish-Stanford series that began in a Rose Bowl way back when but didn't get going for good until 1988. Boston

Few renditions of the Notre Dame–USC rivalry are as memorable for Irish fans as the 1977 game, when Notre Dame broke out green jerseys.

SOUTHERN CAL • NOTRE DAME

October 22, 1977 • Notre Dame Stadium • $2.00

College fits that mold as well—in a matchup that didn't begin regularly until 1992.

Notre Dame's most common opponents through the 2011 season include: 1. Navy (85), 2. Purdue and USC (83 each), 4. Michigan State (75), 5. Pittsburgh (67), 6. Army (50), 7. Northwestern (47), 8. Michigan (39), 9. Georgia Tech (34), 10. Indiana (29).

Which opponents has Notre Dame defeated the most times? Here they are: 1. Navy (72), 2. Purdue (55), 3. Michigan State and Pittsburgh (46 each), 5. USC (43), 6. Army (38), 7. Northwestern (37), 8. Georgia Tech (27), 9. Air Force and Indiana (23 each).

Which teams own the most wins over Notre Dame? Here's the list: 1. USC (35), 2. Michigan State (28), 3. Purdue (26), 4.

Michigan (23), 5. Pittsburgh (20), 6. Navy (12), 7. Boston College, Penn State, and Stanford (nine each), 10. Army, Iowa, and Nebraska (eight each).

While you tally the votes, here's a more detailed look at a handful of Notre Dame's rivalries (in alphabetical order).

ARMY

Jack Swarbrick probably has long since lost track of the number of times he has related this story. But, for the University of Notre Dame vice president and athletics director, it defines what Notre Dame football is all about. It goes a long way toward explaining exactly why the Irish and Cadets returned to Yankee Stadium in 2010.

Let's go back to 1913.

It's the 25th season of football at Notre Dame and the first season under head coach Jesse Harper. Prior to Harper's arrival, Notre Dame teams had a dozen other coaches, some of them player/coaches. Their teams had more than their share of success (8–0–1 in 1903, 7–0–1 in 1909, 7–0 in 1912). But even the most ardent fans might be hard-pressed to identify any particularly noteworthy wins in that era (Notre Dame's first win over Michigan in 1909, after eight straight losses, probably drew the most attention). Notre Dame was just good enough that many more established programs were loath to schedule the school from South Bend.

To that point, Notre Dame road trips in football had been to Midwestern cities and towns. Harper changed all that. In that 1913 season alone he made agreements to send his Notre Dame team to play for the first time at Army, Penn State, and Texas. A year later he and his players traveled to Yale, in 1915 to Rice, and in 1916 and 1917 to Nebraska. The contact with Army actually began based on the prospect of a baseball meeting, with Army defeating Notre Dame 3–0 in May 1913 in the first contest in any sport between the two programs.

But, it was the 1913 Notre Dame–Army football game that put Notre Dame football on the national map.

Ken Rappoport, in his history of Notre Dame football *Wake Up the Echoes*, calls the game "the most significant victory in the history of Notre Dame football."

Army didn't win its first national championship until 1914, but the Cadets clearly were the more established program (though Army didn't field its first team until 1890, three years after Notre Dame did so).

Notre Dame appeared to be as much a curiosity as anything on the Army agenda in that 1913 season. One newspaper, commenting on the Army schedule, suggested "the most interesting home game is likely to be that with Notre Dame."

Here's all you need to know about how Harper and his players made it to West Point. After an initial offer of $600, the Army Athletic Council finally agreed to give Notre Dame $1,000 for expenses. The Notre Dame squad took railroad coaches from South Bend to Buffalo, then transferred to Pullman cars for the rest of the journey. The players brought sandwiches to save funds. Eighteen players made the trip (bringing only 14 pairs of football cleats between them), many carrying their equipment in their arms.

The forward pass had been legalized in 1906 but had been used sparingly, with most coaches looking on that strategy as a desperation tactic. Notre Dame changed all that on that November 1 afternoon on Cullum Hall Field.

With the Cadets prepared for a Notre Dame power attack, Harper's squad crossed them up. After a summer practicing throwing and catching on the Cedar Point beaches in Sandusky, Ohio,

Notre Dame quarterback Gus Dorais and end Knute Rockne took Army apart with their aerial success.

Statistics in those days were unofficial, but reports suggested Notre Dame passed for nearly 300 yards, on something along the lines of 14-of-17 throwing. Harper's charges scored three fourth-period touchdowns, and Notre Dame won 35–13, handing Army its only loss of the season. The New York Times the next day called it "the most sensational football ever seen in the East."

That single game, played some 100 years ago, changed the course of football at Notre Dame for good.

It set the tone for Notre Dame's ongoing philosophy of playing a national schedule. It set the course for Notre Dame succeeding as an independent. In fact, in recent days—with conference memberships changing for lots of programs—when Swarbrick was asked on almost a daily basis why Notre Dame so valued its independent status, he would refer back to that 1913 Notre Dame–Army football game as the one that set out the University's long-term game plan.

Five years later, in 1918, Rockne succeeded Harper as the Notre Dame head coach—and his 13-year record (105 victories) has never been matched in terms of winning percentage.

All you need to know about the early stages of the rivalry is that the first nine Notre Dame–Army games all were played at West Point. The teams met in 1923 at Ebbets Field in Brooklyn, then in 1924 at the Polo Grounds in the game at which Grantland Rice dubbed the Notre Dame backfield the Four Horsemen. A year later, in 1925, the teams played at Yankee Stadium for the first time. Three years later, also at Yankee Stadium, came the famed "Win One for the Gipper" speech that helped prompt a Notre Dame come-from-behind victory over the Cadets. Rockne's teams finished 9–2–1 against Army.

The rivalry flourished in the 1940s when both programs combined to rule the college football world. They played every year from 1938 through 1947, with Notre Dame ranked seventh or better in the Associated Press poll coming into all of those games. In fact, that's how the term "subway alumni" came to be, with fans traveling by train to Yankee Stadium. Army traveled to play in Notre Dame Stadium for the first time in 1947.

In 2010 the two teams gathered again, fittingly in new Yankee Stadium, for the 50th renewal of the Notre Dame–Army rivalry. It marked the 23rd time Yankee Stadium had been the setting for this matchup. For the Fighting Irish, it qualified as a throwback to how they began to become a college football name.

BOSTON COLLEGE

- Number of opponents for Notre Dame in its football history: 141
- Number of those teams with winning records against the Fighting Irish: 14
- Number of those 14 no longer playing in Division I-A: 4 (Chicago, Great Lakes, Indianapolis Artillery, Yale)
- Number of opponents that have played 20 or more games against the Irish: 15
- Value of a rivalry with Notre Dame: apparently, priceless

The questions come from all sorts of sources. The well-intended journalists writing books or DVD scripts about college football want to know who is Notre Dame's biggest rival in football.

Is it USC? What about Michigan? How about Navy—in the longest continuing intersectional rivalry in the country?

What about the 75 games against Michigan State—and the 83 against Purdue—and the 67 against Pittsburgh?

What about Miami in the 1980s? That one heated up when Lou Holtz arrived in 1986.

What about Boston College, the only other Division I-A football-playing Catholic institution other than Notre Dame?

How about Stanford, another school with a highly respected academic culture and a recent string of great seasons?

Does it require a shillelagh (USC and Purdue), a megaphone (Michigan State), or a crystal bowl (Stanford and Boston College) to make it a rivalry?

Those traditional trophies historically have been more fodder for game notes and media guides than postgame, midfield presentations. Still, it was not so long ago that an Irish loss in one of these series prompted the winning school to send an administrator to South Bend early the next week to pick up the trophy in question.

Do green jerseys on Irish players (see USC 1977, 1983, and 1985, Colorado in 1994, Georgia Tech in 1998, Boston College in 2002, Washington State in 2009, Army in 2010, Maryland in 2011) make for rivalry games?

The answers to all these questions are the same: your opinion is as good as anyone else's.

A longtime journalist from Lafayette asked the question in the press box before a recent Irish-Purdue contest: where does the Purdue rivalry fit in at Notre Dame?

Irish football coaches generally make it clear in their comments that Notre Dame's history and tradition seem to make a rivalry of every game on the schedule—based on the way Irish opponents make their assignments against Notre Dame red-letter dates.

Actually, it's challenging to be politically correct in these institutional debates. Coaches, and usually players, strive for politeness in this venue, so as not to create bulletin-board material. Media, on the other hand, seek the raw human emotion involved.

They'd love to have opposing players or coaches go toe to toe, debating the relative importance of a victory over such-and-such team.

Holtz didn't mind telling you that the USC series meant more than any other to him—and he proved it. He'd done his research on the series history, knew the stories of Knute Rockne and Bonnie Rockne and Gwynn Wilson and Howard Jones. He studied up on that particular rivalry—and even gave his freshman players annual quizzes on the series to make sure they grasped its importance.

A couple of other elements have made it easy to judge the relative importance of football series over the years.

Seventeen different games between Notre Dame and USC have been played with both teams ranked in the top 10. That's happened eight times in the Irish-Michigan series (including five out of six years from 1989 through 1994).

Of those 17 Notre Dame–USC matchups, one ended in a tie (21–21 in 1968) and USC has won nine (to seven victories for the Irish). Now, that's the sort of give and take that helps to promote a rivalry.

Television provides some measure, as well. In 48 consecutive Notre Dame–USC games played starting in 1965, 37 have appeared on national television (plus four more shown regionally). All 25 Notre Dame–Michigan games played starting in 1981 have been televised nationally.

Plus, all these things run in cycles. Michigan State came into its game with Notre Dame ranked in the top 10 on nine occasions from 1949 through 1966. That probably contributed to an eight-game Spartan win streak from 1955 through 1963. No one said all that much about Notre Dame–Purdue—other than the natural geographic happenstance—from 1986 through 1996, when the Irish won 11 straight meetings. But it was a whole different story when the Boilers were ranked 16th or better every year from 1965 through 1969 (and defeated the Irish four of those five games)—and with six of the last 14 Irish-Purdue contests decided by a touchdown or less, there's been no lack of interest in that relationship.

If you talk to anyone from Boston College, it's never been anything but a heavy-duty rivalry, even if the teams have played only 21 times through 2011. David Gordon's game-winning field goal in 1993 to defeat a No. 1–ranked Notre Dame team contributed mightily to that thought—and six straight wins by the Eagles from 2001 to 2008 only added an exclamation mark.

Former Irish linebacker Mike Goolsby stood in the bowels of Giants Stadium some years ago—with the exhaust fumes from an Irish-Navy clash still prominent in the rear-view mirror—and immediately he was being asked about the following week's Notre Dame–Boston College contest and what it meant.

So, be it Boston College or Pittsburgh or USC—call them all rivalries, if you will.

For Notre Dame, there doesn't seem to be any other way.

MICHIGAN

Remember Harry Oliver and Tim Koegel? They actually were teammates at Moeller High School in Cincinnati—and they both ended up playing football at Notre Dame.

They combined on one of the more dramatic, game-ending plays in Notre Dame football history in 1980, when Oliver kicked a 51-yard field goal—with Koegel holding—to enable the Irish to defeat Michigan 29–27 in Notre Dame Stadium.

That one play inspired one of the most emotional radio calls in memory from Mutual's Tony Roberts, who was in his very first year of doing play-by-play on Notre Dame broadcasts.

In typical fashion when it comes to Irish football lore, Koegel revels in telling the story of how the wind stopped in Notre Dame Stadium just in time for Oliver to attempt the field goal. There's a now-famous black-and-white photo by Notre Dame student photographer Peter Romzick of that play—and it that shows then–Notre Dame president Rev. Theodore M. Hesburgh, C.S.C., and executive vice president Rev. Edmund P. Joyce, C.S.C., in the stands, watching the game.

For Oliver, then a junior, it marked only the second field-goal attempt in his career with the Irish.

What prompted all the attention to that one single play? It came against Michigan, then the 14th-ranked team in the country.

Remember Desmond Howard? He caught that layout touchdown pass on fourth down and one from the Notre Dame 25-yard line that enabled Michigan to slip past the Irish in Michigan Stadium in 1991.

Sports Illustrated said it "may have been the most memorable college football play in many seasons."

What else has Howard accomplished in his football career? For one, he won the Heisman Trophy in 1991. But, when they throw up the Howard highlights in Ann Arbor, that reception in the end zone against the Irish—with Howard horizontal—begins the reel. Why? Because it came against Notre Dame, then the seventh-ranked team in the country.

The respective Notre Dame and Michigan directors of athletics often have considered some future scheduling options in a variety of sports. Why? They understand the same thing you do: when Notre Dame and Michigan meet on any sort of athletic field, it's meaningful.

The perception is that the Notre Dame–Michigan football rivalry has been one for the ages—when actually the teams have met on

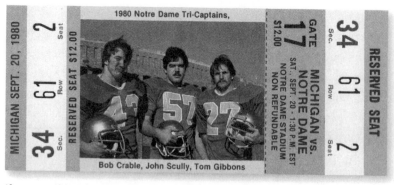

If you own this ticket stub, it means you witnessed Harry Oliver's memorable 51-yard field goal in 1980 to beat Michigan as time expired.

only 39 occasions, far fewer times than the Irish have faced fellow Big Ten members Purdue or Michigan State. The Wolverines actually came to South Bend to play in 1887 in Notre Dame's first-ever varsity football outing. The schools did not meet between 1943 and 1978 (they also didn't face each other between 1909 and 1942), but since then have met on a fairly regular basis (the Irish took on Ohio State instead in that early-season schedule slot in 1995 and 1996 and did the same with Nebraska in 2000 and 2001).

In the last 30 meetings, both teams have been nationally ranked in 21 of those contests—and both teams have been in the top 10 in eight of the 30.

In the 28 meetings starting in 1978 (when quarterbacks Rick Leach and Joe Montana dueled), Notre Dame has won 13 times, Michigan 14—and there's been one tie (1992).

The Notre Dame–Michigan matchups have made for great theatre so often that John Kryk wrote a book (*Natural Enemies*) published in 1994 that detailed the games.

When Kryk updates his tome, who knows whom the heroes will be from the next game?

If the Irish prevail, maybe it will be a Notre Dame player doing his best imitation of Tim Brown, who got his 1987 Heisman Trophy–winning season off to a smashing start in Ann Arbor with a picture-perfect early touchdown reception from Terry Andrysiak to jump-start a 26–7 Irish victory.

Maybe it will be an Irish placekicker, trying to do his best imitation of Reggie Ho, the rookie placekicker whose late field goal provided a 19–17 margin over the Wolverines in 1988 to start Notre Dame on its national championship journey—or of Chuck Male who accounted for all 12 of Notre Dame's points in its 1979 victory in Michigan Stadium.

Maybe it will be a modern-day re-creation of Irish linebacker Bob Crable, who stepped on the back of Michigan's Mike Trgovac (ironically, Trgovac later became a Notre Dame assistant coach) in 1979 to block a potential 42-yard game-winning field goal for the Wolverines with seven seconds left in the 12–10 Irish triumph.

Maybe it will be a Notre Damer returning a kick—as Raghib Ismail did twice for TDs on kickoff returns in 1989 in the rain in Ann Arbor as the Irish maintained their No. 1 ranking.

Maybe it will be a pass interception—in honor of the late Dave Duerson, whose late pickoff in 1982 helped preserve a 23–17 Notre Dame victory over the Wolverines in the first-ever night football game played at Notre Dame Stadium.

Someone will make his mark in any given game as a difference-maker in another Notre Dame–Michigan football game. Count on that individual to merit a chapter title in Kryk's next edition.

NAVY

Truth be told, the major-college intersectional football game seems to, for the most part, have gone by the boards. Bowl Championship Series criteria have stiffened, and Division I programs have decided that—economically and competitively—playing more often at home makes more sense (and cents).

So we're simply not privy to the number of match-ups we used to see.

Check the 2007 season, for example.

On September 1 there were Kansas State at Auburn, Tennessee at California, Washington State at Wisconsin, Oklahoma State at Georgia, and Washington at Syracuse.

On September 8 there were Miami (Fla.) at Oklahoma, Virginia Tech at LSU, and Oregon at Michigan.

Then, on September 15 there were USC at Nebraska and Ohio State at Washington.

Throw in the annual USC–Notre Dame clash, as well as lots of other Fighting Irish games (other than those against the Big Ten). Add the annual service academy contests involving Army, Navy, and Air Force.

Then there's this one: Notre Dame versus Navy. The Irish and Midshipmen do battle either in South Bend or in another neutral locale, including Dublin, Ireland, in 2012.

It's billed as the longest continuous intersectional rivalry in the country. The teams have played in 85 consecutive seasons heading into that 2012 game.

So, maybe make it *the longest continuous intersectional rivalry in the country.*

Or, maybe even, the **LONGEST CONTINUOUS INTERSECTIONAL RIVALRY IN THE COUNTRY.**

Now that's saying something.

The convenient tagline is that Notre Dame's 43-game win streak (1964–2006) marked the longest in college football history by one team over an opponent. The Irish and Mids seldom play without video footage being shown of Roger Staubach leading Navy to its win in 1963 at Notre Dame Stadium.

Although Notre Dame's 72 series victories are 17 more than the Irish have accounted for against any other opponent, the series wasn't always that way.

In 1940 unbeaten Notre Dame needed a 78-yard drive in the final minutes and a fourth-and-goal touchdown run from the seven by Bob Saggau to hold off the Midshipmen 13–7.

Three of the Navy wins came in a four-year period from 1933 to 1936. Five others came within the eight-game, eight-year span from 1956 through 1963. Three more came in a recent four-year span (2007–2010).

The Mids outranked the Irish coming into games in 1941 (a 20–13 win in Baltimore by the seventh-ranked Notre Dame over sixth-rated Navy), 1955 (a 21–7 Irish win in Notre Dame Stadium by the ninth-rated Irish over No. 4 Navy), 1958 in Baltimore (40–20 for the unrated Irish over No. 15 Navy), 1960 in Philadelphia (14–7 for the fourth-rated Midshipmen), 1963 at Notre Dame Stadium (35–14 for the Staubach-led No. 4 Mids, with the Navy signal-caller just a junior and on his way to the Heisman Trophy), and finally 1978 in Cleveland (27–7 for No. 15 Notre Dame over No. 11 Navy).

This is a series that got started in the Knute Rockne era at Notre Dame in 1927 when a Navy assistant coach, Edgar (Rip) Miller, one of the Seven Mules that led the way for the Four Horsemen on the 1924 Notre Dame championship team, convinced Rockne and Navy coach Bill Ingram to match up their teams. They began the rivalry with a handshake, and Miller later became the Navy head coach and also was athletics director in Annapolis for 26 years before he retired in 1974.

Other Notre Dame–Navy connections have included former Naval Academy superintendent Tom Lynch, captain of that 1963 Navy football squad and brother of former 1966 Irish captain and All-American Jim Lynch. Former head coaches Lou Holtz (Notre Dame) and George Chaump (Navy), who were roommates when they were assistant coaches together on head coach Woody Hayes' staff at Ohio State in the late 1960s, also forged a connection.

Former Notre Dame president Rev. Theodore M. Hesburgh, C.S.C., has long championed the relationship between these two programs, both on and off the football field. He often alluded to the fact Navy had plenty to do with Notre Dame surviving during World War II because—with the school reduced to only several hundred students because of the war—the Navy designated the University as a training station for 5,000 of its officers, thus keeping Notre Dame alive and well during a critical time in its history.

The Notre Dame–Navy series has featured games in Baltimore; Cleveland; Philadelphia; Giants Stadium in the New Jersey Meadowlands; Orlando; Chicago (Soldier Field in 1928); Washington, D.C.; and even Dublin, Ireland (1996 and 2012).

Father Hesburgh once raised a few eyebrows around the Notre Dame campus when he suggested it would be good for the Irish-Midshipmen series and relationship if Navy won a game every now and then.

The Irish regularly attempt to prevent that sentiment from becoming reality.

PITTSBURGH

Old-school rivalries are what make college football so delectable.

They give fans of any age the chance to reminisce about games and plays—and players and coaches—of years gone by.

Considering that Notre Dame and Pittsburgh have met more times (67) than any Notre Dame opponent other than Navy (85), Purdue (83), USC (83), and Michigan State (75), let's look back at a few of the connections between the small, private school in the Midwest and the large public institution not far from the banks of the Ohio, Monongahela, and Allegheny rivers:

Consider the great players who came from Pittsburgh/western Pennsylvania to Notre Dame—including Heisman Trophy winners John Lujack (Connellsville) and Leon Hart (Turtle Creek), plus consensus All-America quarterback Terry Hanratty (Butler). And don't forget all-star quarterbacks Joe Montana (Monongahela) and Tom Clements (McKees Rocks).

Other All-Americans from the Keystone State for Notre Dame included Dick Arrington (Erie), Raghib Ismail (Wilkes-Barre), and Mike McCoy (Erie).

Former Irish head coach Joe Kuharich's first coaching job was as line coach of the Pittsburgh Steelers in 1946. Former Notre Dame head coach Bob Davie came from Sewickley, Pennsylvania, while Hall of Famer Lou Holtz grew up in East Liverpool, Ohio, some 40 miles northwest of Pittsburgh. And former Pitt head coach Foge Fazio later came to South Bend as Holtz's defensive coordinator from 1986 to 1987.

Remember some of the more memorable meetings between the Panthers and Irish:

- 1911, when Pitt helped ruin a potentially perfect Notre Dame season with a 0–0 tie. Notre Dame finished 6–0–2, also tying Marquette.
- 1958, when Bill Kaliden's five-yard touchdown run with 11 seconds left gave the Panthers a 29–26 win over the 14th-rated Irish.

- 1962, when Daryle Lamonica tied the Notre Dame record with four TD passes, three to Jim Kelly, in a 43–22 Irish win.

- 1964, when John Huarte completed a 91-yard TD pass to Nick Eddy—longest in Notre Dame history to that point—for the top-rated Irish.

- 1965, when Bill Wolski scored five TDs for fourth-ranked Notre Dame in a 69–13 victory.

- 1968, when 12th-ranked Notre Dame led 49–0 at half (the Irish held halftime advantages of 23–2 in first downs and 399–32 in total offense), as coaches Ara Parseghian and Dave Hart decided to let the clock run in the second half of the 56–7 Irish win.

- 1973, when Pitt freshman Tony Dorsett ran for 209 yards, most ever against a Notre Dame team at that time (the Irish finished second in the country that year in total defense). Notre Dame won 31–10.

- 1974, when Tom Clements' three-yard, off-tackle TD run with 2:49 left gave the fifth-rated Irish a 14–10 win.

- 1975, when Dorsett accomplished what's still the all-time best rushing effort by a Notre Dame opponent player when he ran for 303 yards against the Irish.

- 1977, when the Irish began what turned out to be a national championship season in Pittsburgh against a seventh-ranked Panthers unit that became handicapped when quarterback Matt Cavanaugh (later the Pitt offensive coordinator) broke his left wrist in the first period.

- 1978, when Notre Dame (behind some Montana heroics) overcame a 17–7 fourth-period deficit to win 26–17 in South Bend, as Bob Golic made 22 tackles against ninth-ranked Pitt.

- 1982, when the Dan Marino-led, No. 1–rated, and unbeaten Panthers fell victim to a freshman tailback named Allen Pinkett, whose two TD runs and 112 rushing yards helped the Irish spring the upset in Pitt Stadium.
- 1986, when Jeff VanHorne's 29-yard field goal at the 1:25 mark gave Pitt a 10–9 victory.
- 1989, when the unbeaten Irish shocked the seventh-ranked and unbeaten Panthers in a 45–7 triumph at Notre Dame.
- 1996–1997, when Allen Rossum made life miserable for the Panthers with a 93-yard kickoff return for a TD (1997), an 83-yard punt return for a TD (1996), and a 55-yard punt return for a TD (1996).
- 1999, when Notre Dame played in the final game in old Pitt Stadium. In a 37–27 Pitt win, the Irish highlights came from Bobby Brown's 12 receptions for 208 yards.
- 2003, when Julius Jones set the single-game Irish rushing record with 262 yards against the Panthers in Heinz Field.
- 2004, when Josh Cummings' 32-yard field goal with one second left gave Pitt a 41–38 victory, as Tyler Palko threw five TD passes for the Panthers.
- 2005, when the Charlie Weis and Dave Wannstedt eras opened on the same night in Pittsburgh. Weis' charges won out 42–21, with Brady Quinn completing 11 straight passes and Rashon Powers-Neal scoring three times.
- 2008, when the Panthers survived in a four-overtime 36–33 triumph at Notre Dame Stadium.

When the Panthers visit Notre Dame Stadium for the 31st time in 2012, they will have made more stops to play in Notre Dame's current home facility than any teams other than USC (38), Purdue (36), and Navy (32).

The Panthers' 10 wins in Notre Dame Stadium may not sound like a huge achievement, but the only teams with more are USC (14), Michigan State (13), and Purdue (10).

PURDUE

It wouldn't be Notre Dame–Purdue without the game being a showcase for quarterbacks, would it?

After all, examples such as Purdue's Kyle Orton and Notre Dame's Brady Quinn and Jimmy Clausen are simply the latest signal-callers from either the Irish or Boilermaker camp to find their names in lights:

- Remember Len Dawson? In 1954 he managed only seven pass completions for the Boilers, but four of them went for touchdowns in a 27–14 Purdue win over the top-ranked Irish.
- How about Terry Hanratty? His 63 pass attempts (in a losing cause in 1967 in West Lafayette) still ranks as the all-time single-game Irish high. In fact, three of the top Notre Dame single-game efforts for completions have come against the Boilers (31 by Ron Powlus in 1997 and 29 each by Hanratty in 1967 and by Brady Quinn in 2003).
- Joe Montana? His off-the-bench, come-from-behind effort in 1977 in West Lafayette propelled him into the Notre Dame starting lineup for good in what became a national championship season for the Irish.
- Bob Griese? He connected on an amazing 19 of 22 passes for 283 yards in 1965 in West Lafayette in sixth-rated Purdue's 25–21 win over top-rated Notre Dame.
- Mike Phipps? He led Purdue to an unprecedented three straight victories over the Irish from 1967 to 1969—and the Irish were top-10 teams coming into all three games.

- Brady Quinn? In 2005 he completed an amazing 29 of 36 throws for 440 yards in a 49–28 Irish victory in West Lafayette in a prime-time contest for the 13th-rated Irish over the No. 22 Boilermakers.

If it hasn't been Irish quarterbacks bamboozling the Boilers, it's been Notre Dame receivers. Jim Seymour's 13 receptions—No. 2 on Notre Dame's all-time list—came against Purdue in 1966 and was good for 276 yards in a 26–14 Irish win. The third-best total in that category, 12 catches for 192 yards, came in 1970 by Tom Gatewood in a 48–0 dismantling of the Boilers in South Bend. In

Notre Dame's 26–14 victory over Purdue in 1966 featured 276 receiving yards by Jim Seymour on 13 catches.

that 2005 meeting, Jeff Samardzija caught seven passes for 153 yards and two scores.

Not all the hype turns into proof on Saturdays. In 1980 the 11th-ranked Irish opened the season at home against the ninth-ranked Boilermakers. It might have been the most anticipated meeting of the two schools in recent memory (ABC moved the game a week earlier for national television)—fueled in particular by the participation of Purdue senior quarterback Mark Herrmann, who was being touted as a Heisman Trophy candidate. The only trouble was Herrmann banged a thumb on a teammate's helmet in practice on Tuesday and never played. The Irish won easily 31–10 and went unbeaten in their first 10 games that year.

In 2002, late in a tie ballgame, Kyle Orton saw one of his tipped passes end up in the hands of Notre Dame's Vontez Duff—and 33 yards later the Irish had a game-winning interception return for a score in a 24–17 win.

Consider also that there have been 12 previous series meetings (six of them at Notre Dame Stadium) in which both teams were ranked in the Associated Press poll. Purdue has won eight of the 12—and three of the six in Notre Dame's home facility. The Boilers earned their "Spoilermaker" tag by defeating top-ranked Notre Dame teams in 1954, 1965, and 1967—and by beating the Irish in 1968 when Purdue came in No. 1 by the Associated Press and Notre Dame No. 1 by United Press International.

The 2004 game marked only the fourth time Purdue came into Notre Dame Stadium ranked higher than Notre Dame. It happened previously in 1968 (at least according to AP), 1980 (the ultimately Herrmann-less Boilers ninth, Notre Dame 11th), then in 2000 (Purdue 13th, Notre Dame 21st, with the Irish winning 23–21). That 2000 meeting matched Purdue senior Drew Brees in his final Notre Dame Stadium stop against Notre Dame's Gary

Godsey who was playing in his first college game. Nicholas Setta ended up winning it for the Irish with a 38-yard field goal as time expired.

With all that history in the rearview mirror, much has been made of the fact Purdue has won only a single game (2004) in Notre Dame Stadium since a 1974 victory. That comes in a topsy-turvy series in which the lower-ranked team has won on 18 occasions (with 15 of those 18 chalked up in the Purdue win column).

STANFORD

You've likely heard this story before, yet it bears repeating, maybe more than ever before considering the economy and ongoing employment challenges.

Look at the players on the field in virtually any Notre Dame–Stanford football game—and consider that maybe *every one of them* will graduate from either the University of Notre Dame or Stanford University.

Now that's saying something in a college athletics world where it isn't always easy, much less automatic, to connect the dots between the athlete concept and the student concept.

But, it's safe to say that Notre Dame and Stanford are two of the schools playing major-college sports that are committed to making sure a student-athlete (and preferably all of them) walks away from the campus experience with an education as well as a degree.

Oh, there may well be a player or two off the rosters who doesn't finish up in South Bend or Palo Alto. But, it's much more likely that any potential transfers move to other campuses—not because they have any academic issues at all, but because they simply are seeking a home where they can find more football playing time.

Consider all the recent evidence that backs up the athletic/
academic philosophies of these two institutions:

- In the fall of 2011, when the NCAA released its latest federal graduation numbers, in terms of football, Notre Dame
  stood at 83 and Stanford at 84 (behind only Boston College
  at 87, Northwestern at 86, and Rice also at 84). In terms of
  all student-athletes, Notre Dame ranked first at 91, Stanford
  second at 90.
- In that same survey, which also featured Graduation Success
  Rate (GSR) numbers, Notre Dame ranked first among FBS
  schools in measuring all student-athletes at 99. Stanford tied
  for seventh at 94.
- When it came to football, Notre Dame finished first in the
  GSR standings at 97, while Stanford was 10th at 87.

Go back any number of years to previous federal, Academic
Progress Rate and GSR surveys, and the numbers will be similar. If
Notre Dame or Stanford don't rank No. 1, they almost certainly are
consistently in the top half-dozen in terms of any measurements of
combining athletics and academic success. And that's no accident.

Notre Dame has produced 55 Academic All-America selections in
football—including on-field All-Americans such as Joe Theismann,
George Kunz, Dave Casper, Pete Demmerle, and Ken MacAfee.
Stanford has produced 42 Academic All-Americans in football.

Recent Notre Dame offensive lineman Chris Stewart qualified
as a poster boy for this subject. Owner of a degree in economics
from Notre Dame, he was a first-year student in the Notre Dame
Law School in 2010 while playing his final season. He was featured
in USA Today, in great part because there's no record of a previous
Irish football player combining those two pursuits at the same time.

Notre Dame and Stanford aren't the only programs doing it this way. Look at the graduation surveys, and you'll see many of the same other names year after year. Duke, Northwestern, Boston College, Vanderbilt, Wake Forest, Rice, and the service academies are the names you most often see on list after list.

Scheduling, especially in football, can be an inexact science of sorts. Yet, there are conscious decisions to be made about whom you play from week to week.

Gene Corrigan, who served as Notre Dame's athletics director from 1981 to 1987, made some of those decisions. He decided there was something to be said for playing schools with similar philosophies.

So, Notre Dame—after playing Stanford only in the Rose Bowl following the 1924 season, plus in 1942, 1963, and 1964—began an ongoing series with the Cardinal in 1988.

Corrigan began the Boston College series that started with a single game in 1987 and continued for good in 1992. He scheduled Northwestern for games from 1992 through 1995. He scheduled Rice for 1988. He scheduled SMU for 1986 and 1989. He scheduled Vanderbilt for 1995 and 1996.

You can't legislate academic standards and philosophies at other institutions. But, as Corrigan did, you can make a point to schedule games against programs that treat academics as a welcomed and valued component that goes hand in hand with the athletics aspect of a collegiate experience.

These days, current Notre Dame vice president and athletics director Jack Swarbrick makes the scheduling decisions. He intends to have Notre Dame and Stanford continue playing each other in football. Expect to see Boston College to continue appearing on Irish schedule cards.

Wake Forest played games with Notre Dame in 2011 and 2012.

Call them "sister schools" or peer institutions. What it means is that it's no accident that athletes from these programs generally graduate. It's part of the DNA of the athletic positioning of those institutions.

Pretend you are Brian Kelly or David Shaw—and your football recruiting pitch contains the likelihood that if the young man across the table from you stays for at least four years at Notre Dame or Stanford, the odds are hugely in your favor that he'll walk away with a degree.

In this day and age, that ought to count more than ever before.

USC

We'll begin by presuming you remember what came to be known as the "Bush Push" from Notre Dame Stadium in 2005, when tailback Reggie Bush helped levitate quarterback Matt Leinart over the goal line from the one-yard line with three seconds left to preserve (temporarily) USC's No. 1 ranking.

(We'll forget the Irish version of the story that says replay should have shown the ball being fumbled out of bounds at the 3 on the previous play.)

That's one of the latest thorns the Trojans have injected into the sides of the Irish—and it goes both ways.

USC has beaten Notre Dame more times (35, with Michigan State second at 28) than any other team has defeated the Irish—and the Irish own the most victories over USC (43, with California next at 30).

Some of the Trojan wins over the Irish have been particularly painful. Check out the list of fantastic-finish-style Notre Dame series losses—and you'll find the USC name involved seven times in games decided in the final five minutes (1931, 1964, 1978, 1981, 1982, 1997, 2005), not including the 1996 Trojan overtime win. In former USC coach John McKay's 16 games against Notre Dame, the outcome either determined or helped determine who was the national champion 10 times.

For a little more perspective, we decided to check in with a couple of guys who have more stories about the Notre Dame–USC rivalry than anyone else we know.

Roger Valdiserri was the Notre Dame sports information director from 1966 to 1987 (and remained through the early 1990s as assistant and associate athletics director). He presided over publicity for 20 Irish football seasons that produced a combined 175–66–5 record, three national titles, 30 consensus All-Americans, and a dozen bowl games.

Jim Perry played the same role at USC from 1974 to 1983 (and previously covered USC football for three years, 1971 to 1973, at the old *Los Angeles Herald-Examiner* and also later became an assistant athletics director). His résumé? An 89–25–4 mark. Two national titles. Nineteen consensus All-Americans. Six straight bowl victories (four of them in Pasadena).

Consider some of the rivalry craziness the two publicists witnessed:

Notre Dame's 2005 meeting with USC at Notre Dame Stadium very nearly produced an upset over the top-rated Trojans until Matt Leinart's late touchdown.

1966: Irish national title

1967: Trojan national title

1972: Trojans title

1973: Irish title

1974: Trojans title

1977: Irish title

1978: Trojan fans still revel in the 11th-hour Paul McDonald–led drive that led to Frank Jordan's game-winning field goal with two ticks on the clock. Irish fans are convinced Joe Montana should have been the hero and that McDonald actually fumbled on that late drive. Another Trojan title.

1979: Trojans Heisman winner (Charles White)

1981: Trojans prevail again, this time via a touchdown on a 26-yard Todd Spencer run with less than five minutes to go. Trojan Heisman winner (Marcus Allen).

1982: Trojans fans are certain Michael Harper scored the game-winning TD with 48 seconds left in the game. Irish fans are equally certain Harper never had the football when he crossed the goal line and that Kevin Griffith actually recovered the fumble for Notre Dame.

1987: Irish Heisman winner (Tim Brown)

It didn't take long for the memories to flow for Valdiserri (the USC Trojan Club presented him with a Trojan jersey with the No. 33 on it for the number of Notre Dame–USC games he worked):

- "One year (John) Papadakis for USC had a great game at linebacker (15 tackles in 1970). I was standing in the press box next to Jim Murray (the late *Los Angeles Times* columnist) and some other Los Angeles writers, and I said, 'He's done everything but open a Greek restaurant.' So about five years ago, Emil Hofman (former Notre Dame dean of Freshman Year of Studies) tells me he was in San Bruno, California, and went to Papadakis' Greek restaurant, and the newspaper clipping where I had said that was framed on the wall."

- "In 1967 O.J. Simpson ran for a couple of touchdowns for USC and about 150 yards. I was chatting with Dan Jenkins from *Sports Illustrated*, and I said, 'Now I know what O.J. stands for—oh, Jesus, there he goes again.'"

- "There were two opposing players that I went into the visiting locker room to meet. One was Ernie Davis from Syracuse when he played in South Bend. The other was O.J. out there. He was so great, I just wanted to go in and meet him, and I can still picture him sitting by his locker."

- "In 1977, when we came out in the green jerseys, I've never seen such a reaction in Notre Dame Stadium. It's probably the most memorable a beginning of a home game I've ever been associated with here. The USC players looked around, like, 'What's going on?' I don't think it hit them right away."

Here's what Perry offered, some material from serving as the author for McKay's autobiography *McKay: A Coach's Story* (published in 1974):

- Some quotes from McKay late in his USC career: "When I grew up as a Catholic in West Virginia, I loved Notre Dame and its football team. The Fighting Irish were the first team in any sport I rooted for. I think they've always had that fascination for young Catholic kids, and today I still cheer

In 1970 the greatest passing performance in Irish history—526 yards in the rain by Joe Theismann—went for naught in a 38–28 USC victory.

for them—except when they play us. I've said it a hundred times, and I'll say it again. There's no greater thrill in football than playing in South Bend. I get keyed up and ready to play myself, but thank God that won't happen. I always hope my players are as keyed up as I am. I tell them that if you don't get up for Notre Dame you must be dead."

- After losing to Notre Dame 51–0 in 1966 (which clinched the national title for Notre Dame), McKay watched the film of that game at least once a week for a year—and sometimes every day. Several years later, he said, "It was the only game I've ever coached that I've replayed in my mind long after it was over. I still have that film, and once in a while I'll watch it again."
- McKay always admired Ara Parseghian and thought he was an outstanding coach, but, because of the intensity of the rivalry, they were never close. A couple of years before he died (June 2001, at age 77), he told me he and Ara had now become good friends and talked on the phone about once a week.
- In 1977, in his second year as head coach, John Robinson took his first team to South Bend. The team toured the campus on Friday, and Robinson even bought some souvenirs in the bookstore. USC went out and lost to the Irish 49–19, Robinson's worst loss at USC. He never took the team to campus again, bussing directly to the stadium in 1979 and 1981 and winning both times.

Valdiserri and Perry—now they've *got* some stories. Wonder who will add to their treasure trove of memories next?

First-Time Visitors to Notre Dame Stadium

There's a different sort of wrinkle involved when Wake Forest comes to Notre Dame Stadium in 2012.

Watch the Demon Deacon players as they warm up in Notre Dame Stadium.

Is this just another road trip for the Wake Forest program? That game officially qualifies as Wake Forest's first visit to Notre Dame's current home field.

So, as one opposing coach once kiddingly asked (in reference to Notre Dame's football history), is George Gipp going to come out of the stands to play, or is Knute Rockne going to show up on the other sideline?

Since the expansion of Notre Dame Stadium in 1997, the mural of Christ (maybe better known as "Touchdown Jesus") doesn't loom in view at the north end of the facility quite the way it used to appear.

But, will the Demon Deacons be tempted to be spectators, maybe just a little bit? We'll find out soon enough.

History is not exactly on the side of those first-time visitors who are stopping by for a business trip to the location *Sporting News* in 2011 rated the best place in the country to watch college football (based on the facility, fans, city/surroundings, traditions, and history).

Let's examine the numbers.

Wake Forest becomes the 69th different team to come to Notre Dame Stadium. The statistics suggest it's not easy to win in any team's first attempt at the Irish football facility. South Florida in 2011, Tulsa in 2010, and Connecticut in 2009 did it. But, prior to those contests, 12 straight opponents had fallen to Notre Dame in their first visits to South Bend:

- In 2009 Nevada lost 35–0 in the Notre Dame season opener.
- In 2008 San Diego State fell 21–13 in a similar opener.
- In 2003 it was Washington State losing 29–26 in overtime in the Irish season opener.
- In 2000 23rd-rated Texas A&M found itself on the short end of a 24–10 score against Bob Davie's unranked Notre Dame team (another season opener).
- In 1999 Arizona State lost 48–17.

- In 1998 Baylor fell 27–3.
- In 1997 22nd-rated West Virginia came up on the wrong side of a 21–14 final in Davie's first season with the Irish.
- In 1996 in Lou Holtz's final home game at Notre Dame, his Irish defeated Rutgers 62–0, as Notre Dame outgained the visitors 648–43 in total yards.
- In 1995 Vanderbilt found itself shut out 41–0.
- In 1992 BYU lost 42–16.
- In 1985 Ole Miss was defeated by a 37–14 count.
- And in 1984 Colorado fell 55–14.

So, you have to go all the way back to 1981, when Bobby Bowden brought his barnstorming 20th-rated Florida State team to Notre Dame Stadium, in Gerry Faust's first year at Notre Dame, to find a 19–13 Seminole win. That was the same year Bowden's team played five successive early-season road games at Nebraska, at Ohio State, at Notre Dame, at Pittsburgh, and at LSU (and the Seminoles beat Ohio State, Notre Dame, and LSU).

Actually, Penn State pulled off the trick in 1982 (defeating the Irish 24–14), but the Nittany Lions had made a previous trip to play at Cartier Field in 1926.

So, the current ledger says first-time visitors are only 10–57–1 (.154) at Notre Dame Stadium.

In addition to South Florida, Tulsa, Connecticut, Penn State, (1982) and Florida State (1981), the only other Irish opponents to prevail in their initial stops at Notre Dame Stadium are 14th-ranked Clemson in 1979, Missouri in 1972, Michigan in 1942 (though the Wolverines had made plenty of other visits to Cartier Field), Iowa in 1940, Texas in 1934, and USC in 1931.

Along the way, Notre Dame has dispatched eight ranked teams coming to Notre Dame Stadium for a first look:

- No. 9 Army in 1947 (No. 1 Notre Dame won 27–7).
- No. 20 North Carolina in 1950 (No. 1 Notre Dame won 14–7).
- No. 4 Oklahoma in 1952 (No. 10 Notre Dame won 27–21).
- No. 10 Syracuse in 1961 (the Irish won 17–15 on a final-play field goal that came after a Syracuse roughing-the-kicker penalty).
- No. 7 LSU in 1970 (the No. 2 Irish survived 3–0 on a 24-yard Scott Hempel field goal with 2:54 left in the game).
- No. 10 Alabama in 1976 (No. 18 Notre Dame held on to win 21–18).
- Plus, West Virginia in 1997, Texas A&M in 2000, and No. 15 Utah in 2010.

When you throw in old Cartier Field, the record becomes 103–13–4 (.875) for Notre Dame in games when a visiting team is playing in South Bend for the first time.

So, even though history may not favor Wake Forest in 2012, don't underestimate the Deacs' chances.

The Irish haven't been unbeaten at home since 1998. The decade of the 2000s provided a 39–24 Notre Dame record at home. Brian Kelly wants his Irish to appreciate the importance of "protecting their house."

Wake Forest, nonetheless, will have to buck the long odds in 2012 to keep that from happening.

chapter 4

THE MOST IMPORTANT GAMES IN NOTRE DAME FOOTBALL HISTORY— PART I, 1887–1973

INTERESTED IN RELIVING the best games in all the years of Irish football? Then this section can't be long enough for you. We've boiled the list down to a manageable number (over two chapters)—but even then we've presumably left out at least a few that you'd include.

Understand that there are no bowl games in this section—postseason contests rate their own chapter in Notre Dame football lore (and in this book).

So, sit back and relax and enjoy this chronological, regular-season ride down Irish memory lane:

I. MICHIGAN 8, NOTRE DAME 0
November 23, 1887, at Notre Dame
The First Game Ever Played

The names of the players are not memorable for any particular reason.

In fact, there's no record of who actually scored in the University of Notre Dame's first official football game against the University of Michigan in 1887.

The Wolverines won the game 8–0, the first of eight straight series wins by Michigan (Notre Dame wouldn't beat the Wolverines until 1909).

The Michigan team was treated to lunch and then took off for another game in Chicago. The event was a far cry from what Notre Dame football is about today. In fact, as much as anything it involved the Notre Dame students learning the game of football, which at the time was a fairly new phenomenon.

In any event, it's suggested that there was some amount of passion around campus involving this first-time contest—and that probably shouldn't come as any surprise given what we know about Notre Dame football today.

Here's a compendium of facts and figures (compiled by Notre Dame Monogram Club executive director Beth Hunter) on that very first football event:

- Key stakeholders
  - Brother Paul (Patrick Connors)—born in Ireland—at Notre Dame as a member of the Brothers of the Holy Cross since 1867 and a prefect of the senior department (students age 17 and up)
  - William Warren Harless and George Winthrop DeHaven, Jr.—became friends while students at Notre Dame—from downtown Chicago—studied the same courses and shared a love of sports
- Timeline
  - 1885–1886: Harless and DeHaven leave Notre Dame and enroll together at Michigan in the fall of 1886

Notre Dame's first football team poses prior to its first game, against Michigan on November 23, 1887. Notre Dame lost 8–0 and would remain winless against Michigan until 1909, at which point the rivalry went on hiatus until 1942.

- 1886: Harless tries out and makes the varsity football team as a center
- 1887: DeHaven also joins the varsity football squad as a rush end
- Both become starters for the Michigan team
- Plans are already in place for Michigan to play Northwestern in Chicago in the fall of 1887
- DeHaven stays in contact with Brother Paul
- Brother Paul asks DeHaven if he and Harless could convince the Wolverines to stop at Notre Dame on the way to Chicago to teach some Notre Dame seniors the game of football
- "Ann Arbor boys hold the championship of the West"— Michigan qualifies as one of the leading football teams (almost as good as the leading Eastern teams)

- By mid-November, a game date is set for November 23, 1887—day before the Northwestern/Michigan game (a Thanksgiving Day contest)
- Brother Paul begins to "train" some Notre Dame seniors—but they struggle to learn the game
- A few days prior, Northwestern cancels its game with Michigan—after learning the game from a Michigan player who travels in advance to teach the Northwestern group how to play (Northwestern decided the game was too violent)
- Entire trip to Notre Dame and Chicago was going to cost a total of $150—all funds had been raised by students
- Michigan sends a student representative ahead to Chicago on Monday to find another opponent in Chicago—and so the trip proceeds
- Michigan leaves on Tuesday night—overnight train to Niles, Michigan, arrives at dawn—Michigan group only has until 3:00 PM Wednesday to get back to the train in Niles to go to Chicago
- Michigan arrives—tours Notre Dame campus (arriving at 9:00 AM)
- Michigan wears uniforms (white)—Notre Dame is in "outdoor gear"
- Game is played on "senior campus field"
- Michigan plays all students, no "ringers" (local "townies" who could suit up and play also)
- Stars on Michigan team: Duffy brothers (James E. and John L.)
- Star for Notre Dame team: Harry Jewett
- Entire Notre Dame student body shows up for game—in melting snow, muddy conditions
- 11:00 AM: teams take the field

- Play a mixed game first, so Michigan can teach Notre Dame
- Teams then separate and played a 30-minute game
- Michigan is victorious: 8–0 (two touchdowns, counted as four points each)
- No goalposts, no converted scores, no record who scores the TDs
- Considered a "practice game" at the time
- Both teams have a post-game meal together—Notre Dame president Rev. Thomas Walsh, C.S.C., is in attendance
- 1:00 PM: Michigan leaves for Niles—plays the Harvard School (prep school) the next day in Chicago
- Student enrollment at Michigan: 1,600
- Student enrollment at Notre Dame: 500
- Following the game, a Rugby Football Association is formed on campus at Notre Dame
- In the spring of 1888, Michigan plays Notre Dame in two more games—Friday, April 20, in South Bend and Saturday, April 21, on the Notre Dame campus

2. NOTRE DAME 11, MICHIGAN 3
November 6, 1909, at Ann Arbor
Notre Dame Records First Win over Michigan

After eight straight losses at the hands of Michigan, Notre Dame finally served notice that it could compete against the best of the Midwest. Both teams came in 4–0, with Michigan having lost only five combined games in the last nine seasons. Pete Vaughan and Billy Ryan scored touchdowns for Notre Dame and Red Miller blocked a late Michigan field-goal attempt. Said the *Chicago American*: "All Michigan is in mourning this afternoon." Notre Dame finished the season 7–0–1 in its first season under coach Frank Longman, a former Michigan player.

3. NOTRE DAME 35, ARMY 13
November 1, 1913, at West Point
Notre Dame Uses Forward Pass to Make National Statement

When Army reluctantly agreed to pay Notre Dame $1,000 for its long journey to the plains of West Point in 1913, the good-but-stingy generals conceded the hefty sum would be worth a victory.

Although the Cadets knew coach Jesse Harper's Irish were a Midwestern powerhouse (they'd lost just one game the previous three seasons), most Army fans felt Notre Dame would serve merely as a tasty appetizer for the West Pointers' annual picnic with Navy.

The Irish might be able to give Army a run for its money, but surely the Cadets' gridiron superiority would crush the Hoosier hayseeds who had arrived from their all-day train trip with 18 players—and just 14 pairs of cleats.

Army, which had scouted Notre Dame's 62–0 thrashing of Alma, was expecting a hard-hitting, powerful running attack, led by a strong line. Instead, the Cadets found themselves in the middle of an unrelenting blitzkrieg.

Notre Dame got off to a rocky start. After winning the coin toss and electing to receive (a bold move in those days), quarterback Gus Dorais fumbled during the opening series, and Army recovered on the Irish 27-yard line. But the potent Cadet offense gained just one yard on three tries, and the Army began to realize that $1,000 was a steep price tag for humiliation.

Notre Dame's surprising passing game helped the visitors stake claim to a 14–13 lead at halftime. The Cadets certainly weren't strangers to the aerial toss; in fact, Army was the premier passing team of the East. But the Cadets, along with the rest of the football world, thought passes were thrown only in desperation—as a last resort. The West Pointers couldn't adjust to a team using the pass as its bread and butter.

So the Irish offense continued to shoot rockets in the second half, and Army, with a young cadet named Dwight Eisenhower sitting on the bench, failed miserably on defense.

When Dorais wasn't hurling spirals to Knute Rockne (a technique the pair had mastered during the summer when they worked as lifeguards at the beach resort of Cedar Point, Ohio, where a plaque pays tribute to their summer workouts), Ray Eichenlaub would break through the line for a long gain. Even the Army partisans oohed and aahed at Notre Dame's amazing versatility.

Years later, in a 1930 *Collier's Weekly* edition, Rockne wrote: "We spent a whole summer vacation in 1913 at Cedar Point on Lake Erie. We worked our way as restaurant checkers, but played our way on the beach with a football, practicing the forward pass. There was nothing much else for two young fellows without much

Notre Dame received a $1,000 guarantee from Army in 1913 to make its trip to West Point a reality.

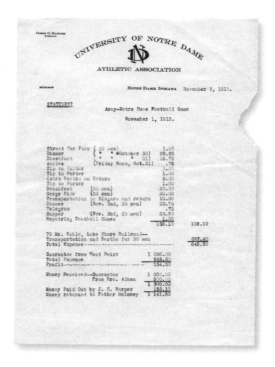

pocket money to do and it made us familiar with the innovation that was to change the entire character of football."

By game's end, Dorais had completed 14 of 17 passes (he misfired on his first two tries) for 243 yards—unheard of totals in 1913. And his 40-yard toss to Rockne was the longest pass ever completed to that day. Notre Dame had rocked the football world with its stunning 35–13 victory.

The win revolutionized college football as the forward pass, a legal weapon since 1906, gained popularity as a legitimate offensive tool. "The press and the football public hailed this new game, and Notre Dame received credit as the originator of a style of play that we simply systematized," said Rockne.

Notre Dame also earned a national reputation with its victory, and teams from all over the East were clamoring for a matchup.

Notre Dame had made it to the big time.

Notre Dame found itself on *Sports Illustrated's* list of the century's greatest games (in all sports), with its 35–13 victory over Army in that November 1, 1913, game checking in at No. 11: "Of all the echoes bouncing around South Bend, this one reverberates loudest. It wasn't just that the unknown Irish whipped the undefeated Cadet juggernaut, it was how they did it—with what had heretofore been a gimmick, the forward pass. ND's Gus Dorais went 14-for-17 for 243 yards and two TDs, one to halfback Joe Pliska, the other to Knute Rockne. Army was so bewitched, bothered and bewildered by the aerial antics that it surely didn't even matter that one of their halfbacks, Dwight David Eisenhower, was out with an injury."

The top spot belonged to the '82 NFL playoff game between San Diego and Miami. The only other college football games on this top 20 list were the 1984 Boston College–Miami game (No. 3) and the 1982 California-Stanford matchup (No. 20).

4. NOTRE DAME 27, ARMY 17
October 30, 1920, at West Point
Gipp Wows Cadets with All-Around Performance

Notre Dame star George Gipp was never better—amassing 480 all-purpose yards against traditional rival and undefeated Army at West Point. Despite a lingering illness, he ran for 150 yards, passed for 123 and a touchdown, totaled 207 yards on kick returns, kicked three PATs, and averaged 43 yards per punt. From a numbers standpoint, it marked Gipp's finest hour.

5. NOTRE DAME 13, INDIANA 10
November 13, 1920, at Indianapolis
That's Why They Called Him 'the Gipper'

In George Gipp's second-to-last game appearance, Notre Dame pulled off a comeback for the memory books. Gipp overcame all sorts of physical ailments and made all sorts of plays that enabled Notre Dame to somehow put two touchdowns on the board in the fourth period to defeat Indiana. Gipp put up modest statistics on this day—52 rushing yards on 16 attempts (a one-yard TD run), 26 passing yards (3-of-5 throwing), one PAT, and an especially valuable nine punts for 351 yards. Yet he did all that with a broken collarbone and dislocated shoulder suffered early in the contest. Notre Dame went on to finish 9–0. A month and a day later, Gipp died.

6. NOTRE DAME 13, ARMY 7
October 18, 1924, at the Polo Grounds
Grantland Rice and Four Horsemen Make History

The box score shows touchdown runs by Elmer Layden and Jim Crowley for Notre Dame. But the score and game details of Notre Dame's victory over Army to a great extent played second fiddle to the next day's newspaper that featured Grantland Rice's sparkling prose in describing Knute Rockne's backfield. Rice's lead that began, "Outlined against a blue-gray October sky, the Four Horsemen rode again," remains arguably the most recognizable passage in sports journalism. It turned Layden, Crowley, Harry Stuhldreher, and Don Miller into football folk heroes (especially after student publicity aide George Strickler posed the four on horseback back in South Bend the next week). That photo became maybe the most recognizable image anywhere in football history—and the combination of Rice's words and the photo that went with it have become part of the heritage of the college game.

7. NOTRE DAME 13, USC 12
December 4, 1926, at Los Angeles Coliseum
Irish Edge Trojans in First-Ever Meeting
between Intersectional Powers

Bonnie Rockne and Marion Wilson should have been proud. The wives of the head football men at Notre Dame and Southern California, respectively, had made great use of a train conversation to bring this long-distance rivalry to fruition—and this was the first game. More than 74,000 fans in the Coliseum watched two excellent teams slug it out until Art Parisien connected with John Niemiec for a 23-yard, game-winning touchdown play with less than two minutes remaining. Parisien participated in all but three plays—even after being told six weeks prior that a heart bruise would sideline him for the rest of the year.

8. NOTRE DAME 12, ARMY 6
November 10, 1928, at Yankee Stadium
"Win One for the Gipper" Carries the Day for the Irish

Knute Rockne was desperate.

His 1928 team, decimated by injuries, already had lost two of its first six games. Three powerful teams—Army, Carnegie Tech, and USC—loomed on the schedule before the season (the worst in Rockne's illustrious coaching career) would mercifully draw to a close.

Rockne knew that if his Ramblers could upend Army—winner of six straight games—in Yankee Stadium, a losing record could be averted. His critics were claiming he'd lost his touch; the magic was gone. But Rockne knew better. The week of the game he quietly told his neighbor that Notre Dame would beat Army. Rockne had a plan. His team might not be able to win on talent, but Notre Dame would win on emotion and spirit. Rockne would deliver what would later become the most famous pep talk in sports history.

After pregame warm-ups, Rockne huddled his players in the locker room. They laid down on World War I blankets that covered the cold, clammy floor. Rockne waited until the room was silent. He lowered his head before speaking.

He began slowly—telling the team about George Gipp, a Notre Dame player who had died during his senior season eight years ago. Although none of the players had known Gipp personally, each and every one of them had heard of his exploits. They knew Gipp had been the greatest player of his time.

Rockne, who had been at Gipp's bedside, repeated the young athlete's last wish.

"I've got to go, Rock. It's all right. I'm not afraid. Sometime, Rock, when the team is up against it, when things are wrong and the breaks are beating the boys—tell them to go in there with all they've got and win just one for the Gipper. I don't know where I'll be then, Rock. But I'll know about it, and I'll be happy."

Rockne continued:

"The day before he died, George Gipp asked me to wait until the situation seemed hopeless—then ask a Notre Dame team to go out and beat Army for him. This is the day, and you are the team."

"There was no one in the room that wasn't crying," recalled line coach Ed Healy.

"There was a moment of silence, and then all of a sudden those players ran out of the dressing room and almost tore the hinges off the door. They were all ready to kill someone."

Army didn't have a chance.

After falling behind 6–0 in the third period, Notre Dame scored two touchdowns and held off a last-chance rally by the Cadets for a 12–6 win.

Jack Chevigny tied the score at 6–6 with a one-yard plunge. As he picked himself up in the end zone, he jumped up and shouted, "That's one for the Gipper."

The emotional Chevigny was helping Notre Dame drive toward its final and winning score in the last quarter when he was injured. Rockne was forced to take him out and replaced him with Bill Drew. Reserve Johnny O'Brien, a willowy hurdler for the track team, took Johnny Colrick's place at left end.

The Irish were 32 yards from the goal line. Left halfback Butch Niemiec took the ball, looked downfield to O'Brien, and flung a wobbly pass over an Army defender. O'Brien hauled the ball in on the 10-yard line, squeezed past two tacklers, and dove into the end zone for the winning touchdown. O'Brien never became a starter in his career with Notre Dame, but "One-Play" was a legitimate hero to Irish fans.

As O'Brien scored, the Notre Dame bench erupted in whoops and hollers. The injured Chevigny cried on the sidelines, "That's one for the Gipper, too."

Even Rockne showed satisfaction with the play.

"You could see a great, big smile on his face," said quarterback Frank Carideo. "He was happy when things created during the week were used to perfection in the ballgame."

But O'Brien's touchdown didn't put the game safely away. Army had another chance with less than two minutes to go. The Cadets drove methodically through the Notre Dame defense, helped by a 55-yard kickoff return by All-American Chris Cagle. Cagle, who had played the entire game, collapsed at the 10-yard line because of exhaustion and had to be carried from the field. Dick Hutchinson took the ball to the 4 and then to the 1. But time ran out before the Cadets could get off another play, and Notre Dame had indeed "won one for the Gipper."

Sporting News released a list of "Top 10 Moments" in college football (November 13, 1999). The No. 3 moment was the legend of Gipp and the famous speech made by Rockne.

9. Notre Dame 26, Navy 2
October 11, 1930, at Notre Dame Stadium
Irish Handle Navy in Notre Dame Stadium Dedication Game

This glossy brick facility, modeled to some extent after the University of Michigan's stadium, had been Knute Rockne's dream. Notre Dame's coach played an intimate role in the planning for Notre Dame Stadium (price tag: $750,000)—then his Irish disposed easily of Navy in the dedication game for the new arena (the first game actually had been a 20–14 win over SMU the previous Saturday). Joe Savoldi scored three touchdowns and rushed for 123 yards.

10. NOTRE DAME 60, PENN 20
November 8, 1930, at Philadelphia
15th Straight by Irish, Three TDs by Marty Brill

In a perfect season that ended up being Knute Rockne's final one in South Bend, this one-sided romp by a powerful Notre Dame unit featured three rushing scores covering 125 combined yards by halfback Marty Brill. The Irish bolted to a 43–0 lead behind their starting unit. That extended Notre Dame's winning streak to 15 on its way to a second straight consensus national title.

11. NOTRE DAME 27, USC 0
December 6, 1930, at Los Angeles Coliseum
Rockne's Last Game Proves a Classic

USC fumbled the ball away on its first play from scrimmage and it was all downhill from there for the Trojans. Notre Dame outgained Southern California 433–140—including 331–89 on the ground. And this was a USC team that came in at 8–1, having allowed only 39 combined points all season. Backup running back Bucky O'Connor ran 80 yards for one touchdown and caught a seven-yard pass from Marchy Schwartz for another. USC coach Howard Jones called it "the greatest Notre Dame team I've ever seen." This win put the finishing touches on the 1930 campaign— with the Irish at 10–0 claiming the consensus national crown. Four months later Rockne was killed in a plane crash in Bazaar, Kansas.

12. NOTRE DAME 13, ARMY 12
December 2, 1933, at Yankee Stadium
Irish Ruin Army's Perfect Season

Notre Dame had been struggling, coming in at 2–5–1 and facing its first losing season since 1888 (1–2). But, with five minutes left in the game, Wayne Millner blocked a Cadet punt and recovered it in the end zone to end Army's bid for an unbeaten campaign. Moose Krause blocked an earlier punt to set up the first Notre Dame score—with Millner carrying four straight times for 19 combined yards to reach the end zone that time.

13. Notre Dame 18, Ohio State 13
November 2, 1935, at Columbus
Irish Pull Off Columbus Shocker Over Vaunted Buckeyes

More than 75 years have passed since Notre Dame's unbelievable 18–13 upset of Ohio State, but the 1935 confrontation is still considered the original "game of the century."

Although both teams were undefeated heading into the clash, the top-ranked Buckeyes were heavy favorites. One sportswriter picked Ohio State by 40 points since coach Francis "Close the Gates of Mercy" Schmidt had his Bucks riding rampant over every foe. The Irish, good but not that good, weren't given much of a chance.

But coach Elmer Layden, a former member of the Four Horsemen, said, "The 1935 team was one that believed in itself to an extraordinary extent. It was fired emotionally because death walked with it in every game."

Captain-elect Joe Sullivan, a starting tackle, had died of pneumonia several months before the season began. His teammates didn't elect another captain. Instead, they dedicated each contest to Sullivan.

Electricity had been generating in Columbus for weeks before the big game. There were parades and pep rallies. University officials and city politicians went into hiding to avoid "friends" seeking tickets. Scalpers were scoffing at any offer less than $50.

On the Friday before the game, Layden took his team to a secluded seminary outside the city for workouts, hoping to avoid

The 1935 Notre Dame–Ohio State game in Columbus probably qualified as the very first "game of the century."

the carnival-like atmosphere on campus. But when the Irish arrived, they were greeted by thousands of Buckeye fans shouting, "Catholics, go home."

When Saturday came, more than 81,000 fans jammed into Ohio Stadium. The Buckeyes got off to a quick start and owned a commanding 13–0 lead at halftime. The pregame predictions seemed to be coming true. Ohio State's offense operated at will, and Notre Dame couldn't do anything right.

"I had never seen a Notre Dame offense so completely stopped," said writer Francis Wallace.

"When the Irish passed, the ball was intercepted and converted into a touchdown. It was difficult to get a running play started against the hard-charging Ohio State line. It was even hard to get a punt away."

In the dressing room, Layden announced that the second team would start the second half. He ended his analytical pep talk by saying, "They won the first half. Now it's your turn. Go out and win this half for yourselves."

The defense finally figured out how to stop Ohio State's razzle-dazzle, and the offense, behind the superb antics of Andy Pilney, got on track. At the end of the third quarter, Ohio State still was ahead 13–0, but the Irish were driving. Notre Dame was on the Buckeyes' 12-yard line.

Pilney passed to Francis Gaul at the 2-yard line. On the next play, Steve Miller went over for the touchdown. The conversion attempt hit the crossbar and wobbled back onto the field, but Notre Dame had cracked the scoreboard.

The Irish were threatening again, but Miller fumbled in the end zone and Ohio State recovered. Notre Dame's hopes dimmed as the Bucks moved downfield. But the defense finally forced Ohio State to punt, and Notre Dame was back in the business of creating miracles.

With three minutes to go, the Irish started from their own 20-yard line. Pilney's zigzag running brought the Irish quickly into Ohio State territory. Then he tossed a 33-yard touchdown pass to Mike Layden. A kick would tie the game. But the Irish missed again, and the Buckeyes clung to a 13–12 advantage.

Layden called for an onside kick, but Ohio State wasn't fooled and recovered the ball. All the Buckeyes had to do was maintain possession for a win. But on Dick Beltz's drive off right tackle, he was hit hard by Pilney and lost the football. Notre Dame's second-string center Henry Pojman recovered on the Ohio State 49.

The crowd was out of control. Layden sent in a play—and the ball came back to Pilney, who dropped back to throw. But all his receivers were covered. He took off, swerving to avoid a rush of Buckeye defenders. They finally forced him out of bounds on the Ohio State 19-yard line. But Pilney didn't get up. He had torn cartilage in his knee and had to be carried from the field on a stretcher.

Bill Shakespeare entered the game with half a minute remaining. He threw straight at Buckeye defender Beltz, who had his hands on the ball, but couldn't hang on.

Layden sent in reserve quarterback Jim McKenna with another play. McKenna had sneaked aboard the team train to Columbus, and his teammates had helped hide him in a berth. When he couldn't scrounge up a ticket for the game, he talked his way into the Notre Dame locker room. When Layden saw him, he ordered the industrious youth to get dressed. He did, but in his excitement he forgot his pads. Now he was bringing in the winning play.

Shakespeare threw another pass. Wayne Millner caught the ball in the end zone. The miracle was almost complete.

"I've thought a lot about the pass. But I wake up nights dreaming about the one before it—the one the Ohio State guy had in his hands and dropped," said Shakespeare years after the game.

"If he'd held it, Wayne and I both would have been bums."

Pilney, the game's hero, missed the touchdown. He was being carried to the locker room.

"While they were carrying me toward the dressing room door, I was trying to turn my head, even though I was in intense pain, to see what was happening," he remembered.

"I heard the crowd and the trainer says to me, 'Andy, it's over. We won.' That's the last thing I remember. Then I went out."

14. No. 11 Notre Dame 26, No. 1 Northwestern 6
November 21, 1936, at Notre Dame Stadium
Notre Dame Chalks Up First-Ever Win over No. 1 Team

In the first year of the Associated Press ratings, Northwestern needed this victory in Notre Dame Stadium to wrap up a perfect season and national title bid. But Notre Dame had other ideas. Notre Dame's defense never allowed the Wildcats to complete a pass. Bob Wilke ran for touchdown dashes of 30 and 34 yards in the first half—and that paved the way for the first of eight Notre Dame wins over No. 1–rated (AP) opponents. This contest joined games against Miami in 1988 and Florida State in 1993 as the only three to take place in Notre Dame Stadium.

15. Notre Dame 28, Iowa Pre-Flight 0
October 17, 1942, at Notre Dame Stadium
Rash of Turnovers Improve Irish Fortunes

The Seahawks came into South Bend unbeaten, but Notre Dame intercepted six passes and recovered three fumbles in whitewashing the visitors. Angelo Bertelli threw 26 yards for one score to Bob Livingstone—and Cornie Clatt intercepted a pass and ran it in 37 yards for another touchdown 47 seconds later. Coach Frank Leahy was at the Mayo Clinic and missed the game due to illness.

16. No. 2 Notre Dame 0, No. 1 Army 0
November 9, 1946, at Yankee Stadium
Late Lujack Tackle Preserves Deadlock with Cadets

Once again Notre Dame found itself in the middle of a classic confrontation. Old rivals Army and Notre Dame were scheduled to meet in New York City's Yankee Stadium in 1946. Although the Cadets had won 25 straight and appeared headed for their third consecutive national championship, World War II was over, Frank Leahy was back from the Navy, and many former Irish players were trading in their military uniforms for football jerseys.

The Army–Notre Dame game would be the game of the year. Yankee Stadium had been sold out since June even though tickets didn't go on sale publicly until August 1. Over $500,000 in refund checks were issued to disappointed fans. Requests for press credentials reached record levels, and many lucky ticket holders were blatantly scalping them for $200.

While Leahy was serving in the Navy, Notre Dame had been whitewashed twice by the Cadets—59–0 in 1944 and 48–0 in 1945. Leahy had listened to those games overseas, and now that he was back, he was determined to change things.

His Irish methodically pounded their first five opponents into the ground, setting the stage for a battle of the unbeatens in Yankee Stadium. The week before the game, his squad would take periodical breaks during practice to chant, "Fifty-nine and forty-eight, this is the year we retaliate." Notre Dame students sent daily postcards to Army coach Earl "Red" Blaik. All were signed "SPATNC"—Society for the Prevention of Army's Third National Championship.

But the game of the year failed to answer any questions about supremacy in the college football world. The brutal, hard-fought struggle ended in a 0–0 tie.

The 1946 Notre Dame–Army game at Yankee Stadium ended in a 0–0 tie and featured probably the most talented two teams in the country.

"I suppose I should be elated over the tie," mused Leahy after the game. "After all, we didn't lose, but I'm not."

Blaik echoed his thoughts. "There is no jubilation in this dressing room. It was a vigorously fought, terrific defensive game. Both teams played beautifully on the defense and that affected both teams' attacks."

Neither squad mustered much of a scoring threat all afternoon. Notre Dame drove all the way to the Army 4-yard line in the second quarter, but the Black Knights stopped the Irish on downs. Notre Dame had moved the ball mostly by running down the right side.

When the Irish got the ball to the Navy 4-yard line, the Irish ran two quarterback sneaks. Following those attempts, the Irish ran two plays to the left, but failed to score.

Notre Dame's defense contained Army's touchdown twins— Doc Blanchard and Glenn Davis—who were often caught behind the line of scrimmage.

But Blanchard, frustrated by an Irish line that refused to budge, made a last-ditch effort to score, and he almost succeeded. Army crossed into Notre Dame territory for the first and only time all day as Blanchard, "Mr. Inside," broke around the end, cut for the sideline, and had a clear path to the end zone. Only one man was in a position to try and stop him. As 74,000 fans leaped to their feet, John Lujack sped across the field, closed in on his prey and dove for Blanchard's ankles. The All-American was dragged down on the Notre Dame 37-yard line.

"They said Blanchard couldn't be stopped one on one in the open field, yet I did it," said an exhausted Lujack after the game.

"I really can't understand all the fuss. I simply pinned him against the sideline and dropped him with a routine tackle."

Army then moved the ball to the Notre Dame 12-yard line and Davis threw an option pass, which was intercepted by future Irish head coach Terry Brennan at the 8-yard line. One play later, Brennan ran the ball past the Irish 30 and Notre Dame was out of trouble.

Even the statistics couldn't pinpoint a clear-cut winner. Notre Dame had 10 first downs to Army's nine; the Cadets gained 224 yards, while Notre Dame managed 219. Each team had 52 yards passing and 40 yards punting. Army completed four of 16 passes; the Irish were five of 17.

Irish in Their Own Words

JOHN LUJACK

Army had Doc Blanchard and Glenn Davis and again was undefeated. There was a huge buildup in the press and on radio, and tickets for the Yankee Stadium game were selling for ridiculous prices.

The way we former players remember it, both coach Leahy and his Army counterpart, Earl Blaik, played very conservatively. We had one good chance, but we were stopped on the 2-yard line. Why coach Leahy didn't call for a field goal, I will never understand, but in those days, there wasn't much emphasis on kicking.

My big play supposedly came on defense when I tackled Blanchard in the open field to prevent a touchdown. It really wasn't a great tackle, and years later I was on a program with Blanchard and he joked that he thought he had killed me on the play.

Irish in Their Own Words

BILL FISCHER

We were looking for a little revenge against Army in 1946. Not only had they beaten us 48–0 the previous year, but they had walloped us pretty good [59–0] the year before I got there. The hype for that game in New York City was tremendous.

Even though the game ended in a 0–0 tie, that was a great game. Do you realize that there were three Heisman Trophy winners—Glenn Davis and Doc Blanchard for Army and John Lujack for us—in that game? [Editor's note: there also were three Outland Trophy–winning linemen in that game: Notre Dame's George Connor and Fischer and Army's Joe Steffey.]

Irish in Their Own Words

JOHN PANELLI

Only the 0–0 tie with Army marred our season. I still tell Johnny Lujack that if he had given me the ball on the 2-yard line, I'd have carried it halfway to Morristown. But we finished undefeated with that one tie.

Irish in Their Own Words

FRANK TRIPUCKA

Even though Frank Dancewicz and George [Ratterman] were ahead of me on the depth chart in 1945, I played enough to win a letter and put myself in position for more playing time the next three seasons. I played quite a bit in 1946 with John Lujack and Ratterman ahead of me. And it was a great season, except for that 0–0 tie against Army in Yankee Stadium. I sat on the bench alongside Ratterman as Lujack played the entire game. The two coaches, [Frank] Leahy and Red Blaik for Army, elected to play a defensive struggle. Instead of playing to win, they played not to lose.

17. No. 2 Notre Dame 14, USC 14
December 4, 1948, at Los Angeles Coliseum
Two Late Notre Dame TDs Produce Tie with Trojans

Notre Dame somehow survived six lost fumbles and used a couple of 11th-hour touchdowns to tie USC, the only blemish on the 1948 scorecard after nine consecutive victories. Frank Tripucka threw 35 yards to Leon Hart for one of the Notre Dame touchdowns. Then, Bill Gay returned a Trojan kickoff 87 yards, and Emil Sitko responded with the tying TD with 35 seconds to go.

18. No. 1 Notre Dame 27, SMU 20
December 3, 1949, at Dallas

Notre Dame had gone 38 straight games without a loss, and this win enabled the Irish to finish a fourth straight season without a loss. But it wasn't easy. Mustang star Doak Walker could not suit up due to injury, but SMU rallied with 20 second-half points to forge a late tie. Bill Barrett's six-yard TD run with eight minutes left provided the margin for the Irish. SMU drove to the Notre Dame four, but Jerry Groom intercepted Kyle Rote's jump pass. Rote scored all three Mustang TDs, threw for 148 yards and ran for 115 more. Irish quarterback Bob Williams finished with 83 pass completions to break the Notre Dame season mark held by Angelo Bertelli.

19. No. 7 Notre Dame 9, No. 2 USC 0
November 29, 1952, at Los Angeles Coliseum
Irish Defense Limits Unbeaten SC to Five First Downs

Southern California had visions of a perfect season, but Notre Dame's defense had no interest. The Irish held the Trojans to only 149 total yards, only 64 on the ground, and five first downs. Notre Dame intercepted five passes—and its one touchdown came after an errant USC pitch on a punt return ended up in the hands of Irish captain Minnie Mavraides.

20. No. 10 Notre Dame 27, No. 4 Oklahoma 21
November 8, 1952, at Notre Dame Stadium
First-Ever Meeting Between Irish and Sooners Worth Saving

There was no shortage of stars in this matchup between what became two of the great traditional college powers. Oklahoma had Billy Vessels, who ran for 195 yards on 17 carries that day and went on to win the Heisman Trophy that year. Notre Dame's John

Lattner, who would win the Heisman a year later in 1953, rushed for 98 and Neil Worden had 75. Vessels scored on a 27-yard reception, a 62-yard run, and a 44-yard run, but his Sooners completed only two passes all afternoon. Plus, the two teams split 10 turnovers in the first half alone. In fitting fashion, the winning points came via the turnover. Dan Shannon's tackle on a kickoff separated Oklahoma's Larry Grigg from the football. Notre Dame recovered at the 24 and Tony Carey ran it in from the one four plays later for the win. It marked the lone loss of the year for Oklahoma, while the Irish parlayed the win into a No. 3 finish in both final polls.

21. NO. 4 NOTRE DAME 23, NO. 17 USC 17
November 27, 1954, at Notre Dame Stadium
Irish Come from Behind on Morse's 72-Yard Run
Notre Dame came from behind three different times in this one—the last time on a 72-yard scoring run by Jim Morse with about five minutes remaining. Morse finished with 179 rushing yards (19 carries), as Terry Brennan's first Irish team survived rain, mud, nine fumbles and two interceptions. Notre Dame's 373 rushing yards carried the day.

22. NO. 4 NOTRE DAME 17, IOWA 14
November 19, 1955, at Notre Dame Stadium
They Called It Hornung's Best Game in an Irish Uniform
The box score says Paul Hornung—who played the entire game without relief—kicked a 28-yard field goal with 2:15 remaining to enable the Irish to defeat Iowa. But that doesn't begin to shape the scope of the Notre Dame comeback required. Down by a touchdown with 10 minutes to play, Hornung received the kickoff and led a 62-yard scoring drive that ended with a 16-yard pass to Jim Morse. After forcing a Hawkeye punt, Hornung found Morse again

on third and 11 down to the Iowa nine. The crowd was the largest to come to Notre Dame Stadium—and after the win the students tore down the goal posts and carried Hornung off the field.

Irish in Their Own Words

JIM MORSE

In our final home game against Iowa, the Hawkeyes went ahead 14–7 late in the game, only to have [Paul] Hornung take over. He directed a long drive to tie the score and then another shorter one to put us in position for a field goal. Even though we were penalized 15 yards for coaching from the sidelines when a manager threw the kicking tee on the field, Hornung still boomed the winning field goal, 17–14, with 2:15 to play.

23. NO. 12 NOTRE DAME 23, NO. 10 ARMY 21
October 12, 1957, at Philadelphia
Stickles' 39-Yard Field Goal Wins It for Notre Dame

Monty Stickles had never before attempted a field goal, but his 39-yarder with six minutes left provided the winning cushion for Notre Dame. The teams met for the first time in 10 years, with star backs Nick Pietrosante (Notre Dame) and Pete Dawkins (Army) doing much of the offensive damage.

24. NOTRE DAME 7, NO. 2 OKLAHOMA 0
November 16, 1957, at Norman
Lynch's Late Run Ends Record Sooners Streak

The odds were stacked heavily against the Irish.

The 1957 Sooners, defending national champions and No. 2 in the weekly polls, boasted the country's longest winning streak at 47 games. Oklahoma had not lost since the 1953 home opener when Notre Dame ruined the Sooners' season debut, 28–21.

Powerful Oklahoma, which had blasted the Irish 40–0 the year before in South Bend, had scored in 123 consecutive contests and was averaging 300 yards a game. The Sooners, playing in their own massive stadium in Norman, Oklahoma, were favored by at least 19 points.

Notre Dame, which suffered through its first losing season in 24 years in 1956, had dropped two straight to Navy and Michigan State (the Irish were outscored 54–12 in those two contests). Coach Terry Brennan was under fire.

Although the Sooners moved all the way down to the Irish 13-yard line on their first possession, the Notre Dame defense dug in and held. Oklahoma would get no closer the rest of the afternoon. Both teams threatened with several offensive drives, but strong defensive stands keep the score at a standstill until late in the fourth quarter.

"I was willing to settle for a scoreless tie in the third quarter," admitted Oklahoma coach Bud Wilkinson. "I felt at the start of the second half we had a good chance. But after we couldn't get going, even with our tremendous punting to their goal, I was ready to settle for a scoreless tie."

The Irish, however, had other plans. With 3:50 left in the game, Notre Dame needed three yards on fourth down to cross the goal line. Quarterback Bob Williams, who had executed nearly each play perfectly all afternoon, faked to Nick Pietrosante in the middle and then pitched to halfback Dick Lynch. Lynch went wide around right end for the touchdown, Monty Stickles kicked the extra point, and Notre Dame had its 7–0 upset.

Williams, who engineered the 80-yard drive in 20 plays, explained, "They were in tight, real tight, just waiting for me to

The Irish in 1957 traveled to Norman and ended Oklahoma's 47-game win streak, still the longest in NCAA history.

give the ball to Pietrosante. Well, I just faked to him and tossed out to Lynch and it worked like a charm."

Brennan, who often called the victory the "greatest thrill of my athletic career," credited the defense with the win.

"We prepared for them in detail," he said. "We didn't have a whole lot of speed and we tried to be as basic as possible. There were only four or five basic plays—and if you stopped them, you had a chance to win. The big thing was to stop their running game."

The Irish indeed halted the Sooners' ground attack. Oklahoma managed 98 yards rushing.

When the team arrived back in South Bend after the victory, the Irish were met by more than 5,000 fans. That hearty welcome was richly deserved as Oklahoma's 47-game winning skein remains the longest in college football.

Irish in Their Own Words

AL ECUYER

That game against Oklahoma was a great defensive struggle. Our coaches, especially Bernie Witucki [tackles] and Bernie Crimmins [backfield], insisted all week long that we could win. And it worked out the way they said. We could stop them, but we had to score, and we finally put together an 80-yard drive with Dick Lynch scoring to give us a 7–0 win. We lost again to Iowa [21–13], but beat the Trojans [40–12] for a great comeback [7–3] season.

Irish in Their Own Words

BOB WETOSKA

We were 4–2 heading to Norman to take on national champion Oklahoma. I'll always remember that game. No one gave us a chance, but our coaches made us believe we could win. I was hurt early in the game and replaced by (Jim) Colosimo. He made a couple of good catches, but we couldn't score. On defense, we shut out the Sooners' ground game, and it was a real struggle until we put together a long [80-yard] drive in the fourth period. On fourth and three, Dick Lynch scored the only touchdown, and that 7–0 victory was the highlight of a 7–3 season.

25. NOTRE DAME 17, NO. 10 SYRACUSE 15
November 18, 1961, at Notre Dame Stadium
"If at First You Don't Succeed" Works Well for Irish

Syracuse had battled back from a 14–0 Notre Dame lead to hold a 15–14 late-game advantage—thanks to a 57-yard touchdown reception by John Mackey on a fourth-and-one play, plus 95 rushing yards from the great Ernie Davis (he won the Heisman Trophy that year). The Irish threw a pair of interceptions in the final five minutes and finally took over at their own 30 with 17 seconds to go. Quarterback Frank Budka scrambled for 20 yards and threw to George Sefcik for 11 more. That set up Joe Perkowski for a 56-yard field-goal attempt. Syracuse's Walt Sweeney crashed into holder Sefcik—and the controversial 15-yard penalty made it a 42-yard attempt. Perkowski connected with no time left on the clock for the Notre Dame victory.

26. NOTRE DAME 31, WISCONSIN 7
September 26, 1964, at Madison
Ara's First Game with Irish Makes for Great Memories

No one knew exactly what to expect from new Notre Dame coach Ara Parseghian with the start of his first season in 1964. Excitement on campus? No question. But the reality of a 2–7 record the previous season in 1963 made for something of a reality check. The Irish were coming off their least successful period in their history and had gone five straight years without a winning record. Ara changed all that. His defense held Wisconsin to minus-51 net rushing yards and intercepted five passes and no Badger ground-gainer netted more than eight yards. Meanwhile, John Huarte set the tone for his Heisman Trophy-winning campaign by throwing for 270 yards—with nine of those caught by Jack Snow for 217 yards.

Irish in Their Own Words

PHIL SHERIDAN

That first game against Wisconsin was fantastic. We went up there knowing that they were a good team from the Big Ten, but honestly it wasn't that hard of a win. We won 31–7, and it was just like being in practice, probably easier. Everything seemed to work. Teams hadn't seen us, nobody knew [receiver] Jack Snow or [quarterback] John Huarte. We were so thoroughly prepared that it wasn't a difficult game. The prior year it seemed like we were in every game but would lose by less than a touchdown. We'd been giving it our all, but we didn't have the confidence or ability to get the job done. That all changed with Ara's preparation.

27. No. 7 Notre Dame 28, No. 4 USC 7
October 23, 1965, at Notre Dame Stadium
Garrett, Trojans No Match for Irish This Time

The crushing loss to USC that ended Notre Dame's 1964 championship bid hadn't been forgotten by Irish students, fans, or players. Trojan back Mike Garrett went on to win the Heisman Trophy that year, but the Irish held him to 43 yards (his career low) on 16 rushing carries. Meanwhile, Notre Dame scored on four of its first five possessions, and Larry Conjar set an Irish record with four rushing scores (he gained 116 net yards). Notre Dame completed only two passes but rolled up 308 rushing yards to 74 (and 10 first downs) for USC. Wrote *Los Angeles Times* columnist Jim Murray, "Outlined against the blue-gray October sky, Notre Dame kicked the bejabbers out of USC on a leaky Saturday afternoon."

Irish in Their Own Words

Bob Meeker

When USC came to Notre Dame for our revenge game earlier that season I noticed on tape during the week that one of the Trojans' defensive linemen changed his feet when he was veering to the inside or the outside. So when (quarterback Bill) Zloch would come to the line of scrimmage he could call an audible, depending on which way the USC line was going. It was the easiest block in the world for me to make because I just had to drive him with his momentum. We scored all four of our touchdowns in that hole because we knew what was coming. All four of our backs outgained Mike Garrett in that game, even though he went on to win the Heisman Trophy. That fact was a source of pride for our line.

28. No. 6 Notre Dame 26, No. 8 Purdue 14
September 24, 1966, at Notre Dame Stadium
Hanratty to Seymour Debuts in Major Fashion against Boilermakers

Irish football fans knew sophomores Terry Hanratty and Jim Seymour had some reasonable amount of potential to impact the Notre Dame offense in a positive fashion. Little did they know it was going to start this well. In their very first varsity game,

Hanratty completed 16 of 24 passes for 304 yards. Seymour caught 13 of them for 276 yards, including TD passes of 84, 39, and seven yards. To that point, only one player in college football history had amassed more receiving yards in a single game than Seymour's 276. Plus, this was no average Boilermaker unit—with Bob Griese (he was 14 of 26 for 178 yards) at quarterback and Leroy Keyes (he returned a fumble 94 yards) helping Purdue to an eventual Rose Bowl win over USC that year. For Notre Dame it proved a grand way to begin what became a national title season.

Irish in Their Own Words

TERRY HANRATTY

After that Purdue game my sophomore year (1966), I went back to the dorm and called my mom, and the first thing she said was how great [Purdue quarterback] Bob Griese was, what a classy kid he was, and how I should try to be like him. She was even calling him Mr. Griese. I tried to tell her that I had just thrown three touchdown passes, but she didn't seem to care. Then Sunday night we watched the film of the game with my chest pumped out, and for the next two hours the coaches just rode me on my footwork and everything. I walked out of that meeting room thinking I had played a terrible game. Ara was just making sure that Jim [Seymour] and I didn't get bigger than the team just from one good game. We realized the team wasn't about Jim and me; it was about everybody. You look at that team and the offensive line was fantastic, the defense was fabulous, and the running game was great. That 1966 team had everything. Jim and I were just the missing links.

29. No. 1 Notre Dame 10, No. 2 Michigan State 10

November 19, 1966, at East Lansing

Another "Game of Century" Ends in Stalemate

When the brutal battle in East Lansing was finally over, there was nothing left but inconsolable emptiness and frustration.

The epic battle between top-ranked Notre Dame and No. 2 Michigan State didn't settle much of anything for either team. When the clock ticked its last second-hand sweep, exhausted and battered players, emotionally drained coaches, and frenzied fans could only look at the 10–10 tie in exasperation and disappointment.

"Nobody can be happy with a tie," said Irish quarterback Terry Hanratty who had to leave the game in the first quarter after Bubba Smith rearranged his shoulder. "It was a helluva ballgame, but we were all so tired. I don't think anyone wanted to go into a fifth quarter."

The Irish, who had rallied from a 10–0 deficit early in the second quarter, had a chance to go for the win. Notre Dame had the ball on its 30-yard line with time for at least four passing plays. The Spartans were expecting the Irish to go for broke. But under coach Ara Parseghian's strict orders, the Irish played it safe.

"We'd fought hard to come back and tie it up," he explained. "After all that, I didn't want to risk giving it to them cheap. They get reckless and it could cost them the game. I wasn't going to do a jackass thing like that at this point."

His players agreed.

"It was the worst kind of depression coming off the field after working that hard and coming out with a tie," remembered pass-catching sensation Jim Seymour, who didn't catch a pass that afternoon.

The 1966 Notre Dame–Michigan State game didn't produce a winner, but the Irish clinched their title a week later with a win at USC.

"What people don't realize is that we couldn't throw the ball because they had set up a specific defense to stop the pass. Our quarterback was so run down because of his diabetic problem that he couldn't throw the ball more than 10 yards. And they were really set for it. So why throw the ball for an interception and really hang yourself? Ara's been questioned many times about that decision.... But there was nothing else he could do under the circumstances."

Seymour was right. The Irish probably were lucky to survive with a tie. Their best halfback, Nick Eddy, had slipped getting off the train in East Lansing and fell on an already banged-up shoulder. He wouldn't even get in the game. Center George Goeddeke's ankle fell victim to Smith in the first quarter, along with Hanratty.

But Coley O'Brien, who required two insulin shots a day to keep his diabetes in check, and sophomore Bob Gladieux proved able replacements.

After the Spartans had taken a 10–0 lead on Regis Cavender's four-yard run and Dick Kenney's 47-yard field goal, O'Brien directed the Irish 54 yards in four plays. He hit Gladieux with an 11-yard strike and Rocky Bleier for a nine-yard gain. O'Brien then lofted a perfect 34-yard spiral to Gladieux, who caught it on the goal line and stepped into the end zone.

The Irish finally caught up with the Spartans on the first play of the fourth quarter. After Notre Dame stalled on the Michigan State 10-yard line, Joe Azzaro kicked a 28-yard field goal to knot the score. Notre Dame was dominating the second half, and the defense hadn't let the Spartans any closer than they were when they had kicked the field goal. Linebackers Jim Lynch and Jim Horney nailed the talented Spartan runners for either minus yardage or no yardage on 16 rushing plays.

With five minutes left in the game, the Irish got a big break. Safety Tom Schoen intercepted a wild Jimmy Raye pass and ran it back to the Spartan 18-yard line. Larry Conjar went straight ahead for two yards. But on the second play, halfback Dave Haley went wide to his left. Smith and Phil Hoag nailed him for an eight-yard loss. O'Brien's third-down pass went incomplete, and Notre Dame had to settle for a 42-yard field goal try.

Azzaro's kick went wide to the right.

Irish in Their Own Words

TERRY HANRATTY

The [10–10] Michigan State game that season was probably a matchup of the two most talented teams on one field in college football history when you look at all the All-Americans out there.

In what I remember as our third series, in comes a play from the sidelines calling for a quarterback draw. I took my three steps back and started to go forward into a sea of green. I knew I wasn't going anywhere and I'd be lucky to get back to the line of scrimmage. A couple Michigan State guys wrapped me up, and out of the corner of my eye I see Bubba Smith just bearing down the line. I knew that wasn't a collision I was going to win. He buried me, and when I got up my left shoulder felt a little weird. So on the next play Ara calls for a pass, a down and out to the left side. The second I threw my left arm up the pain just shot through it because my shoulder was separated. So as I'm coming off the field the first thing Ara says is, "Why the hell did you call that draw?" I told him that he sent it in, but Ara said, "No, that was supposed to be a halfback draw!" So as it turns out it was a screw-up in communication that knocked me out of the game.

Irish in Their Own Words

JOE AZZARO

Even during the Michigan State game there was never any doubt that we were going to win. That game was easily one of the coldest days that I've ever played football in. Before the game I was practicing kicks and [Michigan State head coach] Duffy Daugherty came up to me and started talking, but I didn't know who he was. Duffy was from my neck of the woods and started talking about western Pennsylvania. Trying to keep my mind on my business, I just didn't realize it was Duffy until a half-hour later when I saw him standing on the sidelines.

That stadium was so packed that there was no room on the sidelines. I don't know how all those people got in, but they were down on the field, which made for a lot of disorganization. We had fans sitting on our bench.

I don't remember much about the 28-yard field goal that I made to tie the game at 10–10. What stands out to me is the one that I missed from 42 yards. It didn't seem like a big deal at the time because there was time left in the game. That kick couldn't have gone more than a couple of inches wide right, and the wind even took it a little bit at the end. I thought it was going to go right down the middle, but then it started veering a little bit at the end and just missed. There's no question that if we hadn't lost eight yards on that drive before the field-goal try, that kick would have been good. I still felt that we'd get a shot to kick another one, but that never happened.

When that game was over you looked around and wondered when you were going to play the rest of the game. Somebody had to win, right? There was a sense of emptiness, which I'm sure the Michigan State players were feeling too. That said, I think Ara made all the right decisions in the end. If one of us had won that game instead of it being a tie, I wonder how much people would still be talking about it. Michigan State had a team of great athletes and deserved a lot of recognition. It would have been a shame if someone had lost that game, so maybe it's better that no one did.

Irish in Their Own Words

PETE DURANKO

That was such a disciplined team [1966], and people noted that during the Michigan State game. Even in the second half of the hardest-hitting game of my life, the defensive linemen were down on their knees and the defensive backs had their hands behind them. It looked like the Marines in terms of a disciplined approach to every play. We came out of the huddle and set ourselves the same way every time so we never showed any sign of fatigue. That discipline ran from start to finish that season, and it was a huge part of winning the national championship.

Irish in Their Own Words

KEVIN HARDY

The old cliché is that you never look ahead, but a couple of weeks before the 10–10 tie against Michigan State, we knew what was coming. We were so good that it was assumed we would be No. 1. There was no reason to think we'd be anything but No. I, There wasn't the kind of hype that would make you think the game was the "Game of the Century." We were just reading the *South Bend Tribune*, which always had stories about half the opposing players who wanted to come to Notre Dame and couldn't, so they really wanted to beat us. That happened in every game.

The stadium was so packed in East Lansing that we couldn't even sit on the bench. There were people all around us. There must have been 10,000 sideline passes. If you were a running back headed out of bounds, you weren't going to hit the ground because you were going to land on three bodies.

I had a friend come out for the Duke game the weekend before, and he loved the experience, so I gave him one of my tickets and he hitchhiked up to East Lansing. He wound up watching the game on the field standing next to me. Everybody was so wrapped up in the game that I doubt any usher noticed him climbing over the railings to get down on the field.

I don't think anybody on the defense was all that concerned with the outcome even after [Terry] Hanratty went down and [running back] Nick Eddy and [center] George Goeddeke were out too. We never thought about losing, and it wasn't an issue on the sidelines.

We beat some good teams that season and shut out a lot of people. It never surprised me that we blew out USC [51–0] the very next week. The surprise of the season to me was that we didn't score more against Michigan State. With Hanratty and Eddy out, there were physical reasons for us not scoring more, but I really believe we should have won that game. And yet we were still the national champions and deserved to be.

Irish in Their Own Words

BOB GLADIEUX

My sophomore year I was behind Nick Eddy. When he was injured prior to the 1966 Michigan State game, I looked at it as an opportunity. Nick was graduating after the 1966 season, so this was a way for me to prepare and gain experience. Without a doubt, the defining moment of my career was the touchdown catch at Michigan State. That's how I get introduced all the time: "This is Bob Gladieux. He caught the touchdown pass in the famous 10–10 tie with Michigan State in 1966." We never had the opportunity to review the film of that game. The coaches went right into preparation for USC the next week because it would be for the national title.

I thought I was lined up in the slot on that touchdown [against Michigan State], but when I saw the ESPN Classic broadcast of that game, I was in a twin formation. In the style we played, the half-back was a flanker, too. When Rocky [Bleier] and I weren't in the backfield, we'd be flanked out. All I know is I wasn't the primary receiver on the play. I was supposed to go deep to tie up the safety, but they blew a coverage and Coley (O'Brien) got me the ball.

I got injured later in the game, and it was the hardest I've ever been hit. I had been doing pretty well in the game up to that point with my pass-catching. My recollection is we got into the huddle and came in with the play. When they called the formation, I thought, "What the heck is that?" But I was told, "Harpo, get open." As soon as I released, I didn't recognize the coverage, so I ad-libbed an inside route, which was a no-no. I kept going inside, running against the grain, and Jess Phillips hit me while I was in the air. I got hit in the head and in the leg. My quadriceps muscle was splattered into hamburger meat and my thigh pad busted into four pieces. I couldn't walk. I missed the rest of the game plus the USC game, and I was sidelined the entire next spring.

30. No. 1 Notre Dame 51, No. 10 USC 0
November 26, 1966, at Los Angeles Coliseum
Irish Make Strong Argument for Title by Whitewashing Trojans
So much for Notre Dame's hangover after the frustrating and physically taxing tie at Michigan State the previous Saturday. With the Spartans' regular season finished, the Irish had one last chance to prove their point—and, boy, did they ever take advantage of it. Even with standouts like Terry Hanratty and Nick Eddy sidelined by injury, Notre Dame demolished the Trojans. Backup quarterback Coley O'Brien looked like a star in completing 21 of 31 passes for 255 yards and three touchdowns. Jim Seymour caught 11 balls for 150 yards and two of those TDs. The Irish defense ran back two interceptions for TDs and held USC to minus-12 rushing yards. Notre Dame led 31–0 at the half

and only twice permitted USC to cross midfield. Said USC coach John McKay, "Do you realize there are over 700 million Chinese who didn't even know the game was played?" Despite McKay's assertion, the convincing triumph handed the national title to Ara Parseghian's group.

Irish in Their Own Words

JOE AZZARO

There was no emotional letdown that next week at Southern California. I don't know if I ever saw [backfield coach] Tom Pagna as focused as he was that week. He was really a ball of fire! Maybe that focus kept us from having a letdown. Normally when you're going out to Los Angeles to play the Rose Bowl representative there's a little bit of apprehension because they are a pretty good team. I don't want to say it was men playing against boys, but we just took them apart. There was no doubt in my mind that we were the best team in the country in 1966. I'm sure there were some doubts in some people's minds, but looking at the entire body of work, that was one of the great teams to ever play in South Bend.

31. USC 38, No. 4 NOTRE DAME 28
November 28, 1970, at Los Angeles Coliseum
Record Passing Effort by Theismann
Not Enough to Slow Trojans

Notre Dame's Joe Theismann threw for 300 yards *more* than his USC counterpart. But that wouldn't be enough to keep the Trojans from squashing the title hopes of Ara Parseghian's unbeaten Irish.

USC took control early, with successive TD marches of 70, 51, and 57 yards in an eight-minute span. Then, after the Irish had pulled to within 24–14 at halftime, the Trojans struck quickly by recovering two fumbles in the end zone after Notre Dame miscues. Through the rainy, miserable conditions, Theismann played nearly flawlessly. He completed 33 of 58 passes for 526 yards and two TDs—and also ran for two more TDs, once from 25 yards and once from the one on fourth down. The Irish suffered through eight turnovers and five sacks.

Irish in Their Own Words

JOE THEISMANN

There's no question the 1970 USC game was the most memorable even though we lost. I didn't find out until years later that [Washington Redskins head coach] Joe Gibbs was USC's offensive line coach. He was amazed at how I was able to grip the football and pass for so many yards, but for some reason I've always been able to throw a wet football.

Irish in Their Own Words

TOM GATEWOOD

The most disappointing game for me was at Southern California in 1970 because I felt we were the best team in the country that year. We lost to a team that was not that good [USC finished 3-4 that year in the Pac-8 Conference]. It wasn't our day. We got behind early and couldn't come back in the rain. Later we won the Cotton Bowl and knocked off the No. 1 team [Texas, 24–11], but we fell short [finishing No. 2]. That was the one thing I felt got away. I would have loved to have had that championship ring on my finger. That USC loss was the low point, the worst defeat for me as an athlete.

32. No. 2 Notre Dame 8, Purdue 7
September 25, 1971, at West Lafayette
Ellis Punt Block Saves the Day for Irish

With less than three minutes remaining in the contest played in rain and mud, Notre Dame's Clarence Ellis blocked a Purdue punt and Fred Swendsen recovered the football in the end zone for Notre Dame's lone touchdown. Then reserve quarterback Pat Steenberge found Mike Creaney in the end zone for the two-point conversion that won the game.

33. No. 8 Notre Dame 23, No. 6 USC 14
October 27, 1973, at Notre Dame Stadium
Penick Skirts the Sideline and Irish Dispatch USC

The Irish stemmed the tide. Notre Dame hadn't won against USC in any of its last six attempts, while the Trojans came to South Bend with an overall 23-game unbeaten streak (USC began the year ranked No. 1 but tied Oklahoma 7–7). If this was the biggest win of the regular season, the biggest Kodak moment came almost four minutes into the third period when halfback Eric Penick cut around left end in front of the Notre Dame bench and barreled 85 yards for the touchdown that made it 20–7 for the home team. The Irish ran for 316 yards and forced three fourth-period turnovers by the Trojans. Notre Dame ran 85 plays (to 48 for USC) and set the tone on the first play from scrimmage when a Luther Bradley hit knocked Lynn Swann's helmet loose.

Irish in Their Own Words

FRANK POMARICO

The most satisfying game was the Southern California game in 1973. They were national champs in 1972 and 1974, and when we played them in 1973, we were 5–0. The first four games of that year I had ripped up my ankle and I was in a cast for about a month. I came back for the Rice game and only played on an extra point. I started the Army game and I probably wasn't ready, but I wanted to come back. I knew if I didn't come back for the Army game, I probably wouldn't play against Southern California.

We had such intensity playing against USC in those days, mostly because they were the essence of athletes. They were big; they were strong; they were fast; they were talented. The thing they had, too, was this air about them coming from California. You know, good weather, Hollywood, everything at their fingertips as far as the good life was concerned...that was how we thought about them. Back in South Bend, it was cloudy, it was dingy, it was disciplined as far as school was concerned. We had all this snow in the winter.... It was just a contrast in lifestyles, and we represented more of the middle class, hardworking individuals, not the flashy athletes.

We had a strong ground game. We were going to grind it out. We weren't going to win on the big play. The buildup to that game after Anthony Davis had scored six touchdowns the year before was intense. Playing against them was an emotional, electric time.

Anthony Davis had been on the cover of *Sports Illustrated*, and somebody made copies of that cover and put them all over the crosswalks at Notre Dame. Every time the students at Notre Dame would come across one of those pictures, they'd spit on it or stomp on it. So the intensity wasn't just with the team; it was with the whole University. When Southern California came in here it was like the anticipation of a heavyweight fight.

Remember I said we were going to grind it out against them? Well, we did, but we also had an 85-yard touchdown run by Eric Penick, so we did beat them with the big play as well while limiting Anthony Davis.

Irish in Their Own Words

Tom Clements

We knew we'd be better in 1973, and we obviously ended up being very good. After we beat USC and we were unbeaten and halfway home, we knew we had something special in front of us.

I remember the week before USC we beat Army 62–3 on the road, and you could sense the excitement in that locker room as if we had just won a big game. We knew what was next, and the anticipation started immediately after Army. With all the pep rallies and the posters of Anthony Davis on the sidewalks, every day you were reminded in some way that there was a big game coming up. It built up all week.

When Luther Bradley put that big hit on Lynn Swann early in the game, that set the tone for the day. The most memorable play was Eric Penick's touchdown run at the start of the second half. That was probably the loudest I've ever heard Notre Dame Stadium. The reaction to that run was unforgettable. Once Eric got outside the line, you knew that he was going to go all the way.

Irish in Their Own Words

LUTHER BRADLEY

My most fond memory is the 1973 USC game. That's probably the best game I ever played, and certainly the most intense. [USC wide receiver] Lynn Swann was an All-American, so you get pumped for that challenge. You see him on tape and just know he's a superstar. He was like the guys you see today—Larry Fitzgerald [Pittsburgh] and Mike Williams [USC]—the best in the United States. I was just ready to play.

chapter 5

THE MOST IMPORTANT GAMES IN NOTRE DAME FOOTBALL HISTORY— PART II, 1974–2010

34. No. 15 NOTRE DAME 21, NORTH CAROLINA 14

October 11, 1975, at Chapel Hill

Montana Comeback in Chapel Hill Saves the Day for Irish

These sorts of comeback victories eventually became rather routine for Notre Dame quarterback Joe Montana—but this one qualified as the first on the list. Down 14–6 to North Carolina with 6:04 remaining, Montana relieved starter Rick Slager and promptly hit Dan Kelleher for 39 yards. That set up a one-yard Al Hunter touchdown run, with Montana throwing for the two-point conversion at the 5:18 mark. Carolina missed a field goal, and Montana took the field again with 1:19 remaining. On the second play, Montana fired a quick out pattern to Ted Burgmeier, and the elusive Irish receiver took it 80 yards. Montana was on the field all of 62 seconds in the game, completed three of four passes for 129 yards, and produced the tying and winning TDs. Said Irish coach Dan Devine, "We did everything wrong for the first three quarters. Then we did everything right."

35. No. 15 Notre Dame 31, Air Force 30
October 18, 1975, at Colorado Springs
Another Week—and Another Montana-Led Irish Comeback

Joe Montana sure knew how to make it interesting. The Irish sophomore didn't even enter the game until just before halftime after starter Rick Slager had managed only a single completion in seven attempts for seven yards. And Montana contributed to the drama himself by throwing three interceptions. But he also managed to erase a 20-point deficit by leading Notre Dame into the end zone three times in a seven-minute span—and that proved good enough to eek out a come-from-behind road win for a second straight Saturday. Montana bootlegged it in from seven yards himself for the first of those three scores. Then he found Mark McLane for 66 yards and again for the TD from seven to cut it to 30–24. After the Irish took over at the 4:34 mark, Jerome Heavens ran 43 yards off right tackle and then went the final yard for the game-winning points.

36. No. 12 Notre Dame 24, Georgia Tech 3
November 8, 1975, at Notre Dame Stadium
Irish Victory over Tech Launches Legend of Rudy

Jerome Heavens ran for 148 yards, including a 73-yard touchdown play on the second Irish offensive play of the third period. However, the headlines made that day never could have presaged the fact that a walk-on Notre Dame player named Dan Ruettiger would turn this one game appearance into a major motion picture and speechmaking career. Ruettiger, in his final home game at Notre Dame Stadium, played the final minute and actually sacked the Georgia Tech quarterback on the final play. Eighteen years later, the story

Notre Dame's victory over Georgia Tech in 1975 marked Dan Ruettiger's only game experience and became the basis for the movie *Rudy*.

of Rudy's life hit the big screen, with its debut in South Bend in 1993. The production of *Rudy* marked one of the rare times Notre Dame permitted a movie to be filmed on campus—and interestingly enough, the film to this day forms the perception of Notre Dame for many casual fans who have never been to campus.

37. No. 11 Notre Dame 31, Purdue 24
September 24, 1977, at West Lafayette
Yet Another Montana Comeback Beats the Boilermakers

Never again in Joe Montana's college career would he not be the starting Notre Dame quarterback after the display he put on to pull his Irish up by their bootstraps to defeat Purdue. Montana actually ranked third on the depth chart starting the day. Coming off a loss at Ole Miss the previous Saturday, Rusty Lisch started and struggled, Gary Forystek relieved him only to suffer a career-ending injury, Lisch came on and struggled again—and finally Montana got his chance. In fact, by then, all the Irish signal-callers had been outshone by Purdue's Mark Herrmann who threw for 270 yards in the first half alone. Montana first led a drive to a field goal at the 13:18 mark. After a Luther Bradley interception, Montana connected with Ken MacAfee for 13 yards to tie the game with 10:25 remaining. Fifty-eight yards from pay dirt with three minutes left, Montana made it happen again. Dave Mitchell's five-yard run at the 1:39 juncture ended it. Montana finished 9-of-14 for 154 yards—and Notre Dame never lost again in 1977.

Irish in Their Own Words

JOE MONTANA

We lost to Mississippi in 1977, and Gary Forystek was the quarterback when we went to Purdue. Unfortunately for Gary, he took one of the most devastating hits I've seen in football. Luckily he wasn't seriously injured, and he ended up trying out for the 49ers a few years later. But for me, it was being in the right spot at the right time and having the right things fall into place to be able to get into a game. The one thing I try to tell guys today is that if you're not starting, you've got to practice like you're starting because you may get thrown into a game, and if you're not prepared, you may only get one chance. That chance will blow by you quickly, and you won't get another chance if you're not ready.

Irish in Their Own Words

DAVE REEVE

When Rusty (Lisch) came out of the game at Purdue and Gary (Forystek) went in, you could sense a relief on the sidelines that with Gary in there we were going to win the game. But it wasn't long before Gary took a helmet to the chin. He laid motionless on the field for what seemed like forever as the ambulance came out. We thought he might be dead. Then Rusty goes back in, still couldn't move the team, and then Joe (Montana) got his chance in the third quarter. Joe is just a winner, no matter whether it's football or tiddlywinks.

38. No. 11 Notre Dame 49, No. 5 USC 19
October 22, 1977, at Notre Dame Stadium
Green Jerseys Now Officially in Vogue for Irish Fans

Casual fans may still be confused about the official color palate of Notre Dame football. Blue? Gold? Green? They're all good. Yet, no single football game did more to put green into the Irish record book than Notre Dame's 1977 home win over USC. Every national title season contains at least one signature victory that springboards the success level—and this one certainly qualified in 1977. Dan Devine's squad warmed up in its traditional blue jerseys—then returned to the locker room just before kickoff to find the green versions. "You could feel the noise on your face," noted USC coach John Robinson, talking about the fan reaction when the Irish emerged in green. The game was never close. Notre Dame converted 14 of 19 third-down attempts—and Joe Montana ran twice for scores and threw two TD passes to Ken MacAfee. Bob Golic blocked a Trojan punt—and Ted Burgmeier intercepted a pass, forced a fumble, ran 21 yards on a fake field goal and threw for a two-point conversion after a bobbled snap.

Irish in Their Own Words

Dave Reeve

We kept believing from the Mississippi game on because we had the schedule on our side, including the USC game, which obviously stands out as the green jersey game. I knew about the switch before it happened, and I can't reveal how, but about 10 guys knew. I remember the chills that went down our spines when we came back into the locker room and saw those jerseys. I was one of the last guys off the field after pregame, and when I made it to the locker room some of the guys already had the jerseys on. It looked like the game was over and we'd already won with the jubilation in that locker room.

Of course it was all set up the night before when Digger Phelps went on at the pep rally and told the fans to show everyone the Irish colors by wearing green. When we first got to the locker room they had set out our normal game socks, but instead of the blue and gold stripe, it had two green stripes. Everyone was thinking how cool it was that we had our green. Coming in later to see the entire jerseys, it fired up everyone. There was more emotion in that locker room at that time than there ever was during my career. Changing the uniforms was a masterful decision. Who takes credit for it, I don't know, but I think Digger Phelps had something to do with it.

Irish in Their Own Words

LUTHER BRADLEY

The green jersey game was a favorite memory. We weren't privy to the information that we were going to change jerseys. But I remember walking with Willie [Fry] to the dorm that week and he kept telling people who were passing by, "Make sure you wear green [for the game]!" So when we got into the locker room after warming up and saw the green jerseys hanging there, it was pretty exciting, all the yelling and screaming. That put us over the top.

I was really close to Willie, but he never said a word about it to me. After the game, I said, "Willie, how did you know? When did you find out?" He said the captains had been told about a week earlier, but [Dan] Devine had said, "Don't tell anybody because if it gets out and everybody knows, it's not going to have the same impact."

39. Notre Dame 26, No. 9 Pittsburgh 17
October 14, 1978, at Notre Dame Stadium
Another Magical Fourth Period Ends Well for Irish

Down 17–7 in the fourth period? Hardly a challenge for Joe Montana and Notre Dame who seemingly had done it countless times before. Montana connected on 11 of his 15 second-half throws—after a Pitt touchdown with 13:52 left in the contest appeared to lose the Irish pixie dust. Montana first needed less than three minutes to lead Notre Dame 86 yards, ending in an eight-yard TD toss to Kris Haines. After a Panther punt, Montana fired for 30 yards to Haines and 22 to Dean Masztak, then ran it in from the one for the lead. After a Pittsburgh fumble, Montana converted to Dennis Grindinger with a fourth-down throw, then did the same on fourth down to Vagas Ferguson for a touchdown. Dave Waymer ended the last Panther threat with an interception. Montana finished with 218 passing yards—and connected on seven straight throws for 110 yards in the fourth period.

40. No. 10 Notre Dame 38, No. 20 Georgia Tech 21
November 18, 1978, at Atlanta
Ferguson's Record Running Enough to Wreck Tech

Vagas Ferguson had 188 rushing yards by halftime, and he finished with 255 yards to set the Notre Dame single-game record. Ferguson set the tone by running 68 yards on the second play from scrimmage. Joe Montana filled the gaps by completing 10 straight passes over one stretch to tie Angelo Bertelli's record. The win earned a Cotton Bowl invitation for the Irish.

41. No. 3 USC 27, No. 8 Notre Dame 25
November 25, 1978, at Los Angeles Coliseum
The Montana Comeback That Wasn't to Be

Irish fans don't include this one on the list of great Joe Montana–led comebacks because Notre Dame didn't win the football game—yet, by all rights, it might have been as impressive as any on Montana's list. USC's offense rolled for 538 total yards (most ever against Notre Dame at the time), and it looked bleak for the Irish when the Trojans snared a 24–6 fourth-period lead. Then Montana went to work—first throwing a 57-yard TD pass to Kris Haines. A 98-yard drive included 64 more receiving yards for Haines and a Pete Buchanan score. Taking over at 1:35, Montana found Pete Holohan from two yards out at the 46-second stoppage for a 25–24 Notre Dame lead. Montana threw for 358 yards overall (20-of-41, with 17 completions in the second half). The Irish thought they'd won when USC quarterback McDonald lost the football after a hit by Jeff Weston, but officials ruled it an incomplete pass as opposed to a fumble. McDonald completed a 35-yard throw on the next play, then Frank Jordan knocked through a 37-yard field goal with two seconds to go to dim the memory of Montana's exploits.

42. No. 9 Notre Dame 12, No. 6 Michigan 10
September 15, 1979, at Ann Arbor
Male Field Goals and Late Crable FG Block Defeat Wolverines

This was a defensive struggle par excellence—as Notre Dame managed only seven first downs all day and held Michigan to 94 second-half yards. So the heroes became Irish kicker Chuck Male, who connected on four field goals for all of Notre Dame's scoring (three coming after Michigan turnovers)—and Irish linebacker Bob Crable who made 12 tackles. Vagas Ferguson also contributed 118 rushing yards for the Irish (landing him on the cover of *Sports Illustrated* the next week). Crable made the play of the

Notre Dame defeated Michigan in Ann Arbor in 1979 without benefit of a touchdown—as Bob Crable preserved the win with a late field-goal block.

day when, with six seconds left, he blocked a 42-yard field-goal attempt by Michigan by jumping on the back of Wolverine lineman Mike Trgovac (who later became a Notre Dame assistant coach). The Irish win marked Michigan's first non-conference defeat in 10 years (and that one also came against a Dan Devine-coached team, when Devine was head coach at Missouri).

43. No. 14 Notre Dame 18, South Carolina 17

October 27, 1979, at Notre Dame Stadium

Lisch Borrows Some of Montana's Magic Comeback Dust

By 1979 Joe Montana had graduated and moved off to the NFL. So new Irish quarterback Rusty Lisch borrowed a few of his tricks when it came to comeback victories. South Carolina notched all 17 of its points in the third period, and it looked like the Gamecocks might jump their record to 6–1. But the Irish fielded a punt and took over on their own 20 with 1:36 left. In a 54-second span, Lisch connected with Pete Holohan, Ty Dickerson, himself (for three yards on a deflected toss), then to Dean Masztak for 14 yards and a touchdown. Then he found Holohan for the two-point conversion to finish off the comeback.

44. Notre Dame 40, Miami 14

November 24, 1979 at Mirage Bowl in Tokyo

It's No Mirage—Ferguson Leads the Way for Irish in Tokyo

Notre Dame took a road trip for the ages all the way to Olympic Stadium in Tokyo, Japan, to face Miami. Vagas Ferguson ranked as the crowd favorite and he didn't disappoint in gaining 177 rushing yards and scoring three times. Dave Waymer ran a pair of interceptions back for touchdowns against Hurricane quarterback Jim Kelly in the wet, chilly conditions.

45. No. 8 Notre Dame 29, No. 14 Michigan 27
September 20, 1980, at Notre Dame Stadium
Oliver Makes Memories for Irish,
Makes Life Miserable for Wolverines

Take a poll of the most memorable plays in Notre Dame football history and you'll be sure to get a bunch of votes for the 51-yard field goal launched by Harry Oliver in 1980 to beat Michigan as time ran out.

Why?

At a time when television had not yet come to dominate the landscape, Tony Roberts' radio play-by-play call on Notre Dame's Mutual network might well rank as his most famous of all-time.

Then there was a now-famous black-and-white photograph (yes, black and white) that perfectly captured Oliver's follow-through, as a Michigan defender tried vainly to reach the football. In a day when the Notre Dame Stadium press box barely contained enough room for the media, Fathers Ted Hesburgh and Ned Joyce (then University president and executive vice president) can be seen (in sunglasses) about a dozen rows up in the seats, in the background of the photo. Undergraduate photographer Peter Romzick (he was shooting for the *Dome*, Notre Dame's yearbook) snapped the photo.

Though Oliver died in 2007 of stomach cancer, holder Tim Koegel, also an Irish backup quarterback, has spent countless hours (and settled who knows how many bets) recounting exactly how the wind stopped blowing at exactly the right moment to give Oliver's attempt a better chance to clear the upright.

Oliver's memorable left-footed, soccer-style kick remains one of the longest ever by a Notre Dame player (at any point in a game) and represents one of only seven times in the program's

122-year history that the Irish have won on the final play of regulation. Despite having attempted only one previous field goal in a Notre Dame varsity game, Oliver was up to the task in the waning seconds versus Michigan and went on to have a record-setting junior season in 1980 that included making 18 of 23 field goals, highlighted by two different games when he sent four through the uprights (tying what then was the Irish single-game record).

Both teams seemingly won that '80 Irish-Wolverine clash in the final minutes. Notre Dame's Phil Carter smashed over from four yards for his second touchdown of the game, giving the Irish a 26–21 lead that should have been 28–21 (if not for a missed PAT by Oliver and later a failed two-point try). Michigan's Butch Woolfolk answered on the next drive with a pair of draw plays that gained 57 yards—and the Wolverines went on to crack the end zone with just 41 ticks left on the clock (27–26).

Notre Dame freshman Blair Kiel then drove the Irish downfield, leaving the ball on the Michigan 34-yard line with only 0:04 remaining on the clock.

All of the drama up to that point was more than enough to provide the most fantastic of finishes. But it's always better when Mother Nature gets involved. In this case, Oliver took the field with a brisk 15 mile-an-hour wind in his face as he eyed the goalposts in the south end zone.

"I just remember thinking this wind is very strong and half-thinking I don't have a chance in heck of making this thing," Oliver would later say. But, then, the unthinkable happened—starting with a meteorological shift in which many observers claim that the wind suddenly stepped aside to complement the hushed tone amidst a crowd of nearly 60,000. Michigan's outside rushers crashed in for the attempted block—and one of those players knocked Oliver down and he never saw the ball clear the crossbar (by inches).

46. No. 6 Notre Dame 7, No. 5 Alabama 0
November 15, 1980, at Birmingham
Irish Shut Out Bear Bryant and Tide to Earn
Sugar Bowl Assignment

Alabama had been shut out only four previous times under Bear Bryant and not since 1958 in Birmingham—so Notre Dame's feat earned a blue ribbon. The Tide defense was a match—with Notre Dame's only points coming on a two-yard, second-quarter Phil Carter run after Scott Zettek recovered a fumble on the Alabama four. Zettek stopped Alabama for a two-yard loss on the first play from scrimmage and finished with nine tackles, as Notre Dame recorded a fifth straight game without allowing an opponent touchdowns. "I can't remember when I've ever seen a defense play better," said Irish coach Dan Devine.

47. No. 20 Notre Dame 23, No. 10 Michigan 17
September 18, 1982, at Notre Dame Stadium
Late Duerson Pick Earns Irish a Win in First Night Game
at Notre Dame Stadium

This was a week when the novelty of a night game at Notre Dame Stadium meant the media spent as much time writing about Musco Mobile Lighting from Oskaloosa, Iowa, as they did about the football game. Turns out the football game was rather interesting, as well. The Irish managed 419 yards of total offense—and defensive back Dave Duerson made an acrobatic, late interception to save the day for Notre Dame in its season opener.

48. NOTRE DAME 31, NO. 1 PITTSBURGH 16

November 6, 1982, at Pittsburgh

Pinkett and Irish Surprise Dan Marino and No. 1 Panthers

Notre Dame exploded for three touchdowns in the fourth period to knock off an unbeaten and top-rated Pittsburgh team coached by Foge Fazio (he later became the Irish defensive coordinator under Lou Holtz). The Irish took the lead for good when Blair Kiel handed off to Phil Carter on a sweep, Carter pitched the ball back to Kiel, and Kiel fired it 54 yards to Joe Howard for a touchdown. After a Pitt field goal, rookie Allen Pinkett ran 76 yards for another touchdown. He scored again four minutes later to cap a 65-yard drive and finished with 112 rushing yards. Dan Marino completed 26 of 42 throws for 314 yards, and the Panthers had a 25–10 edge in first downs (88–48 in total plays), but the Irish kept Marino from throwing a TD pass for the first time in 20 games.

Irish in Their Own Words

MIKE GOLIC

Another memorable game was the win against Pittsburgh my sophomore year, when they were No. 1 in the country and we hammered them. Allen Pinkett had a great game. We're coming back from Pittsburgh, and the buses were coming down Notre Dame Avenue, and the streets were mobbed with people. The students were jumping into the buses and I remember thinking to myself, "I wish it were like this all the time. I hope it's like this all the time." As it turned out, we didn't have a moment like that again during my junior and senior years. So that Pittsburgh game was like a championship feeling.

Irish in Their Own Words

LARRY WILLIAMS

One time that we did put it together was at Pitt when they were No. 1 in the country. We played out there and Dan Marino was at quarterback and there was a glimpse of what we could do if we all got on the same page. Allen Pinkett went crazy, the defense played well, the coaching was great, a flea flicker worked, all kinds of things just sort of fell into place, and we won 31–16.

49. NOTRE DAME 38, No. 17 USC 37
November 29, 1986, at Los Angeles Coliseum
Tim Brown's Showcase Performance Highlights
Irish Comeback

The reality of this final game in Lou Holtz's first season was that it meant the difference between finishing 4–7 versus 5–6. But the resulting last-second victory by Notre Dame, thanks to a break-out effort by Irish all-purpose standout Tim Brown, added a sensational ending to a year in which five of the Notre Dame defeats came by a combined 14 points.

Notre Dame trailed 37–20 heading into the final quarter, but Steve Beuerlein, playing his final college game in his hometown, completed 18 of 27 throws for 285 yards and four TDs. Another Californian, Mark Green, added 119 rushing yards. And Brown established himself as a Heisman candidate for the following season with a spectacular all-around effort capped by a 56-yard punt return in the game's waning moments. That set up John Carney for a 19-yard game-winning field goal on the final play.

Irish in Their Own Words

CHUCK LANZA

In terms of the games, the rivalries against Michigan, USC, and Penn State were always fun. The big win in our junior year at USC [1986] was the springboard of our success. It showed the resiliency of our team when we were able to come back in the second half.

Irish in Their Own Words

D'JUAN FRANCISCO

One of the most memorable games for me was the last game of the 1986 season when we went to USC. We came back after being down by like three touchdowns or something like that, and that was the turning point of the program. You sensed it. I was on the punt-return team, and I took pride in blocking for Timmy Brown. Special teams sparked that comeback.

Irish in Their Own Words

MARK GREEN

It was a matter of learning how to win, and I think the real turning point was the last game of the season in 1986 when we beat USC in the Coliseum. That was a real turning point because we came back when they were kicking the crap out of us. Tim Brown made a couple of big punt returns, Steve Beuerlein played well, and we got to the point where we said, "You know what? We can do this!"

We took that momentum right into the next year and won eight of our first nine.

50. No. 9 Notre Dame 31, No. 17 Michigan State 8

September 19, 1987, at Notre Dame Stadium

Brown Returns Two Punts for Scores,
Becomes Heisman Frontrunner

By the end of the opening period Notre Dame had enough points to defeat a game Michigan State team (the Spartans would go on to beat USC in the Rose Bowl)—and Tim Brown had enough style points to win the Heisman Trophy. The electricity began when Michigan State, already down 5–0, punted to Brown with 2:14 left in the first quarter. Brown returned it 71 yards for a touchdown. Exactly two minutes and one second later, the Spartans punted to Brown again and the Irish senior flanker repeated the trick, this time reaching the end zone from 66 yards out. In two-plus minutes Brown had tied an NCAA record. No Irish player had returned even one punt for a TD in 14 years. Michigan State's Lorenzo White, who ended up fourth to Brown in the Heisman voting, managed only 51 rushing yards on 19 carries.

Irish in Their Own Words

Ned Bolcar

The 1987 Michigan State game against Lorenzo White was another great one for us. Tim Brown had two punt returns for touchdowns and White had something like 21 yards when he left the game in the fourth quarter. We basically knocked him out of the game.

51. NO. 4 NOTRE DAME 31, NO. 1 MIAMI 30
October 15, 1988, at Notre Dame Stadium
Terrell's Late Deflection Preserves End of Hurricanes'
36-Game Winning Streak

The edges of the seats in Notre Dame Stadium may be worn thin, but the Stadium's magic remains alive and well. The same could be said for Notre Dame's football program.

That was the end result when Pat Terrell batted away Steve Walsh's two-point conversion pass with 45 seconds to play, as the fourth-rated Irish locked up a stunning 31–30 upset of No. 1–ranked Miami in 1988.

Erased was Miami's mystique and all the embarrassment it had handed the Irish in recent years.

The game had such an impact on Irish fans that they rated it the top moment in Irish history in the 20th century as part of Notre Dame's "Century of Greatness" program. And it came after head coach Lou Holtz had predicted victory the night before at a wild, outdoor pep rally (later claiming "you should never be held responsible for what you say at a pep rally").

Walsh had his most prolific day and found himself saddled with his first loss in 17 college starts. The Miami regular season winning streak ended at 36 games, and its road win streak ended at 20. Notre Dame had lost the previous four emotional encounters by a 133–20 margin—but the Irish made those seem like ancient history with the one-point triumph.

Both clubs made mistakes and caused mistakes. Notre Dame made the big play that counted.

Its defense was on the spot in the final two minutes.

The Irish led 31–24 when Tony Rice was hit hard to force a fumble on third and 17 from the 21. The Hurricanes' Greg Mark recovered, and the Irish were in trouble.

Miami gained four yards in three plays, then faced a fourth and six from the 11. Walsh, who completed 31 of 50 for 424 yards, four TDs, and three interceptions, lofted a pass to the right front corner of the end zone, and Andre Brown made a lunging reception for the touchdown. Miami coach Jimmy Johnson said there was never any doubt about the choice of going for the two-point conversion.

Walsh dropped back and had time. But pressure came from Irish tackle George Williams. He lofted the pass toward tailback Leonard Conley in the end zone. Terrell, in man-to-man coverage, had him blanketed and stepped in front to knock it away. Miami went with an onside-kick attempt—it had won at Michigan, 31–30, after recovering an onside kick—but Anthony Johnson smothered it at the Miami 44. All Notre Dame had to do was ride out 42 seconds to sign another chapter to its glorious history.

For the most part, the Irish couldn't stop Miami unless it took the ball away. It did seven times—three on interceptions and four on fumble recoveries. The Irish gave it back three times.

The most controversial Miami miscue came with seven minutes to go. On fourth and seven at the Irish 11, Walsh hit Cleveland Gary with a short pass. Strong safety George Streeter hit Gary near the end zone and the ball popped loose at the one. Michael Stonebreaker recovered.

Notre Dame, shuffling in eight offensive linemen because of injuries, drew first blood with a 75-yard, 12-play drive capped by Rice's seven-yard run.

Walsh answered early in the second quarter when he drove the Hurricanes 68 yards in eight plays. Brown caught the eight-yard TD pass for a 7–7 tie.

Notre Dame got a couple in the second quarter. Rice hooked up with Raghib Ismail on a 57-yard pass on third and 13 from

RESERVED SEAT

34	7	2
Sec.	Row	Seat

GATE
17

MIAMI vs.
NOTRE DAME
Sat., Oct. 15, 1988
Kick-off time to be announced
Non Refundable

$21.00 NOTRE DAME STADIUM

22 USA

KNUTE ROCKNE

©U.S. Postal Service 1988.
Reprinted with permission of USPS

MIAMI OCT. 15, 1988

34	7	2
Sec.	Row	Seat

GAME 4

When Irish fans voted on the top moments in Notre Dame football history, the 1988 win over Miami finished No. 1.

the Irish 17 then finished off the 80-yard drive with a nine-yard scoring toss to Braxston Banks.

Less than two minutes later, Terrell stepped in front of a Walsh pass that was tipped by defensive end Frank Stams and returned it 60 yards for the score. Reggie Ho's third PAT gave the Irish a 21–7 lead.

Walsh only needed five minutes to erase it, ending one drive with a 23-yard TD pass to Conley on fourth and five, and the other on a 15-yard pass to Gary.

The Irish could have felt good about the halftime tie—had it not been the ease with which Miami punched in its second and third touchdowns.

They started over at half and it got crazier.

Rice was intercepted by Bubba McDowell at the Miami 42. But on first down, Conley was hammered by Jeff Alm, and Stams recovered the fumble.

The Irish got into field-goal range, but Bill Hackett's 43-yard attempt was blocked.

The Irish defense held. On fourth and three at the 47, Miami tried a fake punt and failed. Reserve quarterback Steve Belles made the stop on upback Matt Britton.

From the 46, the Irish took two plays to get in. Rice and Ricky Watters hooked up on a 44-yard pass play and Pat Eilers went the final two yards.

Miami drove again to the Irish 25 where Alm, at 6'6", picked off a Walsh pass two yards off the line.

The Irish took the momentum and marched 65 yards in nine plays before stalling at the 11. Ho hit the 27-yarder to give the Irish their 31–21 lead.

Miami made good on its first possession of the final quarter when Carlos Huerta hit a 23-yard field goal to close the gap to 31–24.

In 2003 CollegeFootballNews.com produced its list of the 100 Best College Football Finishes since 1970, and the 1988 classic between the Irish and Miami at Notre Dame Stadium was ranked fifth in that survey.

Irish in Their Own Words

WES PRITCHETT

Beating West Virginia for the national title was great, but the win over Miami was the pinnacle. There's no question about that for so many reasons. It was symbolic at the end of the day because of how far we had come since the 58–7 drubbing in Miami. Miami was a team that hadn't lost in two years. Jimmy Johnson was at the peak of his career, and we beat 'em, and we really should have beaten them worse. They could argue about the breaks because they went back and forth. But at the line of scrimmage? We kicked their (butts)! Now, was their passing game tough to stop? There's no doubt. But I guarantee you, we kicked their (butts) up front.

Michigan, USC and Miami, those were our three biggest games in 1988. We got in a fight with Miami before the game. We got done with our warm-ups and they came running through the middle of our drill. At the end of warm-ups, everybody would line up in the back of the end zone and we'd punt. They came running right through the middle of the drill and that set the tone because they realized that we weren't going to be intimidated.

Irish in Their Own Words

D'JUAN FRANCISCO

When I look back on some of those pregame fights with Southern California and Miami, it came to a point of personal pride. You want to make a contribution to the team, you want to be recognized and not criticized anymore. It simply reached a point where you couldn't take any crap from those teams anymore. You had to stand up for what you knew was right. So when other teams started to walk through us while we were stretching during pregame, we had to stand up for our rights. We would never do that to an opponent.

Then, when we played Miami and they're walking over to our side of the field...we were running drills and had to start backpedaling because their linebackers kept coming into our drills. I'm getting my helmet fixed, and all of a sudden I see [Irish strong safety] George Streeter and [cornerback] Todd Lyght in their faces. I grabbed my helmet; I had no pads in there because it was getting fixed. I strapped my chinstrap on, and the helmet was moving all around. I wanted a piece of the action because those were my boys, my brothers. That's how the fight in the tunnel started. You have to protect the field. It takes the players to get that respect back.

That's what those fights were about—respect—and we backed it up on the field. Then Coach Holtz said no more fighting, you've got to keep your composure. And then he said, "At the end of the game, save [Miami head coach] Jimmy Johnson for me!" He always knew how to say the right things.

Irish in Their Own Words

TONY RICE

The 31–30 win over Miami was unbelievable. Coach Holtz worked us so hard that week. It was like, "Wow, when are we going to get to the game!" I remember it being so special because of the involvement of everybody on the campus.

52. No. 1 Notre Dame 27, No. 2 USC 10
November 26, 1988, at Los Angeles Coliseum
No. 1–vs.–No. 2 Battle to Close Regular Season
Goes Irish Way

This one had everything you could want—the top two ranked teams in the country, both with perfect 10–0 records, playing in the final regular season game in front of a record crowd at the venerable and tradition-rich Los Angeles Coliseum. Notre Dame's defense carried the day, with Frank Stams and his mates knocking USC's quarterback, Rodney Peete, out of the game, and Irish cornerback Stan Smagala running an interception back 64 yards for a TD right before halftime. Tony Rice ran for one 65-yard score on the option. The Irish ended up prevailing relatively easily, even after sending their leading rusher and receiver, rookies Ricky Watters and Tony Brooks, home on Saturday morning for violating team rules.

Irish in Their Own Words

TONY RICE

Another game that stands out is the victory at USC in 1988. Ricky Watters and Tony Brooks were sent home, and Mark Green stepped up like he had all season. Mark was a great runner. You realize at that moment that anyone can be replaced as long as someone steps up. When [Holtz] sent [Watters and Brooks] home, I was surprised and I thought, "We're going to have to work extra hard or we don't have a chance!" But the captains made a decision to send them home, and whoever was there had to step up and fill the void. One of the big plays in that game was my 65-yard touchdown run. I was shooting for one corner of the end zone. When I made the turn, I saw [USC defensive back] Mark Carrier cut across toward the pitch man, and I said to myself, "OK, that's it." Everybody else was accounted for, and the rest was easy at that point.

Irish in Their Own Words

WES PRITCHETT

If you go back and watch the Southern California game, they moved the ball up and down the field. They were a damn good team. They had the biggest offensive line in the country. Their two tackles were like 340 pounds. I remember when they broke the huddle I was like, "Good Lord, look at the size of those guys!" They were huge, and their defense was in the top three or four in the country. It was No. 1 versus No. 2, 10–0 versus 10–0, Notre Dame versus USC in the last game of the season. How could it be any bigger than that?

Irish in Their Own Words

MARK GREEN

My junior year [1987], Ricky Watters and Tony Brooks arrived at Notre Dame. There's no question about their overall talent. Both of those guys were more talented than I was. But they had to learn the system. I don't think they were quite as disciplined as me, and I had my best year statistics-wise during my junior year. After that, they started to develop and understand what was expected.

But when we went back to the Los Angeles Coliseum to play USC in 1988, Watters and Brooks made a mistake. The coaches put it on the players and said to us, "What do we do?" The consensus at that time was, "Hey, look, we're here, we're abiding by the rules, and we're a team. Those guys don't have the respect for rules, the team, and each other." Everybody in that room agreed that the best thing to do would be to send those guys home. Even with them going home, we still knew we were going to win the football game. We just didn't think anybody could beat us after we got by Miami. After we got by Miami we knew we were going to win the national title.

53. No. 1 Notre Dame 24, No. 2 Michigan 19
September 16, 1989, at Ann Arbor
Rocket's Two Kickoff Returns Doom Second-Ranked Wolverines

Michigan's special teams hadn't given up a kickoff return for a touchdown by an opponent in 32 years. Never had a player returned two to the end zone in a single game against the Wolverines. Raghib Ismail changed all that on a wet afternoon in Ann Arbor and ended up on the cover of *Sports Illustrated* for his work. The headline on the cover read "Rocket Man" and it firmly

Raghib Ismail (25, kneeling) gave Irish fans cause for celebration in 1989 with his two kickoff returns for scores against Michigan. *Photo courtesy of Mike Bennett/ Lighthouse Imaging*

cemented a nickname and reputation for the Irish sophomore. With the Irish holding a 7–6 halftime lead, Ismail brought back the second-half kickoff 89 yards. Two minutes into the final period, with Notre Dame on top 17–12, he did it again, this time from 92 yards back. Somehow, the Irish managed to defeat a Michigan team that would go on to the Rose Bowl by attempting only two passes all afternoon (completing one). In addition to Ismail's return work, Notre Dame got it done on the ground, with 213 net rushing yards including 80 by Anthony Johnson and 79 by Tony Rice. Amazingly, this didn't even count as a first for Ismail—he'd also returned two kickoffs for TDs in a 1988 game against Rice.

Irish in Their Own Words

NED BOLCAR

I loved the Michigan game in 1989 when Rocket [Raghib Ismail] ran back two touchdowns. I had a big game and landed on their quarterback, Michael Taylor, and separated his shoulder. Then Elvis Grbac came in, and that was a big mistake for us. Our offense wasn't moving the ball and I remember being on the sideline saying to the offensive players, "We'll play defense all day. Don't you worry about it. We'll handle it!" I was trying to get our guys [the defense] jacked up.

54. NO. 1 NOTRE DAME 34, NO. 9 TENNESSEE 29
November 10, 1990, at Knoxville
Offensive Shootout Requires Late Interception to Win It for Irish
The lead changed hands five times as top-rated Notre Dame and once-beaten Tennessee put on a nifty show in Knoxville. Ricky Watters enjoyed his best-ever career day with 174 rushing yards, including scoring runs of 66 and 10 yards. The Vols ran off 29 more plays than the Irish—but Notre Dame gobbled yards in big gulps, including a Rick Mirer-to-Rodney Culver pass for 59 yards and a TD and a 44-yard Raghib Ismail TD dash. The Irish allowed 510 total yards, lost an onside kick as well as a fumble inside the Tennessee five—but Rod Smith intercepted a Tennessee pass with 46 seconds left and the Vols at the Notre Dame 20 with a first-and-10.

55. No. 8 Notre Dame 17, No. 22 Penn State 16
November 14, 1992, at Notre Dame Stadium
"Snow Bowl" in South Bend Provides Heart-Stopping Finish

The 1992 Notre Dame–Penn State contest in Notre Dame Stadium merited the attention of Irish fans for a handful of reasons:

- It marked the final home appearance of an impressive cadre of players, notably Rick Mirer, Jerome Bettis, and Reggie Brooks.
- It marked the final scheduled meeting between the two historic programs, mostly due to Penn State's impending entrance into the Big Ten Conference.

- It marked a bizarre weather day in South Bend, with a memorable snowstorm during parts of the contest making for some artistic photos from the event.
- More than anything, the 17–16 Irish victory featured a downright amazing ending.

The Notre Dame–Penn State game from 1992 came to be known as the "Snow Bowl."

A mostly defensive struggle left the teams tied 6–6 at the half. From a 9–9 tie, the 22nd-rated Nittany Lions late in the fourth quarter

Irish quarterback Rick Mirer (seen above under center) ensured his career home finale in 1992 against Penn State would be memorable. *Photo courtesy of Mike Bennett/ Lighthouse Imaging*

took advantage of an Irish fumble to drive 44 yards for a Brian O'Neal scoring run with 4:25 on the clock to give Penn State a 16–9 lead.

The eighth-rated and once-beaten Irish took over at the Penn State 36 and made great use of three plays—a 21-yard gain when Mirer threw to Bettis, a 14-yard run by Mirer, and a Mirer-to-Ray Griggs connection for 17 more.

It finally came down to fourth down and goal from the Penn State 3 with 25 seconds left. And Mirer found Bettis in the end zone to make it 16–15.

That left the Irish to attempt a two-pointer. Mirer had hoped to find his tight end, but he ended up scrambling to his right—and Brooks ran from the left side through the back of the end zone toward the right corner.

Brooks had to lay out almost horizontal to get his hands on Mirer's throw—then he managed to get his feet in bounds for the two points and the Irish victory.

It was an unlikely ending for Brooks, whose entire Notre Dame career had featured only two pass receptions.

56. No. 2 Notre Dame 31, No. 1 Florida State 24
November 13, 1993, at Notre Dame Stadium
Hugely Hyped No. 1–vs.–No. 2 Matchup
Pushes Irish to Top of Polls

This was one matchup where the game lived up to the pregame hype, maybe even beat it. Notre Dame and Florida State entered this latest "Game of the Century" with undefeated records, identical 16-game winning streaks, and the top two rankings in the Associated Press poll (the Seminoles held the top spot).

The buildup for this game was an all-time high, thanks in part to the two teams entering the game undefeated—and thanks in part to the ever-expanding electronic and print media. As each week during the college football season went by, and as the Fighting Irish and Seminoles both remained unblemished, it became clear that November 13 was not going to be just another football game at Notre Dame Stadium.

National media began rolling in for this event on Monday, and by the time kickoff came on Saturday, there were more than 700 media credentials issued. Personalities from television talk show host Regis Philbin to movie producer Spike Lee converged on Notre Dame Stadium, as did athletes like baseball's Roger Clemens and golf's Paul Azinger. On Friday night, the Joyce Athletic and Convocation Center was jam-packed for a pep rally two hours before it was scheduled to start.

And through all the hype, all the glitter, all the celebrities, the most exciting part of the whole week was undoubtedly clear—the actual 60 minutes of football played on the Notre Dame Stadium turf.

"I thought with all the hype, the game might not live up to it," said Notre Dame coach Lou Holtz. "I don't know how it looked from the press box and I don't know how it looked from the stands. But I want to tell you I wouldn't want it any more exciting from the sidelines. I can promise you that."

After controlling and leading most of the game, it all came down—as if the football gods wanted to put a spike in the heart of the hype once and for all—to the final play before the Irish won 31–24.

With three seconds left to play Florida State quarterback and eventual Heisman Trophy winner Charlie Ward had one last chance.

The previous series, on a fourth-and-goal from the 20, he had found a miracle by hitting Kez McCorvey for a touchdown pass

The game ticket for the 1993 Notre Dame–Florida State game showed former Irish athletics director Moose Krause signaling No. 1—and that's where the Irish stood after beating the Seminoles.

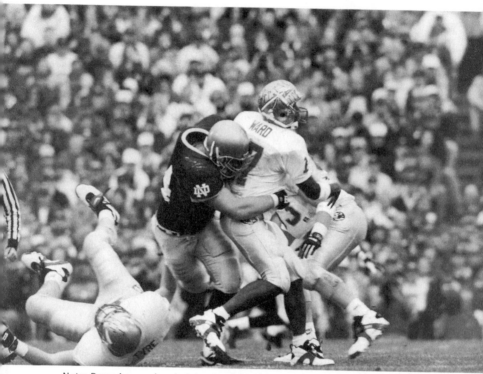

Notre Dame in 1993 handed that year's Heisman Trophy winner, Florida State's Charlie Ward, his lone defeat of the season. *Photo courtesy of Mike Bennett/ Lighthouse Imaging*

that had bounced off the hands of Notre Dame safety Brian Magee to cut the lead to seven with 1:39 left to play.

After a three-and-out series for the Irish, Florida State got the ball back with 51 seconds, no timeouts, and the ball at its own 37. Three plays and 41 seconds later, the Seminoles were at the Irish 14 and Ward's first try for the touchdown was batted down by defensive end Thomas Knight.

That left three seconds and one play.

"I was scared a little bit there," said Irish quarterback Kevin McDougal. "You can have no control when you're on the sidelines and with Charlie Ward on the field, anything can happen. I had watched the drive where they got the touchdown before so I said I'll switch up and not watch it. I just watched the clock and on the last play I waited for the crowd reaction."

He liked what he heard because here's what everyone else in Notre Dame Stadium saw. Ward went back, got some pressure from the Irish defensive line, scrambled, and fired for the end zone toward Kevin Knox. Notre Dame cornerback Shawn Wooden, inserted as a sixth defensive back, batted the pass down, and bedlam followed.

"We had to throw the ball in the end zone," said Ward. "I missed my guy who was wide open [Matt Frier at the 5], but that's part of making the decision and the ball was batted down. I can't go back and rethink what I did."

Said Wooden: "Coach Holtz just told us to stay fundamentally sound, read your keys. Charlie came to my side. I looked at No. 1, he did a square-in, so I just stayed underneath. When Ward was scrambling, I just tried to stay under No. 1. I was staying there, no matter what. The pass was right to me. I was surprised. I just wanted to knock it down and make sure."

Florida State scored on its first possession and then was chasing from behind for the rest of the afternoon. The Irish came right back with an 80-yard drive, capped by a 32-yard romp on a reverse by Adrian Jarrell behind the escort of linemen Aaron Taylor, Ryan Leahy, and Todd Norman downfield.

A 26-yard touchdown run by Lee Becton keyed the second Irish drive and three minutes later, the Irish cashed in on John Covington's interception. Coupled with a personal foul on Florida State, Notre Dame took over on the Seminoles 23, and a third-down pass to Michael Miller from McDougal set up a six-yard TD run by Jeff Burris. Entering the game, the Seminoles had given up just two rushing TDs the entire season.

"I've got no excuses about the game. Notre Dame won the game. I thought they deserved to win the game," said Florida State head coach Bobby Bowden. "They did the things to us I was afraid they were going to do to us. And there's no doubt about the great spirit they have here. I think it helps them. I do not think it hurt us. Their kids just played possessed."

By halftime it was 21–7 Irish, marking the first time in 23 games that the Seminoles had been behind at the half. Ward had been picked off for just the second time in the season, breaking a streak of 159 passes without an interception. It didn't get any better for the Seminoles in the third quarter, as the Irish received a 47-yard field goal from Kevin Pendergast.

But Ward, who was 31-of-50 for 297 yards and three TDs, led Florida State back with an 80-yard scoring drive, concluded with a six-yard pass to Warrick Dunn. Scott Bentley made a 24-yard field goal with 10:40 left for a 24–17 score.

McDougal then went to work through the air. Becton made a one-handed catch on a screen that was good for 15 yards and, on third down, McDougal double-clutched and stepped under a heavy blitz to find Lake Dawson for a first down, setting up Burris' second touchdown of the day.

"Just when it looked like we were going to give them a knockout, they came right back and then it looked like we were on the ropes and we put on an 80-yard drive against the wind," said Holtz.

Becton led all rushers in the game with 122 yards, while McDougal was nine of 18 in the air for the Irish for 108 yards.

Irish in Their Own Words

KEVIN MCDOUGAL

I've never seen anything like the hype for the Florida State game. You had the Heisman Trophy winner [Florida State quarterback Charlie Ward] in the game, Aaron Taylor won the Lombardi Award...probably every major award winner was in that game between No. I and No. 2. Once we won against that caliber of opponent—probably one of the greatest teams ever assembled— we felt we were on our way. We were 10–0 and No. 1.

Irish in Their Own Words

AARON TAYLOR

The Florida State game, with us ranked No. 2 and them No. 1, was by far the biggest game any of us ever played in. They arrived in South Bend and certainly didn't show us any respect. But that comes with the territory with those guys—the cocky swagger they have.... Whether or not they respected us more than any team in their lives, I think they still would have acted that way. That was the makeup of what those Florida teams were about.

I think the message they were trying to pass on, not knowing Bobby Bowden, but I think it was all about, "We're not going to be in awe of what you guys have done." They were coming into Notre Dame and this is South Bend and this is the house that Rockne built, but they weren't going to be in awe. We knew coming in they were talking and they were cocky. (Offensive line coach) Joe Moore said up front that these guys were very good on defense. He said, "They run around and they fly to the ball and they are by far faster than any defense we've faced, and we will probably not be able to run outside on these guys, which is okay because we're going to run it right up their ass!"

When we didn't get a rematch with them in the bowl game after we lost to Boston College, we felt slighted, and that was probably one of the first big issues of the bowls and polls and all this pre-BCS stuff. We beat them in head-to-head competition, yet at the end of the day, they were national champions.

There was a lot of talk about how [the media] had picked Bowden over Holtz for the national title. I don't think there's any question we were the best team in the country that year. Florida State was damn good, and if we had played them again, you could flip a coin. But we knew we deserved to be called national champions.

[Florida State quarterback] Charlie Ward was a special talent, an incredible athlete. That was a helluva ball game, and when it came down to it, we won head to head and we played better than they did that day. All of us felt we should have won the national championship. But you know, we had an opportunity and we didn't do it, so we don't have anybody to blame but ourselves.

57. No. 19 NOTRE DAME 54, NAVY 27
November 2, 1996, at Croke Park in Dublin, Ireland
Irish Look Right at Home in Dublin American Football Display
Seventeen years after playing in Japan, Notre Dame took a football team to Ireland and played in historic Croke Park, normally home only to Gaelic Athletic Association events. The Irish ground game carried the day in Dublin, as Marc Edwards scored three touchdowns and Notre Dame gained 303 yards on the ground.

58. No. 11 Notre Dame 17, Georgia Tech 13
September 6, 1997, at Notre Dame Stadium
New-Look Notre Dame Stadium Works Just Fine in Debut

This game featured a pair of noteworthy storylines—Bob Davie's first game as Notre Dame head coach and the unveiling of the addition of 20,000 seats to an expanded Notre Dame Stadium. Both headlines worked to Notre Dame's advantage, as Autry Denson scored in the final three minutes to push the Irish past Georgia Tech.

59. No. 22 Notre Dame 36, No. 5 Michigan 20
September 5, 1998, at Notre Dame Stadium
*30 Straight Points vs. Defending National Champions
Enough for Irish*

Quarterback Jarious Jackson caught fire in the second half, and Bob Davie recorded maybe his most noteworthy win as Irish head coach as Notre Dame came from behind to tally 30 consecutive points—and those were enough to defeat the defending national champion Michigan Wolverines.

60. No. 6 Notre Dame 34, No. 11 Florida State 24
October 26, 2002, at Tallahassee
High Point of Willingham Era Pushes Irish to 8–0 Mark

Notre Dame had been impressive enough as its irrepressible defense paved the way to seven straight wins to open the season and the Tyrone Willingham era at Notre Dame. A first-ever trip to Tallahassee to face Florida State was expected to be even more of a challenge. But the Irish were up to it as they accentuated their "Return to Glory" season with a dominating second half to defeat the Seminoles. Carlyle Holiday delivered an early message, connecting with Arnaz Battle on a 65-yard scoring play less than three minutes into the game on the first Irish play from scrimmage. After the halftime break, Notre Dame intercepted two passes, recovered two fumbles, shut off the Florida State run game (93 net yards on the day) and forced 'Nole quarterback Chris Rix into a 13-for-32 effort. Ryan Grant ran for 94 yards, including two second-half scores. Florida State coach Bobby Bowden said he and his Seminoles were "bumfuzzled."

Irish in Their Own Words

JEFF FAINE

Coming back to my home state and playing Florida State, I thought about that game for two years going. Knowing that they had a real good defensive line with Darnell Dockett, it was unbelievable. Then we just blew them up, just killed them. It was awesome.

After that game you got an example of Coach Willingham being human and letting go of his guard. I remember getting back on the bus, and I don't remember what the song was, but my man was up at the front of the bus dancing like there was no tomorrow. He's still got some moves. I'd never seen something like that out of him. It was almost like 1,000 pounds were lifted off his shoulders.

Going into that stadium, beating Coach Bowden and beating Florida State, I remember some of their assistant coaches asking me during recruiting why I was going to Notre Dame when I could go to a championship program in Tallahassee. To be able to shake that coach's hand after the game was a great feeling.

61. NOTRE DAME 20, NO. 15 PITTSBURGH 14
October 11, 2003, at Pittsburgh
Jones Runs Wild for 262 Yards'
Worth of Panthers Real Estate

Life hardly looked rosy for Irish football fortunes, with Notre Dame heading to Pittsburgh on the heels of three straight losses to Big Ten opponents. Julius Jones changed all that in one evening at Heinz Field as he obliterated the Notre Dame single-game rushing record by gaining 262 yards on only 24 attempts while helping defeat the Panthers. The ground game made all the difference, as Pitt managed only eight net rushing yards compared to 352 for the Irish. And all that came with Notre Dame wielding a rushing game that ranked 110th in the country coming into the contest. Jones scored both Notre Dame touchdowns, from 25 yards to open the scoring in the first period and from 49 yards to tie the game at 14 midway through the second quarter. He had another 61-yard run in the fourth period, as part of a 68-yard drive that took up more than nine minutes and featured running attempts on 15 of the 16 plays.

62. NOTRE DAME 42, NO. 23 PITTSBURGH 21
September 3, 2005 at Pittsburgh
Weis Era Debut an Eye-Opener
for Both Irish, Panthers

Two new head coaches brought their wares from the NFL— Charlie Weis for Notre Dame and Dave Wannstedt for Pittsburgh—but it was Weis' Irish who showed their stuff most impressively in the prime-time season opener for both teams. Pitt led early 7–0, then it was all Irish from there. Brady Quinn helped the Irish convert 10 of 11 third-down chances and completed 18 of 27 throws (11 straight over one stretch) for 227 yards. Darius Walker ran for 100 yards and scored on a 51-yard delayed screen pass. The Irish sacked Tyler Palko five times, intercepted a pass and recovered a fumble on a kickoff return. The 33 first downs and 502 net yards suggested the Irish offense would be just fine.

63. No. 20 NOTRE DAME 17, No. 3 MICHIGAN 10
September 10, 2005, at Ann Arbor
Irish Hold Off Michigan to Claim Weis'
Road Opener in Ann Arbor

Michigan had won 16 straight home games and hadn't lost a non-conference game in Michigan Stadium since 1998. But Charlie Weis became the first Notre Dame coach to go on the road and win his first two games in his rookie season since Knute Rockne did it in 1918. Brady Quinn led the Irish 77 yards downfield on the opening, no-huddle drive and found Rhema McKnight for five yards for a 7–0 lead. A 72-yard march in the second period ended with a five-yard throw from Quinn to Jeff Samardzija. The Irish survived, thanks to an early Tom Zbikowski interception at his own 1, a Notre Dame defensive stand after Michigan had navigated to the Irish 5—and a late Chad Henne fumble on a fourth-and-goal attempt from the Irish one that Chinedum Ndukwe recovered in the end zone for a touchback.

64. No. 1 USC 34, No. 9 NOTRE DAME 31
October 15, 2005, at Notre Dame Stadium
"Bush Push" Enables Trojans to Squeak Out Victory

Notre Dame didn't win the football game—yet this contest might still have qualified as the most memorable one of the Charlie Weis era, given all the hoopla that accompanied it. With USC ranked

No. 1, more than 45,000 fans showed up for a Friday night pep rally at Notre Dame Stadium, Notre Dame issued a record number of media credentials, and the ESPN *GameDay* show came to town. The game absolutely lived up to the hype, as the Irish rebounded from three different deficits to lead 31–28 with 2:04 left after Brady Quinn ran five yards to put Notre Dame on top. From there, Matt Leinart amazingly found Dwayne Jarrett for 61 yards on a fourth-and-9 play. Corey Mays forced a Leinart fumble, but the ball was placed at the 1 with six seconds remaining (there was no replay for the game because USC coach Pete Carroll had not agreed to it). From there, Leinart traversed the final yard—with a push from behind from Reggie Bush (he ran for 160 yards and three TDs).

65. No. 12 Notre Dame 40, Michigan State 37
September 23, 2006, at East Lansing
Amazing Irish Comeback in Rain Thwarts Spartans

It couldn't have been worse for Notre Dame early on, as the Irish fell behind 17–0 after a period, 31–14 at halftime and 37–21 with nine minutes left. From there, Notre Dame revved things up in the pouring rain. First, Brady Quinn connected with Jeff Samardzija for a 43-yard score. Chinedum Ndukwe forced a Michigan State fumble—and Quinn hit Rhema McKnight on a 14-yard scoring play to cut the margin to 37–33. Then, at the 2:53 mark, Terrail Lambert intercepted a Spartan pass and ran it in from 27 yards out. He added another pickoff in the final seconds to stave off the last Spartan rally. Quinn threw five TD passes overall, as Notre Dame rushed for only five yards in the second half, while Samardzija and John Carlson combined for 234 Irish receiving yards.

66. No. 10 NOTRE DAME 20, UCLA 17
October 21, 2006 at Notre Dame Stadium
Quinn to Samardzija Enough to End Bruins' Upset Bid

If you're a Notre Dame fan, there was a little about the first 59 minutes of this football game you'd care to remember. Brady Quinn had come up short on a fourth-down attempt, and it looked like UCLA was headed for a signature victory. But the Bruins punted it back to Notre Dame, and Quinn had one more shot from his own 20 with no timeouts and 1:02 left on the clock. First, Quinn hit Jeff Samardzija for 21 yards, then he found David Grimes for 14 more to the UCLA 45. Next came a play for the ages—Quinn rolled right, found Samardzija crossing the middle, and Samardzija broke a whole host of tackles on his way to the end zone with 27 seconds left. The victory enabled the Irish to continue what became an eight-game late-season win streak.

67. NOTRE DAME 40, WASHINGTON STATE 14
October 31, 2009, at San Antonio
Irish Begin Tradition of "Off-Site" Games
by Playing in San Antonio

This game didn't feature much in the way of drama, but it qualified in great part because it represented the first of Notre Dame's novel concept of playing an "off-site home game" once per year. Once the NCAA approved an annual 12th home game, the Notre Dame administration eschewed another home contest and opted instead to move a game to an out-of-town location. The original plans were to play in states like Texas and Florida where Notre Dame wanted to establish a recruiting presence. So San Antonio became the initial site—to some extent based on the weather and the attraction of the River Walk area that provided a delightful hospitality venue for Irish fans. The Friday night pep rally took place in front of the Alamo. One of the more memorable images came after the Band of the Fighting Irish played its afternoon pre-game concert in downtown San Antonio, then marched to the Alamodome followed by thousands of fans. The off-site series continued in 2010 against Army at Yankee Stadium and in 2011 against Maryland at FedEx Field. Future assignments include 2012 against Miami at Soldier Field in Chicago and 2013 against Arizona State at Cowboys Stadium in Dallas.

68. Notre Dame 28, No. 15 Utah 3
November 13, 2010, at Notre Dame Stadium
Irish Change Momentum in Big Way by Trouncing Utah

Notre Dame's first win over a ranked team in four years came in unlikely fashion. Just a few weeks removed from unbeaten status and making its first-ever visit to Notre Dame, Utah never managed a touchdown after coming in averaging 41 points per game. Rookie quarterback Tommy Rees threw for three scores in the second and third periods combined, while Utah managed only a 46-yard field goal midway through the opening period. Robert Blanton opened the Irish gates by blocking a first-period Ute punt and running it in from six yards out to give the Irish the lead for good.

69. Notre Dame 27, Army 3
November 20, 2010, at Yankee Stadium
Irish Prevail in First Football Game
Ever at New Yankee Stadium

The 50th meeting between Notre Dame and Army—in Notre Dame's first appearance in the Bronx in 41 years—provided all the color and pageantry imaginable, in the first football game ever played at the new Yankee Stadium. With the Irish players wide-eyed while dressing in the Yankee clubhouse, Notre Dame held an opponent without a touchdown for a second straight week (and that hadn't happened at Notre Dame since 1988). Tommy Rees threw for 214 yards, including a 31-yard scoring toss to Tyler Eifert. David Ruffer kicked a pair of field goals, Robert Hughes scored on a short run, and Darrin Walls ran an interception back 42 yards for a score. The two teams relived glory days of the past with John Lujack and Pete Dawkins serving as honorary captains.

chapter 6

NOTRE DAME IN THE BOWL GAMES

NOTRE DAME MAY WELL not have the richest heritage when it comes to postseason bowls. In fact, there are more than 20 programs that have played in more bowl games than the Irish, led by Alabama—with the Tide participating in almost twice as many postseason events as Notre Dame. (Keep in mind that due to Notre Dame's 45-year bowl embargo, when the Irish were headed to play in their second bowl game in history following the 1969 season, Alabama already had played in 22.)

But don't try to tell any self-respecting Notre Dame football fan that the postseason hasn't produced its share of glory. The Irish had 15 bowl victories heading into the 2012 season—and the memorable moments proved ample in great part because for many years Notre Dame followed through on an inclination to play the highest-ranked opponent it could find:

- Eight of Notre Dame's bowl games have come against teams ranked No. 1 in one or both of the major polls. Seven of those eight opponents also were unbeaten and untied.
- The Irish won five of those matchups against top-ranked teams—and those five wins rank among the most memorable of all Notre Dame football victories.

- In 15 bowl games, almost half the Notre Dame total, the Irish have faced off against an opponent ranked fifth or higher in the AP poll (eight of those equated to Irish victories).
- Nine of those matchups came against unbeaten and untied foes—and Notre Dame won seven of those.

How about some of these highlights?

- A farewell appearance by the Four Horsemen against an unbeaten Stanford team in the 1925 Rose Bowl, at that time the only legitimate bowl game on the calendar.
- A pair of memorable battles with unbeaten Texas teams in the Cotton Bowl in Notre Dame's first two postseason forays after a 45-year absence from the bowl scene.
- Two consecutive wins over top-ranked Bear Bryant–coached Alabama teams in the final two seasons of the Ara Parseghian era.
- Consecutive Cotton Bowl wins in Joe Montana's final two seasons as Irish quarterback.
- Notre Dame's national title won in its first ever appearance at the Fiesta Bowl in 1989.
- Consecutive Orange Bowl matchups with top-rated Colorado.
- A string of nine straight Irish appearances in the traditional New Year's Day bowl games from the 1987 through 1995 seasons.
- Notre Dame's last victories in the so-called major bowls—both against Texas A&M in the Cotton Bowl following the 1992 and 1993 seasons.

Those moments rank among the best ever not only for Notre Dame, but also in many cases in all of college football.

Before we launch into a look at Irish bowl history, here's a quick summary of how Notre Dame changed its postseason policy after playing in only one bowl game until the end of the 1969 season.

Following the 27–10 Rose Bowl win over Stanford that capped the 1924 season, University policy kept Notre Dame out of postseason bowls for 45 years. A revision of that policy, announced on November 17, 1969, permitted Notre Dame to accept an invitation to play Texas in the 1970 Cotton Bowl. Rev. Edmund P. Joyce, C.S.C., Notre Dame's executive vice president at the time, noted that athletes in all other sports at Notre Dame had engaged in NCAA postseason play, and that many football coaches and players had participated in postseason games on an individual basis. "The crucial consideration," Father Joyce said, "was the urgent need of the University for funds to finance minority student academic programs and scholarships.

"Notre Dame's share of the bowl game proceeds will be dedicated to this pressing University need. Plus, bowl-connected activities of the football team will fall largely in vacation time."

THE ONE AND ONLY ROSE BOWL

Bowl games back in 1924 weren't at all commonplace. The Rose Bowl first appeared in 1902, then began offering regular matchups in Pasadena in 1916. But the Orange and Sugar bowls didn't begin until 1935 and the Cotton Bowl in 1937. And Notre Dame's matchup with Stanford marked only the second year the game was played in the Rose Bowl Stadium (previous games had been played at Tournament Park). And what a matchup it was.

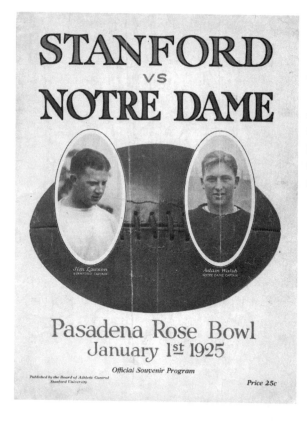

STANFORD vs NOTRE DAME

Jim Lawson
STANFORD CAPTAIN

Adam Walsh
NOTRE DAME CAPTAIN

Pasadena Rose Bowl
January 1st 1925

Official Souvenir Program

Published by the Board of Athletic Control
Stanford University

Price 25c

Knute Rockne and the Four Horsemen made the most of the lone postseason appearance of the Rockne era in the Rose Bowl after the 1924 regular season.

There were no polls back then, but both Notre Dame and Stanford came in unbeaten. Notre Dame had Knute Rockne and the Four Horsemen. Stanford had coach Pop Warner and the great Ernie Nevers.

Notre Dame won this one on defense, with Elmer Layden intercepting two of Nevers' passes (Stanford threw five interceptions altogether) and returning them for scores (70 and 78 yards). He scored a third touchdown on a three-yard run. Notre Dame's other TD in the 27–10 win came on a fumble return—one of three lost fumbles for Stanford.

PLAYING AND BEATING NO. 1

Notre Dame came back into the bowl business in great part because it wanted to ensure it could be part of the national title conversations—and what better way to do that than to match yourself against the top-ranked team in the country, or at least a highly regarded team ranked ahead of you?

So here are all the times the Irish faced off against top-ranked opponents.

1969 Season—Cotton Bowl vs. Texas

The Longhorns finished unbeaten and won the national title—but Notre Dame gave Texas all it could handle. The Irish led 10–0 early on a 54-yard scoring pass from Joe Theismann to Tom Gatewood. Then, Theismann's TD pass to Jim Yoder gave Notre Dame a 17–16 lead with just less than seven minutes to go. Then it was Texas, driving 76 yards in 17 plays for the winning Billy Dale TD with 1:08 left for the final 21–17 margin.

Irish in Their Own Words

MIKE McCOY

Playing in the Cotton Bowl after the 1969 season was something that stirred mixed emotions in me because I wanted to get home after getting picked to play in the East-West All-Star Game, and we had tests after Christmas. Ara said we were going and whoever didn't want to go didn't have to, and unfortunately a couple guys didn't.

Ara made it very clear why we were going to a bowl. Obviously there was the money factor, and if we wanted to stay competitive in recruiting, it was time to change the policy. I had to take some

Notre Dame barely missed out on a victory against top-rated Texas to cap the 1969 season in the Cotton Bowl.

of my books down to Texas because a couple days later we had tests. I wound up skipping the Shrine Game.

We probably should have beaten Texas [Notre Dame lost, 21–17] after recovering a fumble on the 2-yard line, but the refs threw a flag as a Texas player was running onto the field. The refs said that made the play dead, so the fumble we caused and recovered didn't count. To Texas' credit, they drove down and converted their third downs and then punched it in.

After the game a few of us seniors were sitting in the training room, devastated, and in walks Lyndon B. Johnson with the big 10-gallon hat, the belt buckle, and the boots. He was the last person I wanted to see.

1970 Season — Cotton Bowl vs. Texas

A year later, with unbeaten Texas looking for another title, the result was different. This time, the Irish forced nine Texas fumbles, recovered five of them, and limited Longhorns star Steve Worster to 42 ground yards. Meanwhile, Joe Theismann ran for two TDs and threw for a third to Tom Gatewood as they broke to a 21–3 lead two minutes into the second period on their way to a 24–11 triumph. Neither team scored after halftime.

Irish In Their Own Words

WALT PATULSKI

When the school broke its bowl ban in my sophomore year [1969], it was a great, great opportunity because I went there thinking they didn't go to bowls. The experience of travel and staying at a different city for a number of days...that's what college is all about.

When we lost in the final minute to [No. 1] Texas [21–17], I don't think Ara was out of the shower before he told us, "We'll be back here next year, and the score is going to be different!" In spring ball, we put the "mirror defense" in, and we worked on it all spring. He knew we were going back to play Texas in the Cotton Bowl. He knew how the defense worked, and he couldn't wait to use it. He put in new wrinkles that I don't think Texas had seen. Once the game arrived, we were so ready.

After we won [24–11], we were excited at the prospect that we might be national champions. The problem was letting someone else do your work for you. We were 9-0 before losing at USC, but we still had a chance. The [Orange Bowl] between Nebraska and LSU started at 9:00, and we had already gone to the awards ceremony for the Cotton Bowl. When LSU couldn't beat Nebraska at the end, we felt very let down. We were so close. The door was wide open and we had a legitimate claim.

1973 Season—Sugar Bowl vs. Alabama

In the fog that shrouded old Tulane Stadium in New Orleans, this game proved as memorable as they come. The lead changed six different times, the last time on a 19-yard Bob Thomas field goal at the 4:26 mark of the final period that enabled the Irish to prevail 24–23. Even then, maybe the signature play came later as Notre Dame retained possession on an end-zone pass from Tom Clements to reserve tight end Robin Weber. Earlier, Al Hunter ran a kickoff back 93 yards for a score, and Wayne Bullock and Eric Penick added scoring runs to help Notre Dame remain unbeaten and claim the title for the Irish.

Irish in Their Own Words

FRANK POMARICO

My college career culminated with the [24–23] victory over Alabama in the Sugar Bowl to win the national title. It was overwhelming. The culmination of seven years of dreaming ended in the locker room with my father, my grandfather, and my little brother, not yelling and screaming, but just watching everybody go crazy.

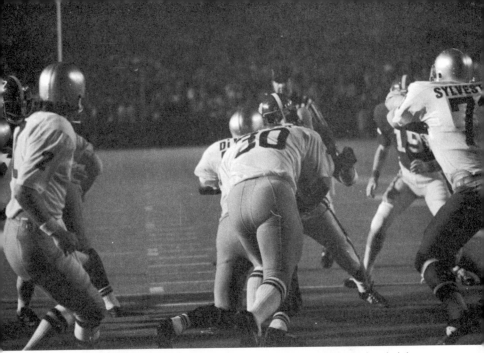

Notre Dame's New Year's Eve Sugar Bowl win over top-ranked Alabama handed the 1973 national title to the unbeaten Irish.

I don't think we had the intensity toward Alabama that we had toward Southern Cal, but it was a humongous victory for us.

Irish in Their Own Words

TOM CLEMENTS

The atmosphere around the Sugar Bowl was very special too because we knew it was going to be for the national title. That's why you come to Notre Dame in the first place, to play in big games. That's why you go to Alabama, USC, or Ohio State. Add in two Hall of Fame coaches [Ara Parseghian and Paul "Bear" Bryant] and there were so many elements that made the game exciting. The buildup over the course of a month made it all the more intense.

•   •   •

Here's Weber's recollections of what went into his late-game reception from Clements that enabled the Irish to run out the clock:

> You know the story. Ross Browner roughs the Alabama punter on fourth-and-20 as he booms a 60-yarder down to our two-yard line with a little over two minutes remaining in the game. Bear Bryant, instead of taking the 15-yard penalty and going for it on fourth and five, decides to let his defense try and win it and gives us the ball on our two-yard line. Prudent choice in my book.
>
> Setting up 'the catch' was a play we had run in the USC game and remaining games with a two-tight end set, a misdirection play called tackle trap [left or right]. One tight end would block down on the tackle and the opposite tight end would take a point step and pull straight down the line looking for penetration and/or a kickout block to lead the back around the end or through the hole. This play was a testament to how fast Dave Casper and I were!
>
> On first down, Pete Demmerle was in for a run play in which we gained a few yards. On second down Ara sends me in with a play that is a slant up the middle that gains a few yards so it is now third and five. I'm watching the sideline for Demmerle to come in, but Ara makes the call from the sideline that is another slant up the middle but with a delayed count to try and draw the defenders offside for a five-yard penalty and a first down and a win. It was not going to be a pass play as reported. We are going to snap the ball using a delayed count. If we don't make the first down by gaining five yards by either running it or drawing them offside, we are going to punt out of the end zone and let our defense try to win it. I get to the line of scrimmage and get set and Tom Clements uses the delayed count that made the defensive tackle between me and

our tackle jump into the gap at which time the ball was snapped. I thought we had just won the national championship by drawing them offside for the first down—and you can see me clap as I come up out of my stance and start walking back to the huddle. Little did I know—and because the Alabama defensive tackle that jumped was blocking my view—that Casper on the opposite end had jumped as well and we had the penalty. Half the distance to the goal line and an obvious passing down at third and eight. Ara makes the call from the sideline, as you can see me in the huddle looking over my shoulder for Demmerle with Clements standing directly behind me outside the huddle getting the call from the sideline.

Clements walks into the huddle and makes the call and it is tackle trap pass left, a play that sets up just like tackle trap run and calls for the left, fast, split end to be pulled in tight and run a speedy, deep 40-yard clearout flag pattern while the opposite main tight end on the right [Casper] drags 10–15 yards deep across the middle as the primary receiver. I had never practiced anything but the drag route on second team from the main tight end position and never been involved in a passing play in practice with the first team. Nothing was said in the huddle other than the play being called by Clements after it was signaled in very quickly from the sideline. In fact, the play call happened so fast after Casper jumped offside, maybe 20 seconds, I didn't even have time to react when I heard the call. So in a matter of a few seconds I go from thinking we had just won the national championship to being told to run a 40-yard flag pattern. Quite a contrast! This time, I didn't even bother to see if Demmerle was coming in and just lined up saying to myself, "I can run a deep flag just like we have all done in sandlot football as kids! You know...Weber go deep!"

The ball is snapped and I fire out at the defensive back, who is lined head up four yards off the line of scrimmage and had me man to man. I will never forget the look on his face as I'm running unchecked straight at him as hard as I can run. His eyes were as big as silver dollars because he thought he was about to get hit. Just as I got in his face, I dipped my shoulder, stepped inside of him then hit the jets, seeing only the safety off to my right who was backpedaling, with nothing but open field and red jerseys on the sideline to my left. Little did I know (and little did I care) that Casper had been stuffed at the line of scrimmage and Clements had progressioned to me. So there I am in the national championship game, all 6'5", 260 pounds of me running unfettered through the Alabama secondary...wheee!

I instinctively made my break where I knew he (the safety) would never catch me and immediately started looking for the ball. I can assure you, I wasn't thinking I was a decoy and hoped Clements was seeing this. Suddenly, I see the ball launched over the jumping Alabama defender and the next thing I know the ball comes whistling in over my left shoulder and I make 'the catch' purely with my hands after I adjusted my speed to his throw. I make sure I have control of the ball and turn upfield and see the goal line 65 yards away with nobody in front of me. Just as I am turning on the afterburners with visions of a TD in my head, I get body-blocked out of bounds by the safety five yards into the Alabama bench. I am laying on my back, clutching the ball, looking up at a bunch of red helmets peering down at me and hearing a bunch of cuss words over the roar of the crowd. I get up from the sideline and flip the ball to the referee and as I'm looking back downfield for penalty flags, here comes a very upset Bryant storming towards me. I see no flags and jump for joy because I know it is checkmate in a national championship game.

Ara was right. He said before the game the team who had possession of the ball at the end of the game would win it. A unique experience to say the least, with an over-the-shoulder pure hands catch, on a play I had never before practiced, thrown by a QB who had never thrown me the ball, not even in warm-ups in practice. From my perspective, quite simply a sandlot play between two good athletes.

And that's how good Tom Clements was.

He never said anything in the huddle in the three years I played with him other than call the play. No rah, rah...pure business. Very much a machine just like what he has created at Green Bay. Best athlete I have ever seen other than Art Best. He could fake you out of your jock with his basketball moves and had a rocket for an arm.

1974 Season—Orange Bowl vs. Alabama

In Ara Parseghian's final game as Irish head coach, Notre Dame continued its hex against the Crimson Tide, defeating an unbeaten and top-rated Alabama team for a second straight season. This time the Irish broke to a 13–0 lead midway through the second period on Wayne Bullock and Mark McLane touchdown runs, then held on to win 13–11. 'Bama could not survive four turnovers—with Reggie Barnett's interception in the final two minutes preserving Parseghian's final ride off the field on the shoulders of his players.

Irish in Their Own Words

TOM CLEMENTS

I never saw Ara's retirement coming. When you're 21 years old playing football in college, you're just concerned with yourself, life in the dorms, and going to school. It would have been hard to make an assessment of how Ara was feeling at the time. When you're that young as a player, you thought Ara would be there for a long time. My first reaction when Ara decided to step down was shock, followed by the fact that I was glad I was a senior and wouldn't have to work with a new regime.

We wanted to send Ara off in his last game with a victory over a tough Crimson Tide team that had the motivation of revenge on their side. Ara handled the situation so well. We practiced for the Orange Bowl over on Marco Island in the morning and then enjoyed the afternoons. Then three days before the game we went over to Miami, got down to business, and were focused. Ara planned the practices very well, and he went out like the champion that he was.

1977 Season—Cotton Bowl vs. Texas

Notre Dame made certain there were no major-college teams left unbeaten by forcing six Texas turnovers in a 38–10 dismantling of the Longhorns that paved the way for the Irish to jump from the five spot in the polls to the top. Heisman Trophy winner Earl Campbell managed 116 rushing yards, but the Notre Dame defense generally frustrated him. Jerome Heavens and Vagas Ferguson countered Campbell with 101 and 100 rushing yards, respectively, as Ferguson scored three times. Bob Golic added 17 tackles for the Irish and blocked an attempted field goal.

Irish in Their Own Words

VAGAS FERGUSON

Receiving the MVP Award in the Cotton Bowl wasn't nearly as important as the win itself. We were underdogs playing against Earl

Campbell, the Heisman Trophy winner; Brad Shearer, the Outland winner; Johnny "Lam" Jones, the fastest guy in football; Russell Erxleben, the best kicker in football.... All we heard all week was how good they were, and it was unusual for us to be underdogs.

Irish in Their Own Words

ROSS BROWNER

My greatest moment in football was beating No. I Texas for the national title in the Cotton Bowl my senior year. Down in Texas we were told we shouldn't even have shown up because Texas was the largest state in the whole U.S.A. Everything in Texas is big, and Texas is No. 1 in everything.

Every place we went, people just said, "You're Notre Dame. You guys are Catholic, you're small, you need to go back home." We weren't very welcome in Dallas. Even at the awards ceremony on the evening before the game, we had to sit in a balcony and all the Texas players sat on the main floor. That burned a spur in our hide. They got their [Cotton Bowl] watches presented to them on time, and we had ours presented the next day. We were upset about being treated like second-class citizens.

They didn't know who they were messing with, which is why we whipped them 38–10. Our whole team just said, "We're not going to take this!" Coach Devine didn't have to give a pep talk or anything because we were ready to tear out the door.

1980 Season—Sugar Bowl vs. Georgia

Notre Dame held unbeaten Georgia to only 127 total yards and only one pass completion in 13 attempts—but Herschel Walker's two touchdowns (and 150 net rushing yards) enabled the Bulldogs to prevail 17–10. The Irish committed four turnovers and also muffed a kickoff return that turned into a one-yard TD drive for Georgia. Notre Dame's defense held Georgia scoreless for the final 43 minutes of the contest, but couldn't muster enough offense to counteract the two-TD edge the Bulldogs grabbed two minutes into the second period.

1989 Season—Orange Bowl vs. Colorado

Notre Dame used a familiar script to romp past unbeaten Colorado 21–6—a rugged, productive running game, a dogged defense, plus a timely big play from Raghib Ismail. The Irish ran for 279 net rushing yards (108 from Ismail, 89 from fullback Anthony Johnson) and also made great use of an early stand after the Buffs had first-and-goal at the 1 and didn't score after botching a fourth-down fake field-goal attempt. No one scored in the first two periods, but the Irish responded with two scoring drives in the first eight minutes of the third quarter. Ismail made the play of the day, dashing 35 yards down the right sideline on a reverse to make it 14–0.

Irish in Their Own Words

RAGHIB ISMAIL

I remember how disappointed Coach Holtz was after we lost to Miami [27–10] in 1989. He called me into his office, and it was the first time I felt like he felt he didn't coach up to his potential. It was like he was going to cry.

He was watching the film of the loss to Miami, and he said, "Son, we should have given you the ball 10 more times." He was heartbroken, and he said, "I'm going to play you at tailback a lot in the [Orange] bowl game [against Colorado]."

I had a bunch of touches in that game [16 carries for 108 yards rushing] and scored on like a 35-yard run in the third quarter that stretched our lead [to 14–0]. That was the same play we ran earlier in the year against Pitt and Tennessee. I wish I remember how the blocking scheme was, but I know it was just so perfectly executed, I don't think I was touched. We went on to win [21–6] to cap what was another great season, but disappointing from the standpoint of losing to Miami.

1990 Season—Orange Bowl vs. Colorado

Notre Dame made a second straight trip to Miami for a second consecutive meeting with a top-rated Colorado team. This will forever be remembered for the Raghib Ismail punt return that didn't count. The Irish almost survived a gaggle of errors—five turnovers, a blocked PAT, and a field-goal attempt that smacked the upright. Trailing by a point, the Buffs punted the ball away with 43 seconds left and Ismail brought it back 91 yards to the end zone—but a clipping call enabled Colorado to hold on for the 10–9 victory. This turned out to be the final college game for Chris Zorich, who won the defensive MVP award and later found that his mother had passed away back in Chicago not long after the game had ended.

Irish in Their Own Words

SCOTT KOWALKOWSKI

My last game in a Notre Dame uniform was the 10–9 loss to Colorado in the Orange Bowl. Losing that bowl game was rough. Rocket Ismail returned about a 90-yard punt for a touchdown that would have given us the win, but Greg Davis was called for a controversial clip.

I personally don't think it was a penalty. I watched it. I saw it on replay. It was questionable. It was the referee's discretion. I felt really bad for Greg at the time. He felt the weight of the loss on his shoulders. Greg was a very quiet guy who just loved to play football. He didn't say much, he just did his job, and I felt bad for the guy. Not being vocal, I figured he would internalize it and suffer that much more.

The Old-School January 1 Bowls: Orange, Cotton, Sugar, Fiesta

Notre Dame stands 11–10 in the old-school major bowls—5–2 in the Cotton Bowl, 2–2 in the Sugar Bowl, 2–3 in the Orange Bowl, 1–3 in the Fiesta Bowl, and 1–0 in the Rose Bowl. So here are some other success stories for the Irish that didn't involve playing top-rated opponents:

1978 Season—Cotton Bowl vs. Houston

This game didn't have much if any effect on the national scene, but—wow—did it ever have dramatic sidebars. Joe Montana's last game as a collegian. Ridiculous weather conditions that left the stands half empty. Hypothermia for Montana, prompting a halftime locker-room warm-up fueled by chicken broth. And, finally, arguably the most amazing comeback in Notre Dame football history. The Irish did little right early in playing poorly, losing Montana to the chills and falling behind 34–12. But Notre Dame righted the ship and scored 23 points in the final 7:37. Montana made the clutch throw at the end, hitting a diving Kris Haines at the edge of the end zone as time ran out. Joe Unis kicked the PAT for the 35–34 Irish win.

Irish in Their Own Words

JOE MONTANA

People probably ask me the most about the 1979 Cotton Bowl when we came back from a large deficit [34–12] to defeat Houston [35–34]. It was probably the coldest game I ever played in. I think there were more people watching the game in the parking lot and in their RVs than there were in the stands.

There were 69 points scored in the game, and the wind was blowing so hard in one direction that I think only 14 points were scored against the wind, one of which was a blocked punt. We were fortunate enough to have the wind in the fourth quarter and have that momentum.

I got a little hypothermia during that game. It was so cold.... I didn't like going from the field to the heater to the field to the heater. But I was doing it that day. My body temperature dropped and we had tried to heat my body core with some chicken soup or some chicken bouillon or whatever was in the locker room at that time. They wouldn't let me come back out until [my body temperature] was back to normal. Fortunately I got to go back out. I wasn't sure if that's what I wanted to do at the time, but we went back and we did the simple things.

We weren't throwing the ball down the field in desperation. We just wanted to go back and end the game on a high note. Typically what coaches do when you're getting beat that badly, they say, "Let's just go back to the fundamentals and let's start showing some progress. If we end the game that way and we're progressively getting better than we were, that's a plus even if we lose the game." But in that game, things really started working in our favor, which they typically do when you take that approach.

Notre Dame's first-ever Fiesta Bowl appearance in 1988 turned into a national title.

1988 Season—Fiesta Bowl vs. West Virginia

Notre Dame had already beaten the teams ranked No. 1 (Miami) and No. 2 (USC)—so the Irish opted for a postseason assignment against unbeaten and third-ranked West Virginia. The unbeaten Irish made life tough for Mountaineer quarterback Major Harris—plus 242 rushing yards and a career-high 213 passing yards from Tony Rice got the job done. The Irish led 23–6 at halftime and rolled to the final 34–21 margin. That proved more than enough to chalk up Notre Dame's 11th consensus national title. Rice ran for 75 yards and also accounted for completions of 57 yards to Ricky Watters, 47 to Derek Brown, 35 to Mark Green, and 29 (and a TD) to Raghib Ismail.

Irish in Their Own Words

MARK GREEN

We went through the practice sessions for West Virginia [in the Fiesta Bowl], and I remember this like it was yesterday. We put in five or six new plays for that game. Our coaches designed these plays, and we were running them in practice. Guys were open by 10 or 15 yards.

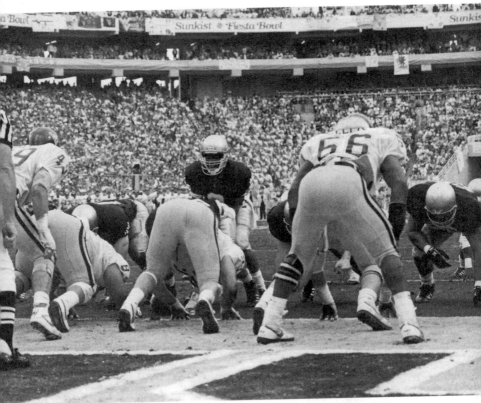

Irish quarterback Tony Rice parlayed his best-ever passing effort (213 yards) into a Fiesta Bowl win over West Virginia. *Photo courtesy of Mike Bennett/Lighthouse Imaging*

We were like, "Come on, man, we're not going to be this open! There's no way it's going to happen like this!" And our coaches were like, "I'm telling you, [West Virginia is] unsound on defense. It's going to work!" Sure enough, we had guys that wide open that game.

Irish in Their Own Words

TONY RICE

The national championship game against West Virginia in the Fiesta Bowl was interesting because they were playing man-to-man the entire time, and we had been practicing that in preparation for the game. For some reason, I was really on that day, and it was like, "Tony, this is your time to shine!" I never lacked confidence in my ability to pass, but there sure were a lot of other people who didn't think I could.

Jerome Bettis dominated the second half versus Florida in 1992.

1991 Season—Sugar Bowl vs. Florida

Lou Holtz drew plenty of laughs for his "What's the difference between Notre Dame and Cheerios? Cheerios belong in a bowl" story. His Irish turned around and proved they belonged, too, utilizing a radical, no-rush, all-cover defensive approach to thwart the Gator passing attack. Then Jerome Bettis and his mates took over in the second half and ran roughshod over Florida. Notre Dame trailed 16–7 at half, but Bettis finished with 150 rushing yards and three fourth-period scoring runs. The Irish rushed for 245 yards in the final two periods and, even though Shane Matthews threw 58 times for 370 yards, the Notre Dame defense stiffened enough to force five Gator field goals. The Irish won 39–28.

Irish in Their Own Words

RICK MIRER

I remember we were ranked 18th and Florida was ranked third for the Sugar Bowl [a 39–28 victory on January 1, 1992]. They were playing closer to home than we were, and it seemed like the stadium crowd was lopsided in their favor, which was weird for us because it wasn't normally like that.

I seem to remember some of the stuff our defense did in that game more than our offense. We would rush two guys once in a while. Our defense just kept coming up with huge plays, and they never expected that kind of defense. Offensively, we just kept hammering away with Jerome [Bettis] making a couple of huge runs. That was a real memorable game because of the anticipation of the bowl game, Steve Spurrier...that was very rewarding. We came out in green [trim on white jerseys]. That might have been the last time we won wearing the green.

1992 Season—Cotton Bowl vs. Texas A&M

Texas A&M came in unbeaten, and both the Aggies and Irish had made their living with blue-chip ground attacks. But Notre Dame's 290 rushing yards carried

The Irish traveled to Dallas after both the 1992 and 1993 seasons.

the day in Dallas, with A&M held to only 165 total yards. Reggie Brooks ran for 115 yards, and Jerome Bettis added 75 of his own. Notre Dame ran off 31 more offensive plays than Texas A&M. Rick Mirer threw 40 yards to Lake Dawson for Notre Dame's first points, then hit Bettis for 26 yards for a 14–0 lead. Bettis' one-yard TD run in the final minute of the third period made it 21–0 and ensured the Irish success story in the eventual 28–3 victory.

1993 Season—Cotton Bowl vs. Texas A&M

After a 10–0 start and a win over No. 1 Florida State, Notre Dame saw its title hopes throttled by a last-second home loss to Boston College. That sent the Irish back to Dallas again, again to face Texas A&M. This time Notre Dame made good use of Lee Becton's 138 ground yards—and the Irish and Aggies found themselves tied at seven, 14 and 21. Kevin Pendergast's 31-yard field goal with only 2:22 on the clock turned out to be the difference. That came after Notre Dame's Michael Miller returned a punt 38 yards to the Aggies 22 to put the Irish in business to account for the winning points in Notre Dame's 24–21 triumph.

Irish in Their Own Words

KEVIN McDOUGAL

I'll never forget when we were getting ready to play in the Cotton Bowl, Coach Holtz walked up to me and said in front of the whole team, "Kevin McDougal, I will never lose you a lead again!" That's when it hit me: he had finally realized what I achieved and what kind of player I was. We had gone through so much during the season. Words were exchanged back and forth. It was like his acceptance of me.

After we won the Cotton Bowl [24–21 over Texas A&M], we got back to the hotel, and when we saw Florida State barely made it past Nebraska, we definitely thought we would be co-champions. Everybody was saying it. Even Coach Holtz was saying, "We'll at least be co-champs!"

We were heading back to the airport the next day when they announced on the radio that Florida State was No. 1 and we were No. 2. That was probably the lowest I'd been, even worse than losing to Boston College. I just felt like the voters didn't do the right thing.

I could accept that Boston College beat us [41–39] on the field fair and square, and we had done everything we could. But how were you going to give the national title to somebody we had beaten? If anything, don't give it to either of us. But it was between two teams that had each lost—and we beat them.

Irish in Their Own Words

AARON TAYLOR

Then we went to the Cotton Bowl to play Texas A&M [a 24–21 victory], and let me tell you, those guys brought it. I struggled in the first half. I had turf toe and they had a guy who took it to me. I was a senior and Joe Moore just smiled at me, put his arm around me, and said, "Let's go play football." I ended up playing very well the second half.

WINNING IN JACKSONVILLE, MEMPHIS, HONOLULU, EL PASO

Finally, let's take a look at the remaining Notre Dame bowl wins from around the country:

1976 Season—Gator Bowl vs. Penn State

Al Hunter scored on short touchdown runs in each of the first two periods—and Notre Dame built a 20–3 halftime lead that gave the Irish all they needed for an eventual 20–9 win over Penn State. Hunter finished with 102 ground yards, while the Irish made effective use of a 65-yard Terry Eurick kickoff return and a Jimmy Browner fumble recovery to account for some of those first-half points. Penn State's only TD came after a blocked punt set the Nittany Lions up at the Irish eight midway through the final period.

1983 Season—Liberty Bowl vs. Boston College

It may not have been Miami or New Orleans or Dallas, but a superior Notre Dame rushing attack helped warm up a 12-degree Memphis night for Irish fans and defeat a Doug Flutie–led Boston College team. Allen Pinkett ran for 111 yards and Chris Smith for a career-best 104 to offset 287 passing yards from Flutie. Pinkett scored twice, and Blair Kiel also threw a TD pass to rookie Alvin Miller. Both teams managed three TDs—but Boston College missed a PAT then failed twice on two-point conversion throws, while Notre Dame had two PAT attempts blocked. The Irish defense prevailed when a fourth-down Flutie throw from the Irish 35 came up short with 1:08 left, leaving Notre Dame on top 19–18.

Irish in Their Own Words

MIKE GANN

When I think back to some of those games, the Liberty Bowl when we beat Boston College [19–18] and Doug Flutie in 1983 stands out. That was a big win for us. It was very cold that night, and I can actually remember looking up in the stands and some fans had built fires in the stands to stay warm. The field was as hard as cement. It was frozen. We were expected to go out there and chase down Doug Flutie on an icy, hard field. That seemed like an impossible task, so when we came out on top, that was a great win for us.

Irish in Their Own Words

LARRY WILLIAMS

We played Boston College in the Liberty Bowl when it was amazingly cold in December of 1983 in Memphis [a 19–18 victory]. I have actually very little recollection of the game because I think my head was frozen. Weren't there fires in the stands, or is that just part of my imagination? My recollection is that people started these little bonfires in the stands. We thought, *Hey, we get to go to a bowl game in Memphis! Sunny, nice...* I didn't think it got that cold in Memphis.

2008 Season—Hawaii Bowl vs. Hawaii

Notre Dame bounced back from dropping four of its last five regular season games and ended a nine-game bowl losing streak with a record-setting performance in a 49–21 whitewashing of Hawaii on the Warriors' home turf. Jimmy Clausen threw for 401 yards and five touchdowns as the Irish put up a postseason win for the first time in 15 years. Golden Tate contributed six catches for 177 yards and three TDs—and the Irish put this one away with four straight TD drives (79, 67, 88, and 50 yards) in the middle two periods, all four ending in Clausen TD passes. Clausen completed 22 of 26 throws and had 300 passing yards by halftime. Armando Allen added a 96-yard kickoff return for a final score.

2010 Season—Sun Bowl vs. Miami

Old rivals Notre Dame and Miami met for the first time in 20 years, and the Irish added a fourth straight victory (after Utah, Army, and USC) to their season total in defeating the 'Canes 33–17. On a chilly day in El Paso, Tommy Rees threw for 201 yards—including two first-period touchdown passes to Michael Floyd—as the Irish rolled to a 27–0 lead before halftime. Floyd finished with six grabs for 109 yards, and Harrison Smith key-noted the Notre Dame defensive effort with three interceptions. Cierre Wood and Robert Hughes combined for 162 ground yards for a balanced Irish attack that also included three David Ruffer field goals (one from 50 yards).

chapter 7

THE 125 MOST
IMPORTANT PEOPLE
IN NOTRE DAME
FOOTBALL HISTORY—
PART I, 1900–1965

THIS SECTION FEATURES 125 individuals who have had a major impact on football through the years at Notre Dame. The number is in tribute to the University's celebration in 2012 of 125 years of football since the first Irish game in 1887.

Let's acknowledge right up front that 125 isn't nearly enough. We've included consensus All-America players, head coaches from Jesse Harper on, plus a smattering of others whose names you will recognize. We've left out dozens of other all-stars and All-Americans who came short of the consensus All-America designation—and dozens of captains and other players whose contributions came in ways not so easy to measure. You can make a case for hundreds of other behind-the-scenes individuals—from athletics administrators to student managers, assistant coaches, athletic trainers, team doctors, equipment managers, and lots of others who have made Notre Dame football what it is. For example, the

Joe Montana legend at the 1979 Cotton Bowl in Houston is not complete without Dr. Les Bodnar and the Notre Dame medical staff that gave him chicken broth.

Still, start with knowing these 125 individuals and your Notre Dame football history lesson is in good stead:

1. LOUIS "RED" SALMON, FB
5'10", 175, Syracuse, New York, 1900–1903

For years Walter Camp selected the most prestigious college football All-America team—and Red Salmon became the first Notre Dame player selected to that squad (third team pick in 1903). A two-time Notre Dame captain, Salmon scored 105 points as a senior and finished with 36 career touchdowns—and both those records stood for more than eight decades. His 250 career points lasted as the Notre Dame record until Allen Pinkett broke it in 1985. A four-year regular, he joined the National Football Foundation Hall of Fame in 1971 after helping Notre Dame to a 28–6–4 combined mark in his four seasons.

2. GUS DORAIS, QB
5'7", 145, Chippewa Falls, Wisconsin, 1910–1913

Maybe no program in the country has a more illustrious list of quarterbacks to its credit—and Gus Dorais qualified as the first to place his name on that chart at Notre Dame as the school's first consensus All-American. The other half of a potent Notre Dame pass-and-catch tandem that featured Knute Rockne on the other end, Dorais started for four straight season at the quarterback spot. He and Rockne, contrary to some reports, weren't the first to throw and receive forward passes in college football—but the Notre Dame victory over Army at West Point in 1913 without question proved that you could win big football games via the forward pass. In fact, there remains a plaque feting Dorais and Rockne at Cedar Point in Sandusky, Ohio, where those two perfected their form in their summer spare time on the beaches of the popular rollercoaster resort. A multi-talented player, Dorais still qualifies as the only Irish player to attempt seven field goals in a game (he made three against Texas in 1913). Over his sophomore, junior, and senior seasons, Dorais' Notre Dame teams compiled a combined 20–0–2 record. He also pitched for the Notre Dame baseball team. Inducted into the National Football Foundation Hall of Fame in 1953 as a coach, Dorais won 150 games at the collegiate level—as head coach at Columbia (Iowa) College (now Loras), Gonzaga, and Detroit—and also spent five seasons as head coach of the NFL Detroit Lions.

3. RAY EICHENLAUB, FB
6'0", 210, Columbus, Ohio, 1911–1914

A second-team All-American as a junior in 1913 on the team named by Walter Camp, Ray Eichenlaub scored 12 touchdowns as a senior in 1913 and finished with 176 career points. While Gus Dorais and Knute Rockne earned most of the headlines in the 1913 win at West Point, Eichenlaub contributed 100 rushing yards of his own and two TDs that day. A four-year Irish starter at fullback (with Notre Dame combining to go 26–2–2 during that period), he won four monograms in football and four more in track. After Eichenlaub's graduation, assistant coach Rockne handed his cleats off to George Gipp. Eichenlaub spent 20 years as a Big Ten Conference football official and was elected president of University of Notre Dame Alumni Association in 1940. He's a 1972 inductee into the National Football Foundation Hall of Fame.

4. JESSE HARPER, HEAD COACH
1913–1917 (34–5–1, .863)

Notre Dame had a dozen head football coaches—only one for more than two years—before Jesse Harper. But Harper, who took over the program in Knute Rockne's senior season, played a major role in putting football on the map. Harper made the decision to take his Notre Dame team to play Army at West Point in 1913—and the victory over the Cadets proved that Rockne and quarterback Gus Dorais and Notre Dame could compete at the same level as the most established programs. Harper and Co. put together an unbeaten season in 1913 and lost only a single game in each of his last three seasons. He retired to his Kansas farm after the 1917 season, returned for a two-year stint as Notre Dame's athletics director after Rockne's death in 1931—and was a 1971 inductee into the National Football Foundation Hall of Fame.

5. FRANK RYDZEWSKI, C
6′1″, 214, Chicago, Illinois, 1915–1917

A consensus All-America pick in 1917, Frank Rydzewski served as a two-year Irish starter at center from 1916 to 1917, Jesse Harper's last two years as Notre Dame coach. A starter on Notre Dame units that ended up 8–1 and 6–1–1 in those two seasons, he joined the pros in 1920 with the Cleveland Tigers followed by stints with the Chicago Tigers, Hammond Pros, Chicago Cardinals, Chicago Bears, and Milwaukee Badgers over a seven-season professional career.

6. GEORGE GIPP, HB
6′0″, 175, Laurium, Michigan, 1917–1920

George Gipp, perhaps the greatest all-around player in college football history, probably would have become a legend even if he had overcome the streptococcic throat infection that led to

While George Gipp emerged as one of Notre Dame's all-time football greats, he actually came to Notre Dame to play baseball.

his untimely death at the age of 25. But ironically, his death on December 14, 1920, assured Gipp's place in Notre Dame's history books. Gipp headed to Notre Dame with ambitions of playing baseball. But one fall afternoon Rockne spotted Gipp, who had never played football in high school, drop-kicking the football 60 and 70 yards just for the fun of it. The persuasive coach, sensing Gipp's natural athletic ability, eventually convinced Gipp to go out for the team. Gipp experienced nothing but success on the gridiron. A four-year member of the varsity, Gipp proved to be the most versatile player Rockne ever had. He could run, he could pass, and he could punt. Still holder of a handful of Notre Dame records in a variety of categories, Gipp led the Irish in rushing and passing each of his last three seasons (1918, 1919, and 1920). His career mark of 2,341 rushing yards lasted more than 50 years until Jerome Heavens broke it in 1978. Gipp did not allow a pass completion in his territory. Walter Camp named him the outstanding college player in America in 1920. Gipp was voted into the National Football Foundation Hall of Fame in 1951.

The Gipp legend emerged again in 1940, when future United States President Ronald Reagan portrayed Gipp in the motion picture *Knute Rockne, All-American* (starring Pat O'Brien in the title role). O'Brien and Reagan were reunited at Notre Dame's 1981 commencement, with Reagan providing the commencement address and O'Brien receiving an honorary degree. A 15-foot Lake Superior stone memorial to Gipp was erected in his hometown of Laurium, located on Michigan's northern peninsula. The memorial was reconstructed in 1999 and features a brick walkway constructed in the shape of a football. *The College Game* in 1974 rated Gipp a first-team back in the 1910–1919 period. The *Sports Illustrated* Web site, SI.com, ranked Gipp the top Notre Dame athlete of all-time (any sport) in its summer 2008 ratings, calling him "perhaps the most versatile player in college football's storied history." The 2008 *Sports Illustrated* book *The College Football Book* listed Gipp as a first-team back for the 1920s on its all-decade teams.

7. KNUTE ROCKNE
LE, 5′8″, 165, Chicago, Illinois, 1910–1913
Head Coach, 1918–1930 (105–12–5, .765)

Knute Rockne first put his personal stamp on the Notre Dame football program back in 1913 when, as a senior end on the Irish roster, he collaborated with quarterback Gus Dorais to help beat powerful Army in a game that firmly attached Notre Dame's name to the college football map. But, it was five years later, when he became the Irish head football coach in 1918, that he began a 13-year tour of duty that saw his star rise to the highest point in the Notre Dame galaxy.

In those 13 seasons, he produced five Notre Dame teams that finished unbeaten and untied, plus six more with only a single loss. His Notre Dame squads produced consensus national titles in 1924, 1929, and 1930. He won 105 games against only 12 defeats—and his all-time winning percentage of .881 remains the best in the history of college football.

Along the way, Rockne coached legendary figures like the Four Horsemen and all-around superstar George Gipp. On 11 occasions, Rockne's players were selected as consensus All-Americans—and eight Notre Dame players that he coached are now in the College Football Hall of Fame.

Originally hired as a chemistry research assistant, Rockne also was a master motivator and marketer whose flair for promotion and the creation of national rivalries against teams like USC furthered the Notre Dame football name.

He also served as Notre Dame's athletics director, business manager, ticket distributor, and track coach. He authored three books, helped design Notre Dame Stadium, opened a stock brokerage firm in South Bend—and was a spokesman for Studebaker.

When the College Football Hall of Fame inducted its first class in 1951, one of the names on the list was Knute Rockne. That came 20 years after he died tragically in a plane crash near Bazaar, Kansas.

Actually, Rockne had a rude introduction to football.

As a young Norwegian immigrant to the Logan Square district of Chicago, Rockne first played the game with his immigrant neighbors on the sandlots. A slender and swift ball-carrier, Rockne

Knute Rockne's lifetime winning percentage (.881) still ranks as college football's all-time best.

broke away from his pursuers for a long run, a sure touchdown. But a rowdy group of fans for the opponents stepped in, stripped the ball away from his cradled arms and mistook his body for a punching bag.

When he finally arrived home, his parents took one look at his tattered body and announced that his football career was over. But a few bumps and bruises would not keep Rockne away from the game he loved for long. With his parents' blessing, he returned to the gridiron in high school and later emerged as the country's most respected, innovative and successful college football coach of all time.

After Rockne finished high school, he worked as a mail dispatcher with the Chicago Post Office for four years and continued his athletic endeavors at the Irving Park Athletic Club, the Central YMCA, and the Illinois Athletic Club. By then he had saved enough money to continue his education and boarded the train for South Bend and Notre Dame. After a difficult first year as a scrub with the varsity, Rockne turned his attention to track where he earned a monogram and later set a school record (12–4) in the indoor pole vault. Those accomplishments gave him incentive to give football another try. This time he succeeded and eventually was named to Walter Camp's All-America football squad as a third-string end. During his senior season (1913) when he served as captain, Rockne and his roommate, quarterback Gus Dorais, stunned Army with their deadly pass combination and handed the high-ranking Cadets a 35–13 setback.

But Rockne—who also fought semi-professionally in South Bend, wrote for the student newspaper and yearbook, played flute in the school orchestra, took a major role in every student play and reached the finals of the Notre Dame marbles tournament—considered himself primarily a student. He worked his way through school, first as a janitor and then as a chemistry research assistant to Professor Julius A. Nieuwland, whose discoveries led to synthetic rubber. Rockne graduated magna cum laude with a 90.52 (on a scale of 100) grade average.

Upon graduation Rockne was offered a post at Notre Dame as a graduate assistant in chemistry. He accepted that position on the condition that he be allowed to help Jesse Harper coach the football team. When Harper retired after the 1917 season, Rockne was named his successor.

Under Rockne's tutelage, Notre Dame skyrocketed to national prominence and became America's team. With their penchant for upsetting the stronger, more established football powers throughout the land, the Irish captured the hearts of millions of Americans who viewed Notre Dame's victories as hope for their own battles.

"The old padre running the university understood marketing. He realized that up the road in Chicago there was a newspaper or two he could use," said longtime ABC Sports college play-by-play veteran Keith Jackson.

"They were in the perfect position to capitalize because they were a private university. You have to remember, they were called the Catholics for a while. The circumstances were just right. They had a coach and an athletic director in Jess Harper who could deliver.

"Then Knute Rockne came along. He was a chemistry teacher and he might have gone to Alaska and sold refrigerators if he hadn't gone into football. He was a salesman and he could have sold anything. Notre Dame had Chicago and New York. Columbia never captured New York City. Notre Dame has always been the dominant college football team in New York City because there are all kinds of Catholics there. Not just the Irish."

During Rockne's 13-year coaching tenure, Notre Dame beat Stanford in the 1925 Rose Bowl and put together five unbeaten and untied seasons. Rockne produced 20 first-team All-Americans. His lifetime winning percentage of .881 (105–12–5) still ranks at the top of the list for both college and professional football. Rockne won the last 19 games he coached. Rockne, who was inducted into the National Football Foundation Hall of Fame in 1951—the first year of inductions—revolutionized the game of football with his wide-ranging ideas and innovations. Rockne was the first football coach to take his team all over the country and initiate intersectional rivalries. The Irish competed in a national arena. He challenged the best football teams in the land and almost always won.

For all of his contributions to the game of football, *Sporting News* recognized Rockne as the 76th most powerful person in sports for the 20th century. In its 2008 book *The College Football Book*, *Sports Illustrated* listed Rockne and Alabama's Bear Bryant as its all-time coaches.

The *NCAA Official Football Records Book* listed 12 major college dynasties from the 20th century, "because of historical significance, and all represent an outstanding record as well as at least one national championship." Notre Dame was one of three schools to place two dynasties on that list (1919–1930 under Rockne; 1946–1953 under Frank Leahy), with Oklahoma (1948–1958; 1971–1980) and Alabama (1959–1967; 1971–1980) also earning double distinction.

Using his medical and anatomical knowledge, Rockne designed his own equipment and uniforms. He reduced the amount of bulk and weight of the equipment, while increasing its protectiveness. He also introduced the gold satin and silk pants that cut down on wind resistance. Rockne foresaw the day of the two-platoon system and often used his "shock troops," a full team of second-stringers, at the start of most games.

Inspired by the precision and timing of a chorus line, Rockne added the Notre Dame shift to his playbook. In the shift, all four backs were still in motion at the snap. Opponents were so dumfounded by the shift that they couldn't find a consistent way to handle it. The rules board finally enacted a law against the shift. Rockne also attempted to outsmart his coaching peers by downplaying his squads' talent. He never boasted about his team or its strengths; rather, he lamented his squad's lack of skill every chance he got. Rockne believed that half of football strategy was passing, while most of his counterparts kept the ball on the ground.

"Rockne is the greatest college football figure of the 20th century, no ifs, ands, buts about it," says ESPN's Beano Cook.

"People recognize his picture now. They know it's Rockne. When he died, if I recall, it was the first funeral ever broadcast nationally on radio. That's the kind of impact he had. For me, it was easy to pick Rockne as the No. 1 coach. He has been dead 80 years and everybody still knows his name."

After the championship season of 1930, Rockne tried to get away for a much-needed rest and vacation. But he was required to be in Los Angeles to make a football demonstration movie. An enthusiastic flier and never one to waste time, Rockne boarded Transcontinental-Western's Flight 599 from Kansas City to Los Angeles on March 31, 1931. Shortly after takeoff, the plane flew into a storm, became covered with ice, and fell into a wheat field near Bazaar, Kansas. There were no survivors.

Rockne became the first athletics coach at any level to be featured on a United States postage stamp on March 9, 1988, when a commemorative stamp in his honor was dedicated at Notre Dame. The stamp honored the 100th anniversary of Rockne's birth.

Approximately 160 million Rockne stamps were printed, with the first-day issue originating from the University of Notre Dame Post Office. Highlighting the unveiling of the stamp was an appearance and speech in the Joyce Center by President Ronald Reagan, who played George Gipp in the 1940 Warner Brothers movie *Knute Rockne, All-American.*

WONDER WHAT THE NAME KNUTE ROCKNE MEANS TODAY?

Do current college students and fans recognize the name? Do they know who he is? What does his name mean more than 80 years after he last coached a football game?

We recently surveyed a Notre Dame film, television, and theatre class—and 25 of 30 students did not recognize the name.

One student knew about him because she's a tour guide on the Notre Dame campus and said her training included a great deal of Rockne information and that student guides are encouraged to talk about him a lot.

Another knew about him from going into the Rockne Memorial Building and seeing the Rockne bust there.

A Saint Mary's College student knew him because three of her male friends at Notre Dame go to his grave every Saturday morning before home football games and drink shots of whiskey (we're not making this up).

One student took a history of sports class in sociology and the instructor devoted a section to Rockne and Notre Dame.

One student, when he was young, had been given a book about Rockne by his father.

Others had seen books about Rockne in the bookstore.

Most knew he was an "old football coach at Notre Dame," but perhaps only one or two had any clue as to the significant accomplishments he had or the impact he had on Notre Dame.

Only one knew how he died.

There may be something of a generation gap in play here, yet consider the many and varied things that have helped keep the Rockne name front and center (not counting the street Rockne Drive that came into existence in 1948 in the Edison Park area southeast of campus in South Bend):

1931 *Rockne's funeral is held at the Basilica of Sacred Heart on the Notre Dame campus, and it's the first live national radio broadcast of a funeral.*

1931 *The small Texas town known previously as Walnut Creek or Lehmanville is renamed Rockne after a vote among community schoolchildren. There's now a Jerry McKenna–produced Rockne sculpture there.*

1932 *The Notre Dame Club of St. Joseph Valley holds its first Rockne Mass and Breakfast. The event continues today.*

1932 *The first Rockne car, manufactured by the Studebaker Corporation, comes off the assembly line.*

1937 *Ground is broken on the Notre Dame campus for the Rockne Memorial Fieldhouse (still in use today on the west edge of campus) after a million dollar fundraising campaign.*

1940 *The movie* Knute Rockne, All-American *premieres in South Bend. It's the last time the University permits filming of a movie on campus until* Rudy.

1951 *Rockne is in the first class of inductees into the College Football Hall of Fame.*

1959 *The Notre Dame Club of Chicago holds its first Rockne Athletic Banquet. The event, now an annual affair, remains the club's largest fund-raiser.*

1961 Rockne appears on the cover of the Notre Dame–Oklahoma
game program (most covers in previous years feature
generic art), then appears again on covers in 1963, 1970,
1972, 1977, 1979, 1981, 1986, 1987, 1991, 1997, 2003, and
2008.

1988 A Rockne commemorative postage stamp is dedicated with
a Joyce Center event featuring President Ronald Reagan
(he played George Gipp in Knute Rockne, All-American) and
actor Pat O'Brien (he played Rockne). It marks the first time
an athletics coach in any sport appears on a U.S. stamp.

1997 The movie Knute Rockne, All-American is selected for the
National Film Registry (others selected that year include
West Side Story, The Bridge on the River Kwai, and Rear
Window).

1999 Sporting News ranks Rockne 76th on its list of the 100 most
powerful people in sports in the 20th century.

2001 ESPN Classic recognizes the 70th anniversary of Rockne's
death with an hour-long special SportsCenter Flashback: The
Death of Knute Rockne.

2002 The Rockne Heritage Fund is created by the Notre Dame
athletics department to help fund expendable scholarships
for student-athletes.

2004 The Rockne family receives the Ellis Island Family Heritage
Award at the Statue of Liberty. The award goes to Ellis Island
immigrants (also honored that year were NFL commissioner
Paul Tagliabue and film director Martin Scorsese).

2004 The Kansas Turnpike Authority unveils a Rockne memorial at
the Matfield Green Service Area (milepost 97), not far from
where Rockne died.

2005 *A sculpture of Rockne by McKenna is dedicated in front of the College Football Hall of Fame in downtown South Bend.*

2006 *A sculpture identical to the one at the College Hall of Fame is dedicated in Voss, Norway, on the 75th anniversary of Rockne's death.*

2006 *The Northern Indiana Center for History in South Bend presents an exhibit titled "Rockne: Crossing the Last Chalk Line" that runs from May until January 2007.*

2006 *Rockne makes the list of "100 Most Influential NCAA Student-Athletes" as part of the NCAA's Centennial celebration.*

2007 *Longtime Rockne crash-site caretaker Easter Heathman of Bazaar, Kansas, is presented with an honorary monogram at a pep rally by the Notre Dame Monogram Club.*

2008 *John Vincent "Jack" Rockne, the last remaining child of Knute Rockne, dies in South Bend. A funeral Mass for him is held at the Basilica of Sacred Heart.*

2009 *Sporting News, on its list of the top 50 coaches of all-time, puts Rockne 10th.*

And another 2009 entry came to fruition with the dedication and blessing of the Rockne sculpture at Notre Dame Stadium. The Rockne sculpture, originally on the east side of the Stadium, moved to the north tunnel in 2010.

For many years, a bust of Rockne sat in a Joyce Center display case. Ara Parseghian once walked past the bust and remarked, "You started all this."

It may have been 80-plus years since he last stalked the sideline at Notre Dame Stadium, but consider Knute Rockne alive and well.

8. EDDIE ANDERSON, E
5'10", 164, Mason City, Iowa, 1918–1921

A consensus All-American for Notre Dame as its 1921 team captain, Eddie Anderson led the squad in catches as both a junior and senior. He played on Knute Rockne's first four Notre Dame teams and contributed on a noteworthy basis during a stretch when Notre Dame won 20 straight games. He led the team in receiving as both a junior and senior, including 26 catches for 394 yards and two touchdowns in 1921. Maybe even more accomplished as a coach, Anderson spent 39 seasons in that profession—including as head coach at Loras (then known as Columbia College), DePaul, Holy Cross (47–7–4 in six seasons), and Iowa. Also a practicing medical doctor, Anderson was named the national coach of the year at Iowa in 1939 (after a 6–1–1 season led by Heisman Trophy winner Nile Kinnick) by the American Football Coaches Association—and two of his Iowa teams defeated Notre Dame. He joined the National Football Foundation Hall of Fame in 1971, qualifying as only the sixth coach in history to claim 200 victories.

9. HEARTLEY "HUNK" ANDERSON
LG, 5'11", 170, Hancock, Michigan, 1918–1921
Head Coach, 1931–1933 (16–9–2, .630)

Knute Rockne remembers Hunk Anderson as one of the interior rocks of his first four Notre Dame teams—with Anderson a four-year starter at left guard. A 1974 inductee into National Football Foundation Hall of Fame, he claimed first-team All-America recognition as a senior in 1921 on teams named by International News Service (INS) and *Football World* magazine. A four-year starter at left guard for Irish, playing on Knute Rockne's first team and blocking for George Gipp, he helped Notre Dame to a four-year mark of 31–2–2. He once blocked a pair of punts against

Purdue and recovered both in the end zone for touchdowns. After serving as an Irish assistant coach under Rockne while also playing professionally for Chicago Bears from 1922 **to** **1926**, Anderson coached at the University of St. Louis from 1927 **to 1928**, then returned to Rockne's staff in 1930. He served as Irish head coach from 1931 **to 1933** following Rockne's death, spent 1934 **to 1936** as head coach at North Carolina State, then coached at Michigan in 1937 and Cincinnati in 1938. He also spent 11 seasons as an assistant with the Chicago Bears. He retired from football in 1951.

10. Grantland Rice and the Four Horsemen

Grantland Rice qualified as a well-known New York, if not national, sports journalist even before he wrote his account of the 1924 Notre Dame–Army football game. Yet his dubbing of the Notre Dame backfield as the Four Horsemen forever linked Rice with those four players—Don Miller, Harry Stuhldreher, Jim Crowley, and Elmer Layden. The nickname of that Notre Dame football quartet remains one of the most recognizable and enduring in college football history. Notre Dame added another chapter to its football history and tradition that year with an unbeaten season and mythical national championship—finished off in Pasadena with a Rose Bowl win over an unbeaten Stanford squad led by all-star Ernie Nevers and legendary head coach Pop Warner. A Knute Rockne student publicity aide named George Strickler had the foresight to take the four Notre Dame players to a South Bend stable the week after that Army game and pose them on horseback—and that photo, too, has played a huge role in cementing their celebrity status.

As it usually is with legends, the Four Horsemen earned their spot in gridiron history. Although none of the four stood taller than six feet and none of the four weighed more than 162 pounds, the Four Horsemen might comprise the greatest backfield ever. As a unit, Stuhldreher, Crowley, Miller and Layden played 30 games and only lost to one team, Nebraska, twice. Stuhldreher, a 5'7", 151-pounder from Massillon, Ohio, was a self-assured leader who not only could throw accurately but also returned punts and proved a solid blocker. He emerged as the starting signal-caller four games into his sophomore season in 1922. He was often labeled cocky, feisty, and ambitious, but his field generalship was unmatched. Crowley, who came to Notre Dame in 1921 from Green Bay, Wisconsin, stood 5'11" and weighed 162 pounds. Known as "Sleepy Jim" for his drowsy-eyed appearance, Crowley outmaneuvered many a defender with his clever, shifty ball-carrying. Miller, a native of Defiance, Ohio, followed his three brothers to Notre Dame. At 5'11", 160 pounds, he proved to be the team's breakaway threat. According to Rockne, Miller was the greatest open-field runner he ever coached. Layden, the fastest of the quartet, became the Irish defensive star with his timely interceptions and also handled punting chores. The 6', 162-pounder from Davenport, Iowa, boasted 10-second speed in the 100-yard dash.

After graduation, the lives of the Four Horsemen took similar paths. All began coaching careers with three of the four occupying top positions:

- Layden coached at his alma mater for seven years and compiled a 47–13–3 record. He also served as athletics director at Notre Dame. After a business career in Chicago, Layden died in 1973 at age 70.
- Crowley coached Vince Lombardi at Fordham before entering business in Cleveland. He died in 1986 at age 83.
- Stuhldreher, who died in 1965 at age 63, became athletics director and football coach at Wisconsin.

- Miller left coaching after four years at Georgia Tech and began practicing law in Cleveland. He was appointed U.S. District Attorney for Northern Ohio by President Franklin D. Roosevelt. Miller died in 1979 at age 77.

All four players were elected to the National Football Foundation Hall of Fame—Layden in 1951, Stuhldreher in 1958, Crowley in 1966, and Miller in 1970.

The Four Horsemen were featured in 1998 on one of 15 commemorative postage stamps that saluted "The Roaring Twenties" as part of the Celebrate the Century program by the United States Postal Service. The stamp was unveiled in ceremonies at the College Football Hall of Fame in South Bend on May 19, 1998, and the stamp went on sale as part of the series nationally on May 30, 1998. Celebrate the Century was a commemorative stamp and education program honoring some of the most memorable and significant people, places, events, and trends of each decade of the 20th century.

The *Sports Illustrated* website, SI.com, rated the Four Horsemen the fourth greatest Notre Dame athletes of all-time (behind George Gipp, Paul Hornung, and Brady Quinn) in its summer 2008 listings.

11. Don Miller, HB
5'11", 160, Defiance, Ohio, 1922–1924

Don Miller followed his three brothers to Notre Dame. At 5'11" and 160 pounds, Miller proved to be the team's breakaway threat and, according to Knute Rockne, was the greatest open-field runner he ever coached. The halfback was a member of the famous Four Horsemen. He gained 472 ground yards as a sophomore, led the team in 1923 with 698 (on 89 carries), and added 763 yards (107 attempts, five touchdowns) in 1924. When he graduated, his

The most recognizable image in the history of college football? It's probably this shot of Notre Dame's Four Horsemen.

1,933 career rushing yards trailed only the total of George Gipp. Also a basketball letter-winner at Notre Dame, Miller served as president of his senior class. Miller went on to coach at Georgia Tech for four years but then left to pursue a career in law. He joined the National Football Foundation Hall of Fame in 1970 as the last of the Four Horsemen to be selected.

12. HARRY STUHLDREHER, QB
5′7″, 151, Massillon, Ohio, 1922–1924

Harry Stuhldreher, a 5′7″, 151-pounder from Massillon, Ohio, proved to be a self-assured leader who not only could throw accurately but also returned punts and proved a solid blocker. The quarterback was one component of the renowned Four Horsemen. He emerged as the starting signal-caller four games into his sophomore season in 1922. As a senior in 1924 Stuhldreher completed 25 of 33 passes for 471 yards and four touchdowns and also rushed for three other TDs (he also ran for five scores as a sophomore in 1922). He went on to coach football at both Villanova and Wisconsin, as well as becoming the athletics director at the latter. Stuhldreher was elected into the National Football Foundation Hall of Fame in 1958.

13. JIM CROWLEY, HB
5′11″, 162, Green Bay, Wisconsin, 1922–1924

Jim Crowley, who came to Notre Dame in 1921 from Green Bay, Wisconsin, stood 5′11″ and weighed 162 pounds. Known as "Sleepy Jim" for his drowsy-eyed appearance, Crowley outmaneuvered many a defender with his clever, shifty ball-carrying. He comprised part of the famous Irish backfield known as the Four Horsemen— rushing for 566 yards and five touchdowns in 1922, then 536 and four TDs in 1923, and finally 739 yards and six scores in 1924. Crowley eventually went into coaching at Michigan State (22–8–3 in four seasons) and then in 1933 at Fordham University, where one of his players was Vince Lombardi. After accumulating an overall 78–21–10 collegiate record, he became both the first commissioner of the All-America Football Conference, then owner and coach of the AAFC Chicago Rockets. Crowley was elected into the National Football Foundation Hall of Fame in 1966.

14. ELMER LAYDEN
FB, 5′11″, 162, Davenport, Iowa, 1922–1924
Head Coach, 1934–1940 (47–13–3, .770)

Best remembered as an All-America fullback and one of the Four Horsemen during his playing days at Notre Dame, Elmer Layden gained 1,296 career rushing yards and then played one year of professional football after graduating following the 1924 season. His greatest college game probably was his final one—when he returned two interceptions for touchdowns and also scored on a short run in the Notre Dame Rose Bowl victory over Stanford. His career numbers in the rushing department included 453 yards in 1922, 420 in 1923, and 423 in 1924—and he scored five rushing TDs as both a junior and senior. In 1925 he became head football coach at Columbia College (later Loras) in Dubuque, Iowa, finishing 8–5–2 in two seasons. He held the same post at Duquesne in Pittsburgh from 1927–1933 and put together a 48–16–6 mark. Layden coached at his alma mater for seven years and compiled a 47–13–3 record after taking over as both coach and athletics director in 1933 following the resignations of coach Hunk Anderson and athletics director Jesse Harper. In 1940 he resigned his Notre Dame post and a year later became commissioner of the National Football League. He left that position in 1946 to start a business career in Chicago. In 1951 he was selected to the National Football Foundation Hall of Fame.

15. EDGAR "RIP" MILLER, T
5′11″, 180, Canton, Ohio, 1922–1924

One of the famed Seven Mules, the linemen who paved the way for the Four Horsemen from 1922 to 1924, Rip Miller helped the Irish to 27–2–1 record in his three years with the varsity squad. A starter at right tackle as senior in the 1924 national championship season, he received the Byron Kanaley Award as the top student-athlete at Notre Dame in 1925 and received his degree in foreign commerce. He spent one season as a football assistant coach at Indiana in 1925, then moved to Navy as an assistant and helped the Midshipmen to the national title in 1926. Miller helped start the Notre Dame–Navy series in 1927 and remained a Navy assistant through 1930 before becoming the Navy head coach in 1931. He spent three seasons as Navy head coach and became the first Mid coach to defeat Notre Dame, developing six All-America linemen as a Navy assistant for 14 years through 1948. Miller served as a Navy assistant athletic director from 1948 through his retirement in 1974. He was a 1966 inductee into the National Football Foundation Hall of Fame.

16. ADAM WALSH, C
6'0", 187, Hollywood, California, 1922–1924

A second-team All-American as a senior in 1924 on teams named by Newspaper Enterprise Association (NEA) and International News Service (INS), Adam Walsh served as captain of the Irish 1924 national championship team. A two-year starter as the Irish center, he also earned monograms in basketball (one) and track (two)—and set an indoor fieldhouse record at Wisconsin in the 45-yard high hurdles. Head coach and athletics director at Santa Clara from 1925 to 1928, Walsh became line coach at Yale from 1929 to 1933, Harvard line coach in 1934, then head coach at Bowdoin from 1935 to 1942 (34–16–6 record). After one season as an Irish assistant in 1944, he coached the Cleveland Rams in 1945 to the NFL title and was named pro coach of the year—and in 1946 as head coach of the Los Angeles Rams, Walsh guided them to a second-place finish in standings. Walsh returned as Bowdoin head coach from 1947 through 1958, winning four league titles. He was appointed by two different presidents as U.S. Marshal for the district of Maine. Born in Churchville, Iowa, he was a 1968 inductee into the National Football Foundation Hall of Fame.

17. JOHN "CLIPPER" SMITH, G
5'9", 165, Hartford, Connecticut, 1925–1927

A consensus All-American in 1927, captain of the 1927 Irish team and a two-year starter at left guard from 1926 to 1927, Clipper Smith played fullback, halfback, center and finally guard for Notre Dame. The Irish went 23–4–2 during his career at Notre Dame. He returned as Irish line coach after graduation for one year before moving on to serve as line coach at Trinity, Georgetown and Duquesne. Smith later became a head coach at Newark Academy, North Carolina State (also serving as athletics director), Duquesne and Villanova. He's a 1975 National Football Foundation Hall of Fame inductee.

18. ART BOERINGER, C
6'1", 176, St. Paul, Minnesota, 1925–1926

A near-unanimous and consensus All-America center as a standout lineman under Knute Rockne in 1926 (on a 9–1 Notre Dame team), Art Boeringer played one of the best games of his career versus Carnegie in 1925 in Notre Dame's 26–0 win by scoring a touchdown. After graduation he became line coach for 16 years under Notre Dame former great Gus Dorais at Detroit. Boeringer also coached as an assistant at Iowa and spent five years as line coach at Cornell (1946–1950).

19. FRED MILLER, T
6'0", 195, Milwaukee, Wisconsin, 1926–1928

A first-team All-American as a senior in 1928 on the team named by International News Service (INS), Fred Miller was a three-year starter at left tackle slot and Irish captain in 1928. He graduated cum laude and boasted the highest academic average of any monogram athlete at Notre Dame. A grandson of the founder of Miller Brewing Company, Miller became involved in real estate, lumber, and investments before becoming president of Miller Brewing Company. He was killed in an airplane crash in 1954 at age 48. Miller was a 1985 inductee into National Football Foundation Hall of Fame.

20. JACK CANNON, G
5'11", 190, Columbus, Ohio, 1927–1929

Elected to the National Football Hall of Fame in 1965 and a consensus All-American in 1929, Jack Cannon was a member of the 1929 Irish national championship team that played all its games away from home due to the construction of Notre Dame Stadium. One of the last Notre Dame players to play without a helmet, Cannon, in the 1929 Army game at Yankee Stadium, had a key block for Jack Elder, who ran an interception for 96 yards and the winning touchdown. Cannon, who played in the 1930 Shrine Game in San Francisco, was called the best guard in Notre Dame history by Grantland Rice in 1947.

21. FRANK CARIDEO, QB
5'7", 172, Mt. Vernon, New York, 1928–1930

A unanimous first-team All-America quarterback in 1929 and 1930, Frank Carideo became a National Football Foundation Hall of Fame inductee in 1954. Quarterback for the 1929 and

1930 undefeated Irish national championship teams (though he didn't lead the team in passing in either season), he scored the only touchdown in a shutout win over Penn State during the 1928 season. In Knute Rockne's last game versus USC in 1930, Carideo called the play that resulted in his receiving a throw from Marchy Schwartz for a 19-yard TD pass in the win. One of the all-time Irish leaders for most total kick returns in a career with 96, Carideo ranked second to Tim Brown in career per-game record at 3.4 (96 in 28). He also was a skilled punter for Notre Dame. Carideo spent three seasons (1932–1934) as head coach at Missouri, coached basketball at Mississippi State, and also served as an assistant football coach at Purdue and Iowa.

22. BERT METZGER, G
5'9", 149, Chicago, Illinois, 1928–1930

A first-team All-American as a senior in 1930 on teams named by Associated Press and United Press, Bert Metzger played key roles on Irish squads that finished unbeaten and won national championships in both 1929 and 1930, his junior and senior seasons. He helped the Irish outscore opponents 410–112 those two years combined. A starter at right guard in 1930 for the Irish, he spent one season as offensive line coach at Catholic University. Metzger was a 1982 inductee into the National Football Foundation Hall of Fame.

23. TOMMY YARR, C
5'11", 195 Dabob, Washington, 1929–1931

Tommy Yarr earned consensus All-America honors in 1931, captained the 1931 Irish squad and was a starter at center on the 1930 national championship team as well. He intercepted two passes versus SMU in 1930 in the closing minutes of the game to insure a win. Yarr played professional football with the Chicago Cardinals and went on to coach at Carroll College. He was a 1987 inductee to the National Football Foundation Hall of Fame.

24. MARCHY SCHWARTZ, HB
5′11″, 167, Bay St. Louis, Mississippi, 1929–1931

A two-time consensus halfback who helped the Irish to the 1930 national title and was a unanimous All-America pick as senior in 1931, Marchy Schwartz ranked second behind only George Gipp on the Notre Dame career rushing list when he finished his career. He led the team in rushing, passing, and scoring during the 1930 and 1931 seasons and still holds record for most punts in a game with 15 versus Army in 1931. Schwartz rushed for 1,945 career yards on 355 carries for 16 TDs and still stands 17th on the Irish career rushing list. He became backfield coach at the University of Chicago and later head coach at Creighton, followed by a stint at Stanford. The National Football Foundation Hall of Fame inducted him in 1974.

25. FRANK "NORDY" HOFFMANN, G
6′2″, 224, Seattle, Washington, 1930–1931

A first-team All-American as a senior in 1931 on the Associated Press team, Nordy Hoffmann never played football in high school but became a regular for the Irish in 1931 at right guard, playing next to another future Hall of Famer, center Tommy Yarr. Hoffmann led the 1931 team in interceptions with three—and he also competed in the shot put for the Irish track team. He became sergeant-at-arms of the United States Senate before retiring in 1984. Hoffmann was a 1978 inductee into National Football Foundation Hall of Fame.

26. JOE KURTH, T
6'2", 197, Madison, Wisconsin, 1930–1932

A three-year starter at right tackle from 1930 to 1932, Joe Kurth was a first-team All-American in 1931 and a unanimous selection in 1932. A regular on Notre Dame's 1930 national championship squad in Knute Rockne's final season as coach, he was a participant in the 1933 East-West Shrine game and went on to play for the Green Bay Packers for two years. He transferred to Notre Dame from Wisconsin and in 1930 became the first sophomore to start on a Notre Dame championship squad.

27. JACK ROBINSON, C
6'3", 200, Huntington, New York, 1932, 1934

The Irish starter at center in 1932 and 1934 and a consensus All-America pick in 1934, Jack Robinson had serious eye problems that kept him from playing during the 1933 season. He had five pass interceptions in 1934 as a senior.

28. BILL SHAKESPEARE, HB
5'11", 179, Staten Island, New York, 1933–1935

A first-team All-American as a senior in 1935 on the team named by the All-America Board, Bill Shakespeare was the Irish starter at left halfback in 1934 and 1935. He threw the winning touchdown pass to Wayne Millner in the final minute of the landmark 18–13 win at Ohio State in 1935. He set Notre Dame career punting records with 91 kicks for 3,705 yards and 40.7-yard average, including an 86-yarder versus Pittsburgh in 1935 that still ranks as the all-time longest punt by an Irish player. Shakespeare averaged 41.0 yards per kick as a junior in 1934 on 41 punts and ranked as Notre Dame's career punting leader until 1987. He completed

19 passes, rushed for 374 yards on 104 attempts to lead the team in that category, and scored four touchdowns as a senior in 1935. Notre Dame's passing leader in both 1934 and 1935, throwing for 230 yards and two TDs in 1934 and 267 yards and three TDs in 1935, he also led the team in kickoff returns in both 1934 and 1935. Notre Dame's first-ever No. 1 NFL draft pick in 1936 by Pittsburgh, Shakespeare went from private to captain in World War II, winning four battle stars and the Bronze Star. Shakespeare was a 1983 inductee into the National Football Foundation Hall of Fame.

29. WAYNE MILLNER, E
6'0", 189, Salem, Massachusetts, 1933–1935

A consensus All-America pick in 1935, Wayne Millner caught the game-winning pass in the 1935 Ohio State game with less than two minutes remaining on the clock in a contest still referred to as the original "game of the century." A three-year starter at left end from 1933 to 1935, he participated in the 1936 College All-Star Game. An eighth-round pick by Boston in the first NFL draft in 1936, Millner played for the Boston/Washington Redskins from 1936 to 1941. He returned to his alma mater in 1943 as assistant line coach under Frank Leahy, then was named head coach of the Philadelphia Eagles in 1951 but resigned shortly thereafter due to health problems. Millner was elected to the National Football Foundation Hall of Fame in 1990.

30. CHUCK SWEENEY, E
6'0", 179, Bloomington, Indiana, 1935–1937

The Irish starter at right end while earning consensus All-America honors in 1937, Chuck Sweeney played both football and basketball at Notre Dame, working with the Irish hoops squad in 1935–1936. He played in the 1938 College All-Star game, helping defeat the Washington Redskins as well as playing in the East-West Shrine game.

31. Ed Beinor, T
6'2", 200, Harvey, Illinois, 1936–1938

A unanimous All-America tackle in 1938 and also a first-team pick in 1937, Ed Beinor recovered a Georgia Tech blocked kick in a 14–6 Irish win in 1936. He tossed the shot 47–11 to win the 1938 Lithuanian Olympics. A participant in the 1939 College All-Star game, Beinor played pro football with the St. Louis Gunners, Washington Redskins and Chicago Cardinals. He retired from pro football after entering the U.S. Marine Corps in 1942.

32. Bob Dove, E
6'2", 188, Youngstown, Ohio, 1940–1942

A consensus All-American in 1941 and 1942, Bob Dove was inducted into the National Football Foundation Hall of Fame in 2000. A standout on Frank Leahy's first two teams at Notre Dame, he caught 15 passes from future Heisman Trophy winner Angelo Bertelli for 187 yards in 1939 as a freshman. Dove claimed the Rockne Trophy as outstanding college lineman of 1942 and played in the 1943 East-West Shrine Game. A fifth-round selection by Washington in the 1943 NFL Draft, he spent eight years in the pros with the Chicago Rockets and Chicago Cardinals. An assistant coach for four years with the University of Detroit, he then followed with two years with the NFL Detroit Lions as end coach. Dove retired as an assistant athletics director and football coach at Youngstown State University.

33. FRANK LEAHY
T, 5′11″, 183, Winner, South Dakota, 1928–1929
Head Coach 1941–1943, 1946–1953 (87–11–9, .855)

Frank Leahy's very first Notre Dame team in 1941 finished unbeaten. His last Notre Dame team in 1953 also finished unbeaten. In between, Leahy's Irish produced four consensus national championship seasons. So, it should be no surprise that Leahy still has the fourth-highest career winning percentage (minimum 10 seasons) in the history of college football.

He produced six Notre Dame teams that finished without a loss. Nine of his 11 teams ended up sixth or higher in the final Associated Press polls. His 11 years in South Bend produced 87 victories against only 11 defeats—and his all-time winning percentage of .864 (including two seasons as coach at Boston College in 1939–40, producing a 20–2 combined mark and Cotton and Sugar Bowl appearances) trails only Knute Rockne among major-college coaches.

Along the way, Leahy coached four Heisman Trophy winners in Angelo Bertelli, John Lujack, Leon Hart, and John Lattner. And he coached a pair of Outland Trophy winners in George Connor and Bill Fischer. On 20 occasions, Leahy's players were selected as consensus All-Americans—and 13 Notre Dame players that he coached are now in the College Football Hall of Fame.

After World War II, his Irish teams put together one of the more remarkable runs in the history of college football. In 1946 Notre Dame finished 8–0–1, followed by a perfect 9–0 season in 1947. In 1948 the Irish finished 9–0–1 and then in 1949 a perfect 10–0. So, in those four combined seasons, the Irish went 36–0–2. The seniors on the 1949 squad, including Hart, Jim Martin, and Emil Sitko, spent four years at Notre Dame and never lost a football game.

Irish coach Frank
Leahy coached 13
players now in the
College Football Hall
of Fame, including
four Heisman Trophy
winners.

Known as a stern taskmaster, Leahy's practices often were more demanding than the games. But his players loved him and they created the Leahy's Lads group that erected the Leahy sculpture (dedicated September 19, 1997) on the east side of Notre Dame Stadium and continue to raise money for scholarships at the University.

A tackle on Rockne's last three Notre Dame teams and a 1931 graduate, Leahy was selected to the National Football Foundation Hall of Fame in 1970. Before becoming a head coach, he had been an assistant at Georgetown, Michigan State, and Fordham. He missed two season at Notre Dame (1944 and 1945) while serving as a lieutenant in the Navy during World War II.

A recent *NCAA Official Football Records Book* listed 12 major college dynasties from the 20th century, "because of historical significance, and all represent an outstanding record as well as at least one national championship." One of those was Notre Dame's 1946–1953 period when Leahy was head coach.

Irish in Their Own Words

Ed Sullivan

Frank Leahy was one of a kind. As a player, you didn't get too close to him. Even the varsity people who played four years for him had very little one-on-one contact with him. He was the kind of guy who would say, "Coach [Bill] Earley, Coach Earley, ask that lad not to do that again!" He wouldn't talk directly to you.

But he was such a great coach, such a great organizer. He also had such a great staff and was so organized that Frank Leahy could have been ignorant of football and still been successful.

Irish in Their Own Words

Frank Tripucka

I'll always remember my first touchdown pass as a quarterback. It was in the Tulane game in New Orleans [in 1945]. I threw it to Johnny Agnone and it helped us win 32–6.

What I remembered most about that game was that Frank Leahy (dressed in his Navy lieutenant commander uniform) came into the locker room after the game and came up to me and said, "Francis, that was a good pass you threw." He called me by name, formally, too, and I didn't even know how he knew who I was. Then he said, "Please sit with me on the bus back to the hotel." Boy, did I ever shower quickly and get to that bus! And sure enough we rode together. That was the first time I ever saw him. But it wouldn't be the last.

We started getting ready for 1946 right after our final game. Leahy was back on campus from the Navy and said, "We will work out in the old upstairs gym in the fieldhouse." I didn't even know where it was. We were so busy with studies and football, we didn't even know the campus.

Well, I found it all right, and we worked and worked inside until spring practice started in March. And then all the veterans came back from the war and we had a long and tough spring practice. We scrimmaged every day, or at least it seemed like it.

The one thing I remember about the spring of 1946 was that [quarterback] George Ratterman was on the tennis team and Leahy didn't like it one bit. He would say, "George Ratterman, oh George Ratterman, when are you going to get out of those short pants and play a really tough sport like football?" Leahy knew, and we all knew, that Ratterman was a great athlete. He was tough and smart, as he later proved in pro football. But Leahy demanded unquestioned loyalty.

Practices at Notre Dame were rough, but occasionally Leahy would have surprises for us. Sid Luckman of the Bears, the T formation master quarterback for George Halas, came down one time to work with us. Luckman confided in us one time, "I don't know why coach Leahy wants me here. That Lujack knows the T formation better than I do. And he can pass better, do the mechanics better, and he surely can outrun me."

Leahy's quarterbacks always called their own plays. Oh, sometimes he would send in a message with a player or the trainer, but we had regular sessions on calling the plays.

I was the punter, and in one game it was fourth and short, and I called a short pass play. It worked for the first down, only the player—(John) Panelli, I think—fumbled, and we lost the ball. It was only a minute or so until half-time, and it didn't hurt us a bit. But Leahy came up to me and said, "Francis, you don't like me! You don't like Notre Dame! You don't like our Blessed Mother on top of the dome! Why would you call such a play?"

Boy, he was tough to play for, but everyone respected him and knew that he and his coaches were the very best. And we won and won and won.

34. CREIGHTON MILLER, HB
6′0″, 187, Wilmington, Delaware, 1941–1943

A consensus All-America pick in 1943, Creighton Miller led the nation in rushing as a senior in 1943 with 911 yards, the second-best single-season figure in Notre Dame history at that time. He finished fourth in the 1943 Heisman Trophy voting—as Irish starter at halfback in 1942 and 1943. Nephew of Four Horseman Don Miller, he rushed for 911 yards on 151 carries in 1943, plus 13 touchdowns. Miller played in the College All-Star game in 1944 and was a first-round pick by Brooklyn in the 1944 NFL Draft. He was elected to the National Football Foundation Hall of Fame in 1976.

35. ANGELO BERTELLI, QB

6′1″, 173, Springfield, Massachusetts, 1941–1943

Frank Leahy's switch to the T-formation starting in 1942 made a star of Angelo Bertelli and helped him win the Heisman Trophy as a senior despite playing in only six of Notre Dame's 10 games. Bertelli's Irish career began as a single-wing tailback in 1941 as his 1,027 passing yards (and a .569 completion percentage that led the nation) propelled his team to a 9–0–1 record. As a junior, he switched to quarterback in the T and ended up throwing for another 1,039 yards and 10 touchdowns. In a 27–10 win over Stanford that year, he threw four touchdown passes and completed a record 10 straight passes. Runner-up to Minnesota's Bruce Smith for the Heisman as a sophomore and sixth as a junior behind winner Frank Sinkwich of Georgia, Bertelli's play enabled Notre Dame to average 43.5 points in its first six games in 1943 before the Marine Corps called him into service. Still, he threw 10 scoring passes in those six contests and helped Notre Dame claim the national title despite a final-game loss to Great Lakes while Bertelli was in boot camp. He played three seasons with Los Angeles and Chicago in the All-America Football Conference before a knee injury ended his career. Bertelli ran a beverage distributorship in Clifton, New Jersey. He joined the National Football Foundation Hall of Fame in 1972. Bertelli died on June 6, 1999.

Irish in Their Own Words

FRANK TRIPUCKA

In 1946 I got a chance to meet the man who would become such an important part of my life—[1943 Heisman Trophy winner] Angelo Bertelli. He came back to campus from the Marines and joined (John) Lujack and me in a little passing session on the practice field. He actually could have come back and played in 1946, but he finally decided against it. Lujack told me that there never was a passer as accurate as Angelo. He was just the best and had won the Heisman Trophy in 1943 after playing in only six games.

The Boston Yanks had drafted Bertelli in 1944, but he ended up playing in the new All-American Conference with the Los Angeles Dons and then the Chicago Rockets. He eventually gave up because of injuries, but back home in Jersey, I discovered he was going to coach Paterson in one of the minor leagues. That was right near my home, and I got to know him well. Eventually we became partners in business. Angelo was like a brother to me. We were the only boys in our families, and Bert was like the brother I never had. It was the same for him.

36. PAT FILLEY, G
5′8″, 178, South Bend, Indiana, 1941–1944

A consensus All-America pick in 1943, Pat Filley was the first two-time Irish captain (in 1943 and 1944) in 25 years. A member of the 1943 national championship squad, he was the Irish starter at left guard in 1943 and 1944. A 12th-round draft pick of Cleveland in the 1944 NFL Draft, he went from assistant coach in 1945 at Cornell to athletics director in 1954 and business manager in 1961.

37. JIM WHITE, T
6′2″, 210, Edgewater, New Jersey, 1942–1943

A starter at left tackle on the 1943 Irish national championship team and a consensus All-American, Jim White finished ninth in the Heisman Trophy voting in 1943 behind teammate and winner

Angelo Bertelli. White played in the College All-Star game versus the Chicago Bears in 1944, then played five years with the New York Giants from 1946 to 1950.

38. John Yonakor, E
6'4", 222, Dorchester, Massachusetts, 1942–1943

A consensus All-American in 1943, John Yonakor was a starter at right end on the 1943 Irish national championship team. He caught a 30-yard touchdown pass in the 1943 Army game in a 26–0 Irish win. Yonakor won the National AAU indoor shot put title that same year with a toss of 50'2½". Selected for the 1944 College All-Star Game versus the Los Angeles Rams, he became a first-round pick of Philadelphia in the 1945 NFL Draft and then played in the pros with the Cleveland Browns and the New York Yanks. Yonakor spent one year with the CFL Montreal Alouettes before returning to play with the Washington Redskins.

39. Zygmont Czarobski, T
6'0", 213, Chicago, Illinois, 1942–1943, 1946–1947

A first-team All-American as a senior in 1947 on teams named by International News Service (INS) and Newspaper Enterprise Association (NEA), Ziggy Czarobski started for the Irish on their 1943 national championship team, spent two years in the military, then returned to play right tackle on the 1946 and 1947 national title teams. A seventh-round pick of the Chicago Cardinals in the 1945 NFL Draft, he played two seasons with the Chicago Rockets and Hornets of the All-America Football Conference. Czarobski later became administrative assistant to the Illinois Secretary of State. He was a 1977 inductee into the National Football Foundation Hall of Fame.

40. John Lujack, QB

6'0", 180, Connellsville, Pennsylvania, 1943, 1946–1947

John Lujack took over at quarterback for Notre Dame as a sophomore in 1943 when Angelo Bertelli joined the Marines—and he ended up helping the Irish to three national titles and establishing a reputation as one of the great T-formation signalcallers in college football history. In his initial start versus Army in 1943, he threw for two scores, ran for another and intercepted a pass in a 26–0 victory. He spent nearly three years of his own in the Navy but returned in time to earn consensus All-America honors as a junior and senior on Notre Dame teams in 1946 and 1947 that did not lose a game. No slouch as a runner (he also played halfback as a sophomore), Lujack also punted—and probably made his greatest individual play on defense. He preserved a scoreless tie in 1946 between the second-ranked Irish and top-ranked Army by making a touchdown-saving tackle of Cadet fullback Doc Blanchard from his defensive back position. As a junior, he finished third in the Heisman voting behind Army's Glenn Davis. As a senior, he earned the Associated Press Male Athlete of the Year award.

Lujack played four years with the Chicago Bears, leading the team in scoring each year, tying a record with eight interceptions as a rookie, throwing for a record 468 yards in one game in 1949 and playing in the NFL Pro Bowl his last two seasons. An Irish backfield coach for two years following his retirement in 1952, Lujack then ran an automobile dealership in Davenport, Iowa, until he retired in 1988. He was elected to the National Football Foundation Hall of Fame in 1960. ESPN's Beano Cook and longtime *Sports Illustrated* college football expert Dan Jenkins tabbed him as their selection as their best all-time quarterback. Lujack rated as the top defensive back by longtime *Dallas Times-Herald* and *Dallas Morning News* columnist Blackie Sherrod. In its 2008

The College Football Book, Sports Illustrated selected Lujack as a first-team back on its 1940s all-decade squad.

Irish in Their Own Words

JOHN LUJACK

When I was in grade school in Connellsville, Pennsylvania, I would never miss a Notre Dame game on radio. Players such as Andy Pilney, Bill Shakespeare, and Wayne Milner were our heroes, and we listened every Saturday in the fall. It was my dream to play for Notre Dame someday, but after high school, I really didn't think I was good enough to play there. Many schools contacted me, but I didn't hear from Notre Dame.

My congressman had an interest, too, and he got me an appointment to West Point. But I didn't want to play football for Army, just Notre Dame. My dad couldn't understand why I wouldn't accept an appointment to Army, but I had absolutely no interest in becoming an Army man, even though World War II had started. Finally, a man by the name of Henry Opperman decided he would help. He contacted his friend, Fritz Wilson, who ran a men's clothing store in Pittsburgh. Fritz had a brother who was a Notre Dame priest, and Fritz became sort of a bird dog for Notre Dame in the Pittsburgh area. Wilson took an immediate interest and arranged for a visit to Notre Dame, and when I met coach Frank Leahy for the first time, he offered me a scholarship. That was a big moment for me, but I wondered a little about Coach Leahy and why he would offer me a scholarship. I had been a single-wing halfback at Connellsville, and in 1942 Coach Leahy had decided to switch Notre Dame to the Chicago Bears' T formation. I guess he envisioned me as a quarterback and passer.

The Bears sent their quarterbacks, Sid Luckman and Bob Snyder, to help us. Sid was there mostly for show, but Snyder stayed on as an assistant coach to help Angelo Bertelli and me make the switch to T quarterback. Angelo had been there for spring practice, and he was really getting the T down pat.

Freshmen were not eligible, so I had to learn the job on the practice field. We scrimmaged almost daily against the varsity. It wasn't a great season. There was a [7–7] tie at Wisconsin and then a [13–6] loss to Georgia Tech. And not only that, but Coach Leahy came down with a back ailment that sent him to the Mayo Clinic for treatment. We lost to Michigan [32–20] and also tied Great Lakes [13-13] for a 7–2–2 record. Notre Dame had several Navy programs on campus, and we were enrolled as future officers.

What has been so rewarding for me is the great associations that I have had at Notre Dame. At first we had "Ziggy reunions" with Zygmont Czarobski, our fun-loving and talented tackle, and then it became an annual gathering of Leahy's Lads. We raised a scholarship for our coach and had a larger-than-life sculpture erected alongside the stadium. It was our tribute to him.

I get back to Notre Dame as often as I can, usually for early-season games. When I went into the automobile business in Davenport, Iowa, it was only about 250 miles from campus. My buddy Creighton Miller was an attorney in Cleveland, also about 250 miles away, and we would get together for golf games before Notre Dame home games.

Every time I get back there, it's like a spiritual retreat. It's such a great place and brings back so many memories. Creighton Miller died some years ago, and I was able to put together a scholarship fund in his name. My wife, Pat, and I have other scholarship funds that total about $1 million. I have been fortunate in life, but I owe much of that to Notre Dame. Any time I get a chance to help the university and its people, I do. What a great place! It helped shape me into the person I am today.

41. BILL FISCHER, G
6′2″, 226, Chicago, Illinois, 1945–1948

A consensus All-America pick in 1947 and 1948, Bill Fisher was a first-team All-American as a senior in 1947 on teams named by Associated Press, United Press, Newspaper Enterprise Association (NEA), *Sporting News*, and *Look*. Captain of the 1948 Irish national championship team, he was a three-year starter who won the Outland Trophy in 1948 as the top lineman in the country. Fisher helped the Irish to unbeaten seasons in 1946, 1947, and 1948 and tied for the team lead in minutes played in 1947 with 300. He played in the East-West Shrine all-star game, captaining the East team—then was named MVP for his team in the 1949 College All-Star game. A first-round pick of the NFL Chicago Cardinals in the 1949 draft, Fischer played professionally with the Chicago Cardinals from 1949 to 1953 and was a Notre Dame assistant coach from 1954 to 1958. He was an all-pro player in 1951 and 1952. Fisher became president of the Notre Dame Monogram Club. He was a 1983 inductee into the National Football Foundation Hall of Fame.

Irish in Their Own Words

BILL FISCHER

If I had used that Illinois Central train ticket I had in my hand in 1945, I would have been called a Fighting Illini from Illinois instead of a Fighting Irish from Notre Dame. Fate and Notre Dame assistant coach Gene Ronzani intervened. That South

Shore train to South Bend left from the same 12th Street Station, but Ronzani, who was working for Irish interim head coach Hugh Devore, persuaded me to come to Notre Dame instead of going to Illinois.

Ronzani and Devore had visited me at Chicago Lane Tech High, but Ray Eliot, the Illinois coach, was more persuasive. He sent me the one-way ticket to Champaign-Urbana. I liked both schools. But I thank my lucky stars that Ronzani showed up at the station. I rode with him to the [Notre Dame] campus and have never regretted it one bit.

About a month after I made that decision in the train station, Notre Dame played Illinois in South Bend. I kicked off that day and we won [7–0], as we did the next year in Champaign [26–6]. I started both of those games. Other than that game my first year, most of my memories come from 1946 to 1948, when we never lost a game and tied twice and won a couple of national titles.

42. Jim Martin, E/T
6′2″, 204, Cleveland, Ohio, 1946–1949

A first-team All-American as a senior in 1949 on teams named by Associated Press, Newspaper Enterprise Association (NEA) and International News Service (INS), Jim Martin played for the Irish during a four-year period when they did not lose a game. A four-year starter who played both ways, his first three years at end and his senior season at tackle, he served as co-captain of the 1949 national championship team. Martin led the team in minutes played in 1949 with 405—and he received the George Gipp Award as top athlete on campus that year. Martin also played in the East-West Shrine and College All-Star Games. He won a Bronze Star in the Marine Corps during World War II, then became a second-round pick of the NFL Cleveland Browns in the 1950 NFL Draft.

Martin played one season with Cleveland, then 11 more with the Detroit Lions (1951–1961), earning all-pro honors in 1961 when he also led team in scoring with 15 field goals and 25 PATs. He became a court officer for the 48th Michigan District Court. Martin was a 1995 inductee into the National Football Foundation Hall of Fame.

43. GEORGE CONNOR, T
6'3", 225, Chicago, Illinois, 1946–1947

Winner of the Outland Trophy in 1946 as the outstanding guard or tackle, George Connor became a key component of the 1946 and 1947 Irish national championship teams and won consensus All-America honors both seasons. He was voted No. 49 on collegefootballnews.com Top 100 list of all-time college players. When sportswriter Grantland Rice saw him play, he said, "Connor is the closest thing to a Greek god since Apollo." Senior captain of the unbeaten 1947 squad, he was a 1948 participant in the East-West Shrine game. A first-round draft pick in 1946 by the NFL New York Giants, Connor played eight years in the NFL with the Chicago Bears. In 1963 he was elected to National Football Foundation Hall of Fame. For many years Connor worked with Lindsey Nelson on the C.D. Chesley Sunday replays of Irish football games.

44. LEON HART, E
6'4", 225, Turtle Creek, Pennsylvania, 1946–1949

Leon Hart and Larry Kelley of Yale (the 1936 winner) rank as the only linemen ever to win the Heisman Trophy. Joining Irish teammate and tackle Jim Martin as the last of the two-way players with the advent of two-platoon football, Hart gained a reputation as an outstanding blocker and superb rusher on defense in addition to his estimable pass-catching skills. A four-time letter-winner, Hart never played on the losing side during his years in a Notre Dame uniform as the Irish went 36–0–2 and claimed three national championships. He became a three-time first-team All-American and a consensus choice as a junior and senior. In 1949 he was voted the Associated Press male athlete of the year, outpointing such famous names as Jackie Robinson and Sam Snead. He also received the Maxwell Award as top collegiate player in 1949. A mechanical engineering major, Hart called defensive signals and often played fullback as a senior to confuse defenses. He went on to play eight seasons with the Detroit Lions, helping the team to three NFL titles and earning all-pro honors on both offense and defense in 1951. He was elected to the National Football Foundation Hall of Fame in 1973.

45. EMIL "RED" SITKO, FB
5'8", 175, Fort Wayne, Indiana, 1946–1949

A two-time consensus All-America selection at fullback Emil Sitko was a unanimous pick while helping the Irish to the 1949 national title. He finished eighth in the 1949 Heisman Trophy voting behind teammate Leon Hart and never played in a losing game while at Notre Dame. During the 1947 national championship season he carried the ball 60 times for 426 yards and five touchdowns. In 1948 he led the team with 742 yards on 129 carries and nine TDs, caught seven passes for 70 yards and returned one kickoff 76 yards. Sitko won the 1949 Walter Camp Trophy as the outstanding college player. He carried 363 times for 2,226 career yards and 26 TDs, caught 16 passes for 188 yards, and returned seven kickoffs 217 yards and one punt 23 yards—and still stands 11th on the Notre Dame career rushing chart. A member of the 1950 College All-Star team, Sitko played three seasons in the NFL with the San Francisco 49ers and the Chicago Cardinals. He was a 1984 National Football Foundation Hall of Fame inductee.

46. BOB WILLIAMS, QB
6'1", 180, Baltimore, Maryland, 1948–1950

Bob Williams finished fifth in the Heisman Trophy voting as a junior in 1949 (also a consensus All-American) and sixth as a senior in 1950. He carried 34 times for 63 yards and one touchdown in 1949; completed 83 of 147 passes for 1,374 yards and 16 TDs; punted 42 times for a 39.2-yard average. Williams had 80 career carries for 189 yards and five TDs, completed 190 of 371 passes for 2,519 yards and 28 TDs, one kickoff return for 12 yards and had 86 punts for a 39.12-yard average. He set the then single-game record for completion percentage by hitting 13-of-16 versus Michigan State in 1949. His 161.4 passing efficiency rating from 1949 still ranks as Notre Dame's best in a season (tied with Jimmy Clausen in 2009). Williams ranked sixth in NCAA total offense stats in 1949 and 10th in passing in 1950. He was a first-round selection of the Chicago Bears in the 1951 NFL Draft and played for three seasons. He was a 1988 National Football Foundation Hall of Fame inductee.

Irish in Their Own Words

BOB WILLIAMS

It was just after my junior year in high school, and when I was visiting an aunt in Chicago, I persuaded her to drive me to see Notre Dame for the first time. I was a very good high school player, but I didn't think I was good enough to play at Notre Dame. But I went over to the athletic department anyway. Most of the coaches were on vacation, but line coach Joe McArdle was there. I'm sure he thought I was too small and too slight of build to play for the Irish.

He was pleasant—later I got to know other sides of him—and he told me to work hard at my game that fall and to send him some newspaper clippings of our games. There weren't any high school game films in those days. I did send along some clippings during the year, but I didn't hear a thing from the school. Finally, in the late spring, I received a letter from Ed "Moose" Krause encouraging me to apply for admission.

I knew a little bit about Notre Dame because my older brother, Hal, was a 1938 graduate and was a newspaperman in Baltimore. Hal didn't know anyone in the athletic department except for Charlie Callahan, the sports information director. So Charlie at least knew my name and maybe he put in a good word for me, but I arrived on campus and reported for the freshman team.

The surly old equipment manager, Jack MacAllister, gave me some ratty equipment, including a pair of shoes, one size about 6 or 7 and the other one 10 or 12. When I complained, Mac snarled, "What's the difference? You'll be gone in a week anyway!"

The freshman coaches in 1947 were some varsity seniors who wouldn't make the team that were coming back from the 1946 national championship. They put the green-shirted frosh through their drills.

I had met some of the assistant coaches, but not Coach [Frank] Leahy himself. One day he came over and watched the freshmen for a while, and he came up to me and said, "Robert Williams from Baltimore!" For me it was like meeting God, and he even knew my name!

After a while, we had practiced enough to work against the varsity. Before the scrimmage, they would line up the freshman backs and send them down a line to be tackled by varsity players. Here I was, skinny little me, trying to run the gauntlet against big veterans like Leon Hart, Jim Martin, Marty Wendell, some of the real hitters. I tried to protest that I was a quarterback and not a running back, but they said, "Get in the line!" Football practice under Leahy was really something. He scrimmaged every day, and when the varsity wasn't beating up on us little freshies, they were going head to head, first team against second team.

The craziest thing I was ever involved in was the day before Army arrived on campus that fall in 1947. It was the biggest game of the year after that 0–0 tie in 1946. On Fridays, most teams just have a light workout, brushing up on assignments or maybe a little kicking practice. But Coach Leahy was so intense. He must have thought the team wasn't ready. They scrimmaged against us. And brother, they were really ready. They stuffed every play we ran, and they ran all over us on offense. It was some show.

After that freshman season of getting battered around, I moved into the No. 2 spot at quarterback. John Lujack had graduated, and Frank Tripucka was the quarterback. I actually got to play in the opener against Purdue because Coach Leahy liked to dabble in a little trickery. He came up with the idea of two quarterbacks behind the center. One would pivot left and the other right, trying to confuse the defense. After a few plays the strategy didn't work and Coach Leahy went back to the regular formation.

I was the punter, too, and I remember on my first punt, the ball popped off my foot almost straight up in the air. It didn't travel 15 yards. I came back to the bench and figured the coaches would be all over me. But little was said, and when the next punt was called for, Leahy just said, "Robert, get in there and kick!" I boomed a good one and the job was mine the rest of the year.

Coach Leahy wanted his quarterbacks to call the plays. Occasionally, someone would come in and mention a particular play, but generally, we called everything. The most unusual play I ever called was in the North Carolina game in Yankee Stadium in 1949. We were leading 6–0, but we were pinned back at our own 6 and we were going to punt. I called a screen pass from the punt formation and it worked, despite the fact the receiver, Larry Coutre, had terrible vision. Throwing a fourth-down pass to a nearly blind man was not very sound judgment, but it worked out OK.

We won all 10 games that year and were threatened only once, in the final game at Southern Methodist. They had Kyle Rote at halfback, who was playing for injured Heisman Trophy winner Doak Walker, and they played a great game. Jerry Groom and Bob Lally saved us and we won, 27–20. [It was Notre Dame's 38th straight game without a loss.]

The key game of that 1949 season was at home against Tulane. They were ranked No. 4 and we were No. 1. Our scouts, particularly end coach John Druze, did a fantastic job on that game. We were able to key on their defensive alignment. When they went left, we went right, and as a result, we rolled up a 28–0 first-period lead and won easily 46–7.

Our undefeated streak came to an end at 39 against Purdue in the second game of the 1950 season. We were outmanned and finished 4–4–1, which was Leahy's worst season. It was kind of sad the way that season went. But in truth, a cutback in scholarships in 1948 and 1949 left us with no reserve strength. But we knew that the freshmen of 1950—John Lattner, Neil Worden, and some good linemen—would be able to bring the team back.

47. JERRY GROOM, C/LB
6′3″, 210, Des Moines, Iowa, 1948–1950

Captain of the 1950 Irish squad and a consensus All-America pick that year, Jerry Groom started at linebacker for the Irish in both 1949 and 1950, helping the 1949 team to the national championship. He played 465 career minutes—86 percent of the total time Notre Dame played. Groom played in the 1951 East-West Shrine game and College All-Star game. A first-round selection of the Chicago Cardinals in the 1951 NFL Draft, he played with the Cardinals from 1951–55. He was a 1994 National Football Foundation Hall of Fame inductee.

Irish in Their Own Words

JERRY GROOM

As for how I ended up at Notre Dame, Bishop Jerry Bergin from Des Moines had called Coach Leahy to see if he would come and give a speech for the Dowling High School football banquet, and Coach Leahy agreed.

Army, Navy, Southern California and Iowa had expressed an interest in me, and coincidentally all four schools were on the Notre Dame schedule. Coach Leahy offered me a scholarship. But an old Notre Damer, Dr. Eddie Anderson, was the Iowa coach, and he went all out to get me to go to Iowa. Iowa created the Nile Kinnick scholarship, named after the deceased World War II flyer and Iowa great, and I was awarded the honor. But I told Dr. Anderson that I had promised Coach Leahy that I would visit. What a visit it was! Johnny Lujack was Notre Dame's star player, but he was away from the campus making a speech somewhere. In his absence, his room was turned over to me and I hit it off with the coaching staff and the players. The school just fit.

When the 1948 season began, I was in the battle for the No. 1 center job with Bill Walsh, who was the incumbent, and Walt Grothaus. I held my own at No. 2 but played more as a middle linebacker. A year later, Leahy switched mostly to platoon football and I was the number-one middle linebacker and again the number-two center.

We continued to win, although a 14–14 tie with Southern California in the Coliseum at the end of the 1948 season cost us a third straight national title. In 1949 Coach Leahy fielded one of his best-ever offensive teams, and we were again No. 1.

I was elected captain in 1950, but I knew it was going to be a tough season. When I came in for the 1947 school year, there were only about 15 other scholarship freshmen, and it was pretty much the same in 1948. On the practice field, you could see the lack of numbers. We had good, solid No. 1 units, but the backups were not nearly as good. When injuries hit, and they always do, the reserves just didn't match up.

We struggled in the opener against North Carolina and won [14–7] to increase our undefeated streak to 39 games. But then we played Purdue in the rain at home. Purdue's quarterback, Dale Samuels, had a good day and we lost 28–14. We suffered some injuries in that game and a few more the next week [a 13–9 victory over Tulane]. The rest of the season was a struggle. We lost to Indiana [20–7] and Michigan State [36–33], we tied Iowa [14–14], and then lost a low-scoring game to Southern California [9–7] in Los Angeles.

It was tough being regarded as the captain of the worst team that Coach Leahy ever fielded. He didn't blame me or the team—just the fortunes that came from the recruiting cutbacks a few years earlier. And he vowed to come back.

My feelings toward Notre Dame have never changed. I just love that place. It was very good to me and to my family. Without it, I wouldn't have been an All-American, been in the College Hall of Fame, or had the all-pro experience in the National Football League.

48. EDWARD "MOOSE" KRAUSE
T, 6'3", 220, Chicago, Illinois, 1931–1933
Athletics Director, 1949–1981

Fans who enjoy strolling the Notre Dame campus during a football weekend have a popular site to include in their agenda, as a bronze sculpture of legendary Irish student-athlete, head coach and athletics director Edward "Moose" Krause stands in front of the Joyce Center, looking over at Notre Dame Stadium. While Krause arguably had a greater impact on the Irish basketball team than he did for Notre Dame football, he nonetheless headed up and represented the Notre Dame athletics administration for more than three decades.

The sculpture—dedicated in September 1999—shows Krause sitting on a bench, looking toward Notre Dame Stadium, and was produced by Jerry McKenna of Boerne, Texas, a 1962 Notre Dame graduate who also created the sculptures of the Notre Dame national championship coaches at the Notre Dame Stadium gates.

Krause's many honors include being inducted into the Knights of Malta—the highest honor a layman can receive in the Catholic Church—at ceremonies conducted in New York's St. Patrick Cathedral by Cardinal Terence Cook. The City of Hope National Medical Center honored Krause in 1997 and established an

Edward Krause Research Fellowship, in recognition of his service to that organization's philanthropic interests.

Krause was named Man of the Year by the Walter Camp Football Foundation for his lifetime achievements and received the 1989 Distinguished American Award from the National Football Foundation and Hall of Fame. He served as the University Division representative for district four of the National Association of College Directors of Athletics and was elected to the Honors Court of the NCAA, in addition to serving on the National Football Foundation Hall of Fame honors court.

He earned three football monograms as a tackle at Notre Dame in 1931, 1932, and 1933, in addition to earning second-team All-America honors in 1932. But his biggest college athletic heroics were accomplished on the basketball court as a center, and he was inducted into the Naismith Memorial Basketball Hall of Fame in 1976. Krause earned All-America honors in both basketball and football and also earned a monogram in track. After graduating in 1934, Krause returned to Notre Dame in 1942 as an assistant basketball and football coach.

During Krause's tenure, the Notre Dame football team played in nine bowl games and won four consensus national championships. The basketball team advanced to the NCAA Final Four in 1978 and made a total of 16 appearances in the NCAA Championships. Krause helped spearhead the building of the multipurpose Joyce Center, which opened in 1968, by a fund-raising tour that saw him visit 175 cities. He also saw 10 new sports reach varsity status at Notre Dame and handled the establishment of women's varsity sports beginning in 1974.

Krause passed away December 10, 1992, one day after attending the Notre Dame athletics department Christmas party and just weeks before he planned on attending Notre Dame's appearance in the 1993 Cotton Bowl.

49. JOHN LATTNER, HB
6′1″, 188, Chicago, Illinois, 1951–1953

John Lattner claimed the Heisman Trophy in 1953 during his senior year in the second-closest Heisman balloting in history, despite the fact he didn't lead the Irish in rushing, passing, receiving or scoring. A jack of all trades who barely nosed out Minnesota's Paul Giel for the award, Lattner benefitted from helping Leahy's final Notre Dame team to a 9–0–1 record that earned the Irish national title recognition from all selectors but the two wire services (they named unbeaten Maryland). He received the Maxwell Award as the top collegiate player as both a junior and senior and finished fifth in the Heisman voting as a junior behind Oklahoma's Billy Vessels.

A consensus All-American as both a junior and senior on offense and defense, he made his mark by running, catching, and punting the football, while also returning punts and kickoffs and intercepting 13 career passes. He established a record for all-purpose yards from rushing, receiving, and runbacks—a mark that stood until Vagas Ferguson broke it in 1979. He finished with 321 kickoff return yards on only eight returns (two for touchdowns) as a senior. Lattner played one year with the Pittsburgh Steelers before entering the service and suffering a career-ending knee injury in a military game. A former restaurant owner in Chicago, he became an executive for a business forms company. Lattner was elected to the National Football Foundation Hall of Fame in 1979.

Irish in Their Own Words

JOHN LATTNER

When I was playing halfback at Fenwick High in the tough Chicago Catholic League, I knew I wanted to play college football, but I didn't know where it would be. I certainly wasn't convinced that it would be Notre Dame. Notre Dame had just completed four years of football without a loss, and as much as people tried to sell me on Notre Dame, I wondered if I'd be good enough. My coach at Fenwick, Tony Lawless, said to me, "Notre Dame? If you go down there to look the place over, make sure of one thing: don't let them time you!"

At a time when the great emphasis in college football was on speed, I really wasn't fast. I could run pretty well and I could pass a little. I punted, too. But make no mistake about it, I was not a burner. When I visited Notre Dame, they offered me a scholarship and I quickly accepted. I didn't want them to change their minds.

I was a freshman in 1950. The varsity wasn't having a good year and Coach Frank Leahy believed in lots of scrimmages. We went up against the varsity almost every day. Neil Worden was from Milwaukee and was a small fullback. We were the workhorses among the freshmen, and we were called on regularly to scrimmage against the varsity. My coaches thought I could play, maybe not as a runner but probably as a defensive back. Leahy was a slow convert to two-platoon play, and the defensive coaches wanted me with them despite my lack of speed.

Assistant coach Bill Earley was my primary offensive position coach, and that's why I ended up with No. 14. For four years, Emil "Six Yard" Sitko had worn that number, and Earley assigned that number to me, hoping I could replace that All-American back.

Those would be pretty big shoes for me to fill, but when you're young, you think nothing is impossible. I wanted to play and I wanted to be another Sitko. When Sitko finished playing for the Irish in 1949, only the famous George Gipp had gained more yardage.

All I wanted was a chance to play as a sophomore in 1951. Starting was just something to dream about. Leahy had converted to platoon football, but he liked players who could go both ways. I quickly became one of the three defensive backs. In those days, the Irish were playing sort of a 5–3–3 defense, and I was one of the halfbacks. On offense, the right halfback ahead of me was John Petitbon, a real speedster from New Orleans. He was the fastest player on the team, and he also could play defense. He once had been timed at 9.6 in the 100-yard dash. On my best day, I was no better than 10.2, 10.3, maybe worse.

Notre Dame was coming back from its worst season and everyone was working hard. Because of the Korean War, freshmen were eligible again in 1951, so there were a lot of sophomores and freshmen trying to make the team. I got to play a lot, most of the time on defense, but I also became the punter and had plenty of action at halfback. My buddy Worden was the regular fullback, and in our first game, he scored four touchdowns and we won handily over Indiana [48–6], and then we went to Detroit to play in a night game against the University of Detroit [a 40–6 victory].

Those first two games were easy, but we found out about our defense in the third game. Southern Methodist came to Notre Dame, and Fred Benners threw on every down. We tried to match them pass for pass, but our quarterback, John Mazur, was no match. Our freshman quarterbacks, Tommy Carey and Ralph Guglielmi, got to play in that game. We lost only 27–20, but we knew we had to play much better in order to win. We ended up

7-2-1 that year, which was an improvement over the previous season.

The game I remember from 1951 was the Iowa game, which ended in a 20–20 tie. I will always remember that game because two seniors on our team, captain Jim Mutscheller and tackle Bob Toneff, defied the coaching staff late in the game. We were behind and on fourth down, and we were supposed to punt. There wasn't much time left, and the seniors said, "We are not going to give them the ball and lose the game! Lattner, go back to punt and throw the ball!"

I was shaking in my boots, but I threw a wobbly pass that Mutscheller caught for a first down, and we went down the field to tie the score on Bobby Joseph's extra point. Coach Leahy never said a word to me afterward, but he probably talked to Mutscheller.

The 1952 season was a memorable one. I'll never forget our trip to Texas for the second game of the season [a 14–3 victory]. To prepare for the heat, Coach Leahy got Texas to agree to let us sit on the same side of the field, so we wouldn't be facing that blazing sun. [Guards coach] Joe McArdle went out that morning and bought every Frank Buck–type hat in Austin, and we sat on the bench with our heads shaded by those big hats.

Then there was the Purdue game in 1952. Fumbles were the big story of the game. There were 22 in all, 13 by Purdue. We had nine and lost six. I was charged with five lost fumbles. We won the game 26–14, but at our Monday meeting, I caught the wrath of Coach Leahy. "Oh, John Lattner!" he said to me. "How could you commit those five mortal sins for Our Lady's school? Do you hate her? Don't you like your teammates?" My punishment was to carry a football with me to my classes all that week.

After that season and despite a 7-2-1 record, we were voted No. 3 in the nation. In voting for the Heisman that year, I was placed fifth, mostly because I had played both ways. A year later, after an undefeated season, I beat out Paul Giel of Minnesota for the 1953 Heisman Trophy.

50. ART HUNTER, T
6'3", 221, Akron, Ohio, 1951–1953

A consensus All-America pick in 1953, Art Hunter was a three-year starter for the Irish, opening at center in 1951, right end in 1952, and right tackle in 1953 as a senior. He caught 16 passes for 246 yards and a touchdown in 1952—then led the team in minutes played in 1953 with 423 and made three fumble recoveries. A participant in the 1954 East-West Shrine game, he played on the College All-Star team versus the Detroit Lions in 1954. A first-round selection of the Green Bay Packers in the 1954 NFL Draft, Hunter also went on to play for Cleveland, Los Angeles Rams, and Pittsburgh.

51. RALPH GUGLIELMI, QB
6'0", 180, Columbus, Ohio, 1951–1954

A three-year Irish starter and unanimous All-America quarterback as a senior in 1954, Ralph Guglielmi was inducted into the National Football Foundation Hall of Fame in 2001. He completed 208 of 435 career passes for 3,073 yards and 18 touchdowns, carried 187 times for 200 yards and 12 TDs, kicked five PATs, made 10 interceptions for 98 yards and one TD, recovered two fumbles, and returned two kickoffs 15 yards. Guglielmi finished fourth in the Heisman Trophy voting in 1954. A member of the 1955 College All-Star team, winning MVP honors, he also played in the East-West Shrine game. The No. 1 draft pick of the Washington Redskins in the 1955 NFL Draft, he then moved on to play with St. Louis in 1961, the New York Giants in 1962, and for both New York and Philadelphia in 1963.

Irish in Their Own Words

RALPH GUGLIELIMI

When I was a senior quarterback and baseball player at Grandview High in Columbus, Ohio, I visited some 12 to 15 schools. I got to meet such famed coaches as Paul "Bear" Bryant at Kentucky, General Bob Neyland at Tennessee, Biggie Munn at Michigan State, and a rookie coach who had yet to field a team at Ohio State—Woody Hayes. When she found out that Notre Dame was a nonfraternity school, she quickly decided that Notre Dame was the best place for her son. There was one small problem: Notre Dame wasn't showing much interest in me. That all changed one day in May.

We lived in a house that was attached to the house my grandmother lived in. When I got home that day, Ohio State graduate John Igel was on my front porch talking to my mother. On the adjoining porch was my grandma with Notre Dame coach Frank Leahy. It couldn't have been much of a conversation. Grandma couldn't speak a word of English, and I'm sure Coach Leahy didn't know Italian. I remember Coach Leahy telling me, "I think you will be able to play for us this year." This was during the time of the Korean War, and freshmen were eligible to play in 1951. My mother was happy that I was going to be taken care of at Notre Dame. But what really clinched things was that after Coach Leahy left, Grandma came over and in Italian told me, "You go with that man. I liked him and I just feel that it will be best for you."

So I joined other freshmen such as Joe Heap, Dan Shannon, Jack Lee, Frank Varrichione, Tommy Carey, and two other Ohio players, Sam Palumbo and Dick Szymanski, at Notre Dame that fall. Coming up as sophomores were Johnny Lattner, Neil Worden, Art Hunter, and Jim Schrader, all highly regarded players.

Notre Dame had been 4–4–1 in 1950, and nobody was satisfied with that. John Mazur was the quarterback, and we had some solid veterans like Jim Mutscheller, our captain; big Bob Toneff at tackle; and John Petitbon at halfback.

Carey, Don Bucci, and I battled for the backup role behind Mazur. We beat Indiana in the opener [48–6] and then Detroit in a night game [40–6]. Then came my baptism by fire. Southern Methodist came to town and their quarterback, Fred Benners, passed on the first 26 plays. I came in for Mazur and played like the inexperienced freshman that I was, and we lost [27–20].

We were 5–1 going against No. 5 Michigan State. They scored on their first play and beat us 35–0. I don't think I ever got into that game. It was awful. But a week later I started and we won at North Carolina [12–7 for Notre Dame's 400th career victory] with Carey alternating with me. After we tied Iowa [20–20], Mazur started at Southern California. I came into the game early and we won in the Coliseum [19–12]. That's when Woody Hayes at Ohio State learned that my girlfriend was at Ohio State, and he asked me if I'd transfer. I really never considered it seriously. I had some thoughts about going to medical school, but I really liked Notre Dame. Plus, [1947 Heisman Trophy winner] John Lujack had retired from the Chicago Bears and was now Notre Dame's quarterbacks coach. He taught us how to read defenses and to call plays.

We started slowly in 1952 with a tie, a win, and a loss. We worked our way up to 4–1–1 and played No. 4 Oklahoma at home and won [27–21]. Tommy Carey played a great game. I don't think we would have won without him. We lost to Michigan State [21–3] but beat Iowa [27–0] and Southern California [9–0] to finish 7–2–1. We were voted No. 3 in the country because we had beaten the champs of the Southwest, Big Seven, Big Ten, and Pacific Coast conferences.

52. REV. THEODORE M. HESBURGH, C.S.C.
President

& REV. EDMUND P. JOYCE, C.S.C.
Executive Vice President
1952–1987

Former Notre Dame president Rev. Theodore M. Hesburgh, C.S.C., and longtime executive vice president Rev. Edmund P. Joyce, C.S.C., never played a down for the Irish nor coached a game. But the two Notre Dame administrators had huge impacts not only on Irish athletics but also on collegiate sports at large.

Father Hesburgh headed the Knight Commission from 1990 to 1996—while Father Joyce for years was a central figure within the College Football Association. Both men had much to do with the philosophy of college athletics, especially the importance of combining academics with athletics—and both men have received some of the NCAA's and college football's most prestigious awards. They retired from the University of Notre Dame on May 31, 1987, after 35 years in their respective positions.

Hesburgh's effect on the University's growth was profound, whether measured in public esteem, academic distinction, physical expansion, or operating budget and endowment. Considered one of the most influential Americans in the areas of education and religion, he has been deeply involved in key social and moral issues, most notably civil rights. Hesburgh's 35-year term marked the longest of any University president in the country, and he holds a record for receiving more than 150 honorary degrees. His many distinguished honors include becoming the first recipient (in 2003) of the NCAA's President's Gerald R. Ford Award, honoring an individual who has provided significant leadership as an advocate for intercollegiate athletics on a continuous basis. Father

Hesburgh served as co-chairman of the Knight Commission on reform of intercollegiate athletics, whose landmark report was issued in May 1991.

Following their joint retirements, Hesburgh and Joyce, who died in 2004, spent six months touring the country in a recreational vehicle before serving as co-chaplains for a 1988 world cruise on the Queen Elizabeth II. Hesburgh now works out of an office in the Hesburgh Library (named in his honor in 1987) and devotes much of his time to the Institute for International Peace Studies. Hesburgh was presented with the Congressional Gold Medal in 2000 in Washington, D.C., the highest honor bestowed by Congress. The medal has been awarded to only approximately 300 persons in the history of the republic, with Hesburgh the first recipient from higher education. Father Hesburgh added to his distinguished life's work in 2002, when he carried the Olympic torch as it crossed the Notre Dame campus en route to Salt Lake City for the 2002 Winter Olympic Games. He previously received the Medal of Freedom, the nation's highest civilian honor, bestowed by President Lyndon Johnson in 1964. The only other Notre Dame graduate to receive the Congressional Gold Medal was Dr. Thomas Dooley in 1961.

Joyce, a central figure in Notre Dame's athletic success for nearly four decades, passed away May 2, 2004, at age 87. He was an influential voice in the NCAA, particularly dealing with educational integrity in college athletics. He was instrumental in forming the College Football Association and served as its secretary-treasurer. The National Football Foundation honored Father Joyce with its Distinguished American Award. Notre Dame's double-domed home for basketball, volleyball and other sports (hockey until the 2011 opening of the Compton Family Ice Arena) was named the Edmund P. Joyce Athletic and Convocation Center (now the Joyce Center) by vote of the Board of Trustees on May 8, 1987. The Joyce Center, which houses Notre Dame's athletics offices, opened in the fall of 1968 and has seen numerous exciting upsets and momentous sports occasions.

53. MIKE DeCICCO
Academic Advisor

Notre Dame's name can be found atop almost any list of athletic graduation rates—and one key individual who played a major role for decades in that success is longtime former Irish fencing coach Mike DeCicco. DeCicco, a 1949 Notre Dame graduate, returned to his alma mater to serve as assistant fencing coach in 1954. He became Irish head coach in 1962 and multiple NCAA titles ensued prior to his 1995 retirement.

As DeCicco tells the story, Notre Dame executive vice president Edmund P. Joyce, C.S.C., asked him to create an academic advising program for the Irish athletic department. So DeCicco called around the country, thinking he could find examples at other schools after which he could model the Notre Dame program. He didn't find any. So DeCicco set out creating what remains arguably the most successful Academic Advising for Student-Athletes program in the nation. More than a few former Irish athletes have paid tribute to DeCicco and his staff (and successors Kate Halischak and Pat Holmes) for their help in keeping them on the straight and narrow path to the classrooms. Graduation rates have received much more publicity in recent years—as the NCAA has been in the business of releasing details of the Academic Progress Rate, Graduation Success Rate and the Federal graduation figures. In DeCicco's day, one of the very few awards was the Academic Achievement Award in football presented by the College Football Association (since taken over by the American Football Coaches

Association). Notre Dame won the award (it began in 1981) in 1982, 1983, 1984, 1988, 1991, and 2001.

Irish in Their Own Words

MIKE GOLIC

One other guy who scared the crap out of me when I got there was Mike DeCicco, who was the academic adviser for athletics and also the fencing coach. The fencing team was always fantastic.

I remember the freshman scholarship athletes gathered in the auditorium with DeCicco. He comes into that meeting with us, and he has one of his swords in his hand! Here we are all scholarship athletes, the kings and queens of our high schools, or so we thought, and we're all obviously quite full of ourselves.

In comes DeCicco with this sword, and he begins to go into this thing about how he doesn't care if we get in for one play or play one minute, but we will graduate and we will get our diplomas. He talked about all the available help and what we needed to do, how you needed to budget your time. And he's saying this as he's drilling this sword into one of the desks! You want to talk about some cocky freshmen, sitting up straight with their eyes wide saying, "Who is this nutcase with the sword?"

But he got our attention and he let you know, "OK, you're the cream of the crop athletics-wise, which is one of the reasons you're here. But another reason you're here is because of your academic side and the person that you are. Don't forget that, and that's going to carry you farther than your participation in sports."

I still love seeing Mike today. I give him a big bear hug every time I see him because I appreciate what he was saying. Sometimes you don't appreciate things until after you leave. But I certainly look back at what he meant to that school. He was fantastic.

54. Wayne Edmonds, T
6'0", 205, Canonsburg, Pennsylvania, 1953–1955

Notre Dame's football program for the first time had a pair of African Americans on its roster in 1953 in Wayne Edmonds and Dick Washington. Edmonds returned to campus for the 2008 Notre Dame opener against San Diego State and outlined some of the challenges and struggles he faced as a student-athlete some 50 years before. Edmonds, a 1956 Notre Dame graduate and the first black football player to win a monogram while competing for the Irish, presented the flag prior to that Notre Dame–San Diego State contest. He was joined by Paul Thompson, son of Frazier Thompson, a 1947 Notre Dame graduate and former Irish track standout who was the first black graduate of the University and the first black monogram-winner in any sport at Notre Dame. Edmonds played defensive end, tackle, and guard for the Irish in 1953 (helping Notre Dame to a 9–0–1 mark and No. 2 final national ranking), 1954 and 1955—starting at left tackle as a senior in 1955 and winning monograms each of those three seasons. Listed at 6' and 210 pounds and originally from Canonsburg, Pennsylvania, he was selected in the ninth round of the 1956 NFL Draft by the Pittsburgh Steelers but instead went to graduate school at the University of Pittsburgh and later became the dean of students at the School of Social Work at Pittsburgh.

55. Paul Hornung, QB
6'2", 206, Louisville, Kentucky, 1954–1956

An outstanding all-around athlete who played quarterback, left halfback, fullback, and safety, Paul Hornung remains the only

Paul Hornung won the Heisman Trophy in 1956 and remains the only player from a losing team to do so.

player from a losing team (Notre Dame finished 2–8 in 1956) ever to win the Heisman Trophy. As a sophomore, Hornung served as the backup fullback and also averaged 6.1 points per contest while earning a basketball monogram. As a junior, he finished fourth nationally in total offense with 1,215 yards and fifth in the Heisman voting behind Ohio State's Hopalong Cassady. Hornung ran for one score, threw for another, and intercepted two passes in a victory over fourth-ranked Navy and then brought the Irish from behind against Iowa with a TD pass and game-winning field goal in the final minutes. In a loss to USC, he threw and ran for 354 yards, an NCAA high that year. As a senior, he ranked second nationally in total offense (1,337 yards), accounted for more than half the Irish scoring, and converted 67 times on either third or fourth down as a junior and senior combined. A bonus pick of the Green Bay Packers, he led the NFL in scoring in 1959, 1960, and 1961. He retired after the 1966 season, as physical problems kept him from joining New Orleans as an expansion pick. Hornung joined the National Football Foundation Hall of Fame in 1985 and the Pro Football Hall of Fame in 1986. In addition to various business enterprises in Louisville, Hornung has been involved in numerous television and radio projects.

Irish in Their Own Words

PAUL HORNUNG

I chose Notre Dame because of my mother, plain and simple. Back in the fifties, even before that, the majority of kids went to colleges because of where their parents wanted them to go. I don't think it's like that today. But I really wanted to go to Kentucky.

Bear Bryant was the head coach at Kentucky, and I was going to play my first year, so I was excited about playing for the Wildcats. At Notre Dame, freshmen were ineligible then, so that was the main reason I wanted to go to Kentucky. I had been with Bear Bryant maybe 30 or 40 times during the recruiting season.

He offered every senior on my football team in high school a scholarship if I would go to Kentucky, and we had 19 seniors. So he really put the pressure on me. Of course, back then, you could run [players] off. If you saw *The Junction Boys*, you knew he was going to run them off anyway.

But he did want five kids from my high school football team and Notre Dame wanted five of them. I went [to Notre Dame] along with another teammate who had a scholarship. We went together, and we've been like brothers ever since. The way it turned out, I was glad. I made the right decision.

The 1956 season was a very unusual year. The top 10 guys in the Heisman balloting that year were, in my opinion, the best 10 guys who have ever come out of college football in one year. All 10 of those guys went into the College Football Hall of Fame. Six went into the Pro Football Hall of Fame. So we're really talking about an excellent group. I was very fortunate to win the award.

I had gathered more votes as a junior than any other junior in 1955, so theoretically, I was kind of like the favorite entering the 1956 season. But the Heisman Trophy wasn't promoted the way it is today. You never saw an article until November about the Heisman Trophy back then.

Like most things that occur during your life, at the time, I really didn't have a full appreciation for the opportunity that was presented to me at Notre Dame. I knew I was at a school with a great amount of tradition.

I loved Frank Leahy. He recruited me and he said some awfully strong things about me when I was a freshman and a sophomore-to-be. I was hoping I would have an opportunity to play for Coach Leahy, and it was very disappointing when I didn't have that chance. He was one of the great recruiters in America and one of the greatest coaches that ever lived. When [Leahy retired], the guy they gave the opportunity to was Terry Brennan, and I loved Terry. I thought Terry did a great job.

Irish in Their Own Words

ED SULLIVAN

They had a testimonial for Paul Hornung a while back, and the things they said about him were just over the top. He was heaped with praise that night, and you know what? Everything they said about him that night was true! He was a phenomenal football player. He was a great player on both sides of the ball. I led the team in tackles in 1956, but Paul was second. He was just a great football player.

I don't think he was affected by winning the Heisman. In fact, he may have been affected by it more if he hadn't won it because he had great confidence in himself. People said he was cocky and had a big head. He was cocky, but he didn't have a big head. He knew what he would do and he produced.

The best play we had in 1956 was when Paul would go back to pass and everybody would be covered. In other words, we couldn't run a play that was better than keeping it in Hornung's hands.

56. TERRY BRENNAN, HB
6'0", 170, Milwaukee, Wisconsin, 1945–1948
Head Coach, 1954–1958 (32–18–0, .640)

Terry Brennan played under Frank Leahy at Notre Dame, graduating in 1949. He started for three seasons at halfback and led the Irish in receiving and scoring in 1946 and 1947 while also rushing for 1,269 career yards. After winning three straight city championships at Mount Carmel High School in Chicago, he returned to Notre Dame in 1953 to coach the freshman squad under Leahy. He succeeded Leahy as head coach in 1954 and his five-year 32–18 record included 9–1 and 8–2 records his first two seasons that ranked the Irish fourth and ninth, respectively, in the final Associated Press polls. In 1959 he became the player conditioning coach for the Cincinnati Reds in spring training and eventually joined a Chicago investment banking firm.

57. AL ECUYER, G
5'10", 190, New Orleans, Louisiana,1956–1958

A consensus All-America pick in 1957, Al Ecuyer served as a 1958 Irish co-captain. A three-year starter at right guard from 1956 to 1958, he shared the honor of most tackles (88) in 1958 with teammate Jim Schaff. His best game versus Iowa in 1957 featured 18 tackles. A 1959 participant in the Hula Bowl, Ecuyer was selected in the 18th round of the 1959 NFL Draft by the New York Giants.

58. MONTY STICKLES, E
6'4", 215, Poughkeepsie, New York, 1957–1959

A three-year starter at end from 1957 to 1959 and a two-time first-team All-American (consensus in 1959), Monty Stickles finished ninth in the Heisman Trophy voting as a senior in 1959. He had 11 catches for 183 yards and three touchdowns in 1957; led the team in scoring with 11 PATs, one field goal, and three TDs for 32 points; made 27 tackles and broke up two passes. Stickles led the team in minutes played in 1958 and scored 60 points while making 31 tackles. He paced the Irish in receiving in 1958 with 20 catches for 328 yards and seven TDs—and accumulated 42 career receptions for 746 yards and 12 TDs, kicked 42 PATs and five field goals, made 110 tackles, broke up six passes, recovered three fumbles and blocked one kick. Stickles participated in the 1960 College All-Star and East-West Shrine games. He became a first-round NFL draft choice in 1960 by San Francisco.

59. JOE KUHARICH
Head Coach, 1959–1962 (17–23, .425)

Joe Kuharich played professional football with the Chicago Cardinals from 1940 to 1941. He served in the Navy for the next four years and in 1946 became line coach for the Pittsburgh Steelers. He moved on to become line coach at the University of San Francisco in 1947, then became head coach of the Chicago Cardinals. In 1953 he scouted for various clubs. From 1954 to 1958 he served as the head coach of the Washington Redskins, earning pro coach of the year honors in 1955. After his four-year stint at Notre Dame, from 1958–1962, Kuharich became supervisor of officials for the National Football League. From 1964 to 1969 he was head coach and general manager of the Philadelphia Eagles. Kuharich's best teams at Notre Dame all finished 5–5—in 1959, 1961, and 1962. His teams twice knocked off USC teams that ranked in the top 10—in 1959 (16–6 over seventh-rated USC) and in 1963 (17–14 over seventh-ranked USC), both games at Notre Dame Stadium.

60. DARYLE LAMONICA, QB
6'2", 205, Fresno, California, 1960–1962

When the subject of Notre Dame quarterbacks comes up, Daryle Lamonica generally is not the first name that comes to mind. Lamonica suffered in terms of recognition and publicity from playing during one of the least-successful eras of Irish football (he started for Notre Dame in 1960, 1961, and 1962, when his teams combined for 12 wins against 18 losses). However, Lamonica—though he seldom draws comparisons to Joe Montana or Joe Theismann or even Angelo Bertelli or John Lujack before him—made his own mark in an Irish uniform and then became one of the most amazing passers in the history of the gun-slinging American Football League. First, Lamonica won third-team All-America honors as a senior in 1962 from the Associated Press. That year he completed 64 of 128 throws for 821 yards and six touchdowns. Next, Lamonica joined the pre-merger AFL version of the Buffalo Bills, playing in an era of wide-open offense and pass-happy play-calling. Despite qualifying as only a 24th-round AFL and 12th-round NFL draft selection, he played for the Bills from 1963 to 1966, then with the Oakland Raiders from 1967 **to 1974**. He threw 30 TD passes in 1967, 34 more in 1969—earning AFL MVP honors both seasons. He helped Buffalo to AFL titles in 1964 and 1965 and Oakland in 1967. A five-time Pro Bowl selection, Lamonica threw for 19,154 career yards and 164 TDs in his professional career.

Irish in Their Own Words

DARYLE LAMONICA

When it came time for me to choose a school, it was between Southern California and Notre Dame. I knew more about USC and I wasn't sure I wanted to be as far away from home as I would be at Notre Dame. Coach Kuharich had come from the pro ranks and had been in San Francisco a few years earlier, so both he and line coach Dick Stanfel, who also was a California native, knew the talent in the area. In the end, I picked Notre Dame because it was a prestigious school and its football program was well known.

But for most of my freshman year, I had doubts whether I would ever see action for the Irish varsity. I had suffered some torn ligaments in my leg and was sent to see a specialist in Chicago. The specialist said my leg would be all right but that I would never be able to compete in sports again. Needless to say, that wasn't the opinion I was looking for, and I asked to see another doctor. The South Bend doctor had been an athlete himself and had suffered a similar injury. He prescribed a walking cast, and for several months I hobbled to and from classes and eventually to the football field.

Once I got back on the field, I started to have some doubts about playing football for Notre Dame. School was great. I liked it, but on the football field, I began to have some doubts. At Notre Dame, there was no quarterback coach and about all the strategy we ever got was in team meetings. I decided to make the most of it and became the starting quarterback in 1960.

My first game was against, ironically, the Cal Golden Bears from back home. We won [21–7] and everything seemed to be settling in nicely. But it got much worse after that. We lost to Purdue [51–19], and that was the first of eight losses in a row. We pushed North Carolina all over the field in Chapel Hill but still lost [12–7]. Finally, in the last game of the season in Los Angeles in a driving rainstorm, we beat USC [17–0]. After that game, we were determined never to have a season like that [2–8] again.

We started fast in 1961 with wins over Oklahoma, Purdue and Southern California, but Michigan State, Northwestern and Navy beat us after that. We had a good group of players with people like [end] Jim Kelly and [linebacker] Nick Buoniconti. But we never seemed to put it all together and finished 5–5.

We started fast again in 1962 with a win over Oklahoma [13–7]. I think I called more automatics in that game than we even had. But the following week against Purdue, I didn't play; [halfback] Ed Rutkowski didn't play.... As I recall, about five or six players who helped beat Oklahoma weren't even used against Purdue [a 24–6 loss]. I think Coach Kuharich's explanation was that he thought [quarterback] Frank [Budka] had a much better week of practice than I did. We ended up 5–5 again.

61. John Huarte, QB
6'0", 180, Anaheim, California, 1962–1964

John Huarte's Heisman Trophy victory ranks as one of the biggest upsets in the history of the award considering he missed much of his sophomore season due to injury and didn't even play enough as a junior to win a monogram. Behind the aerial efforts of Huarte and fellow Californian Jack Snow (he caught 60 passes that year for 1,114 yards and a record nine touchdowns), Ara Parseghian in his first year turned Notre Dame from a 2–7 team in 1963 into a 9–1 squad that came within minutes of the national title. Huarte threw for 270 yards in the 1964 opening-game upset of Wisconsin—including TD tosses of 61 and 42 yards to Snow—and ended up finishing the year ranked third nationally in total offense (2,069 yards). He set 12 Irish records that year, and also earned back of the year and player of the year honors from United Press International. A second-round draft pick of the New York Jets, Huarte played sparingly in the pro ranks for eight years with Boston, Philadelphia, Minnesota, Kansas City, and Chicago, prior to retiring from the World Football League Memphis entry in 1975.

Irish in Their Own Words

John Huarte

Dick Coury, my high school coach at Mater Dei in Santa Ana, California, was a Notre Dame graduate, as was my older brother David. For me it was a clear decision that I wanted to go to Notre Dame, with not only my family's influence but also the enormous, rich tradition. As a teenager growing up and listening to Notre Dame on the radio, I remember the team ending the win streak of

Oklahoma. I remember names like Joe Heap and Ralph Guglielmi. Those traditions made it a dream for me to go to Notre Dame. It didn't matter to me what the team's current record was. Going to Notre Dame was a simple choice. I remember being on my first flight going to Notre Dame and telling the people sitting next to me that I had never been to the East before. South Bend sure was east of California without me ever realizing that you had to keep going to actually get to the East. I was just a farm boy from California.

I remember our first practice my freshman year in 1961. Joe Kuharich called everybody out and then started dividing players into position groupings and told the linebackers and quarterbacks

John Huarte emerged from relative obscurity at Notre Dame to win the 1964 Heisman Trophy and jumpstart the ultra-successful Ara Parseghian era.

to come with him and to bring a football. I thought that was a little unusual, but I grabbed a football and ran over to where he was standing. I was told to put a couple of tackling dummies five yards apart. Then when the whistle blew, you had to pick up the football and run through a confined area. He used the quarterbacks for tackling practice, and when you're just a young kid out of high school, you don't know what to think. Kuharich would just stand there and grumble about how quarterbacks had to be tough. Of course, he was exactly right. It was a surprise to go through that in your first practice, but if you're going to play football at Notre Dame, you had to learn how to hold on to the ball.

[When I was] a sophomore, Kuharich had his structure to practices, and in my mind he really had a good eye for talent. But we were not a smoothly running team. I think he expected more maturity from us as players. [Backfield coach] Don Doll always stood out to me as a clear-eyed disciplinarian. But that year I didn't get to play, other than in scrimmages.

My junior year was just a really poor season. I started near the top of the quarterback depth chart, moved to second string, and then through a 10-week cycle I think I went down to third, fourth, then fifth string. For one game, I didn't even travel. Then I started moving back up. I wound up playing a little bit in the first and last games, including the Syracuse game in Yankee Stadium [a 14–7 loss]. Going into the House That Ruth Built to warm up made for some great memories. Unfortunately, we were a poor football team at 2–7.

I absolutely believe that team had some talented pieces with Nick Rassas and Jack Snow and Paul Costa. We had some backs that could catch the ball, and I knew I could throw the ball. One game against Northwestern I was stuck leaning on my helmet on the sidelines watching their quarterback throw the ball into the flat and moving the offense. I knew I could do that. Little did I know that that same Northwestern coach was going to be on my side of the field one year later and off we'd go.

When Ara [Parseghian] arrived that winter you had the sense that things were going to get pointed in the right direction in a hurry. During the spring we could advance the ball and were able to do some things right off the bat. When the coach is new you're sensitive to what he's thinking. At some point I did something that was OK, and I glanced over at Tom Pagna and Ara, and I couldn't hear what they were saying because I was 15 yards away. But I knew it was good. It seemed like they thought whatever I was doing was going to work.

62. Jack Snow, SE
6′2″, 210, Long Beach, California, 1962–1964

A consensus All-American in 1964, Jack Snow finished fifth in the Heisman Trophy voting as a senior in 1964 behind teammate John Huarte. He caught nine passes for 217 yards and two touchdowns in the 1964 opener versus Wisconsin—and those 217 receiving yards set an Irish single-game best at the time. Snow had 60 pass receptions in 1964 for 1,114 yards and nine TDs and ranked second nationally in receptions in 1964 while setting the Irish single-season record for catches and yards and also set the record for receiving TDs that wasn't broken until 1994. A 1965 member of the College All-Star team, Snow became a first-round NFL draft pick in 1965 and played for the Los Angeles Rams through 1975.

63. Dick Arrington, G
5′11″, 230, Erie, Pennsylvania, 1963–1965

A consensus All-America pick in 1965, Dick Arrington played both offense and defense in 1965, racking up 36 tackles. A starter on the offensive line in 1964 when John Huarte won the Heisman Trophy, he had 40 tackles and blocked a Syracuse PAT attempt in 1963. Also a heavyweight wrestler at Notre Dame, he became an 18th-round pick of Cleveland (NFL) and a fourth-round pick of Boston (AFL) in the 1965 draft. He finished third in the NCAA Wrestling Championships in 1965 as a heavyweight—and ranked as one of the elite few Irish athletes at the time to earn monograms in multiple sports.

64. NICK RASSAS, DB
6′0″, 180, Winnetka, Illinois, 1963–1965

A two-year starter at safety from 1964 to 1965 and a consensus All-American in 1965, Nick Rassas began his career at Notre Dame as a walk-on. He made 106 career tackles, returned eight kickoffs for 185 yards, 39 punts for 612 yards and three touchdowns and had seven interceptions for 220 yards and one TD. Rassas led the Irish in punt returns as a junior and senior, with his 459 yards and 19.1-yard average in 1965 leading the nation. His three TDs on punt returns in 1965 were a single-season best and remain tops with Allen Rossum and Tim Brown—and he ranked eighth in 1965 in NCAA interception stats. Rassas participated in the 1966 College All-Star game, then became a second-round selection by Atlanta and San Diego in the 1966 NFL and AFL Drafts. His son, Todd Rassas, played for the Notre Dame lacrosse team and graduated in 1998.

65. ARA PARSEGHIAN
Head Coach, 1964–1974 (95–17–4, .836)

After a two-year pro career with the Cleveland Browns was halted by injury in 1949, Ara Parseghian worked at his alma mater as an assistant coach under Woody Hayes at Miami of Ohio in 1950. In 1951 he became head coach at Miami, where he stayed until 1955. After an eight-year career with Northwestern he became the head coach at Notre Dame in 1964. He resigned in 1974 for health reasons after 11 years at Notre Dame, where he won two consensus national championships and also guided the Irish to victories in the 1971 Cotton Bowl, the 1973 Sugar Bowl, and the 1975 Orange Bowl. Named national college coach of the year in 1964 after guiding his first Notre Dame team to a 9–1 season, his overall 24-year college coaching record stood at 170–58–6 (.739). He worked as a color commentator with ABC Sports from 1975 **to** 1981 and served as college football analyst for CBS Sports through the 1988 season. He was voted into the National Football Foundation Hall of Fame in 1980.

I WAS NINE YEARS OLD

Starting fourth grade at Jefferson Junior High School in South Bend in the fall of 1964, I found that one of my classmates was Mike Parseghian. His dad happened to be the new football coach at Notre Dame.

I went to the first Notre Dame home game that fall. Notre Dame beat Purdue 34–15. Then I saw the Irish beat UCLA and Stanford, and neither game was close. Later they beat Michigan State, that one coming after the Spartans had beaten Notre Dame in five straight seasons. At the time, I didn't understand how much that one meant, but it wouldn't be long before I did.

I didn't know all that much about football, but sitting in the stands at Notre Dame Stadium—or watching from any other vantage point, for that matter—I quickly figured out that this was pretty good stuff. I remember watching the final game of that 1964 season on television and feeling distraught when USC won in the final two minutes (presumably nowhere near as distraught as Ara).

But, that game not withstanding, that 9–1 first season quite obviously was the start of something. I attended 42 more home games over the next eight seasons combined—and Notre Dame won 36 of them. No coach in America would turn down a winning percentage (.869, including one tie) like that.

This Ara Parseghian guy, he really had it going.

I wasn't the only one who noticed.

In its annual football review issue for 1964, Notre Dame's *Scholastic* (the University's weekly student magazine) wrote: "The magnitude of what this team accomplished can't be measured fully by its won-and-lost record or by the impression it made on one fan. Before the season began, the 1964 Irish were labeled mediocre by every football expert in the country. Yet the Irish won nine games and nearly won them all.

"In doing so they totally dominated the 1964 football season. Their feats daily filled the sports pages of newspapers in every section of the country, and stories appeared in nearly every national magazine. Notre Dame captured and focused the attention of sports fans everywhere. The story of this team, a team that came out of nowhere to revive a football legend was the sports story of the year."

Even *Sports Illustrated* underestimated the turnaround Parseghian would concoct. "Ara Parseghian is an impatient, determined man, convinced he can return Notre Dame to its position of dominance in college football, and he undoubtedly will one day—but not in 1964. This year he will hope for the best, which could be a break-even-season," it printed in September.

The media called Parseghian a "miracle worker" and they called that 1964 season alone "one of the greatest comebacks in football history." The tradition of that season—and those that came after—lives on in part because Parseghian, as well as four of his assistants (Brian Boulac, Tom Pagna, John Ray, Joe Yonto) remained in South Bend even after they finished coaching.

Pagna, in his book *Era of Ara*, recalled when the team came home from that loss in 1964 at USC:

> When we landed that night we were asked to remain on the plane for a few minutes. We had no way of knowing what was planned, but the short delay made final arrangements possible. The route of the buses that would take us to campus had been publicized, and all along the way people had their porch lights on and were standing out applauding us in nine-degree temperatures. We expected to go to the main entrance of campus, as usual, but instead the buses headed straight for the Old Fieldhouse.
>
> Assembled there was a larger crowd than for any (pep) rally. The overflow was forced to stand outside in the snow. As soon as the fans spotted us, they erupted. We were escorted to our normal place in the balcony with the cheers still building. This lasted for at least 20 minutes. There were no speeches planned, but Ara made an attempt at one. He fought to get the words out as he considered the tribute these people were paying us. "We wanted to bring you back the national championship," he stammered. "You did, you did, you did..." they roared. He couldn't continue.
>
> That had to be the most stirring event any of us ever lived through. I looked around at the team and the other coaches. None of us, including Ara, could hold back the tears. We were all that touched and hurt that we couldn't have pulled it off.

That first season proved only a beginning. Eleven seasons produced 95 combined victories and only one year with as many as three losses. The 1964 squad won the MacArthur Bowl from the National Football Foundation, the 1966 and 1973 teams won consensus national titles—and the bowl wins over Texas (1971 Cotton Bowl) and Alabama (1973 Sugar and 1975 Orange) rank among Notre Dame's all-time greatest.

More than 200 of Parseghian's players returned to campus in 2007 to pay tribute to him, in recognition of the sculpture of him unveiled at Notre Dame Stadium. There were captains and All-Americans (a handful who qualified in both categories), student managers and trainers, assistant coaches and administrators, and others who were part of the Irish program at some point during those 11 campaigns.

They came to feature a Hall of Fame coach who has enjoyed the heights of professional accomplishment and the depths of personal tragedy.

Mike's dad turned out to be someone special, after all.

—John Heisler

Irish in Their Own Words

PHIL SHERIDAN

Ara's arrival was like flipping a switch. He had his rules, but he didn't make a big deal out of them. Ara told us that if we didn't live by his rules, we'd be gone. He made a couple examples out of guys who tested him. That let you know that Ara meant business.

He was so organized. For example, we might spend exactly 22 minutes on the offensive line, then we'd run to a new drill with everything done by whistle. Before, the ends would be down at one end of the field and the coach would be doing a demonstration while everyone else took a knee. Ara believed in entire units working through drills as a group with everyone moving. Our practice time went from three and a half hours to an hour and a half. Everybody knew you'd be on the field at a certain time and off the field at a certain time.

Ara not only organized the program, he upgraded it, too. The first thing he said was we were going to get lighter shoulder pads, new pants, and new shoes. Everything was geared to make the uniform lighter with an emphasis on speed. Ara made a big deal out of the shoulder pads because the old ones must have weighed 12 pounds and you wanted to get them off after a half hour of practice.

It was really nice to leave the program on the upswing because it felt like part of a rejuvenation. You knew things were only going to get better for Notre Dame because of Ara. It was gratifying to know that you were part of a revitalization because the football program's rise made the whole campus more alive. Everything was better, even going to class.

Ara's organizational skills were what made him such a success in my mind. He could have been successful in whatever avenue of life he wanted to get into. Put his organization with his ability to gain the respect of the people around him, whether players or assistant coaches, and you really had something. Ara had a knack for obtaining the respect of everybody around him, and that made you want to work hard for him. We weren't used to seeing assistants up to all hours working like that staff did. You knew he was going to be successful. If you have a program that's so well organized and everything is so well timed, it gives you the feeling things are going to happen. Then when you add in hard work, the bottom line is going to be success.

Irish in Their Own Words

ARA PARSEGHIAN

The best time of my life, for my family and me, was the 11 years at Notre Dame. My family was in the formative stage where our three children were being educated. Plus there was a lot of excitement around the Notre Dame family that football was resurrected.

We didn't belong to a conference and we didn't even go to bowl games when I arrived. You throw those dimensions in and it was really tough because there was no way you could recoup from an early season loss to win the national title. If we lost the second game—which we did several times in the sixties to Purdue—all of a sudden we fell in the rankings, we couldn't make it up with a conference title or go to a bowl game, and we had to fight our way back up the ladder.

That's why one of our proudest accomplishments was the fact that in 11 years, we never lost two games in a row during the regular season. That was a pretty impressive achievement considering how deflating and devastating just one loss could be as far as ending the main goal you work toward.

I found it unfair at times when the games we lost were often classified as the "big ones." How do you determine what is a big one? Going into 1964, Notre Dame had lost eight in a row to Michigan State, five of its last six to Purdue, three of four to Navy, and four of six to Pittsburgh. We won against all those teams in our first year. Were those "big games" or not? When we lost to Southern California in the final minute after going 9–0, that became "the big game."

So we beat Southern California the next year [28–7] and lost to Michigan State—the team that became the national champion—and

Ara Parseghian wasted no time turning around the Notre Dame football program, leading the Irish to a 9–1 record in 1964, his first season in South Bend.

now that was "the big game." In 1966 we beat USC [51–0] out there to clinch the national title, but the 10–10 tie the week before at Michigan State was "the big game." From 1969 on, we played five bowl games and four of our opponents were undefeated and ranked No. 1. We won three of them. Were those big games or not? If you won, great, that stigma of "not winning the big one" goes away temporarily, but you're never better than your last game.

Can somebody coach at Notre Dame beyond 11 years? That's a good question and I don't know if I can answer it. The answer probably is yes—but unlikely. The demands at Notre Dame and the expectations would have to be built around the physical, emotional, and psychological abilities of the person we're talking about.

In my case, I was emotionally involved. My very nature is emotional. While that probably helped me motivate the team, it also probably was a drain over 11 years. Some coach would have to have all these qualities to last a long time: emotional stability, great strategy, great motivating skills, great recruiting skills, a great relationship with the administration, a great relationship with the alumni, and great sentiment between the families of his players. To be able to do all those things and be balanced in all, that's going to take a very significant person. It's not easy.

I had two mottoes I lived by, and they were there to complement each other. One was for the success we achieved, and the other was for the adversity you face in life. When things weren't going well, it was: "Adversity elicits talent, which under prosperous conditions would have remained dormant." When you're down, it doesn't mean you have to stay down. It might stimulate you to be back on top.

For success it was: "Remember this your whole life through, that tomorrow there will be more to do. And failure waits for all who stray, with some made yesterday." That addressed the guys riding high. When you reach the high spot, you better recognize that somebody is trying to knock you off from there and a little humility might help you.

I didn't get tired of coaching. I enjoyed it and I missed being on the field and developing the techniques and game strategies. I was always a guy for today and tomorrow, and I'd let history speak for itself. I'd always tell my squad, "Last week's game against that opponent we beat badly has nothing to do with today or what we have coming up on Saturday. That day is for historians." I still felt I was creative and I still felt we were innovative. The demands to live up to the expectations were difficult. They became a burden in a sense. It was an accumulation of things over 11 years.

After I left coaching, I became amazed by all the eulogies people were presenting and the respect they had for what happened in those n years. I became more respected, more recognized, and more appreciated after I left coaching. I remember saying to [1949–1981 Notre Dame athletic director Ed] "Moose" Krause when he was retiring, "Moose, you're going to be amazed at how respected you're going to be and how honored you're going to be now that you're leaving." We both laughed about it because during his time, he took a lot of heat for his coaches and administration.

It's true that after you're gone, people have an opportunity to look back and they have measuring sticks: how did you do when you came in compared to your predecessor? How did you do compared to your successors? All of those things fall into place after a period of time.

The respect from accomplishment is not only from the alumni and people who were part of it, but the respect from the players, which has been very encouraging for the former coaching staff.

What you feel good about is when they tell you how well prepared they were, how they never went onto a field sensing they were going to be surprised by anything. They knew what the opponent was going to do on both sides of the ball, and we weren't going to make glaring mistakes on the sideline to make it more difficult for them. That kind of attitude and respect has been prevalent since I've left coaching.

If people know me well enough, they know that receiving praise isn't what is most important to me. The word I most closely identify with is respect. The important things for me were to do the best possible job I could and to have a unity of team spirit and chemistry, a strong relationship with our staff, and respect for each other all around. All of those factors will lead to the successes.

Irish in Their Own Words

FRANK POMARICO

I knew all about Ara before I got there. Ara was a very, very impressive guy. He's got these piercing eyes that make you stand at attention, and everything he said was gobbled up because we felt if we wanted to be successful as a team, as individuals we were going to try to emulate his intensity, his character. That was something that we believed in. Even if you lost games, you would still win by showing your character and strong will.

Ara instilled in us that the game may be over and we may have lost the battle, but we didn't lose the war. We were always trying to achieve and improve on the athletic field, as individuals, or in the classroom. So it was never really lost: time just ran out. He used to talk about not having a breaking point.

Irish in Their Own Words

MIKE McCoy

Looking at the success of Ara, there were several things that made him such a great coach. One aspect was the combination of his hands-off style when we lost and how hard he would work us after we won. Another was his knowledge of the game and how he could be up in that tower and before the snap of the ball he could tell if the middle linebacker, Bob Olson, was too far to the left or if I wasn't lined up right. He knew everybody's position and assignment because he wrote the book.

Another strength was Ara's ability to change a game plan on the run, something all the great coaches do. If you've got a drop-back quarterback and try to make him an option passer, that's never going to work. He knew how to mold the players and suit them to the system, which for him meant putting the best athletes on defense.

Through his personality Ara developed an atmosphere where you could go in and tell him things. You knew he wouldn't put you down to third team because you did something wrong. He drew the line short of being your buddy, and you knew he wasn't following you around checking up on your work all the time. But he let you know what was expected of you. You knew if you didn't get those things done that you wouldn't play. He had the authority, but you knew you could approach him too.

Irish in Their Own Words

BRIAN BOULAC

I really don't know why we couldn't get over the hump. But as an assistant coach sitting in on meetings in 1964, I felt Ara's approach was different than Coach [Joe] Kuharich's. He was maybe more at ease in communicating with young kids, whereas Kuharich was used to working with the professional athlete. Kuharich knew his Xs and Os, and he and his staff worked hard. But I felt the difference immediately when Ara arrived, with his enthusiasm and preparation, the way we approached the game, and the way you could pick that up as a player.

Prior to Ara, we competed and were rarely out of games. When Ara came, they competed, they were in games—and they won. He got us over that hump. I guess coaching at times does make a difference. Prior to Ara, the talent was there, the spirit was there, but it took the master chef to put it together.

Irish in Their Own Words

JOE THEISMANN

Whenever someone would come up to me and say, "Coach wants to see you," I would get a big knot in my stomach. Sitting in front of Ara was, to me, like having an audience with the pope. You get a feeling when you're in his presence that this is not just another football coach, this is not just another man, this is someone who is bigger than everything else.

He used to sit in the tower, offense on one side, defense on the other. I'd run a play, screw up, and I'd quickly look up to see if he was looking—and he'd be facing the other way. I'd think, "Whew, I dodged a bullet!" I'd break the huddle, come walking out, and he'd say, "Joe, don't make the mistake you just made!" I'd think, "How did you know?" To this day, I'm uneasy in his presence.

Irish in Their Own Words

JOE AZZARO

I dealt with Ara more than any other coach. Every day he'd bet me milkshakes in practice when he'd kick alongside me, but he never paid off. It took him a long time to gain trust in me, but once I had that, there wasn't much that could take it away. He'd work with me every day, throwing stuff at my feet, telling the snapper to snap it poorly, and trying to get me off my game. He wanted to make sure I could handle the pressure, and that's something he tried to do with everybody.

Irish in Their Own Words

JOHN HUARTE

Ara was another guy who would test his players. During one scrimmage in a spring practice, he stopped play and put me in at middle linebacker. It was a goal-line defense situation, and I had never played linebacker in my life. The coaching staff just wanted to see if I could hit somebody. We ran about six plays and I did all I could, diving onto the pile. And then they pulled me out. They just wanted to see if their quarterback could hit. Ara didn't know what kind of players he had, so that was a good way to figure it out.

When I talk about the job that Ara did, I mean Ara and his assistants. The jobs that John Ray [defensive line/linebackers], Paul Shoults [defensive backs], Doc Urich [offensive line], and especially Tom Pagna [offensive backs] did...this was a management team that came in. They all knew each other and they made a lot of decisions as a group on moving guys around from the year before, breaking up the elephant backfield, for example, or lining Jack Snow up at end.

To me, Tom Pagna was the key guy on that staff when it came to my success, along with Ara of course. Tom spent a lot of time with me. Every time I saw him I told him how lucky I was to have him as a coach. He, of course, told me how lucky he was to have me as a player.

Tom was very skilled at handling young college kids. Tom's style was very fundamental and reassuring. He wasn't a rah-rah cheerleader, but more of an execution guy. He really drilled the little things, like the importance of getting deep off the line and staying precise with your footwork. That was a particular point that Tom really worked with me on. He was a gently encouraging coach who was a fun guy but serious at the same time.

About four days before the first game in 1964, I was walking into a meeting with Ara and a couple players. Ara put his arm around me and said, "John, this Saturday I want you just to relax and play like you can. If you make a mistake, don't worry about it. I'm going with you." Those words were really, really important to me. Ara had enough experience handling young kids to tell me that, especially after the year before when I had been bounced around and just shattered.

Irish in Their Own Words

Walt Patulski

Reflecting back, what Ara Parseghian did was put the best athletes on defense, and that enabled us to be in every game. The offense is more of a regimentation where you can be more disciplined.

Irish in Their Own Words

Terry Hanratty

From consensus All-Americans to the guys who never got in a game, nobody could ever say anything bad about Ara. He was an extremely fair and caring person. He helped make my Notre Dame football experience very special.

66. Alan Page, DE
6′4″, 230, Canton, Ohio, 1964–1966

Former Notre Dame All-America defensive end Alan Page, now a Minnesota Supreme Court Justice, has been honored as much for what he has done away from football as he has been for his gridiron exploits. Previously the recipient of an honorary doctor of laws degree from Notre Dame, Page was honored at the 2004 Notre Dame commencement ceremony with an honorary doctor of humane letters degree. Earlier in 2004, Page became the 37th recipient of the Theodore Roosevelt Award during the NCAA Honors Dinner. The coveted "Teddy," named for the 26th president who played a key role in founding the NCAA, is presented annually to a distinguished citizen of national reputation and outstanding accomplishment.

After his All-America career at Notre Dame—which included a three-year record of 25-3-2 that was capped by winning the 1966 national title—Page became a key member of the Minnesota Vikings' famed "Purple People Eaters" defensive line. He appeared in nine Pro Bowls during an NFL career that spanned 15 seasons, including 11½ as a member of the Vikings and 3½ with the Chicago Bears. In 1971 the four-time NFC Defensive Player of the Year became the first defensive player in NFL history to earn the league's Most Valuable Player award. Page— elected to the NFL Pro Football Hall of Fame in 1988 and the National Football Foundation and College Hall of Fame in 1993—worked his way through law school as a full-time student while maintaining his career as a pro football player. He earned his juris doctorate from the University of Minnesota Law School in 1978 and worked as an associate with Lindquist & Vennum in 1981 before fulfilling responsibilities as a special assistant attorney general in Minnesota's employment law division. Page served as assistant attorney general from 1987 to 1993, when he was elected to Minnesota's Supreme Court.

A vocal proponent of education and frequent speaker at elementary schools, Page and his wife Diane established the Page Education Foundation in 1988 to help provide educational grants for students of color to attend colleges in Minnesota. As a condition of receiving the funds, the so-called Page Scholars serve as role models and mentors for younger children with the goal of changing the future. The foundation has awarded nearly 5,000 grants to students, totaling some $3 million. The 540 Page Scholars in 2011–2012 combined to provide 28,000 hours of community service in terms of tutoring and mentoring children of color—and they received a combined $775,000 in grants.

Irish in Their Words

KEVIN HARDY

My first memory of Notre Dame football is clear: Alan Page. I had never been around anyone that big before. I might have been even bigger than he was, but you don't look at yourself like that. When I walked into the room with Page, I didn't know what I was getting into. Of course all these other guys were probably looking at me thinking about how I was one big SOB.

67. NICK EDDY, HB
6'0", 195, Tracy, California, 1964–1966

A unanimous All-America pick in 1966, Nick Eddy was the leading Irish rusher on the 1966 national championship team as well as in 1965. He rushed for 553 yards in 1966 and 582 in 1965 and also led the Irish in kickoff returns in 1966. Eddy finished third in the Heisman Trophy voting for 1966 and helped the Irish lead the nation in scoring in 1966 and rank third in total offense. A 1967 participant in the College All-Star game, he became a second-round selection of the Detroit Lions in the 1966 NFL Draft and played with the Lions from 1968 to 1972.

68. JIM LYNCH, LB
6'1", 225, Lima, Ohio, 1964–1966

Captain of the 1966 national championship squad, Jim Lynch was the recipient of the Maxwell Award in 1966 as well as being a unanimous first-team All-American. A CoSIDA Academic All-American in 1966 and recipient of a postgraduate scholarship from the National Football Foundation, he played in the 1966 East-West Shrine game and 1967 College All-Star game. Lynch's career totals included 255 tackles; six passes broken up; four interceptions for 12 return yards while recovering one fumble. He was a second-round draft choice of the Kansas City Chiefs in the 1967 NFL Draft and helped the Chiefs win the Super Bowl in 1970. Winner of the NCAA Silver Anniversary award, he was elected to the National Football Foundation Hall of Fame in 1992. Lynch also served as president of the Notre Dame Monogram Club from 1983 **to 1984.**

69. TOM REGNER, OG
6'1", 250, Kenosha, Wisconsin, 1964–1966

A consensus All-America pick in 1966, Tom Regner was a two-year regular at left offensive guard from 1965 to 1966 after starting at right defensive tackle as a sophomore in 1964. He had 68 tackles in 1964 then moved to offensive guard and was a member of the 1966 Irish national championship team. A 1966 CoSIDA Academic All-American, Regner was a member of the 1967 College All-Star team. He was picked by Houston in the first round of the 1967 NFL Draft as the 23rd overall selection and played for the Oilers through 1972.

70. TOM SCHOEN, DB
5'11", 178, Euclid, Ohio, 1965–1967

A consensus All-America pick in 1967, Tom Schoen earned a letter as a backup Irish quarterback in 1965 then started the next two seasons at safety. He led the Irish in punt returns and interceptions as a junior and senior—and had seven interceptions for 118 yards and two touchdowns in the 1966 national championship season (also leading in punt returns with 29 for 252 yards and one TD). In 1967 he had 52 tackles and 11 passes broken up, four interceptions for 108 yards, recovered one fumble, and returned 42 punts for 447 yards and one TD. He ranked sixth in the final NCAA stats in punt return yards as a senior in 1967. Schoen still holds the single-game record for punt return yards with 167 on nine returns versus Pittsburgh in 1967. He played in the 1967 East-West Shrine Game.

chapter 8

THE 125 MOST IMPORTANT PEOPLE IN NOTRE DAME FOOTBALL HISTORY— PART II, 1965–2011

71. ROCKY BLEIER, HB
5′11″, 195, Appleton, Wisconsin, 1965–1967

Irish running back Bob "Rocky" Bleier never qualified as a Notre Dame football superstar. He played three seasons under Ara Parseghian, including the 1966 national title campaign, rushing for 784 career yards and catching 36 career passes (for 422 yards). His most productive year came in 1967 as a senior captain when he rushed 77 times for 357 yards (five touchdowns) and caught 16 passes for 171 yards (two TDs).

However, Bleier's story after he left Notre Dame qualifies as truly remarkable. Following his 1968 graduation and draft selection by the Pittsburgh Steelers (16th round), Bleier also was drafted by the U.S. Army in December 1968 and sent to Vietnam in May 1969. While serving with the 4th/31st of the 196th Light Infantry Brigade of the American Division, Bleier found himself stationed in Chu Lai, South Vietnam. In August 1968 he suffered serious leg injuries in Heip Duc and eventually was awarded both the Purple Heart and a Bronze Star.

After his amazing recovery from his combat injuries, Bleier made the Steelers' active roster in 1972 and two years later won a spot in the starting Pittsburgh backfield. In 1975 he rushed for 163 yards in a game against Green Bay and a year later joined Franco Harris to become only the second pair of NFL backs to both gain 1,000 rushing yards in the same season. He scored the go-ahead touchdown in Super Bowl XIII in 1978 and ended up a four-time Super Bowl champion with the Steelers before retiring in 1980. He worked in television in the Pittsburgh market and remains a highly sought-after motivational speaker. After being told he likely would never walk normally again due to his battle wounds, Bleier ended up accounting for 3,865 rushing yards in his NFL career (plus 136 receptions and 25 TDs). His autobiography, *Fighting Back*, eventually became a television movie.

72. TERRY HANRATTY, QB
6′1″, 190, Butler, Pennsylvania, 1966–1968

A three-year starter for the Irish at quarterback in 1966–1968 and a consensus All-America pick in 1968, Terry Hanratty finished sixth in the 1966 Heisman Trophy voting, 10th in 1967 and third in 1968 (he and Angelo Bertelli are the only Irish players to finish in the top 10 three years running). The starting quarterback for the 1966 national championship team, he took the Irish to an 8–0 mark before suffering a shoulder injury. Hanratty teamed with Jim Seymour to form a great passing duo—in the 1966 Purdue game they combined for a 42-yard gain, 84-yard TD run, 39-yard TD, and another for a seven-yard score. In his career he completed 304 of 550 passes for 4,152 yards and 27 TDs—and carried 181 times for 586 yards and 16 TDs. Hanratty still holds the Notre Dame records for pass attempts in a game with 63; pass attempts per game in a season with 28.1; pass completions per game for a season with 16.6 and is second for career with 11.69; and he is second in passing yards per game in a career with 159.7. He set Irish marks on a career basis for pass completions, passing yards, and TD passes.

A 1969 College All-Star participant, Hanratty became a second-round selection of Pittsburgh in the 1969 NFL Draft. He played with Pittsburgh from 1969 to 1975 and Tampa Bay in 1976. Hanratty has a daughter, Kelly, who played soccer at Notre Dame from 1988 to 1989, and a son, Conor, who is currently an offensive lineman in football for the Irish.

Irish in Their Own Words

TERRY HANRATTY

I was almost signed, sealed, and delivered to Michigan State coming out of high school because of [Spartans head coach] Duffy Daugherty, a wonderfully charismatic person who was hard to say no to. Who knows, I could have been on the other side of that 10–10 tie.

I had a high school coach who told me not to go to California or Florida because back during my high school days, to go that far for school was almost unheard of. My coach told me to be true to these college coaches who were recruiting me, so Michigan State was a local favorite with Daugherty's Pennsylvania ties.

I visited Michigan State a couple of times, and the Spartans' coaches came to see me at Butler High School. Woody Hayes came to Butler, too, but at that time he threw the ball twice a game if Ohio State was down by 30 points. I had a real fatherly comfort with Duffy, even though John Ray was recruiting me for Notre Dame. But after Ara Parseghian saw my film, he told John to call me and set up a meeting.

We met at the Hilton Hotel in Pittsburgh in a little dining room, and I remember looking at the menu and seeing the steak sandwich, which was $3.95. I said to myself, "I can't get that because they'll think I'm trying to gouge them." So I went for the club sandwich that was $1.25. Just spending an hour or two with Ara right then was all I needed.

Duffy had told me that if I didn't start at quarterback by my sophomore year I could start at wide receiver. All Ara told me was that I had a good chance to play as a sophomore. That's all he could guarantee.

How I made the best decision of my life to go to Notre Dame, I'll never know. I'll never forget the night that I picked Notre Dame. I called Ara, but then I had to call Duffy and tell him. For the next hour Duffy went on and on about how great Notre Dame was and what a great guy Ara Parseghian was. He made the call so easy for me, and I always had the utmost respect for Duffy Daugherty from then on.

But for me to go to Indiana from Pennsylvania after not going as far as Pittsburgh until my junior year in high school, I knew it was going to be an adjustment. Then when you arrive and can't play as a freshman, all you have is practice and you get beat up by the varsity every Monday. Not until the spring of my freshman year when I won the starting job, did playing football at Notre Dame start to become fun. We had some scrimmages, and I got hot, which was the key to it all.

Jim Seymour and I used to practice in that old fieldhouse, and in there, if I had to throw the ball 40 yards, I'd have to arc it over two or three rafters. The lighting in there was horrible, but we got our timing down. If you could catch the ball in there, you could catch it anywhere.

73. GEORGE KUNZ, OT
6′5″, 228, Arcadia, California, 1966–1968

A consensus All-America pick in 1968, George Kunz was a two-year starter at right offensive tackle and co-captain of the 1968 Notre Dame team. He played both at tight end and tackle in 1966 and caught seven passes for 101 yards. Kunz participated in the 1968 East-West Shrine game, 1969 College All-Star Game and Hula Bowl. A first-team CoSIDA Academic All-American in 1968 and recipient of postgraduate scholarships from the NCAA and the National Football Foundation, Kunz became a first-round selection of the Atlanta Falcons in the 1969 NFL Draft as the second overall pick. He played six seasons with Atlanta and five more with Baltimore. Kunz was an eight-time Pro Bowl pick and a three-time (1972, 1973, 1975) NFL All-Pro selection. He now lives in Las Vegas, Nevada, where he has been affiliated with McDonald's for many years.

74. MIKE McCOY, DT
6′5″, 270, Erie, Pennsylvania, 1967–1969

A unanimous first-team All-American as a senior in 1969, Mike McCoy finished sixth in the 1969 Heisman Trophy voting. A two-year starter at left defensive tackle from 1968 to 1969, he was named Lineman of the Week by *Sports Illustrated* after the Irish defeat of Northwestern in 1969. Named Lineman of the Year by Associated Press in 1969, McCoy accumulated 203 career tackles, two for losses, and intercepted two passes. A 1970 participant in the College All-Star Game, he was chosen by Green Bay in the first round of the 1970 NFL Draft as the second overall player selected. He played 11 years in the NFL—seven with Green Bay (twice leading the Packers in sacks), two with Oakland, one with the New York Giants, and one more with both New York and Detroit. Appointed by President Ronald Reagan to the Council on Sports for a Drug Free America, McCoy now serves as president of Mike McCoy Ministries and lectures widely in Catholic schools.

Irish in Their Own Words

Mike McCoy

I came out of Erie, Pennsylvania, from Cathedral Prep High School, which was an all-boys' Catholic school known for academic and athletic excellence. I didn't go there until my sophomore year, after spending my freshman year in the seminary studying to be a priest. I thought that's what God called me to do, so I spent a year at St. Mark's, a local seminary in Erie. I can probably give you 10 reasons why I left, but I still really don't know why. But, when I decided to leave, I couldn't get into Cathedral because it was full.

I planned to go to a public school, but somehow word got to Monsignor McDonald that there was a seminarian who had some football experience and a size-15 cleat, or at least that's the story that I've been told. I had never played a down of football. But after spending less than a month on the junior varsity and averaging 15 yards a carry as a fullback, I moved up to the varsity on Labor Day back in 1963. They put me at nose tackle because I had no experience at all, and I started working with Tony Zambroski, who played under Frank Leahy and was my high school line coach.

I was playing both ways by my junior year, which was about the time Zambroski started asking me where I was thinking about playing in college. I didn't know what he was talking about. I was so naïve it was incredible. When Tony mentioned Notre Dame, I didn't even know where it was.

I wound up visiting Penn State, Syracuse, and Indiana, while getting hundreds of letters. Then I went back to Notre Dame on a visit and sat down with Ara [Parseghian]. That meeting pretty much sealed it for me.

Where Notre Dame was headed at that time after Ara's first two years of winning, as well as the academics, just fit for me. I think I was the first freshman to sign that year so I could get it out of the way. I still have the picture on my wall that Ara gave me. He wrote on it, "Mike, welcome to the Notre Dame family." The great thing about Notre Dame is that you really felt like that was the truth. You felt the whole Notre Dame mystique right when you walked on campus.

My first practice on the freshman team consisted of getting killed for about an hour and then Wally Moore calling out some guys and sending us to go scrimmage the first-team defense. I was working at offensive tackle, and on my first play I had to trap Alan Page. Then I had to block Kevin Hardy. On my third play Pete Duranko went right by me. Those were my first three plays, and they left me with three stitches under my eye and I couldn't talk that night.

75. Joe Theismann, QB
6'0", 170, South River, New Jersey, 1968–1970

Joe Theismann launched an attack on the Irish passing record books, setting 19 school marks while leading the team to its first bowl appearance in 45 years in 1969 and a 10–1 record capped by a Cotton Bowl victory in 1970 over top-rated and unbeaten Texas. A first-team All-America selection as a senior by Associated Press, Theismann was the runner-up in the Heisman Trophy voting in 1970. A participant in the 1970 Hula Bowl, Theismann set school records for passing yards in a game (526), yards in a season (2,429), and touchdowns in a season (16), among others. He ranked second in the nation in total offense as a senior at 291.3 yards per game—and that year he helped the Irish as a team average 510.5 total yards per game and 252.7 passing yards per game, two marks that remain all-time Notre Dame bests. In three seasons, Theismann led the Fighting Irish to a 20–3–2 record while completing 290 passes on 509 attempts for 4,411 yards, a mark that still ranks fifth in school history. Honored for his classroom prowess, he earned Academic All-America honors in 1970 and was later named to the GTE Academic All-America Hall of Fame.

Following graduation, Theismann embarked on a 15-year professional career, his final 12 years in the NFL as a member of the Washington Redskins. Upon retirement, he became a highly successful businessman as well as a prominent television sports analyst for ESPN. Theismann in 2003 became the eighth Notre Dame quarterback selected to the National Football Foundation Hall of Fame, joining Frank Carideo in 1954, Harry Stuhldreher in 1958, John Lujack in 1960, Angelo Bertelli in 1972, Paul Hornung in 1985, Bob Williams in 1988, and Ralph Guglielmi in 2001.

Irish in Their Own Words

JOE THEISMANN

I was 5′10″, 152 pounds when I entered college. I weighed 172 when I graduated, and I played almost my entire 15-year career in professional football under 195.

When I arrived here on a recruiting trip, [defensive coordinator] Johnny Ray kept looking for this Joe Thees-man kid. He thought I was a student manager or water boy. [Defensive line coach] Joe Yonto, who recruited me, said, "No, that's the quarterback." Johnny said, "You gotta be kidding me!"

I was interested in Penn State [Joe Paterno's first year as head coach], Notre Dame, Wake Forest, North Carolina, and North Carolina State. Wake's campus is very similar to ours the way they configured the quadrangles. I signed with North Carolina State because my high school coach was a guy named Ron Wojcicki, who played behind Roman Gabriel at North Carolina State [1959–1960]. I was impressed with that.

I didn't enter college, in all honesty, for an academic reason. I was a good enough student to get by in high school, but I really wanted to play ball. Even though I signed a grant-in-aid, the fact that Notre Dame was an independent gave me the opportunity to change my decision back then. Had I gone to another conference school, I would have lost a year of eligibility.

The reason I switched was I made another trip to Notre Dame. It was a typical November day in South Bend: rainy, overcast… dismal. Rocky Bleier was my chaperone. I flew back home and got off at Newark, New Jersey; my mom and dad were there, and my dad said, "What do you think?" I said, "I have to go to Notre Dame!" He said, "Why?" I told him, "I can't tell you why." I just felt like that was where I belonged. I'm sure you've had feelings where you're someplace and it's where you have to be—with no real logical explanation. That's what happened to me.

Notre Dame was an all-male institution where I could concentrate on athletics and academics. That was it. I knew I had to be a better student. I went to study hall and I graduated as an Academic All-American. I went out on two dates my first two years at Notre Dame. The thing I appreciated about the university was that the standard for athletes was higher than for regular students.

Joe Theismann, the 1970 Heisman Trophy runner-up, helped Notre Dame that season average 510.5 total yards per contest.

You had to carry a 2.0 to stay eligible to play football. My youngest son, Patrick, graduated from Notre Dame [in 2003], and what I told him was you have to find a routine that works for you, and then you manage your time to get your studying done. It's a great time to learn how to deal with life without Mommy and Daddy taking care of you. That's what it meant to me.

When I arrived, Terry Hanratty and Coley O'Brien already had quarterbacked a national title, and a third guy, Bob Belden, would be drafted by the NFL. However, Ara [Parseghian] gave me the chance to play, and part of it was by moving Coley to halfback. When Terry got hurt in the latter part of my sophomore season [1968], that's when I got the chance to start.

It wasn't until the final game [at USC in 1968] that I felt I could play big-time college football. I always used the University of Southern California as the barometer of excellence, just as I did the Dallas Cowboys when I played as a professional. When I played well against those two teams, then I felt I belonged.

The first pass I threw in the 1968 USC game was picked off by Sandy Durko and run back for a touchdown. As I walked by Ara, I said, "Don't worry about it. I'll get it back." Ara told me later that it was at that moment he became very comfortable with his decision to have me be his quarterback. We went ahead 21–7 and ended with a tie against the No. 1 team in the country.

I've always had great belief in my abilities because I'm willing to outwork anybody. I've never been the most talented person; I've never been the biggest person; I've never been the fastest person. But if you want to match me work for work, I'll work you into the ground. You can't stay with me. I'll work harder than anybody until I get it right, until I feel comfortable with where I am in my ability to do my job the best I possibly can.

The change in pronunciation for my name...I believe it happened when a reporter was watching spring practice and kidded [sports information director] Roger Valdiserri, "Is that Theismann like in Heisman?" Roger stored that away and called me into his office to ask if we could change it from Joe Thees-man. I asked my dad how we pronounced our last name, and he wanted to know if I was nuts.

Roger changed my name; Ara changed my life. He has a reverence about him that is regal. We were so prepared, and he was willing to take chances, too. He gave me all the freedom in the world. I called a lot of the plays during my senior season. He would give me a block of four or five plays, and I could make decisions about what I wanted to do at the line of scrimmage.

Irish in Their Own Words

TOM GATEWOOD

I don't think there was anything immediate in my chemistry with (Joe) Theismann. He had a very, very accurate arm. He could get you the ball in the area it had to be. It didn't always have a full head of steam, it didn't always have the perfect spiral, but it was always where I had an opportunity to get it.

The first year we played [1969], Joe was maybe 170 pounds. He didn't have the strongest arm, but he really worked at it. He came from a working-class family like I did. He was always out early, always willing to stay late. His senior year [1970], his arm was much stronger and even more accurate—plus he could run. Because he was always a threat to take off, it made my routes easier. The chemistry evolved, and after a while we could just read each other.

He could do check-offs, and we had a signal system where I could tip him off what I was going to do by using certain gestures. We could read each other and communicate in a stadium with 70,000 people, and we would know exactly what was going to happen. It was fun. It was magic.

76. LARRY DiNARDO, OG
6'1", 243, Queens, New York, 1968–1970

A consensus All-America pick in 1970, Larry DiNardo served as captain of the 1970 Irish team. He helped that 1970 squad to the all-time Notre Dame record for total offense with an average of 510.5 yards per game. DiNardo was a seventh-round selection of the New Orleans Saints in the 1971 NFL Draft. His brother Gerry later was also an Irish All-America lineman. A CoSIDA Academic All-American who also earned postgraduate scholarships from the NCAA and National Football Foundation, DiNardo went on to earn his law degree from Notre Dame in 1974 and currently is a partner in the firm of Jones Day in Chicago.

Irish in Their Own Words

FRANK POMARICO

Notre Dame was a simple choice for me. When I was growing up in New York, Gerry DiNardo and I were classmates in grade school and high school, and his brother, Larry, was someone we looked up to. Larry was a great baseball player, and then when he went to St. Francis Prep, he was a model for us to look up to. He was a great student, a great shot-putter, great rugby player.... He was three years older than me, so when he was a senior, I was a freshman. Larry was just the model that we wanted to be like. He did everything the right way. He was a sound individual; he did well with adjustments; he did well with his own classmates....

So now I get to high school, Larry goes to Notre Dame, Gerry and I are sophomores in high school, and Larry comes back talking about this guy named Ara Parseghian. Of course, Larry could have gone to any school he wanted. All the academies, Harvard... but he picked Notre Dame because I think he thought that was his greatest challenge athletically as well as academically. Our goal was, "Maybe someday that can happen to us."

I had a pretty good senior year at St. Francis Prep, and remember, I modeled my stance, the way I approached things, everything was geared to being like Larry. Finally, I had achieved my goal!

77. WALT PATULSKI, DE

6'6", 235, Liverpool, New York, 1969–1971

Walt Patulski finished ninth in the 1971 Heisman Trophy voting as a unanimous All-American that year. A three-year starter at left defensive end and a 1971 Irish co-captain, he was the 1971 United Press International Lineman of the Year as well as the first Lombardi Trophy recipient. Patulski started every game in his collegiate career, made 186 tackles, 40 for minus-241 yards; broke up 10 passes; recovered five fumbles; and returned one blocked punt 12 yards. He played in the 1972 College All-Star Game and Hula Bowl, then became a first-round draft pick in 1972 by Buffalo as the first overall selection (he played four seasons with Buffalo and one with St. Louis).

Irish in Their Own Words

WALT PATULSKI

I spoke at a pep rally when Notre Dame played at Syracuse [in 2003], and the topic was why I chose Notre Dame. Here's what I said: First of all, they have a fight song that brings you up no matter what frame of mind or mood you're in, and you never get tired of hearing it.

Second, they have an alma mater that is so comforting and beautiful that it brings tears to your eyes every time you sing it.

Third, they have meaningful symbols like Touchdown Jesus, No. 1 Moses, a Golden Dome, leprechauns, shillelaghs, green jerseys, and a Grotto where candles burn 24 hours a day, symbolizing eternal hope.

They have tradition and academic excellence where all students graduate. They have fans, not just any fans, but superfans who plan their weddings, vacations, and travel schedules around Irish home games. Finally, they have a spirit that defies description; it can only be experienced. There is a sense of community that melds people together from different races, different faiths, and different economic circumstances in life.

I took a really hard look at nearby Syracuse University because they were going to play me at fullback. That's when Ben Schwartz-walder was there, and they had a great tradition with the running game. But they were in the twilight of Ben's years, and that figured into my decision.

Michigan State was kind of the same with Duffy Daugherty. Duffy told me to go to Syracuse just to keep me away from Notre Dame, whom he had to play every year. My goal was to play fullback. Duffy told me, "At Syracuse, you will play fullback; at Notre Dame, you won't." He was right.

The other school I looked at pretty hard was Boston College. I narrowed it down pretty quickly to Notre Dame, Syracuse, and Boston College, even though I was a high school All-American and recruited all over the country.

The Notre Dame coaches said I would get a good look and opportunity at fullback, but I lasted all of two weeks. I was 6′6″, 235, when I enrolled. Being the good foot soldier that I was, I took it okay. There was room at defensive end, and there wasn't a hell of a lot of room at running back. The competition was less severe and things opened up right away at defensive end. The starters in my freshman year [1968] were Bob Kuechenberg and Chick Lauck, and they were both seniors.

The coaches told me I was a natural to play defensive end, that I would get much bigger, and that there was nobody who was going to be in my way. I could start right out of the gate. [Defensive line coach Joe] Yonto told me, "You're still at fullback, but we're lining you up on the opposite side, and you have to go get the ball." The logic didn't quite work, but it was amusing.

When I was with the freshman team [1968], we played Michigan State twice and Tennessee once, and I played a little tight end, too. Today, kids are much more ready for early action and are more sophisticated than we were at that time. The offenses and defenses have become more complex; the players have more coaches and are better instructed. I think it's easier to play with the varsity today than in my time. When we played, it was better to have the transition time with the freshman team. The level of sophistication is so much higher now than when I played.

There was a lot of pride defensively. Regardless of what the offense was doing, we knew we could limit what another team could do against us. It was more of a defensive game in our era. We played LSU at home in my junior year [1970] and won 3–0— and that was with Bert Jones and Joe Theismann as the quarterbacks. I don't know if you hear about great defenses as much as you used to.

78. CLARENCE ELLIS, CB
6'0", 16, Grand Rapids, Michigan 1969–1971

A consensus All-America pick in 1971, Clarence Ellis was a three-year regular in the Irish secondary from 1969 to 1971. He made 93 career tackles, broke up 32 passes, made 13 interceptions for 157 return yards and one touchdown, returned five punts for 33 yards, caught one 37-yard pass, and intercepted seven passes in 1970. A participant in the 1972 College All-Star Game and Senior Bowl, he became a first-round draft pick by Atlanta in 1972 and played three seasons with the Falcons.

79. Tom Gatewood, SE

6′2″, 203, Baltimore, Maryland, 1969–1971

A consensus All-America pick in 1970, Tom Gatewood served as a 1971 Irish co-captain. He led the Irish in receiving in 1969 with 47 grabs for 743 yards, in 1970 with 77 for 1,123, and in 1971 with 33 for 417. Gatewood set records for most passes caught in a season (77 for 1,123 yards); passes caught in a career with 157 for 2,283 yards; most catches per game in a season with 7.7; most touchdowns by reception in a game (three) and was second in a career with 19. He played in the 1972 Hula Bowl. Gatewood was a two-time CoSIDA Academic All-American who also earned postgraduate scholarships from the NCAA and National Football Foundation. He was selected in the fifth round of the 1972 NFL Draft by the New York Giants and played two years in New York. Gatewood is owner of Blue Atlas Productions, a New York ad specialty company.

Irish in Their Own Words

Tom Gatewood

I was considering going to Yale because my high school quarterback, Kurt Schmoke, went there and later became the mayor of Baltimore [1987–1999]. He became a Rhodes scholar, and we were pretty close. A chance to go to Yale on an academic scholarship can be enticing. Like most players at Notre Dame, I was recruited by hundreds of schools.

I was recruited very late by Notre Dame and didn't take my visit until February. The Maryland area wasn't a hotbed for recruitment, but I was a *Parade* All-American and got some attention. My high school coach, George Young, who would go on to become the general manager of the New York Giants, was very progressive and strongly connected.

George had a great deal of ambition and was very smart. While he was coaching at my high school, he was working with the [Baltimore] Colts and Don Shula during his off time. That was good for us because the benefits rubbed off: we had game footage, our practices were taped, we had pro sets, and all kinds of things were highly influenced by the NFL. I'm pretty sure he sent my tape to Notre Dame because I wasn't really sure how they found out about me.

My high school was all-male, and 600 boys came out for football. It was a college prep school and highly integrated. We dominated the state championships in every sport. I was a three-sport athlete, and we won the state in football and basketball, and we had a very good baseball team. Therefore, Notre Dame was a very attractive school because it had a similar allure with academic status, graduating athletes, and a national ranking in football.

What I was looking for was: 1) an opportunity to be independent by being away from home, and 2) getting a strong enough education to go anywhere in the country. I wanted a national presence. My degree was more important to me than football. I had heard of too many cases where players who had injuries or other problems didn't finish school and people just forgot about them. I didn't want to be a statistic.

I spent most of the time on my visit with academic advisers and counselors and talking to students on campus to find out what it was like at Notre Dame. What locked it up was Ara Parseghian. I didn't see Ara until the last two hours of that weekend. We had about 20 minutes together. Basically, he said, "We've seen film of you, I've got feedback from people who have talked to you and know your personality and how you would blend into the Notre Dame program, and we'd like to offer you a scholarship to play with us. We think you would make a contribution and be a proud addition to our family. We feel certain we can offer you things that will help you with your future."

When I think about it now, he said just what I wanted to hear in comparison to what I heard from other coaches around the country. Those places told me I was guaranteed to be an All-American, guaranteed to be a starter…. That's nice stroking for a kid who's 17 or 18 years old, but I've got to tell you, I was like a 22-year-old analyzing what people were saying. Woody Hayes was telling me he was going to change his offense to a high-powered passing attack. Ben Schwartzwalder [Syracuse] said the same thing. It went in one ear and out the other. I was not immature enough to buy it.

Parseghian wasn't guaranteeing I would be an All-American—he wasn't even guaranteeing I would be a productive part of the team! He never called me again, and I didn't have people from Notre Dame on the phone harassing me, whereas I had high-pressure tactics from several schools. I guess in some instances players take that as ego strokes and feel good about it. I would have felt it annoying, so I was the right personality for that low-pressure sales pitch. But it was a quality sales pitch, and it answered the questions I needed to know. I was the right fit at the right time for the right coaches.

In high school, I was a tight end in a two-tight-end set. They would throw me a two-yard pass and I would run 90 yards for a touchdown. But when I was recruited by Notre Dame, it was strictly as a running back. I didn't know that at the time because nobody said, "Hey, you're going to be a great running back at Notre Dame." The tip-off for me was when I arrived in August. They gave me my jersey and assigned me No. 44. I said, "Why am I 44? Don't they have any 80s left?" They said, "We don't give 80s to running backs." I said, "No, you must have me mixed up with someone else." Next thing I know I'm in line with the halfbacks and full-backs, learning how to take handoffs I had never taken in my life.

Learning the skills and techniques at running back felt mechanical. I was trying to develop the instincts that other guys who had been playing running back since they were in Pop Warner—like Bob Minnix and Ed Gulyas—already had. I didn't have that cutback instinct, and I was trying to learn. That's something you can't really teach. You have to figure it out and feel it.

When our scout team played the varsity [in 1968], I wore No. 32, meaning I was O.J. Simpson when we prepared for USC, Leroy Keyes from Purdue...I was all these top-name backs, except I was getting slammed around by Bob Olson, Mike McCoy, and all the varsity guys. Once we were done with that, we would get to do our regular freshman practice.

I became my own best salesman. I kept telling the coaches, "You're missing the boat here. I'm a really good receiver." Every day I went out early to practice and was in line with the receivers so I could have quarterbacks throw balls to me. I kept trying to demonstrate myself to the coaches. I was thinking, *Please look! Please look!*

Finally, they got tired of me nagging them. They lined me up, sent me out wide, and said, "Theismann, throw long to this guy!" I just took off and Joe lofted one that I caught over my shoulder. They wanted me to do it again to see if it was a fluke, and we did the same thing. That's how it started in the spring of 1969. Jim Seymour was graduating, and his spot was open.

80. GREG MARX, DT
6'5", 249, Redford, Michigan, 1970–1972

A unanimous first-team All-American in 1972 as the Irish co-captain, Greg Marx made 82 tackles and broke up two passes as a sophomore starter in 1970. He was second on the team in tackles in 1972 with 96, leading the team with six for lost yardage. Marx made 263 career tackles (24 for minus-105 yards) and broke up six passes. He's a two-time CoSIDA Academic All-American who earned postgraduate scholarships from the NCAA and National Football Foundation. He played in the 1973 College All-Star and Hula Bowl contests, then became a second-round pick of the Atlanta Falcons in the 1973 NFL Draft.

81. DAVE CASPER, TE
6'3", 243, Chilton, Wisconsin, 1971–1973

A consensus All-America pick in 1973, Dave Casper was the 1973 co-captain of the Irish national championship team. A member of the Pro Football Hall of Fame, he played two seasons at the offensive tackle slot for the Irish then moved to tight end. Ara Parseghian called him the best athlete he'd ever coached. Casper's career totals included 21 pass receptions for 335 yards and four touchdowns. He was a 1974 participant in the College All-Star Game and Hula Bowl. Selected by Oakland in the second round of the 1974 NFL Draft, he played for 11 years with Oakland, Houston, Minnesota, and the Los Angeles Raiders. Casper earned postgraduate scholarships from the NCAA and National Football Foundation and was selected to the CoSIDA Academic All-America Hall of Fame in 1993. He received the NCAA Silver Anniversary Award in 1999. Casper was selected to the College Football Hall of Fame in 2012.

82. MIKE TOWNSEND, DB
6'3", 183, Hamilton, Ohio, 1971–1973

A consensus All-America pick in 1973 and one of three captains of the 1973 Irish national championship team, Mike Townsend started at cornerback as a junior in 1972 and set the Irish single-season record with 10 interceptions for 39 return yards. He led the nation in interceptions in 1972, then made his mark during his senior season in 1973 with 26 tackles, three interceptions for 47 return yards, and three fumble recoveries from his free safety position. His brother, Willie, was an Irish wide receiver, and both walked on to the Irish basketball team in 1971–1972 and 1972–1973. He played in the 1974 Hula Bowl, then became a fourth-round selection of the Minnesota Vikings in the 1974 NFL Draft (but opted to play in the World Football League with the Jacksonville Sharks).

83. Pete Demmerle, SE
6′1″, 196, New Canaan, Connecticut, 1972–1974

Pete Demmerle led the Irish in receiving in 1973 with 26 catches and again in 1974 with 43 grabs for 667 yards. A consensus All-America pick in 1974, he was a member of the 1973 Irish national championship team. In the 1973 Sugar Bowl, he caught three passes in the first quarter, setting up the first Irish touchdown. Demmerle caught 70 career passes for 1,076 yards and 12 TDs. A participant in the 1975 College All-Star Game, he was an Academic All-American in 1974 as well as winner of postgraduate scholarships from the NCAA and National Football Foundation. He was a 13th-round draft pick of the San Diego Chargers in 1975. A Fordham Law School graduate, Demmerle was honored by the Notre Dame Monogram Club with its 2003 Moose Krause Award, in recognition of his distinguished service that included serving as a tireless advocate for ALS awareness and research funding.

84. Tom Clements, QB
6′0″, 189, McKees Rocks, Pennsylvania, 1972–1974

Tom Clements was a three-year starter for the Irish at quarterback, in Ara Parseghian's final three seasons at Notre Dame, leading the 1973 Irish squad to the national title. He led the Irish to

Tom Clements never had gaudy statistics, but his 29–5 record as Notre Dame's starting quarterback served as an impressive legacy.

a combined 29–5 record as the starting signal-caller and finished fourth in the Heisman Trophy voting as a senior in 1974. Clements claimed first-team All-America notice as a senior from the Football Writers Association of America. He threw eight touchdown passes in each of his three seasons—accounting for 1,163 yards in 1972, 882 in 1973, and 1,549 as a senior. He was named MVP of Notre Dame's 1973 Sugar Bowl win over Alabama that clinched the national title for the Irish. Clements played in the Canadian Football League through 1987—winning Grey Cups in both Ottawa and Winnipeg and earning league MVP honors in 1987. His pro career included more than 39,000 passing yards and 252 TD passes. He left a law career in Chicago to return to Notre Dame as an assistant coach from 1992 to 1996. He's been an assistant in the NFL ever since, working in New Orleans, Kansas City, Buffalo, and Pittsburgh and currently serves as the Green Bay Packers' offensive coordinator.

Irish in Their Own Words

TOM CLEMENTS

I didn't always think I was going to Notre Dame, at least not until my senior year in high school. Up until that time, I felt I was going to be a college basketball player instead of a quarterback. I had played basketball longer than I had played football by at least four years. I felt I was a lot further along in basketball and a better basketball player than football player. But, of course, I had a lot more room to improve in football.

I had an older brother who went to Notre Dame but didn't play football. I started following the football program when he was there. Then, when Ara [Parseghian] arrived and Terry Hanratty decided to go there out of western Pennsylvania where I'm from, that added to my interest in the program and the university. When I was recruited by Notre Dame and visited the campus, it fit my mental picture of what a college was supposed to be like with the trees, the buildings, and the campus beauty.

I didn't visit a lot of schools because playing basketball in the Pittsburgh Catholic League meant games on Wednesday and Saturday nights. I had interest in a lot of other schools, but I couldn't visit many places until after the basketball season.

I narrowed it down to Notre Dame, Pittsburgh, and North Carolina. If I picked North Carolina, it was going to be to play basketball, and if I picked Pitt, I was going to try to play both. It was a tough choice between Notre Dame and North Carolina.

My first year wasn't a frustrating one in part because we had freshman games against Michigan, Michigan State, Tennessee, and then a Mexican All-Star team in Mexico City, an interesting experience in itself. We were down there for about four days, and it was like a mini-bowl trip. We played in Aztec Stadium, which at the time held about 120,000 people, and about 90,000 to 100,000 fans showed up for this freshman game. We ended up beating them 82–0 with our roster of about 32 players, so there wasn't much substituting we could do. The one thing that really was funny to me was listening to the Mexican players call out signals in Spanish.

That year really let you get acclimated to college football and let you learn the ropes. The varsity in 1971 had a good ranking going into the year [No. 2 in the AP] with a good defense, but the offense struggled a little bit at times with different quarterbacks playing. I just concentrated on what I was doing on the freshman team and the prep team.

I'll never forget going out as freshmen and wearing those white football practice pants. Everyone on the varsity wore gold pants, and when you graduated from the white pants to the gold pants, you knew you were stepping up. But there was still a growth process in moving up to the varsity.

Spring practice during my freshman year was my chance to win a spot on the varsity roster. The quarterback job was an open competition during that spring, and I thought I played well. But, going into the fall, Ara hadn't named a starting quarterback. It wasn't until the week before the [1972] opener [versus Northwestern] that I finally won the job.

Sometimes things went well that season and sometimes they didn't, as you might expect for a team with an inexperienced quarterback. We were up and down in 1972 [8–3]. We had some good games but we lost a few, too, and then in the Orange Bowl, Nebraska beat us badly, 40–6.

The USC game was a little different because, up until the last quarter, we had played pretty well and they were No. 1. They scored a number of points in the fourth quarter and beat us handily [45–23], but it was a good game for three quarters. The Trojans were just a better team than we were and deserved to win. You never like to lose, but the feeling there was different from the one we had against Nebraska. In that game the Cornhuskers just put it to us, and they were better, as well. Everyone was just waiting for the spring to try to improve.

Any time you lose your last game in the fashion we did, it makes for a long off-season for everyone. The winter workouts were harder, and there wasn't much levity around the team. Spring practice was serious business. We knew we'd be better in 1973, and we obviously ended up being very good. After we beat USC and we were unbeaten and halfway home, we knew we had something special in front of us.

85. GERRY DiNARDO, OG
6′1″, 242, Howard Beach, New York, 1972–1974

A consensus All-America pick in 1974, Gerry DiNardo was a member of the 1973 Irish national championship team. He helped the Irish rank fourth nationally in total offense as senior. A three-year starter who in 1973 helped Notre Dame to 3,502 rushing yards, an all-time Irish record, he's the younger brother of Irish All-America lineman Larry DiNardo. He served as head football coach at LSU (1995–1999 with a 33–24–1 record), Vanderbilt

(1991–1994 with a 19–25 record), and Indiana (2002–2004 with an 8–27 mark). He's currently an analyst for the Big Ten Network.

86. STEVE NIEHAUS, DT
6'5", 270, Cincinnati, Ohio, 1972–1975

Steve Niehaus finished 12th in the Heisman Trophy voting as a senior in 1975. He was a two-time first-team All-American who was a unanimous selection as a senior in 1975. Niehaus had 95 tackles, 13 for minus-82 yards; broke up two passes, and recovered one fumble in 1974. His career totals at Notre Dame included 290 tackles, 25 for minus-128 yards, two broken-up passes, and one fumble recovery. Niehaus played in the 1976 College All-Star Game, then became a first-round choice of Seattle in the 1976 NFL Draft as the second overall selection.

87. ROSS BROWNER, DE
6'3", 240, Warren, Ohio, 1973, 1975–1977

A consensus All-America pick in 1976 and 1977, Ross Browner was inducted into the National Football Foundation Hall of Fame in 1999. A four-year Irish starter who played on the 1973 and 1977 national championship teams, he was the 1976 Outland Trophy recipient and 1977 Lombardi Trophy winner. A unanimous first-team All-America end in both 1976 and 1977, Browner finished fifth in the 1977 Heisman Trophy voting. He holds Notre Dame records for tackles by a front-four lineman (since 1956) in a career with 340; tackles for minus yardage (since 1967) in a single season with 28 for 203 yards; tackles for minus yardage in a career with 77 for 515 yards; and fumbles recovered in a career with 12. He had 340 career tackles (77 for 515 yards in losses), broke up 10 passes, recovered eight fumbles, blocked two kicks, scored two safeties and one touchdown. Browner participated in the 1978

Japan and Hula Bowls, then became the eighth overall selection in the 1979 NFL Draft as a first-round pick of Cincinnati Bengals, and played through the 1987 season. He ranked No. 84 in college football.com's top 100 players of all-time. Voted into the Gator Bowl Hall of Fame in 1999, he also won the Maxwell Award in 1977 as the top player in college football.

Irish in Their Own Words

ROSS BROWNER

During the recruiting process, I evaluated the school, education, coaches, and the publicity the school was receiving. Notre Dame had TV and radio going, and I grew up watching [Joe] Theismann–to–[Tom] Gatewood on the highlights. But it was one man who did it for me: Ara Parseghian. I really liked his leadership. He had genuine honesty and strong character.

Woody Hayes made a lot of trips to our house, and I said, "Coach, I just met a very impressive gentleman at Notre Dame who was a player of yours." And he said, "Yeah, Ara Parseghian... a good kid! But I'm the coach you should be playing for! Ohio kids should stay in Ohio! Look at Archie Griffin! We gave him a chance to start as a freshman [in 1972, the first year the NCAA made freshmen eligible for the varsity again], and look at what he's done!"

I was at Archie Griffin's first start against North Carolina [1972] when he ran for 200-plus yards, and I had a chance to meet him. I was impressed because they weren't shy about playing rookies. Ohio State has a very impressive campus, but 86,000 students or whatever it was really concerned me, compared to just 6,000 at Notre Dame.

The night before my signing, I had to hide at my Aunt Mary's house. She lived about two streets away, and I told Notre Dame to meet me there. Michigan, Ohio State, Michigan State, and, I think, Nebraska were at my parents' door the next morning. They were pretty surprised when I wasn't there, and they confronted my mom and dad. My parents talked with all of them and said, "Ross has made a decision we allowed him to make on his own. He's decided to go to Notre Dame." The schools weren't too happy about that because they all thought I would go to their place.

Ohio State, Michigan, and Michigan State wanted me as a tight end. Michigan State was graduating an All-American in Billy Joe DuPree, and they told me I could follow in his footsteps. Ara said he was looking at me as a tight end because I had good speed, good hands, and height, but he also asked me what I wanted to play.

I said, "Coach, if you're going to give me a choice, on offense you have to kind of accept the punishment, whereas on defense you get a chance to dish it out. I prefer to dish out. I like tackling people. If you would, I'd love to play defensive end." He just said, "Okay, that'll be a good position for you."

I just loved destroying offenses. I loved catching people in the backfield, throwing the whole thing off, and giving our defense an advantage. For my freshman year I was just thinking of being a kamikaze guy on the kickoff team and showing them I could hit. After a couple of days of practice, [defensive line coach] Joe Yonto told me, "We're looking at you a little more than just being on the kickoff team, Ross. I want to start you."

After our first scrimmage with the varsity, that's when they moved up about six freshmen, mostly on defense. Our offense had Tom Clements, Wayne "the Train" [Bullock], Dave Casper, Steve Sylvester, Gerry DiNardo…so many great players, but they weren't able to do anything against our freshmen.

After Willie Fry and I made a couple of tackles in the backfield, Ara's eyes lit up and he said, "Hey, we've got a good corps of freshmen here. We can't let these guys just play freshman ball. They've got to play varsity." [Defensive back] Luther [Bradley] and I started with the first team from then on. Winning the national title that year was the most tremendous award we could give back to Coach Parseghian.

88. LUTHER BRADLEY, SS
6'2", 200, Muncie, Indiana, 1973, 1975–1977

A consensus All-America pick in 1977, Luther Bradley played on the 1973 and 1977 Irish national championship teams. In 1975 he intercepted a pass versus Purdue and returned it 99 yards for a touchdown for the second-longest interception return in Notre Dame history. Bradley had 153 career tackles (five for 30 yards in losses), broke up 27 passes, recovered two fumbles, and blocked two kicks. He holds the all-time Notre Dame individual record for most interceptions in a career with 17 for 218 yards; most yards gained by interceptions (one game) with 103 versus Purdue on two in 1975; highest average for yardage by interception return (one game) with 51.5 and in a season with 33.8. A 1978 Japan Bowl participant, Bradley was drafted in 1978 in the first round by Detroit and played in the NFL through 1981.

Irish in Their Own Words

LUTHER BRADLEY

The major Big Ten powers, Michigan and Ohio State, weren't recruiting me at all when I was a senior in high school. Where I really wanted to go was the University of Tennessee because they were becoming a national powerhouse. My high school coaches sent my films down to Tennessee, but the Volunteers weren't interested. That kind of hurt my feelings.

Then my dad talked to the Penn State coaches because he was a graduate of the school. My coach sent them films—and the Penn State people said they weren't interested, either! So, when we played Penn State in the 1976 Gator Bowl [a 20–9 victory], I was pumped big-time. The schools that recruited me—Indiana University, Purdue University, the University of Minnesota, and the University of Cincinnati—looked at me mainly as a running back. All Ara said was, "We want you to be a defensive back because we have real needs there."

The other school that kind of wanted me to be a defensive back was Indiana. That was the same time they had Quinn Buckner, who was the point guard for the basketball team. But he was also a defensive back. They tried to entice me by saying I might have a chance to play on the basketball team, as well.

Purdue had a selling point of me playing a multiple role. They had an All-American by the name of Leroy Keyes [1966–1968], who played both sides of the field as an offensive back and defensive back. They said I could be like him. But I didn't want to be a running back. I figured my long-term football future would be as a defensive back, and it fit my personality better, too.

Notre Dame wanting me as a defensive back was one of the reasons I signed there. Second, they were always on the hunt for national championships and major bowls. The Big Ten back then sent only one team to a bowl. It would either be Michigan or Ohio State going to the Rose Bowl, and the rest were "wannabes." I wanted to play in big bowls and for national titles.

The third thing was the quality of education. One of the things Notre Dame did that other schools didn't was send a coach to look

330 ALWAYS FIGHTING IRISH

at me in track and field. I was probably in the top five in the state and had run a 9.7 in the 100-yard dash. I don't think the other coaches or schools even knew I ran track, but Notre Dame was amazed at how fast I was when the coach—I think it was Denny Murphy, the freshman coach—saw me compete. After a couple of weeks on the practice field at Notre Dame, it all started to fit. I didn't feel uncomfortable; I didn't feel like a fish out of water. I felt like I deserved to be there and was pretty good at what I did. After the first week, Ross [Browner], myself, and a bunch of freshmen— Willie Fry, Al Hunter, Tim Simon, Marvin Russell—were put on the second team. After the second week, Ross and I were with the first team, and Willie alternated with Jim Stock at right defensive end.

A week before our opener, the freshman team had a game up at Michigan. Ross and I were standing on the sideline and watched them as they were preparing to go to Michigan. We said to one of the coaches, "Why don't you let us go up to Michigan and play this weekend to get the bugs out?" He said, "Are you kidding? If something happened to you two, I'd get fired!"

89. KEN MACAFEE, TE
6'5", 251, Brockton, Massachusetts, 1974–1977

A three-time first-team All-American from 1975 to 1977 and a unanimous pick in 1977 as a senior, Ken MacAfee was a 1997 National Football Foundation Hall of Fame inductee. He finished third in the 1977 Heisman Trophy voting and was the first lineman to win the Walter Camp Player of the Year Award in 1977. During the 1977 national championship season, he caught 54 passes for 797 yards and six touchdowns—and caught 128 career passes for 1,759 yards and 15 TDs, ranking third on the Notre Dame career receiving chart. A 1978 participant in the Hula and Japan Bowls, MacAfee was a first-round pick by San Francisco in the 1978 NFL Draft.

90. DAN DEVINE
Head Coach, 1975–1980 (53–16–1, .764)

Dan Devine was no stranger to either the college or professional football world when he came to Notre Dame. Following three seasons at Arizona State in the 1950s, 92 victories in 13 seasons at Missouri, and four years as coach of the Green Bay Packers, Devine took over the Irish in 1975.

Three seasons later he had Notre Dame once again on top of the college football world.

Devine's second season in 1976 ended in a Gator Bowl win over 20th-rated Penn State. The following year, the Irish dropped their second game of the 1977 season at Ole Miss. A week later, quarterback Joe Montana came off the bench in an epic comeback win at Purdue—and he never left the starting lineup again.

In a critical midseason home game against fifth-ranked USC and in one of the most memorable scenes in the history of Notre Dame Stadium, Notre Dame's team emerged wearing green jerseys. That served as one of the catalysts in a 49–19 Irish victory that day.

The fifth-ranked and once-beaten Irish earned an eventual Cotton Bowl berth against undefeated and top-rated Texas—and a historic defensive effort against Heisman winner Earl Campbell helped Notre Dame knock off the Longhorns 38–10. That propelled the Irish from fifth to first in the final polls and earned Devine and his Irish Notre Dame's 10th consensus national championship.

A year later, the Irish won eight straight regular-season games, including victories over ranked opponents Pittsburgh, Navy, and Georgia Tech. That sent 10th-ranked Notre Dame back to the Cotton Bowl to meet Southwest Conference champ Houston. In the ice and cold of Dallas, it was Montana who generated a miracle comeback, as the Irish overcame a 34–12 deficit, with Montana throwing the game-winning touchdown pass as time ran out.

Devine announced his retirement prior to the 1980 season—then a week into that campaign Harry Oliver's record 51-yard field goal enabled the Irish to defeat Michigan. Unbeaten Notre Dame rose to No. 1 in the nation by November, shut out fifth-ranked Alabama in Birmingham to cinch a Sugar Bowl invitation—then barely missed out in a 17–10 loss to top-rated Georgia and Herschel Walker in New Orleans, in what would be Devine's final game as a head coach.

He coached an Outland Trophy winner in Ross Browner in 1976—and a year later Browner won both the Lombardi and Maxwell awards. He also coached the 1977 Walter Camp player of the year in Ken MacAfee, as well as consensus All-Americans Luther Bradley, Browner, Bob Crable, Vagas Ferguson, Bob Golic, Dave Huffman, Steve Niehaus, and John Scully. During Devine's tenure in South Bend, Jerome Heavens in 1978 and then Ferguson in 1979 became Notre Dame's all-time leading ground-gainers.

Five years after his retirement, Devine was selected to the College Football Hall of Fame. His tenure at Missouri (1958–1970) made him part of the only string of three coaches at an institution that all made the Hall of Fame—the other Tigers coaches being Don Faurot (1935–1942, 1946–1956) and Frank Broyles (1957). He's also one of the links at two other schools with consecutive Hall of Fame coaches—with Ara Parseghian (1964–1974) at Notre Dame and with Frank Kush (1958–1979) at Arizona State.

Irish in Their Own Words

VAGAS FERGUSON

Like any successful coach, Coach Devine was good about getting the best people around him. He let them do their thing, and he collectively kept everybody together. That's what it takes, because you can't coach every position. Even with Joe Montana, we didn't throw the ball that much. Devine just liked to pound the ball. It was about concentrating on assignments and hitting the spots you were supposed to hit.

Irish in Their Own Words

ROSS BROWNER

I didn't know what to expect when I came back and there was a new coach. Once I met Coach Devine, I was impressed with his professionalism and how he handled players. I also had the same position coach, Joe Yonto. We still had Father Hesburgh, Father Joyce, [Ed] "Moose" Krause, Colonel Jack Stephens, and Roger Valdiserri at the same positions. To me, Notre Dame hadn't really changed other than the head coach.

91. DANIEL "RUDY" RUETTIGER, DE
5′7″, 184, Joliet, Illinois, 1975

Walk-on Dan Ruettiger played all of 27 seconds in one football game in his Notre Dame career, working briefly in the waning moments against Georgia Tech in 1975 in the final home game of his senior campaign. Yet his life story became one of the enduring representations of football and campus life at the University of Notre Dame based on the movie *Rudy*. Ruettiger showed enough personal persistence to convince Hollywood producers to make the film—and university administrators were convinced of the merits of the script to such an extent that they permitted the movie's producers to film on campus for the first time since the filming of *Knute Rockne, All-American*. Some of the movie's game action scenes were shot at halftime of a Notre Dame home game in 1992 against Boston College. Actor Sean Astin played Ruettiger in the film that was crafted by *Hoosiers* screenwriter Angelo Pizzo and director David Anspaugh.

92. JOE MONTANA, QB

6′2″, 191, Monongahela, Pennsylvania, 1975, 1977–1978

Of the countless fabled names in Notre Dame's football past, the one that still prompts as many questions as any other in the Notre Dame media relations department is that of Joe Montana, quarterback of Notre Dame's 1977 national championship team. Many visitors to Notre Dame's Heritage Hall often are surprised to discover that Montana never received All-America status and was not selected until the third round of the National Football League draft. Interest in Montana's exploits remained keen partly because of his stardom in the NFL (he was a first-ballot inductee into the Pro Football Hall of Fame and was enshrined in July 2000) and partly because his five years at Notre Dame were so eventful.

Here's a look at Montana's Notre Dame career statistics:

Year	G/GS	Time	PC-PA-Yds.	TD/Int.	TC-Yds.-TD
1975	7/3	92:37	28-66-507	4/8	25-(−5)-2
1977	9/8	198:38	99-189-1,604	11/8	32-5-6
1978	11/11	280:30	141-260-2,010	10/9	72-104-6
Totals	27/22	571:45	268-515-4,121	25/25	129-104-14

Joe Montana passed for 4,121 yards in his career at Notre Dame. He was a key factor in Notre Dame's 1977 national championship season and will be long remembered for rising from a reserve quarterback with the Irish to a multiple Super Bowl champion with the NFL's San Francisco 49ers.

Irish in Their Own Words

JOE MONTANA

Choosing Notre Dame was easy for me. As soon as they said I had a scholarship, I was here. I had visited a few other universities prior to that, but I had always wanted to come here. It was part of a dream growing up.

When I came to Notre Dame, there were a lot of people from western Pennsylvania here. Notre Dame was having great years in football. It seemed like Notre Dame was on TV Saturday, Sunday, Monday, and Tuesday, although it was really the game Saturday and the replay on Sunday. I just had a love for Notre Dame from a very early age. When I had the opportunity, I took it. I canceled the rest of my visits. If it had not been for [Notre Dame], who knows where I would have been? I might have played basketball.

Winning at Notre Dame every year is not easy. Number one, this is Notre Dame, and when Notre Dame shows up on someone's schedule, you're a target, no matter what kind of year you're having. When you're winning, they obviously want to beat you, and when you're down, they want to kick you while you're down. It's a matter of remembering those guys who are kicking you when you're down to help motivate you to get back to the other side of that table.

Being at Notre Dame, you're going to take away some great memories. You're going to take away some great friendships that will last a lifetime. And you're going to take away an education that no matter how long your career is, or if you're just coming out of college and you know your football career is over, you're going to fall back on that education at some point in time, as I've learned after my [pro football] career.

Irish quarterback Joe Montana had a knack for serving as the architect for an amazing series of comeback wins, including in his last collegiate game against Houston in the 1979 Cotton Bowl.

There are certain places where no matter what type of team you have or they have, there's a certain amount of respect, and Notre Dame's great rival, USC, happens to be one of those places. It's like a brother. You constantly fight, but when it comes down to it, you're best of friends when you're not in that mode. I have the utmost respect in the world for [former USC star] Ronnie Lott. He is the godfather to our youngest son. So that tells you what I think of Ronnie, and I think the world of 'SC. They've got a tremendous program, it's a great university, but when it comes to being out on the field, nobody likes anyone until it's over.

People talk about all the great comebacks we had at Notre Dame, but my best advice is to try not to get in those situations where you have to come from behind. When you go about trying to overcome an obstacle that sometimes seems further away than you would like it to be, or not within your grasp, people try to reach and do things that they typically wouldn't try to do and are outside of their capabilities. Where I have had the most success is trying to go almost opposite of that. I'm going to do whatever I can within my ability. There will be a certain time for desperation somewhere along the line, but most of those situations aren't desperation at all. It feels like there isn't a lot of time, but there is.

93. BOB GOLIC, LB
6′3″, 250, Cleveland, Ohio, 1975–1978

A unanimous All-American as the Irish senior captain in 1978 and a member of the 1977 national championship team, Bob Golic made 146 tackles, broke up five passes, blocked one kick, made three interceptions, and returned one punt that season. He added another 152 tackles in 1978. He set the Irish single-game tackle mark with 26 against Michigan in 1978, after making 17 tackles against Texas to earn the defensive MVP honor in the 1978

Cotton Bowl. One of the nation's top wrestlers with a three-year record of 54–4–1, he finished third in the NCAA meet in 1976 and fourth in 1977 as a heavyweight. For his football career Golic made 479 tackles, broke up eight passes, made six interceptions for 22 return yards, recovered two fumbles, blocked one kick, and returned one punt 16 yards. A 1979 participant in the Hula Bowl and Japan Bowl, he was defensive player of the game in the Hula Bowl. A second-round selection by the New England Patriots in the 1979 NFL Draft, Golic played in the NFL from 1979 to 1992 with New England, Cleveland, and the Los Angeles Raiders (he was a three-time Pro Bowl selection with the Browns). He then became an NFL analyst for NBC Sports and also acted in *Saved by the Bell*. His younger brother, Mike, was an Irish captain in 1984, and brother Greg was a Notre Dame offensive lineman.

Irish in Their Own Words

MIKE GOLIC

When I was a kid and Bob was playing, I came to every home game and went to most of the away games that were pretty close to our home. My parents never missed a home game from Bob to Greg to me. We were always there. I was in the stands, I was hanging around outside the locker room, all the things kid brothers do.

I was incredibly proud of Bob. Here's a kid who comes in and starts as a 17-year-old freshman. Bob was an All-America high school football player and an All-America high school wrestler. It was a natural progression for him to go on and be successful at a top college. When I was offered a scholarship by Notre Dame, I wanted to go play and prove that I was that caliber of a player, as well.

94. DAVE HUFFMAN, C
6′5″, 245, Dallas, Texas, 1975–1978

A consensus All-America pick in 1978, Dave Huffman was a three-year starter at center at Notre Dame from 1976 to 1978. A member of the 1977 national championship team, he played in the 1979 Japan Bowl and Hula Bowl. Huffman made sure his family could identify him by wearing signature red elbow pads in games. A second-round selection by the Minnesota Vikings in the 1979 NFL Draft, he played with the Vikings from 1979 through 1990. Huffman's younger brother, Tim, played guard for the Irish from 1977 to 1980 and younger brother Steve played center in 1986.

95. VAGAS FERGUSON, HB
6′1″, 194, Richmond, Indiana, 1976–1979

A consensus All-America pick in 1979, Vagas Ferguson finished his career as Notre Dame's all-time leading ground-gainer with 3,472 rushing yards and 32 touchdowns. The first Irish rusher to gain more than 1,000 yards in consecutive seasons with 1,437 in 1979 following 1,192 in 1978, he was a member of the 1977 national championship team. Named outstanding offensive player of the 1978 Cotton Bowl with 100 rushing yards and three TDs against top-rated Texas, Ferguson finished fifth in the 1979 Heisman Trophy voting. He set the all-time record for rushing yards in a game with 255 versus Georgia Tech in 1978, and in a season with 1,437 (an average of 130.6 per game) and still has the record for rushing attempts in a season with 301 as well as the per-game record at 27.4. He appeared on the cover of *Sports Illustrated* after leading Notre Dame to a win at Michigan in 1979. A participant in the 1980 East-West Shrine Game and Japan Bowl, Ferguson was selected in the first round of the 1980 NFL Draft by the New

England Patriots as the 25th overall pick and played four years in the NFL with New England, Houston, and Cleveland.

Irish in Their Own Words

VAGAS FERGUSON

My mother passed away when I was eight years old, and because my father was in the military, I didn't really see him much. My aunt also passed away at an early age. So my grandparents, Hattie and Joe Walker, took 10 of us in—seven children from my family and three from my aunt's. Here my grandmother was, after raising two sons and two daughters herself, taking in 10 more kids.

The way we were raised was to care for each other and to work together. We were taught that you reap what you sow. Now my grandmother is in her eighties, and even though she has had her setbacks, she's never alone and never lacking in love because of what she did for us. She is surrounded by grandchildren and great-grandchildren. It shows that if you do the right things for people, it comes back to you.

I'm noted for a lot of rushing records, but I didn't achieve anything by myself. From the assistant coaches to the practice players—which I was at one time—they all had a role in helping me get to where I did, so I've never looked at it as "my records." I don't even purchase the football media guides to look up my records. When I saw Julius Jones break my single-game rushing mark, I was proud of the young man, not because of that but because he came back to Notre Dame when he could have left and quit. That's what it's really about.

I didn't follow college football much until my sophomore year in high school, and I didn't know where Notre Dame was located, to be truthful. Where I lived you heard more about Ohio State, Michigan, Purdue, and Indiana because it was Big Ten country in central Indiana. After my junior year I was being contacted by all those schools, as well as Notre Dame. The decision wasn't so much football-based. My guidance counselor and grandparents were pushing me toward an education and a degree. When I looked at schools, I listened to them from the standpoint of athletes graduating and academics. Lee Corso was the Indiana coach then, and he talked to me about being his star player and choosing my own number. But the hype and those kinds of things weren't important to me.

The final three schools were Ohio State, Michigan, and Notre Dame. Ohio State wanted to play me at defensive back. Most of the schools were kind of saying that, but I wanted to try running back because that's what I mainly was in high school. When Ohio State was emphasizing strictly defensive back, I kind of shied away from them. Even when I visited them, I was kind of overwhelmed because it's such a big school.

Michigan was pretty much the same way: defensive back, but running back possibly. The thing I liked about Michigan was they talked about academics, too. Notre Dame came in the door talking about how we want you as an athlete but we want you to be a student first and an athlete second. That impressed me.

My hosts were Luther Bradley and Ross Browner. One of the first things they said was, "If you're going to come to Notre Dame, you're going to be a student first. If you're not going to come to study and graduate, then don't come." That really hit me because everywhere I had been, it was about going out, showing me a good time, and encouraging me to come.

[Running backs coach] Jim Gruden started recruiting me at Indiana University when he was the running backs coach for Corso. The first time I met him, I thought so much of him. I wanted to play for him, and then he ended up at Notre Dame after Hank Kuhlmann left. He taught me so much about the game, reading defenses, reading blocking schemes...it really led to my success. I couldn't believe the things I was able to do once he taught me. We became good friends long after I left the game. He was an inspiration to me and a good friend.

His son, Jon, was just a kid running around all the time at practice with his brother. He's just like his dad all over again: a hardworking, determined guy. He worked us to death, but he loved us at the same time. Just watching his son, you could see he picked up some of those traits. It was nice to see Jon go back to Tampa, where his dad lives. I was really happy for Jim.

I never understood why most schools wanted me at defensive back. I guess I was physical and wasn't afraid to come up and hit people. They were looking at my physical ability and felt I could play at safety. I didn't think I was that fast and couldn't really outrun anybody. I was about 6', 190 coming in, so I wasn't that big.

I was moved to fullback because Jerome [Heavens] got hurt in the third game [of 1976] and was out for the year. Al [Hunter] was the starting tailback, and I didn't mind blocking and hitting people. The coaches saw that I could block, which is why they didn't have a problem putting me at fullback.

The week before the Alabama game, I had been playing sparingly, but never did I think I would start as a freshman. I kind of worked my way into fullback, and they told me midweek that I would start. But they brought me along the right way during the season. They didn't throw me into a lot of pressure situations early and kind of let me play my way in. So it wasn't really a big deal, other than the fact we were playing Alabama and Bear Bryant. When it came time to play, it was just basically doing the things you did in practice and learning some new assignments.

When Al got the 1,000 yards [in 1976], it wasn't a big deal for us. It wasn't about records for us, and I never understand why it is for other people today. When I look back, we didn't relish those kinds of things. We didn't talk about breaking records in the locker room. If it happened, you were recognized for it and you moved on. That's just the way we were.

We had good chemistry. We worked hard to make each other successful. If we had an assignment to block somebody, we made sure we got to that assignment. When we looked at film after games, we wanted to make sure we got our blocks to help that other back be successful. It wasn't about me getting the ball and running for 100 yards. We were there to complement each other.

96. JOHN SCULLY, C
6'5", 255, Huntington, New York, 1977–1980

A consensus All-American in 1980, John Scully served as the Irish starting center in 1979 and 1980 and tri-captain of the 1980 team. In 1977 he was a backup tackle for Notre Dame's national championship team, then played in 1978 as a backup left tackle. Scully moved to center in 1979 and started all 11 games. He received an invitation to play in the East-West Shrine Game, then became a fourth-round NFL Draft pick in 1981 by Atlanta and played guard with the Falcons (he started 82 games) until 1990. A standout pianist, he wrote "Here Come The Irish," a song that has come to be closely identified with Notre Dame athletics.

97. BOB CRABLE, LB
6'3", 225, Cincinnati, Ohio, 1978–1981

A near-unanimous All-America pick in both 1980 and 1981, Bob Crable had 521 career tackles—still a Notre Dame record.

He still holds the records for most tackles in a season (187 in 1979) and in a game (26 versus Clemson in 1979). His 26 tackles tied the Notre Dame (Bob Golic also had 26 in a game) and the NCAA record. Crable recovered a Houston fumble in the 1979 Cotton Bowl, leading to an Irish TD and comeback victory. In 1979 he preserved a win at Michigan with a last-second field-goal block. A 1982 participant in the Hula Bowl, Crable became a first-round draft pick of the NFL New York Jets in 1982. He played six years with the Jets until injury cut his career short—then later became head football coach at Cincinnati Moeller High School, his alma mater.

98. GERRY FAUST
Head Coach, 1981–1985 (30–26–1, .535)

Gerry Faust began as a three-time letterman as a quarterback at the University of Dayton. His 18 years of coaching at Moeller High School in Cincinnati (1963–1980) produced a 174–17–2 record to go with seven unbeaten seasons, four national prep titles and five Ohio state titles in his last six seasons. He coached Notre Dame to a 30–26–1 record, including a 1983 Liberty Bowl victory over a Doug Flutie–led Boston College team and an 1984 Aloha Bowl appearance, before resigning at the end of the 1985 season. He appeared on the cover of *Sports Illustrated* in 1984 after an Irish road win at seventh-ranked LSU. Among his other big wins was a 1982 triumph on the road at top-rated Pittsburgh—plus victories over USC in each of his last three seasons. Faust spent the next nine seasons (1986–1994) as head coach at the University of Akron and finished with an overall record of 43–53–3 at the school.

Irish in Their Own Words

LARRY WILLIAMS

My relationship with Gerry [Faust] was probably different than most folks. It was much less coach-and-player and more friend-and-mentor. Gerry tried to help me out way beyond the football field. [Faust] was always thinking about the whole person and not just the player. And we came [to Notre Dame] in the same year, so we sort of had a bond. We were both trying to figure this thing out on the fly. He didn't have a lot of experience at the college level to rely on, and I didn't, either. He had sort of a special bond with our class in that we all tried to learn together, and there were some pretty rough times.

Now I was a young guy from Southern California, and I wanted to get on the football field and was going to do anything the coach asked me to do. So, when Gerry said to me one day, "Hey, listen, I ran into this coed. She's from California; I know you're from California. Why don't you give her a call and see what happens?" I thought, *Holy smokes, am I being asked to do charity work? Whatever. I'm not sure how this whole thing works, either, so I'll call her.* As it turned out she became my wife [former Irish tennis player Laura Lee], and it worked out great.

99. ALLEN PINKETT, TB

5′9″, 181, Sterling, Virginia, 1982–1985

Allen Pinkett finished his Notre Dame career as the all-time leading ground-gainer (he held that distinction until Autry Denson surpassed his mark in 1998) after becoming the first Irish player ever to gain 1,000 rushing yards in three straight seasons. He burst onto the scene as a freshman by gaining 112 yards in an upset road win over a top-ranked and unbeaten Pittsburgh team led by Dan Marino. Pinkett then rushed for 1,394 yards and 16 touchdowns in 1983; 1,105 and 17 in 1984; and 1,100 and 11 in 1985. He also caught 73 career passes for 774 yards and three TDs. Pinkett finished eighth in the Heisman Trophy balloting as a senior and was Notre Dame's MVP three straight times. He finished with 4,131 career rushing yards and 49 career rushing TDs—with *Football News* naming him a first-team All-American in both 1983 and 1985. Pinkett was a third-round pick of the Houston Oilers and played six years in the NFL. He's currently the analyst on IMG national radio broadcasts of Notre Dame football games.

Irish in Their Own Words

ALLEN PINKETT

Choosing a college to attend was easy because Notre Dame provided me the best opportunity to have success at the end of four years. There wasn't even another school that came close, and that was whether I played football or not.

I also wanted a school that had national recognition with regard to athletics, a chance to win a national championship, and a very sound academic program. Notre Dame, Notre Dame, Notre Dame!

I considered North Carolina and Penn State. I didn't want to stay in state. I guess my perspective was always broader than staying in Virginia. Coach [George] Welsh came into Virginia the year I was a senior in high school, and he had turned that program around after coming in from Navy. But I just didn't believe they could win a national championship.

At Penn State, they sent you a letter offering you a scholarship, but Joe [Paterno] does not like that kind of formal stuff. He put a P.S. on the end of it and said how happy he was to do this. They were the first school to offer me a scholarship. I took several unofficial visits up there, and you knew he was a legend way back then. But to me it just didn't compare to Notre Dame.

Certainly Gerry Faust's enthusiasm was a factor, but I think you have to go to the school because of the school. Coaches come and go. [Defensive line coach] Greg Blache did most of the recruiting, and then Faust took over. It felt like home, it felt like the place I wanted to be, and the campus was all that and more.

From the outset, I figured I would have to wait my turn. I just wanted to try to get to third-string my first year. I came in and had a pretty good camp, but if Greg Bell had not been injured, shoot, I might not have touched the field. After the success I had during camp, I knew I was going to get a shot at traveling [to road games]. But once you get a taste of starting, you don't ever want to come out of the lineup. I was fortunate to have such success so early.

You go through stages where you're happy to be on the team, and then you're happy to get in, and then you start to notice the crowd and that kind of stuff. When you become a full-time starter, you don't even see the crowd. Now it's a job; now you're going to work. Your focus is totally different. Once you get a taste of it being a job, you don't ever want to be on the sideline.

The Pitt game during my freshman year, no doubt, was a thrill. What a lot of people don't remember is that the week before the Pittsburgh game, I had gained more than 100 yards against Navy.

LSU in 1984 was sort of a similar situation to the Pitt game in 1982. Before that LSU game, we had lost three games in a row. LSU was undefeated at 6–0–1, ranked sixth in the country, and we were playing down at their place. We went down there and we thumped 'em [30–22]. That was the thing under Coach Faust; we didn't win a lot of games, but we always found a way to win a big game.

100. TIM BROWN, SE/FL
6'0", 195, Dallas, Texas, 1984–1987

Tim Brown burst onto the scene as a junior with a scintillating season-ending performance in a come-from-behind upset of USC, then used back-to-back punt returns for touchdowns in an early-season 1987 game against Michigan State to cement his Heisman Trophy bid. Listed as a flanker, Brown utilized his ability as a pass receiver, rusher out of a full-house backfield, and punt and kickoff returner to rank third nationally in all-purpose yardage as a junior (176.5 per game) and sixth as a senior (167.9). He finished his junior campaign with 254 all-purpose yards in the 38–37 win at USC (including a 56-yard punt return that set up the winning field goal), then returned punts for 66 and 71 yards for a pair of touchdowns in an early romp over eventual Big Ten and Rose Bowl champion Michigan State.

Brown finished his career as Notre Dame's all-time leader in pass-reception yards (2,493) while also returning six kicks for touchdowns (three punts, three kickoffs). Despite constant double and triple coverage as a senior, he earned a reputation as the most dangerous player in college football—and became the first wide receiver to win the Heisman. Brown was a first-round pick of the Los Angeles Raiders (sixth player chosen overall) in the 1988 NFL Draft. He was selected to play in the NFL Pro Bowl on nine occasions. He played through the 2004 season, mainly with Oakland/Los Angeles and ended his pro career with 14,934 receiving yards and 100 TD receptions. Brown joined the National Football Foundation Hall of Fame in 2009 and then in 2012 received the NCAA Silver Anniversary Award.

I REMEMBER TIM BROWN.

I remember sitting in the press box at the brand-new Hoosier Dome in Indianapolis in 1984 for Notre Dame's football season opener against Purdue. The official, printed play-by-play from the game says Brown (then a freshman playing in his first college game) fielded the opening kickoff at his 10, fumbled at the 12, and Purdue recovered at the Irish 11.

The Boilermakers ran three plays and kicked a 31-yard field goal for a 3–0 lead 1:44 into the contest. Purdue went on to win 23–21.

Fortunately for Brown and Irish fans, lots of better days loomed ahead. Three years later Brown won the Heisman Trophy in 1987 as a senior flanker and kick returner.

I remember the final game of Brown's junior season in 1986, a 252-all-purpose-yard effort that helped beat USC, keynoted by a brilliant punt return.

I remember that prime-time performance in 1987 against Michigan State (25 years ago it was Brown returning consecutive Spartan punts for touchdowns).

If you're much of a football fan, you probably already know the football legacy left by the Dallas, Texas, product.

I also remember the Tim Brown I heard speak as one of the featured guests in 2009 at the celebration of 60 years of successes by black athletes at Notre Dame. Brown that evening shared some experiences about which you might not have heard:

"When I think about how I got to Notre Dame, it's pretty unique. I come from two parents who at the ages of 14 or 15 had to drop out of high school to pick cotton in Louisiana. So, the one thing they always wanted for their kids was education.

"I wanted to perform well in athletics, but I was more concerned about my grades. At my house you couldn't bring a C home. So my passion has always been education. I never thought about going to Notre Dame or the NFL. I just thought about getting a degree from a great university.

"My brother happened to be one of these subway alumni guys, and he used to watch the replays of the games on Sunday. He loved Notre Dame and knew all the history. When I got my first letter from Notre Dame my junior year, he said, 'That's where you're going.' He told my mom all about the educational background, and once she heard it all, she said, 'That's it, that's where he's going.'

"When I came to Notre Dame I came here with one focus only. I was going to get a great education, go back and marry my high school sweetheart, and become a deacon in the church. It all worked out in a totally different way.

"When I was in high school, I hadn't really been recruited that much by Notre Dame. They were recruiting another player from my rival high school, Dante Jones, who went on to play linebacker at Oklahoma. One night Notre Dame came to see him play, and I scored four touchdowns, a couple on long plays and kick returns. That was a Thursday night game—and Friday morning Notre Dame was sitting at the door trying to find out who this Tim Brown kid was. If they'd come the week before, I didn't score at all. The week after, I scored one touchdown. The only time I ever scored four touchdowns at any level was that night.

"One of the big things I remember learning here came my junior year. I'm going to be a senior in Cavanaugh Hall with one of the first choices of rooms—so I'm going to take one of the rooms with a bathroom. It was all good. In my haste I wrote down 403 instead of 408. Somebody came up to me and said, 'Hey, Tim. Why didn't you take the room with the bathroom?' I checked, and I chose the wrong room.

"I went to see Father [Matt] Miceli [the hall rector], and he said, 'Tim, that's too bad. You need to pay attention to what you're doing.' That taught me a lesson. Dot your i's and cross your t's. You put something in writing and you commit to it wholeheartedly. You have to live with it.

"In football things took a dramatic turn when Lou Holtz got here. Before that I was literally just a guy—I was playing the game with not much of a future that I could see. He got here and started saying such great things about me that I started thinking maybe I did have the talent.

"But it might not have happened, I might not have won the Heisman Trophy if not for an unfortunate situation my freshman year. Alvin Miller got hurt, tore his knee up—and he was one of the most incredible athletes you'll ever be around. Because of what happened to him, all he did was encourage me. This is a guy who could have taken the same path I ended up taking. But he took the time to encourage me, and that was monumental to me—and that's what Notre Dame is all about.

"At Notre Dame, I realized how important my family structure was. The last 15 years I have been holding a mentoring minicamp with 150 fatherless boys matched with mentors. At the end of the day, to see these kids light up, it's amazing how good you feel inside."

I remember Tim Brown, arguably the most productive player in Notre Dame history when you consider both his college and pro careers (17 years, nine NFL Pro Bowls, 100 TD receptions).

We all remember him now as a College Football Hall of Famer.

—*John Heisler*

101. Frank Stams, DE
6′4″, 237, Akron, Ohio, 1984–1988

A consensus All-American in 1988, former Irish fullback Frank Stams developed into an all-star defensive end on the 1988 Notre Dame national championship team. He started all 11 games at full-back as a sophomore in 1985, then switched to defense when Lou

Holtz became head coach. Stams was named MVP of the 1988 Miami game after forcing two fumbles and recovering another against the top-rated Hurricanes—then was named the 1989 Fiesta Bowl Defensive MVP for his two sacks and three tackles versus unbeaten West Virginia. In his career he had 47 rushes for 172 yards and three touchdowns; 14 receptions for 100 yards and a 7.1 average; 65 tackles and eight sacks for minus-63 yards. Stams became a second-round choice of the Los Angeles Rams in the 1989 NFL Draft—played for three years with the Rams before moving on to Cleveland, to the Kansas City Chiefs, and then back to Cleveland.

Irish in Their Own Words

FRANK STAMS

It never really was one thing for me when it came to selecting Notre Dame. It was a collection of three or four things. For me, it started at home with my parents. When I took my visit to Notre Dame, the person in charge of admissions said, "If you were to go out to football practice the first day and you broke your leg and never played football again, where would you want to be?" Plus my dad was in high school in the late '40s, and he'd always talk about the Notre Dame legends.

There was a guy here in town who was a good friend of my dad's and a good friend of Ara Parseghian's. His name was Eddie Niam, and he and Parseghian were high school buddies. They both went to South High School here in Akron. My dad was a teacher for 30-some years, and his high school was right across the street from this guy's little diner.

Eddie was around a lot when I was in high school, and there was that whole Notre Dame influence. Plus the fact that Notre

Dame was a nationally recognized school and they weren't in a conference.... You know, you're playing all over the country, and wherever you went, it was like playing a home game. It wasn't a Catholic thing. I remember some of the competing schools made reference to the Catholic institution. It wasn't about that for me, the religious aspect, but it was a handful of other things.

Who finished No. 2? That's a good question. In hindsight, if I hadn't gone to Notre Dame, I probably would have gone to Michigan because of Bo Schembechler. I had good feelings about him as a coach. But it wasn't about any one person. It was the whole thing.

Notre Dame is a great school, and I enjoyed my time there. I broke my ankle there on Cartier Field in minus-20 degree weather in the spring of 1986. It was a bad break and it was a good break because that ultimately affected where I was going to play on the field. Had I not gotten hurt, I probably wouldn't have been around for 1988. I never really expected to move from fullback, but you know, it was a change that I, at the time, welcomed. I wasn't a frustrated fullback or anything like that. I just didn't enjoy the whole offensive experience there, and I was much more suited for the defense.

I think it clicked better for me with a defensive mind-set. Foge Fazio was the coordinator, and then Barry Alvarez was brought in as the coordinator the next year, and it all really fell into place for the whole defense when Barry became the coordinator. A big part of the success we had as a team was because of the groundwork that Foge laid, and then Barry was able to take the whole of that and take it one step further. The players really responded to him defensively. I think the coordinators' personalities brought out the best in the defensive players. The players just kind of fed off their attitude and their personalities.

102. Lou Holtz
Head Coach, 1986–1996 (100–30–2, .765)

Lou Holtz's first season as head coach at Notre Dame in 1986 saw the Irish lose five games by a combined total of 14 points. The next year, the Irish won eight games and played in the Cotton Bowl. The following season, Holtz's Irish won 12 games and the national title—and 20 years after that championship season, Holtz in 2008 was inducted into the College Football Hall of Fame.

Holtz coached 11 seasons at Notre Dame and guided his teams to 100 wins—second only to Knute Rockne in total victories. He remains in the top 10 on the NCAA all-time win list for Division I-A coaches (with 249). Holtz took his Notre Dame teams to nine straight New Year's Day bowl games from 1987 through 1995 and coached the Irish to finishes of sixth or better in the final Associated Press poll in five seasons.

Holtz was named the national coach of the year in 1988 and saw his team play the most difficult schedule in the country three different years. His teams won 32 games against teams ranked in the AP top 25 during his career with the Irish, and Notre Dame also won a record 23 straight games from 1988 to 1989.

He coached 19 first-team Irish All-Americans, a Heisman Trophy winner in Tim Brown, two Lombardi winners in Chris Zorich and Aaron Taylor, a Walter Camp player of the year in Raghib Ismail, and a Johnny Unitas winner in Tony Rice.

The Kent State graduate also coached at William & Mary, North Carolina State, Arkansas, Minnesota, and South Carolina—and then joined ESPN as a studio analyst.

In 33 seasons as a college head coach, Holtz compiled 249 wins and took a record five different programs to bowl games. He saw 22 of his teams qualify for bowl games and 18 finish in the final AP top 25.

Lou Holtz's top accomplishment at Notre Dame? He took the Irish to traditional New Year's Day bowl games in nine consecutive seasons (1987–1995). *Photo courtesy of Mike Bennett/Lighthouse Imaging*

In 2008 he received the Moose Krause Man of the Year award from the Notre Dame Monogram Club for his off-the-field contributions.

A sculpture of Holtz was dedicated in 2008 at Notre Dame Stadium's Gate D, which honors the Irish national championship football coaches. The Holtz sculpture shows the former Irish coach calling a play on the sideline, with two Irish players (Tim Brown and Skip Holtz were the models) beside him. The sculpture complements bas relief portraits of the five Notre Dame national championship coaches—Rockne, Frank Leahy, Ara Parseghian, Dan Devine, and Holtz—that are located at Gate D, designated the national championship coaches gate.

Irish in Their Own Words

CHUCK LANZA

Obviously, Coach Holtz had a huge impact on me as a co-captain my senior year. That was important to me, and a rewarding situation because [fellow co-captain] Byron Spruell and I had to spend a lot of time with [Holtz], attending certain functions for the school and getting an opportunity to visit with him a lot one on one. That was important and meaningful to be involved with him as much as we were.

Irish in Their Own Words

MARK GREEN

Coach Holtz used to say if you can't bench-press 400 pounds, you better be able to throw it and catch it. So we had guys working their rear ends off in the weight room. He also talked about being seen rather than heard. That one stuck with me because it fit me the best. He said it's better to be seen than heard, meaning keep your mouth shut on the football field. Show people what you're capable of doing; don't tell them what you're capable of doing.

He used thunder as an example. All the loud roar and all the noise thunder makes, yet thunder on its own doesn't do a thing. It does absolutely nothing. And he said take the sun, the most powerful visible entity in the world. The sun doesn't make a sound, but look at the power that it has behind it. I liked those analogies. They applied to my approach to playing the game.

It was obvious from the start of Coach Holtz's tenure that we were getting better. It was a project of continuous improvement. Once we got the fundamentals down, then we could begin to use that athleticism that we all were supposed to have as football players at Notre Dame.

Irish in Their Own Words

WES PRITCHETT

You've probably heard the story of Holtz's first meeting with us, and as I look back on that, it's really amazing. Gerry [Faust] said good-bye to us in the little meeting room there in the Joyce Center, and everybody slouched down. [Faust and Holtz] must have crossed each other in the hallway. Gerry is crying, "Good-bye, good-bye!" and within 30 seconds it was like, "Here's your new head coach, Lou Holtz."

All of a sudden it's, "Sit up straight in your chairs! You look at me straight in the eye! Things are going to change from this point forward!" Lou's going crazy. He said, "Things are going to be different. These are our four priorities: God, family, academics, and football." I think that was it. He put seven or eight things on the board. "These are going to be our priorities. We're going to do it this way. I'm not a patient man. You're going to do it my way or the highway." All of the cliches everybody came to know and love. And he never changed. He stuck to his guns every step of the way.

Holtz always had you up emotionally for a game. We knew how to prepare. We made adjustments at halftime.

Irish in Their Own Words

BOBBY BROWN

Coach Holtz's last home game at Notre Dame against Rutgers [1996] was big. The emotion that surrounded it.... I can remember vividly him calling us up as a class and telling us what his next step was and the emotions surrounding it that were pretty profound. I'll never forget all of the 6'4", 300-pound football players reduced to tears because we had come to Notre Dame, and we had come to believe in a coach, and he wouldn't be there when we came to the finish line. It was emotional, and I'll always remember that.

Irish in Their Own Words

RICK MIRER

Coach Holtz had a very disciplined, very professional way, an old-school kind of way of treating the team. I think the guys who were part of his programs during that time period grew up a little faster than maybe some other guys who went to other places where it was a little looser. Because of that, it wasn't fun and games every day. It was very serious, and sometimes we didn't get to enjoy our victories a whole lot. Every time we would win, we would seem to downplay it.

Coach Holtz recruited guys who he knew could handle that, and therefore he was coaching a pretty mature group of people. It wasn't flashy, we didn't get caught up in our successes, and his attitude kind of filtered into everybody else's quotes in the paper. We just kind of kept our mouths shut and played. I've been around a lot of coaches since, and [Holtz] commanded your attention and respect.

Irish in Their Own Words

NED BOLCAR

Lou [Holtz] was a godsend for Notre Dame. It took a guy like him to change that program around. The discipline he instilled...that first team meeting...Chuck Lanza had been voted team captain, and he had his feet up on the stage. I'm not even sure Holtz asked him his name. He said, "Son, how long have you been playing football?" Chuck said something like 14 years. And Lou said, "If your ass isn't pushed up against the back of that seat, your career will come to an end in two seconds!" And you heard 115 guys' rear ends hit the back of the seat.

I tell that story because it proves a point about leaders. In the next four years, I never saw anybody slouch in a meeting. If anybody ever fell asleep in a meeting, Lou was quick to send him out. Nobody let their eyes wander away from him or he would send them out of the meeting. Lou was a leader by his discipline, and he knew how to organize a great coaching staff, he knew how to motivate the players, and he knew how to pull them together.

Those morning workouts...the only person you had to cling to was your teammate. They ran us to death, and it was painful. But it was for a purpose: to bring the team together and to break down the barriers that were formed through dissension and years of losing.

I once heard the phrase, "Men want to be led...just not off a cliff." They want good leadership. If you have success with it, they'll gain confidence and do it harder. If you have somebody beating his head against the wall and there aren't any results, after a while he's going to say, "This is wrong," and then he's going to doubt everybody. But give them a program that works, give them something where they can experience success and build some confidence, and that's what our coaches—led by Lou Holtz—did. All of a sudden a team that couldn't find itself became a great football team, and I was proud to be a part of it.

Irish in Their Own Words

Scott Kowalkowski

Playing for Coach Holtz was tough but good, and I think most people I played with at Notre Dame would agree with me. He tried to make it as hard as possible in practice so that when game time came it was easy. He's like that. Bill Parcells is like that. Bobby Ross was like that [with the Detroit Lions]. Old school. I liked playing for a guy like that because you always knew where you stood. There was no gray area. The other reason I enjoyed playing for a coach like that was because I didn't know any differently. My high school program was like that, and my dad was that way.

When I think back about playing for Coach Holtz, that guy was kind of amazing. He would will it to happen, and that rubs off on your players. I found myself to be that way. I was that way, anyway, because my dad was that way. So it was learned behavior. But that rubs off on a team. You usually take the personality of your coach, and I think that was the case with us.

Irish in Their Own Words

Pete Chryplewicz

Playing for Coach Holtz, to sum it up in one word, was exhilarating, both in a positive and negative way. He was a very demanding coach. He expected excellence, expected the best from his players on and off the field. He put so much pressure on you during the week of practice that Saturday seemed like a scrimmage.

He felt that, if he could count on you Monday through Friday in practice, under his scrutiny and watchful eye, he knew he could count on you on Saturday in third-and-1 and fourth-and-1 situations with the ballgame on the line.

For a lot of guys, that was a very difficult situation to understand and comprehend. The physical labors as well as the mental part of it were difficult. More than anything, it was a mental challenge every day. But at the end of the day, after you've weeded through everything, you know whom you can count on and who's going to be out there on Saturday.

He wasn't just a football coach. He was a mentor in life, as well. He had so many good stories and teachings—philosophies on life that to this day hold true. He didn't just produce football players; he produced young men who were ready to go out into the real world if you listened and understood what he was saying.

103. MICHAEL STONEBREAKER, LB
6'1", 228, River Ridge, Louisiana, 1986, 1988–1990

A two-time consensus Irish all-star and a unanimous first-team All-America selection in 1990, Michael Stonebreaker finished third in balloting for the Butkus Award as the top linebacker nationally in 1990. He started all 12 games for the Irish, ranking second on the squad in tackles with 104 in Notre Dame's 1988 national title season—then was the top Irish tackler in 1990 with 95. Stonebreaker had 220 career tackles with eight passes broken up, five interceptions for 103 yards and one touchdown, four forced fumbles, two fumble recoveries, and five sacks for minus-29 yards. He played in the 1991 Japan and Hula Bowls—then was drafted in 1991 by the Chicago Bears and signed with Atlanta in 1993 and New Orleans in 1994. He also played for the World League in Frankfurt in 1995.

104. Tony Rice, QB
6′1″, 200, Woodruff, South Carolina, 1987–1989

Irish signal-caller Tony Rice was the starting quarterback on Notre Dame's 1988 national title team, led the Irish to a record 23 straight wins from 1988 to 1989, and finished fourth in the Heisman Trophy voting as a senior in 1989. A magician in terms of running Lou Holtz's option attack, Rice became the starter

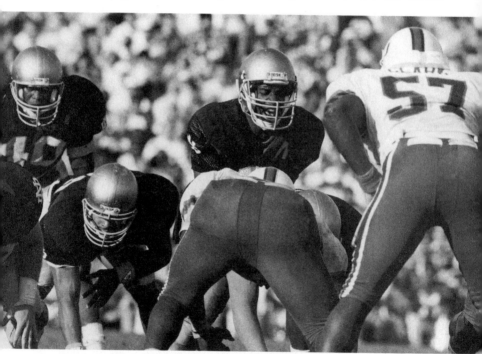

Quarterback Tony Rice served as architect of Notre Dame's record 23-game football win streak from 1988 to 1989. *Photo courtesy of Mike Bennett/Lighthouse Imaging*

midway through the 1987 season after a shoulder injury to Terry Andrysiak, then held that job throughout the record-setting 1988 and 1989 campaigns. In 1988 Rice completed 70 of 138 throws for 1,176 yards and eight touchdowns—then added 68-for-137 in 1989 for 1,122 yards and two TDs. He rushed for 700 yards and nine TDs in 1988, 884 yards and seven TDs in 1989. His career totals included 173-of-357 passing for 2,961 yards and 11 TDs—to go with 384 rushing carries for 1,921 yards and 23 TDs. He earned MVP honors in the 1989 Fiesta Bowl win over West Virginia when he threw for a career-best 213 yards and ran for 75 more. Rice won the Johnny Unitas Award in 1989 and was a *Football News* first-team All-American. Undrafted by the NFL, he played for Saskatchewan in the Canadian Football League and also for Barcelona in the World League (1991–1992) and Munich (1994) in the Football League of Europe.

Irish in Their Own Words

TONY RICE

Rickey Foggie was from Lawrence, South Carolina, about 20 minutes away from me. We played against each other in high school, and I think he was the one who made the referral. He told Coach Holtz about me when they were at Minnesota [Gophers] together. Then [Notre Dame recruiting coordinator] Vinny Cerrato came to see me play in a couple of high school basketball games, and we spent a lot of time just talking about my involvement with Rickey and being a quarterback. [Cerrato] was the guy who really helped me understand about Notre Dame.

Finally Coach Holtz came down and spoke with my grandmother, and he won her heart. I was like, "Wow, okay, I'll take a visit to Notre Dame!" Once I got up there, I fell in love with the place. I took three visits, not five. Pittsburgh was one of them, and the North Carolina Tar Heels was the other. Notre Dame was my second visit, and I already knew I was going there. Being from a small town in South Carolina and never having traveled much, I went ahead and took my visit to Pittsburgh.

People always said that I was the perfect fit for Coach Holtz's offense. But when I went to Notre Dame, I didn't really know Coach Holtz's history and what type of offense he was looking for and what he was most comfortable running. I'd seen Rickey Foggie play, and he ran the option, so I was interested to see what type of scheme Coach Holtz would want to run with me. He didn't really let me know at the time. He had [quarterbacks] Steve Beuerlein and Terry Andrysiak there at the time, and those two guys were passing quarterbacks. When I came in, I was more of a passer/runner.

When I entered the lineup in place of Terry Andrysiak, who went down with an injury my sophomore year [1987], it was a difficult adjustment because I had missed the full year before and hadn't taken a hit in live competition for two years.

People always ask me about how I got along with Coach Holtz. My relationship with Coach Holtz was wonderful. My first year, my sophomore year, I wasn't playing at the beginning of the season, but he didn't just coach one quarterback. He worked with all of us, and I think he made a concerted effort to spend more time with me, trying to get me focused, trying to make me ready for when it was my turn.

There was always this attitude that the practices were the hard part and that the games were the easy part. I thought [Holtz] did a great job doing that, and I've taken that into my life. When you're up against the wall, you take the attitude of, "Hey, I've been through worse things before." He was hard on me, hard as hell. But that just brings out the best in people. As an athlete, you want to improve each and every day, and Coach Holtz provided plenty of motivation for me. He knew how to press the right buttons.

When I look back on that 23-game winning streak, it's still hard to believe. But while it's happening, you don't think about winning 18, 19, 20, 23 games in a row. I didn't realize what we accomplished until I graduated. We were on a roll, and you don't focus on what you're accomplishing as it's happening. When it's all final and done with, it's like, "Man, we did have a great team!" I go back and look at the tapes and I still get excited, even though I know who won the game!

105. Todd Lyght, CB
6′1″, 184, Flint, Michigan, 1987–1990

A two-time consensus All-American in 1989 and 1990 and a unanimous pick as a junior in 1989, Todd Lyght began his Notre Dame career with more playing time in 1987 than any other freshman, making 29 tackles, causing one fumble, breaking up two passes, and making one interception. He was a three-year Irish starter at cornerback from 1988 to 1990. Lyght led the team in tackles in the 1989 Fiesta Bowl win over West Virginia for the national championship. One of the captains for the 1990 season and a finalist for the 1989 Jim Thorpe Award, he had 161 career tackles, caused one fumble, broke up 20.5 passes, and had 11 interceptions for 55 return yards and one TD. Lyght ranked eighth in the final NCAA standings in 1989 for interceptions. He played in the 1991 Hula Bowl and Japan Bowl, then became a first-round pick of the Los Angeles Rams in the 1991 NFL Draft and played for the Rams through 2000 and with the Detroit Lions from 2001 to 2002.

106. RAGHIB ISMAIL, FL

5'10", 175, Wilkes-Barre, Pennsylvania, 1988–1990

A two-time first-team All-American as a sophomore in 1989 and junior in 1990 and a unanimous pick in 1990 when he finished second in Heisman Trophy voting behind BYU's Ty Detmer, Raghib Ismail became a starter on the 1988 national championship squad with 12 catches for 331 yards and two touchdowns, while returning 12 kickoffs for 433 yards and two TDs. He had 64 rushing carries for 478 yards and two TDs in 1989 and caught 27 passes for 535 yards—and returned 20 kickoffs for 502 yards and two TDs with seven punt returns for 113 yards and one TD in 1989. Ismail was the Walter Camp Player of the Year in 1990. He had 67 rushing carries for 537 yards and three TDs in 1990, 32 pass receptions for 699 yards and two TDs, 14 kickoff returns for 336 yards and one TD while returning 13 punts for 151 yards. His career totals included 273 all-purpose attempts for 4,187 yards and 15 TDs—a 15.3 yards-per-attempt average.

Ismail holds records for pass-reception yards per catch in a career with 22.0 (71 for 1,565); kickoff returns for touchdowns in a game with two (vs. Michigan in 1989 and again vs. Rice in 1988, also an NCAA record), and in a career with five; and kick-return yards per attempt in a career with 22.6 (17 for 1,607). He appeared on the cover of *Sports Illustrated* after his two kickoff returns for TDs helped the Irish win at Michigan in 1989. He originally played with the Toronto Argonauts of the Canadian Football League and was a fourth-round draft pick of the Los Angeles Raiders in the 1991 NFL Draft. He joined the Raiders beginning in 1993, played for the Carolina Panthers from 1996 to 1998, and became a member of the Dallas Cowboys in 1999. He's listed as the 75th greatest football player of all-time by collegefootball.com.

Raghib Ismail's abilities as a runner, receiver, and kick returner made him a legitimate threat to provide dramatics any time he touched the ball. *Photo courtesy of Mike Bennett/Lighthouse Imaging*

Irish in Their Own Words

RAGHIB ISMAIL

When I first moved to Wilkes-Barre, Pennsylvania, from northern Jersey, I met a guy by the name of Brian Dwyer, who had just moved to Wilkes-Barre, too. We both played football, and Brian and I struck up a friendship when we were like 12 years old.

I remember one weekend I stayed at his house and we stayed up all night playing this Spider-Man game. My next memory flowing into my consciousness was the voice of the Notre Dame band director saying, "The University of Notre Dame proudly presents..." and the Notre Dame fight song started blaring, although I didn't know that's what it was. It scared me!

I woke up, and on the couch was Brian's dad, Wayne Dwyer, and this cat looked like he was straight out of Ireland. Red hair, glasses on, pipe, sitting in the rocking chair with this big grin... and he said to me, "Do you hear that, laddy? That's the greatest band in the land!" And the seed was planted.

From then on, it was all Notre Dame. All I thought about was playing football at Notre Dame. If I hadn't gone on to Notre Dame to play football, it would have been the biggest disappointment and letdown. At the time, "Wake Up the Echoes" was out and was really big. Mr. Dwyer pulls out the "Wake Up the Echoes" tape, and it was the best advertisement Notre Dame could have ever had with me.

I was a tiny guy. In eighth grade, when I was finally able to go out for freshman football, I was so small that I couldn't hold on to the ball. If I caught the ball five times a game, I fumbled it three times. The summer between my sophomore and junior year in high school, something happened to me. I went from running like a 4.7 to 4.3. Syracuse University started to pursue me after I went to their football camp. I remember going up to the camp in the Carrier Dome, and they had all the guys lined up. I ran my 40, and the coaches looked at their watches, looked at each other, and said, "What did you get?" Then they asked me, "Could you run that again?" So I did, and the time was the same. From that point on, everything took off. Yet in my mind, it was Notre Dame or bust. They didn't have to send anybody to recruit me. If I qualified, I was going to Notre Dame.

I wore big shoulder pads and tried to look big, but I was probably 5'8", 160. By the end of my senior year, I think I weighed 166. Coach [Joe] Paterno from Penn State came to the high school, then Coach Holtz came to the high school, and when Coach Holtz came...you know how you meet someone and you can tell when they're excited to meet you? Well, you also know when they're not excited to meet you, or they're disappointed. I could see in Coach Holtz's face, even though he was smiling, that he was disappointed because I was so small. I felt like, *Oh, man, I just lost my chance to go to Notre Dame!* I was so afraid. I should have worn some lifts in my shoes. But my speed was such a factor that, even though I was small, they had to take a chance on me.

We won every game my freshman year [1988] at Notre Dame, and then we won the first 11 games of 1989. Then we finally lost to Miami at the end of 1989, and then we lost a couple times in 1990. I really didn't know how to handle that after all the success. When you win right off the bat, you don't have the character ingrained within you because you didn't earn it, per se. Experiencing it and not liking it, that's the key. I didn't understand that until my junior year.

I injured my thigh against Michigan State in 1990 [a 20–19 victory] and aggravated it against Purdue [a 37–11 victory]. Then we played Stanford, I didn't play, and we lost [36–31]. It was a home game, and we had a whole bunch of turnovers. It wasn't until later in my pro career—I would say my third year with Carolina—before I realized how to push through an injury, and I regret not playing in that Stanford game.

My most memorable moment on the field at Notre Dame had nothing to do with any of the successes we had or what people would define as great moments. The most memorable moment was my very first game and the week leading up to it. It was Michigan at night in 1988 [a 19–17 victory]. I felt like I was having a surreal moment. They were thinking about putting me back there to return kicks. But I don't think I had caught one deep ball at receiver in three weeks. Coach Holtz was like, "I don't care if you catch it or not, I'm going to put you out there [at receiver] and put the fear of God in [Michigan]."

My mind was going 100 miles per hour the whole week. I remember coming out of the tunnel for pregame, and I felt like I was in the movie *What Dreams May Come* with Robin Williams and Cuba Gooding Jr. When they stepped into the afterlife, it was like walking into a painting, and that's how I felt when I came out of the tunnel. I felt like I was walking into a painting, and it felt like static electricity was in the air. It was a clean, brisk feeling, and everything was hyper-colored. I remember my legs feeling so weak that I didn't know if I could walk. I was stumbling around in our pregame warm-up. I didn't catch a pass. I remember the Irish Guard seeming like they were eight feet tall. Every player for Michigan looked like he was as big as Greg Skrepenak, who was their big [6'8"] tackle.

The first time I stepped on the field, I ran deep. Tony Rice called the play, and my heart was beating so fast. He looked at me and winked to try to relax me, but then when I lined up, here came the emotions again. The DB looked at me, and I remember running up on him and flying past him. I turned for the ball and I could feel the anticipation of the crowd. I looked up into the night sky and there was a small dot. All of a sudden I became so overwhelmed that [the football] hit me in the hands and I dropped it, and I literally felt the air in the stadium from the fans go out.

I came to the sideline, and Coach Holtz said, "Son, I told you I didn't care whether you caught the ball or not. You did exactly what I needed you to do." The next time he had me go in was the second half to return a kickoff, and I was determined to make up for that mistake to show Coach Holtz I could do it. If I ran a 4.1 on my best day, I think I ran about a 3.9 on that return. Then I got hit so hard by a player from Michigan that I felt my organs smashing up against the front part of the inside of my body. It was like all of the air decompressed from my body, and my head hit the ground first. It was dead silent. I looked up at the sky and hundreds of white specks were flashing in front of my eyes. I got up, walked toward the sideline, and everybody looked at me like they had just seen me get hit by a car. I think they were afraid to talk to me.

I had the fullest intention of coming back for my senior year [in 1991]. I hadn't made my decision when we came back from the Orange Bowl [a 10–9 loss to Colorado], and Rodney Culver [who would captain the 1991 squad] and myself, and I think Derek Brown, were talking about what good captains we were going to be. That night I had a dream that my brother woke me up and that the mother of one of my teammates had died. At least I think it was a dream. The next thing I know my brother is coming into my room, waking me up and saying, "Chris Zorich's mom died." That changed my perspective on everything.

Your whole life you've been thinking about how your skills and abilities will be able to get your mom a new house. That's when it hit me. You don't know what's going to happen tomorrow. If I would have gone through what Chris did, I would have been devastated because I didn't have the opportunity to do for my mom what I had wanted to do since I was a little boy. I think it was right then that I made up my mind that I had to turn pro, even though I had no idea what I was getting into, even though I had no idea about the drama that was going to intensify. When I looked back on Notre Dame, I was really sheltered and had a protection mechanism in place, even though it was a pretty intense magnifying glass. But the death of Chris' mom is what provoked the decision.

107. CHRIS ZORICH, NT
6'1", 266, Chicago, Illinois, 1988–1990

Former Irish All-American Chris Zorich reached the pinnacle of his collegiate career with his 2007 selection to the National Football Foundation Hall of Fame. Zorich played professionally in his native Chicago (for the Bears), came back to law school at Notre Dame, then returned to Chicago to live and work. He built his reputation on a relentless, dominating, play-after-play style of performance on defense. Zorich gave the impression he'd be happy to stand toe to toe at any time with an offensive lineman, grit his teeth, snarl, and go "Grrrrrrrr..." He came from the Chicago Public League, taking up football at a relatively late age, and never imagined Notre Dame might be in his future.

Zorich never played as a true freshman in 1987. He came to campus with braces on his teeth and fighting a stuttering challenge. He didn't initially project the sort of confidence or swagger that later defined him. That changed quickly.

A linebacker in high school, Zorich transitioned to defensive tackle as a collegian—and by the end of his career he was as good as anyone in the country at his craft. After toiling with the prep team in 1987, his collegiate debut in 1988 at home against Michigan produced 10 tackles and a sack and a half. He immediately became part of an ultra-talented defense that set the tone for Notre Dame's 1988 championship season. Zorich's junior and senior campaigns produced consensus All-America recognition. *Sporting News* called him the toughest player in the game. He had become the most dominant Notre Dame defensive lineman since Bob Golic played from 1977 to 1978.

Zorich returned home from the 1991 Orange Bowl, his last collegiate game, to find his mother Zora dead in her south Chicago apartment. Chris later established a Notre Dame scholarship in her name—and his contributions to his Chicago community through his foundation became legendary. For all the sports magazines on whose covers he appeared, he probably was more proud of making the front of *Reader's Digest* for what he was doing away from football. Shy around microphones when he came to South Bend, he became a powerful speaker—with a profound story to tell. The university continues to present an award in his name for community service by Irish student-athletes.

108. MIRKO JURKOVIC, OG
6'4", 289, Calumet City, Illinois, 1988–1991

A consensus All-America pick in 1991 and two-year starter at offensive guard in 1990 and 1991, Mirko Jurkovic earned a monogram as a defensive tackle on the 1988 national championship squad, then made the move to guard his sophomore season and played more minutes than any other offensive lineman other than the starting five. He was named Notre Dame lineman of the year by the Moose Krause Chapter of the National Football Hall of Fame as a senior in 1991. Jurkovic played in the Hula Bowl in 1992 and was a ninth-round selection of the Chicago Bears in the 1992 NFL draft. He now does commentary on Irish football for various UND.com productions.

109. RICK MIRER, QB
6'2", 217, Goshen, Indiana, 1989–1992

Rick Mirer played behind Tony Rice at quarterback in 1989, then spent three record-setting years as the starting Irish signal-caller. He left Notre Dame as the all-time Irish leader in touchdown passes

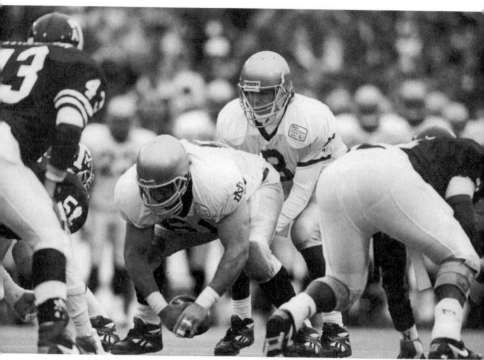

At a school that has produced far more standout quarterbacks than most, Rick Mirer left Notre Dame having thrown more touchdown passes than any other.

Photo courtesy of Mike Bennett/Lighthouse Imaging

with 41. As a sophomore in 1990, he completed 110 of 200 throws for 1,824 yards and eight TDs. Then as a junior he hit 132 of 234 for 2,117 and a single-season record 18 TDs (also running for 309 yards and nine more TDs). Then as a senior in 1992 Mirer served as an Irish captain and completed 120 of 234 passes for 1,876 yards and 15 TDs. He put together a 29–7–1 record as a starter and set the Notre Dame career record for total offensive yards (6,691). His career numbers included 377-of-698 passing for 5,997 yards and those 41 TDs—plus 253 carries for 694 yards and 17 TDs. Mirer appeared on the cover of *Sports Illustrated* after the top-rated Irish defeated fourth-ranked Michigan in the 1990 opener. Mirer was invited to play in both the East-West Shrine Game and the Hula Bowl. He became the second overall player selected in the 1993 NFL Draft by Seattle. He set an NFL rookie record for passing yards in 1993 with 2,833—and played four NFL seasons in Seattle, to go with stints in Chicago, Green Bay, San Francisco, Oakland, Detroit, and with the New York Jets.

110. JEFF BURRIS, FS
6'0", 204, Rock Hill, South Carolina, 1990–1993

A consensus All-America pick in 1993, Jeff Burris served as a 1993 tri-captain of an Irish squad that went 11–1 and finished second in the final polls. He led the 1992 team in interceptions and minutes played and consistently ranked nationally in 1991 as a punt returner with a final 12.6-yard average. Burris played more minutes in 1993 than any other Irish defensive player and was voted MVP by his teammates in 1993. His career totals: 89 tackles, 14 passes broken up, 10 interceptions for 67 yards, 29 carries for 136 yards and 10 TDs as goal-line tailback, one pass reception for three yards and a TD, 11 kickoff returns for 132 yards, and 19 punt returns for 287 yards and one TD. Burris was selected the Irish MVP in the 1993 win over top-rated Florida State. He played in the Senior Bowl, then became a first-round NFL selection in 1994 by the Buffalo Bills. He played with the Bills through 1997, then had stints with Indianapolis and Cincinnati. His 10-year pro career featured 19 interceptions and 529 tackles.

111. AARON TAYLOR, OT
6'4", 280, Concord, California, 1990–1993

A unanimous first-team All-America selection in 1993 as a senior offensive tackle after earning consensus honors as a junior in

1992 as offensive guard, Aaron Taylor was winner of the 1993 Lombardi Award and was one of three finalists for the Outland Trophy that same year. He also had been a Lombardi finalist as a junior in 1992. Taylor was voted by his teammates as recipient of the Nick Pietrosante Award, which is given to the player who best exemplifies the courage, dedication, and pride of the late All-America fullback. Captain of the team his senior season, he started 30 games straight to end his college career. A member of the 1994 Hula Bowl team, Taylor was drafted by the Green Bay Packers in the first round of the 1994 NFL Draft, playing on the Packers team that won the Super Bowl in 1997. He played for the San Diego Chargers in 1998 and 1999 before retiring from professional football. Taylor was voted one of the top 25 players from 1970 to 2012 by collegefootball.com.

Irish in Their Own Words

AARON TAYLOR

Going to Notre Dame was probably the best decision I ever made in my life, and if I could replay time and had to make the decision again, I would do it. It was absolutely a positive experience. Notre Dame was as advertised. That was the first trip I had taken, and I came in on the banquet weekend. Something like 80 to 90 percent of the guys who ended up signing with Notre Dame that year came in that weekend. We all talked and decided there was a fairly good chance we were going to go to Notre Dame. It was interesting because, after we left that weekend, we already had a pretty good idea among ourselves that we were going to be there. So we knew who our teammates were going to be.

When my plane landed in South Bend for my visit and I was heading to the campus from the airport, I was in a car with Dean Lytle, and I remember seeing the Golden Dome for the first time lit up at night. Something about that triggered a visceral response in my body that let me know that this was right. Literally, the moment I arrived on campus, my gut, my instincts, the bells, all that stuff was going off. I knew this was a special place and this was where I wanted to be. My athletics director in high school was a Notre Dame alum, so the sell job was very easy because every day I got a different story about Notre Dame, what the experience

Irish tackle Aaron Taylor joined exclusive company when he won the Lombardi Award in 1993. *Photo courtesy of Mike Bennett/Lighthouse Imaging*

was like for him, what it could mean for me. He was by far Notre Dame's best PR agent. He had a little key chain that played the Notre Dame fight song. He'd call me into his office before practice and he'd play the fight song for me. So I was kind of brainwashed a little toward Notre Dame.

Notre Dame was the first of five trips I had scheduled. The others were South Carolina the very next week; and UCLA, Washington, and Cal were up in the air: all West Coast and Notre Dame. I committed to Coach Holtz the Friday afternoon they brought us in for that banquet. My decision was made. Coach Holtz was an incredible speaker, witty, kind of an intense guy in the sense that he meant business. I was in awe of him. He was a legend. I had heard so many different stories about who he was, what he was about, he was this, he was that...to finally meet the man as a 17-year-old, snot-nosed kid was an experience.

I was shocked when I got to the NFL and saw how bad and how fundamentally unsound the players were. How did these guys even make it to the NFL with the bad technique they had? Common sense, basic fundamental football: keeping your hands inside, staying low, bending your knees, keeping a good base...those things were beat into you over and over, which is why it came naturally when I went to the NFL. For me, when I got hurt [in the NFL], I couldn't physically dominate people anymore. I had to position block and outsmart them and know where they were going, cut them off, and give them one angle. I was able to hang around as long as I did because I had good fundamentals.

112. BRYANT YOUNG, DT
6'3", 277, Chicago Heights, Illinois, 1990–1993

Bryant Young won first-team All-America honors from *Sporting News* as a senior in 1993 while serving as one of the Irish captains that season. A four-time monogram-winner, he finished fourth in tackles as a sophomore in 1991 with 50 (32 solo) and led the Irish in sacks. He played more as a junior in 1992 than any other defensive linemen and ended up with a team-high 7.5 sacks and 51 tackles (37 solo). He finished third in tackles with 67 as a senior in 1993. The seventh overall pick in the first round of the 1994 NFL Draft, Bryant played 14 seasons with the San Francisco 49ers before retiring after the 2007 campaign with 89.5 career sacks. He was the 1994 UPI NFC Rookie of the Year and the 1999 NFL Comeback Player of the Year. Young spent a year as a graduate assistant coach at Notre Dame in 2009, coached the San Jose State defensive line in 2010, and is currently the defensive line coach at Florida.

113. DICK ROSENTHAL
Athletics Director, 1987–1994

University of Notre Dame athletics director Dick Rosenthal, along with longtime NBC Sports executives Dick Ebersol and Ken Schanzer, changed the face of college football on television when they collaborated to create the landmark deal that enabled NBC to televise all Irish home games beginning with the 1991 season. That relationship continues today (with Notre Dame's home schedule under contract with NBC through the 2015 season).

There may have been no bigger change in the college football broadcasting landscape than what came about on a Monday in February 1990 when Notre Dame and NBC Sports jointly announced that the University had sold the rights to televise home football games for the next five years (1991–1995) to the network. The NCAA had long held the television rights, meaning even the most successful programs in the country appeared only once or twice per season (one regional, one national) on a broadcast network. The last NCAA contract allowed for five appearances over a two-year period—and the rest of a team's games went untelevised.

The universities of Georgia and Oklahoma ended that relationship when they filed suit against the NCAA and won on a 1984 Supreme Court ruling. The College Football Association, under the direction of former Big 8 Conference commissioner Chuck Neinas, inherited the national rights for a handful of years for most major conferences (except the Big Ten and Pac-10 conferences). However, the CFA's plan to look at a schedule of more regional games prompted Notre Dame to have a conversation with NBC, with whom it already had a relationship in men's basketball.

The Notre Dame–NBC agreement shocked the college football world, mainly because it came as a surprise to most and qualified as the first national television deal involving a single institution. Arguably, the deal increased the number of national appearances for college football at large, considering NBC had not been in the college football business other than for events such as the Rose, Cotton, and Orange bowls. The deal also became a precursor to various individual conference agreements with various broadcasting entities.

The Irish home games received solid visibility to begin the series, in part because NBC assigned Dick Enberg and the late Bill Walsh as its initial broadcast team. NBC alternated announcers within individual seasons for a number of years, before settling on play-by-play veteran Tom Hammond and former USC quarterback Pat Haden as its team. When Haden in 2010 returned to his alma mater, USC, as its athletics director, NBC replaced him with veteran NFL analyst Mike Mayock.

The top-rated Notre Dame game on NBC was the 1993 Notre Dame–Florida State contest with a 16.0 rating (39 share). Second on the list is the 1994 Notre Dame–Michigan game (8.0 rating, 22 share).

Any way you look at it, the Notre Dame–NBC relationship is a long way from the old days of a couple of television appearances per season under the NCAA rules. As *Sports Illustrated*'s Dan Jenkins put it, "The long-suffering multitudes have been conditioned to watching Brigham Young vs. Wyoming when the world knows that at that very moment Notre Dame is playing USC for the whole store."

114. BOBBY TAYLOR, CB
6'3", 201, Longview, Texas, 1992–1994

Named the 1994 Defensive Back of the Year by the Columbus (Ohio) Touchdown Club, Bobby Taylor was a consensus All-America pick for the 1994 season, earning accolades from the American Football Coaches Association, United Press International, Walter Camp Foundation, *College and Pro Football Newsweekly*, *Sporting News*, and *Football News*. He started 28 games over his three-year career, moving into the free safety position as a freshman. Taylor had five career interceptions, returning one for a touchdown against Navy. He became a second-round draft choice of the Philadelphia Eagles in 1995 and the 50th pick overall.

115. RON POWLUS, QB
6'2", 223, Berwick, Pennsylvania, 1994–97

A four-year starter at quarterback for the Irish from 1994 to 1997, Ron Powlus was a two-time captain who set 20 school records at Notre Dame. He started all 44 regular season games (plus two bowl games) in which he played and completed 558 of 969 passes for 7,602 yards and 52 TDs. Among records he set included the Irish single-game mark for TD passes in a game with four (three times), and at one point he completed 14 straight passes. He set single-season records in 1997 with 182 completions and 298 pass attempts. Powlus' college career was bothered by a broken collarbone suffered in preseason 1993 and a broken bone in his left upper arm late in the 1995 season. He appeared on the cover of *Sports Illustrated* late in the 1997 season.

Powlus originally signed as a free agent in 1998 with the Tennessee Oilers and then was on the Detroit Lions' preseason roster in 1999 and the Philadelphia Eagles' roster in 2000. Powlus played with the NFL Europe Amsterdam Admirals in the spring of 2000. In 1992 he was hailed by *Parade* as the prep player of the year and by *USA Today* as the offensive player of the year. Powlus returned to Notre Dame in 2005 as the team's director of personnel development, then became the Irish quarterbacks coach through the 2009 season. He spent two seasons as quarterbacks coach at Akron and in 2012 began his first year as quarterbacks coach at Kansas.

116. BOB DAVIE
Head Coach, 1997–2001 (35–25, .583)

Bob Davie came to Notre Dame in 1994 from Texas A&M as Lou Holtz's defensive coordinator and three years later succeeded Holtz as Irish head coach beginning with the 1997 season. Davie's very first defense in 1997 allowed the fewest total yards of any Irish defense in 17 years—and he took the Irish to three postseason bowls. He twice was a finalist for *Football News* coach of the year, and all five of his Notre Dame teams spent time in the national polls, most notably in 2000 when Notre Dame finished the regular season ranked 10th. His Irish team of 2000 went 9–2, including an overtime loss to top-ranked Nebraska, and Notre Dame played in the 2001 Fiesta Bowl in its first-ever Bowl Championship Series appearance. That Irish team tied a 34-year-old NCAA record by finishing the season with only eight turnovers. Davie served 10 years as an ESPN college football analyst from 2002 to 2011. The 2012 season marks his first as head coach at the University of New Mexico.

117. SHANE WALTON, CB
5′11″, 185, San Diego, California, 1999–2002

A four-year monogram-winner, Shane Walton was a 2002 unanimous All-American, becoming the first Irish player to earn that distinction since cornerback Bobby Taylor in 1994. Walton had an incredible senior year for the Irish, who finished with a 10–3 record. He finished the year fifth on the team with 68 tackles, including 46 solos. He recorded seven interceptions, returning two for touchdowns, and seven pass breakups. He was named one of five finalists for the Bronko Nagurski National Defensive Player of the Year Award, becoming the first Notre Dame player ever nominated for the award. He also was voted the Irish team MVP and one of four team captains for the 2002 season. Walton set a Notre Dame record with three interceptions in the 2002 opener against Maryland. He also played soccer at Notre Dame as a freshman in 1999, earning second-team All–Big East honors and leading the team in scoring with 10 goals and seven assists. A fifth-round selection in the NFL Draft by the St. Louis Rams, he played with St. Louis in 2003 and Pittsburgh in 2004.

118. TYRONE WILLINGHAM
Head Coach, 2002–2004 (21–15, .583)

In his inaugural season with the Irish in 2002, Tyrone Willingham wasted no time reversing the tide of the Irish program, leading Notre Dame to a 10–2 regular season record and a trip to the 2003 Gator Bowl. In the process, Willingham became the first coach in Notre Dame history to win 10 games in his initial campaign. He was recognized for his efforts when he was named the ESPN/Home Depot College Coach of the Year, the Scripps College Coach of the Year, the Black Coaches Association Male Coach of the Year, and the George Munger Award College Coach of the Year by the Maxwell Football Club. Willingham also made history when he became the first college football coach to earn the *Sporting News* Sportsman of the Year award in 2002. The Irish coach that same year was named the sixth most influential minority in sports by *Sports Illustrated.*

Willingham's first Irish squad won its first eight games in 2002, including defeating ranked opponents Maryland, Michigan, Air Force, and Florida State. Notre Dame's four wins over ranked opponents tied the Irish for the most victories over top 25 teams in the nation (along with Miami) during the regular season. Notre Dame also achieved its first top 10 ranking since 1999, topping out at No. 4 after the Florida State game. In 2003 the Irish featured Julius Jones (who set the Irish single-game rushing record with 262 yards versus Pittsburgh and finished the season with 1,268 yards), defensive end Justin Tuck (who set the Notre Dame single-season record for quarterback sacks with 13.5), and rookie quarterback Brady Quinn (who set Irish freshman records for passing yards, completions, and attempts). In 2004 Willingham led the Irish to a 6–5 regular season record and a berth in the Insight Bowl. The Irish knocked off No. 8 Michigan and also beat No. 9 Tennessee in Knoxville. Willingham came to Notre Dame after seven seasons as head coach at Stanford and also spent four years as head coach at Washington (2005–2008).

119. JEFF SAMARDZIJA, WR
6′5″, 220, Valparaiso, Indiana, 2003–2006

Jeff Samardzija was named to the 2006 NCAA consensus All-America team after leading Notre Dame for the second-straight

By the time he graduated from Notre Dame, Jeff Samardzija had caught more passes than any player in Irish history. *Photo courtesy of Mike Bennett/Lighthouse Imaging*

season in receptions (78) and yards (1,017) and adding 12 touchdown catches. He became the first Irish player to post multiple seasons of at least 1,000 yards receiving and was one of three finalists for the Biletnikoff Award, given annually to the top college football receiver. He left Notre Dame the school's all-time leader in receptions (179), receiving yards (2,593), and touchdown receptions (27). His junior campaign total from 2005 featured 77 catches for 1,249 yards and 15 TDs. Samardzija's 2005 yardage total made him the first Irish receiver to gain 1,000 yards in a season since Tom Gatewood in 1970. He had nine career 100-yard receiving games, became the first Irish player (in 2005) to catch TD passes in eight straight games—and became part of a lethal passing duo with quarterback Brady Quinn.

Samardzija doubled as a standout pitcher for the Notre Dame baseball squad, and in January 2007 he signed a five-year deal with the Chicago Cubs. Heading into the 2012 season, Samardzija had made 128 appearances with the Cubs (five starts) and owned a 12–9 record and 4.40 ERA. In 2011 he pitched in 75 games and finished 8–4 with a 2.97 ERA.

120. BRADY QUINN, QB
6'4", 231, Dublin, Ohio, 2003–2006

Brady Quinn left Notre Dame as the most productive quarterback in Notre Dame football history. He broke 36 school records and when he graduated ranked in the top 10 in the NCAA records book in career passing yards (11,762), passing touchdowns (95), and pass attempts (1,602), and ranked 11th in career pass completions (929). Quinn was a two-time captain and won 29 games as a starting quarterback, tying him for first at Notre Dame with Tom Clements and Ron Powlus. He won the Johnny Unitas Award and the Maxwell Award in 2006 and finished third in the Heisman Trophy voting.

Quinn proved particularly impressive as a junior in 2005 (a single-season record 292-of-450 for a record 3,919 yards and 32 TDs) and a senior in 2006 (289 of a single-season record 467 for 3,426 yards and a record 37 TDs) in leading Notre Dame to consecutive Bowl Championship Series games. He threw for a career-high 487 yards against Michigan State in 2005—and completed a record-tying 14 straight passes in the 2006 Fiesta Bowl against Ohio State. He also threw for a single-game record six TDs against

BYU in 2005. Quinn holds the Notre Dame record by completing a pass in 49 straight career games. He was a first-round selection (22nd overall) in the 2007 NFL Draft by Cleveland, played three seasons with the Browns, two in Denver, and signed with Kansas City prior to the 2012 season.

121. CHARLIE WEIS
Head Coach, 2005–2009 (35–27, .565)

Charlie Weis, a 1978 Notre Dame graduate and owner of four Super Bowl–champion rings as products of a stellar 15-season career as a National Football League assistant coach, wasted no time putting his signature stamp on his alma mater's program in his first two years as Irish head coach in 2005 and 2006. Weis and his Irish followed up a 9–3 record in 2005 and BCS appearance in the Tostitos Fiesta Bowl with a 10–3 overall mark in 2006 and a second consecutive BCS invitation, this time to the All-State Sugar Bowl. That marked the most prominent two-season bowl qualification since the Irish played in the Fiesta and Orange Bowls after the 1994 and 1995 campaigns. Weis' 19 combined wins in his first two seasons were the most by a Notre Dame head football coach in his first two years (the previous high was 17 by both Terry Brennan in 1954–1955 and Dan Devine in 1975–1976).

For the second straight season in 2006, Weis was one of three finalists for the George Munger Award presented by the Maxwell Football Club (of Philadelphia) to the college coach of the year. Notre Dame scored more points in 2005 (440) than in any previous season in school history. Notre Dame finished ninth in the final Associated Press poll for 2005 (its first AP top 10 finish since the Irish were runners-up following the 1993 season), 11th according to *USA Today*. The Irish ended the 2006 season rated 17th by AP and 19th by *USA Today*. His team's 2005 success

Charlie Weis took his 2005 and 2006 teams to Bowl Championship Series appearances in Tempe and New Orleans, respectively. *Photo courtesy of Mike Bennett/Lighthouse Imaging*

helped make Weis winner of the 2005 Eddie Robinson Coach of the Year Award, as national college coach of the year as selected by the Football Writers Association of America. Weis saw his Irish offense flourish right out of the gate in 2005—as Notre Dame set a school record by scoring at least 30 points in all but two outings. After leaving Notre Dame, Weis spent a year as the Kansas City Chiefs' offensive coordinator, a year as the offensive coordinator at Florida, then in 2012 became the head coach at Kansas.

122. GOLDEN TATE, WR
5′11″, 195, Hendersonville, TN, 2007–2009

A former running back, Golden Tate exploded onto the Notre Dame scene as a sophomore and junior, becoming one of the most electrifying players to ever wear a Notre Dame uniform. He finished his college career first in Irish history with 2,707 career receiving yards, ranked second in career touchdown receptions with 26, and was tied for third with 157 career receptions. Tate also owned the school record with 15 games of at least 100 receiving yards and ranked in the top 10 at Notre Dame in career all-purpose yards (4,130 yards, sixth in school history), total career kick/punt-return yards (1,196 yards, seventh), and kickoff-return yards in a career (909 yards, eighth).

In 2009 Tate became Notre Dame's first Biletnikoff Award recipient, presented annually to college football's top wide receiver. He was named Notre Dame's 31st unanimous All-American after recording the best receiving season in Fighting Irish history with 93 receptions for 1,496 yards, and 15 receiving TDs. He set single-season school records for receptions, receiving yards, most games with at least 100 receiving yards (nine), highest receiving yards–per-game average (124.7), consecutive games with a TD receptions (eight), and tied the Notre Dame record for receiving TDs in a season. Tate was selected with the 60th overall pick by the Seattle Seahawks in the second round of the 2010 NFL Draft. He also played baseball at Notre Dame in 2008 and 2009, hitting .329 in 55 games in 2009. He was picked in the 50th round of the 2010 MLB Draft by San Francisco.

123. JIMMY CLAUSEN, QB
6'3", 223, Westlake Village, California, 2007–2009

Jimmy Clausen completed 68 percent of his passes in 2009 for 3,722 yards with 28 touchdowns. He ranked second nationally in passing efficiency (161.42), third in total passing yards (3,722), and tied for third in fewest interceptions (four). Clausen's 3,722 yards ranked as the second most in a season in Notre Dame history, and his 28 TDs were third best. He eclipsed 300 yards passing seven times in 2009—a single-season school record. He led Notre Dame to a school record four fourth-quarter comebacks in 2009. Clausen completed 62.1 percent of his passes (77-of-124) for 1,045 yards and 11 touchdowns while rushing for two other scores in fourth quarters in 2009. When tied or trailing in 2009, Clausen accounted for 20 TDs (18 passing TDs, two rushing TDs) and only three turnovers. After passing up his final season of eligibility, Clausen in three seasons of play ended up second behind Brady Quinn on Notre Dame's career lists for attempts (1,110), completions (695), passing yards (8,148), and TD passes (60). He set the Irish single-game record with 37 completions against Navy in 2009 (for a career-high 452 yards)—and he remains Notre Dame's career leader in completion percentage (.626) and single-season leader in passing efficiency rating (161.4 in 2009) and completion percentage (.680 in 2009). The Carolina Panthers made him a second-round pick in the 2010 NFL Draft.

124. MICHAEL FLOYD, WR
6′3″, 224, St. Paul, Minnesota, 2008–2011

In 2011 Michael Floyd set a Notre Dame single-season record with 100 receptions and led the Irish with a career-high 1,147 receiving yards and nine touchdown catches. His 179 receptions over his last two seasons (2010–2011) are the most by any Notre Dame player in consecutive seasons—and Floyd became just the second Irish player to record two seasons with at least 60 receptions. Owner of five career school records, Floyd left Notre Dame as the most prolific wide receiver in school history. He registered the most career receptions (271), receiving yards (3,686), touchdown receptions (37), receiving yards–per-game average, and 100-yard receiving games (17) as a four-year starter. His junior year in

2010 featured 79 receptions for 1,025 yards and 12 TDs. Floyd caught a career-high 13 passes against Michigan in 2011—and recorded a career-best 189 receiving yards (four catches) against Nevada in 2009.

125. BRIAN KELLY
Head Coach, 2010–present (16–10, .615)

Brian Kelly led the Fighting Irish to bowl games in each of his first two seasons as head coach (2010 and 2011) and became the first head coach in Notre Dame history to guide the Irish to a bowl game victory in his first season. Under Kelly, the Irish won 16 games over two years, equal to the combined number of victories Notre Dame earned in the three seasons prior to Kelly's arrival. His Irish came on strong to finish the 2010 season with four straight wins, including a victory over 15th-rated Utah, a win at USC, and a convincing Sun Bowl triumph over Miami.

Prior to being named head coach at Notre Dame in 2009, Kelly was the architect of two consecutive Bowl Championship Series appearances at the University of Cincinnati, including a perfect 12–0 regular season in 2009 that earned him national coach of the year honors. Kelly currently is the fifth-winningest active coach in the NCAA Football Bowl Subdivision, with 187 victories. Since 2001, only two active FBS head coaches have registered more wins than the 110 victories Kelly's teams have recorded. Kelly's honors include Big East Conference Coach of the Year in 2007, 2008, and 2009. He previously coached at Central Michigan for three years (19–16 from 2004 to 2006) and at Grand Valley State (1991–2003) where he won NCAA Division II championships in 2002 and 2003.

•   •   •

Even as Notre Dame celebrates 125 years of football in 2012, detailing the exploits of 125 people connected with the Irish program doesn't do it justice. It ignores the contributions of dozens more Irish standouts to the Notre Dame heritage—so stay tuned to see who earns their way onto the chart next.

chapter 9

THOSE IRISH CHAMPIONSHIP SEASONS

YOU CAN ARGUE FOREVER about national championships, especially since the Associated Press media poll didn't begin until 1936—and, even then, it wasn't until 1968 that the AP first waited until after the bowl games to issue its final poll (it expanded to 25 teams in 1989). The United Press International poll of coaches (replaced in 1991 by the ESPN/*USA Today*/CNN version) began in 1950 (it began with a final poll after the bowls in 1974). That left plenty of seasons without the AP and UPI versions—so you need to be conversant with the other selectors to make sense of the national title races.

Notre Dame lists 11 consensus national titles—and you can make decent arguments for a handful of other seasons that qualified as near-misses and/or featured at least some mention from one or more of those polls. Check these out:

1924

The 1924 Notre Dame football team will always be known best for *New York Herald-Tribune* sportswriter Grantland Rice's account of the Notre Dame vs. Army game played October 18 at the Polo Grounds in New York:

Outlined against a blue-gray October sky, the Four Horsemen rode again.

In dramatic lore they are known as famine, pestilence, destruction, and death. These are only aliases. Their real names are Stuhldreher, Miller, Crowley, and Layden. They formed the crest of the South Bend cyclone before which another fighting Army team was swept over the precipice at the Polo Grounds this afternoon as 55,000 spectators peered down on the bewildering panorama spread out on the green plain below.

Quarterback Harry Stuhldreher, fullback Elmer Layden, and halfbacks Jim Crowley and Don Miller were the cornerstone of a team considered one of the best in college football history.

The Fighting Irish won the Army game 13–7, as the Four Horsemen played magnificently.

Miller rushed for 148 yards, Crowley for 102, and Layden for 60, while Stuhldreher orchestrated the offense masterfully from the quarterback position. It was the third victory of the season for the Irish, it came against a foe considered the toughest on the schedule, and it spurred the Irish on to a perfect 10–0 season and the school's first recognized national championship.

Rice's account led to near-mythic status for the Irish backfield, but the Seven Mules, who did the blocking, and the Shock Troops, who were perhaps the best second string in the game, played indispensible roles, too. Each week in 1924, seventh-year Notre Dame coach Knute Rockne started his second-stringers, his Shock Troops.

When Rockne felt his Shock Troops had done their job, he brought in the Four Horsemen and the Seven Mules, a group so good "that the Holy Ghost couldn't have broken into that lineup," said Harry O'Boyle, a kicker and reserve halfback on the Shock Troops. Center Adam Walsh was the heart of the Seven Mules, a unit that also included ends Ed Hunsinger and Chuck Collins, tackles Rip Miller and Joe Bach, and guards Noble Kizer and John Wiebel. Walsh clinched the win over Army with a late interception—which he made with two broken hands.

The combination of the Shock Troops, the Seven Mules, and the Four Horsemen worked 10 times in 10 tries in 1924 against a national schedule that took the Irish to New York; Princeton, New Jersey; Madison, Wisconsin; Chicago; and Pittsburgh during the regular season while giving them only four home games. In addition, at the end of the season, Rockne was able to convince the university administration to permit the football team to travel to California to play Stanford in the Rose Bowl, where the Irish clinched the Helms Athletic Foundation's national championship with a 27–10 victory.

In the Rose Bowl—Notre Dame's only bowl appearance until the team began making regular bowl trips with the 1970 Cotton Bowl—the Irish were faced with stopping an undefeated, once-tied Stanford team that included legendary coach Pop Warner and quarterback Ernie Nevers. Rockne was concerned his players might not be ready physically for the heat of the West Coast, so he arranged for a slow, cross-country train trip that included stops in Louisiana, Texas and Arizona so players would have time to adjust to warmer, more demanding weather.

It worked, as Elmer Layden scored Notre Dame's first touchdown on a three-yard run and returned interceptions of Nevers' passes 78 and 70 yards for two more touchdowns. The Irish took advantage of eight Stanford turnovers and made a critical goal-line stand in the fourth quarter to come up with the 17-point win.

"That would always be my favorite team," Rockne once said. "I think I sensed that the backfield was a product of destiny. At times they caused me a certain amount of pain and exasperation, but mainly they brought me great joy."

1929

If the Great Depression wasn't reason enough for Notre Dame football partisans to be a little down, then the fact the Irish were without a home for the 1929 season was surely enough to bring some anxiety into the minds of both the team and its followers. Plans were underway at Notre Dame for a new stadium to be built, and 1929 was the transition year in which the Irish had no home facility.

That didn't keep Notre Dame from winning, however, something the team had accomplished only five times in nine tries in 1928. Knute Rockne had promised to return Notre Dame football in 1929 to what had become its customary level of excellence, homefield advantage or not. He would not be stopped from fulfilling that promise.

The closest the Irish came to having a home game in 1929 were three games contested at Soldier Field in Chicago. The Irish defeated Wisconsin there 19–0 on October 19, then Drake 19–7 on November 9, and finally USC in the most important game of the year, 13–12 before 112,912 fans on November 16.

The lack of home turf was not the only major difficulty of the 1929 season for Notre Dame. The team's legendary coach was in a battle with phlebitis, which doctors said stood a 50-50 chance of taking Rockne's life if he tried to coach that season. But coach the team he did, through one dramatic victory after another, either by telephone from a hospital bed or from a wheelchair on the sideline.

An announcement was made that he would not accompany the team on its trip to Baltimore to face Navy. Line coach Tom Lieb took over for Rockne that day, as the Irish won 14–7. But back in South Bend, doctor's orders couldn't keep Rock away from practice at Cartier Field, where he set up his command post in his car and used a loudspeaker to direct activities.

By the time the USC contest rolled around, the Irish were 6–0 and recognized as one of the top teams in the nation. Running back Joe Savoldi had earned acclaim in the Wisconsin game with dazzling touchdown runs of 71 and 40 yards, and he provided the only score of the game in Notre Dame's 7–0 win at Carnegie Tech on October 26.

When the Irish faced USC at Soldier Field, Rockne's status was as bad as ever, but the team needed him. The Notre Dame–USC tradition was already a great one, and the first half foretold the kind of game everyone expected, with the teams battling to a 6–6 tie.

In the locker room, the Fighting Irish were in desperate need of one of Rock's famous speeches, but he was nowhere to be found. So former Irish running back Paul Castner stepped up to do what he could, and in the middle of his oration, who should two Irish managers wheel into the room but Rockne himself. He was in great pain and had undergone quite a strain—not only from making the trip to Chicago but also from watching his team struggle in the first half.

He gave an impassioned speech with what strength he had, during which a blood clot in one leg broke loose, passed through his heart and settled safely in the other leg. His speech worked, as the Irish escaped Chicago with a 13–12 win and an unblemished 7–0 record.

The Irish still had traditional foes Northwestern and Army left. Northwestern fell relatively easy, as the Irish posted a win on the Wildcats' home field. But the November 30 matchup with Army at Yankee Stadium proved to be a real battle.

The game was played on turf that was frozen solid, and neither team was able to accomplish anything. It was 8 degrees at game time and a biting wind cut across the field as the players dashed out for the opening kickoff.

The first quarter was scoreless, but in the second period Army drove deep into Irish territory. When Red Cagle lofted a pass for end Carl Carlmark, it looked like a certain score for the Cadets. But Notre Dame's Jack Elder came out of nowhere to snatch the ball away. He took it 93 yards for the game's only touchdown. The extra point was added to make it 7–0 Irish, and that's the way it stayed. Notre Dame ended up 9–0 and the season was over. The team had survived without a home, Rockne had survived his illness, and Notre Dame had its second consensus national championship.

1930

Brand new stadium, same old result—another national championship for the Notre Dame football team.

The 1930 football season marked the opening of Notre Dame Stadium, just another in the long line of Knute Rockne masterpieces, only this was a football stadium instead of a team. With typical meticulosity, he had supervised every minute detail of the construction of the stadium.

In addition, Rockne had for the first time a full-time equipment manager, a trainer, a doctor who traveled with the team, a business manager, several secretaries, and a staff to handle the complex sale and distribution of tickets. On top of all that, Rockne was healthy again. The doctors at the Mayo Clinic had given him a thorough going-over from head to foot during the off-season and a clean bill of health. All the Rock had to do was coach, and what a job he did.

On October 4, 1930, the Fighting Irish opened their season in the imposing new stadium—an impressive amphitheatre of sandy-colored brick trimmed with limestone. Rockne had the original sod from Cartier Field transplanted just for good measure.

The Irish christened the good earth with a 20–14 win over Southern Methodist. The stadium was officially dedicated the following week, as Notre Dame trounced Navy 26–2. In the third week of the season, Notre Dame played its third straight home game, defeating Carnegie Tech 21–6 to cap off a successful first homestand.

Preseason national prognosticators considered the 1930 Notre Dame team to be Rockne's strongest yet. Rockne had said as much himself prior to the start of the season, and he had good reason for such high expectations. Frank Carideo, Marchy Schwartz, Marty Brill, and Joe Savoldi made up a latter-day version of the Four Horsemen in the backfield, and all of them earned All-America status on one team or another for that season.

The Fighting Irish not only were stocked with an explosive collection of running backs, but the team also sported a tremendous crew of linemen. Center Tommy Yarr, guards Nordy Hoffman and Brent Metzger, tackles Joe Kurth and Al Culver, and end Tom Conley all made All-America teams either that season or the following one.

The Irish left home three times in the fourth through eighth weeks of the season but continued to roll. Notre Dame traveled to Pitt and beat the Panthers 35–19. A 27–0 romp over Indiana followed before the Irish visited a 60–20 walloping on Pennsylvania. Marty Brill, who had transferred to Notre Dame from Penn, played the greatest game of his career that day, breaking loose for three touchdowns on runs of 45, 52, and 65 yards.

The Notre Dame winning streak stood at 15 games over two seasons, and it quickly grew to 17 as the Irish sprinted past Drake and Northwestern. All that remained between Notre Dame and another national title were games against Army and USC.

On a November 29 afternoon that saw rain and sleet turn Soldier Field into a swamp, the Cadets and the Irish squared off, and it appeared that neither team was going to budge. Near the end of the game, however, Schwartz broke loose for a 54-yard scoring run. The all-important extra point gave the Irish a 7–0 lead. Army scored quickly thereafter, though, on a blocked punt, and it appeared that things would be knotted up. But Notre Dame blocked the extra point, and that's the way it ended.

To finish off the season, Rockne used all his psychological expertise in a ploy that helped the Irish get ready for USC. Injuries during the season left the team with only one healthy fullback, Dan Hanley. So Rock decided to turn Bucky O'Connor, a second-team halfback, into a first-string fullback. However, in practice, Rock had O'Connor and Hanley trade jerseys, and not a single soul suspected anything unusual.

When the game got underway, Notre Dame had one of the speediest fullbacks the Trojans defense had ever seen. O'Connor scored two touchdowns, including one on an 80-yard dash, and the Irish dominated the favored home team to the tune of 27–0.

It was a fitting script to what turned out to be Rockne's final game as the Notre Dame head football coach.

The team won its second consecutive national championship, and that winter Rockne died in a plane crash in Kansas.

1943

At the beginning of the 1943 season many experts called Notre Dame's schedule its most difficult in school history. The Irish faced seven teams that year that were ranked among the nation's top 13 teams in that season's final Associated Press poll.

Frank Leahy's squad only had two returning starters from the 1942 squad that finished 7–2–2. To make matters worse, seven of the 10 games in 1943 were on the road.

The Irish were still in the early stages of adjusting to the T formation, which Leahy installed the season before, moving away from the traditional Notre Dame "Box Formation." The new offense enabled the 1943 team to score 340 points, 156 more than the season before. The T formation also led to the emergence of Angelo Bertelli, who moved from tailback to quarterback to lead the Irish offense. Bertelli directed the Irish to a 6–0 start as the team outscored its opponents 261–31. Included in that stretch were key victories over second-ranked Michigan and third-ranked Navy.

A record crowd of 85,688 witnessed the 35–12 Irish win in Ann Arbor. Bertelli was brilliant, completing five of eight passes for two touchdowns, while All-America running back Creighton Miller averaged 16 yards per play against Michigan.

The Irish were led by Bertelli and All-America tackle Jim White, both of whom finished in the top 10 in the Heisman balloting that year. The team rolled to a 50–0 victory over Wisconsin and a 47–0 bashing of Illinois following the win over Michigan, extending their record to 5–0.

Those wins were followed by a colossal matchup between top-ranked Notre Dame and third-ranked Navy in Cleveland. The Irish cruised to a 33–6 win but lost their quarterback. The Marine Corps called Bertelli into service with four games left in the season. Leahy called on a sophomore to be Bertelli's replacement in the following week's game against Army, then the third-ranked team in the country.

All Bertelli's replacement did was throw for two touchdowns, run for another, and intercept a pass to lead the Irish to a 26–0 win. A new star was born—the incomparable John Lujack.

With Lujack calling the signals, the Irish defeated a pair of top 10 teams in the following two weeks, Northwestern and Iowa Pre-Flight.

All that stood between Leahy's first undefeated and untied season was Great Lakes, a team the Irish had tied in their two previous meetings during the 1918 and 1942 seasons. Notre Dame scored first but trailed 12–7 late in the fourth quarter. Miller capped off an 80-yard drive with a touchdown to put the Irish ahead 14–12 with 1:05 to play.

With 33 seconds remaining, Great Lakes quarterback Steve Lac connected on a 46-yard pass to Paul Anderson, who fielded the ball at the 6-yard line and then went into the end zone for the game-winning score, ruining Notre Dame's perfect season.

After the game, Leahy told his team, "You're still champions to me, boys. You fought your hearts out every inch of the way in the greatest drive I've ever seen. Nobody is to blame for that last Great Lakes touchdown. It was just a fine play, splendidly executed."

Despite the season-ending loss, Notre Dame picked up several awards that would become commonplace for the school. The Irish were crowned national champions by the Associated Press for the first time ever, and Bertelli became the first Notre Dame player to win the Heisman Trophy. Bertelli easily outdistanced Bob O'Dell of Pennsylvania and Otto Graham of Northwestern for the Heisman.

Irish in Their Own Words

John Lujack

Our opening game in 1943 was in Pittsburgh, and Coach Leahy decided to start me at quarterback ahead of Bertelli. When Leahy explained to Bertelli that I would be playing before my folks from Connellsville, Angelo agreed. To hear him explain it later, he said he told Leahy that if he didn't want to win the game, he should go ahead and start Lujack. I don't think he was too happy about it.

I did start, but Bertelli came in and played most of the game, and we won easily [41–0]. Halfback Creighton Miller, who became my best friend and was a great running back, liked to tell a story of how I turned the wrong way and missed the handoff to him. It actually happened twice.

We were having a good season in 1943. We won the first two games and then went to Michigan for the big game of the season. Creighton had just a fantastic game, and we won easily [35–12]. After that loss, Michigan wouldn't play us for 35 seasons.

We had won six straight and were ranked No. 1 in the nation. But after we beat Navy [33–6], the Marines called Bertelli to active duty, and I was going to get my first real action against Army. I had a pretty good day, passing for two touchdowns and running for another, and we won [26–0]. Two games later, we nipped No. 2 Iowa Preflight 14–13 on Fred Earley's extra points. But the next week at Great Lakes, the Sailors came from behind on a long pass play to beat us [19–14]. Despite that loss, we were still picked as national champs.

That would be my last Notre Dame game for a long while. The Navy sent me to Asbury Park, New Jersey, and then Columbia, where I graduated from midshipman's school and became an ensign. They sent me to the Pacific where I was aboard a 110-foot, wooden sub chaser.

1946

World War II had finally ended, and the United States was ready to think about something more pleasant than international conflict for a change—like Notre Dame football. The year was 1946, the coach was hard-driving Frank Leahy, and it was the beginning of a dynasty for Notre Dame football.

In 1943 Leahy had guided the Fighting Irish to their first wire-service national championship, and fourth overall, behind Heisman Trophy winner Angelo Bertelli and future Heisman winner

John Lujack. World War II took many football players from college, including Bertelli in the middle of his Heisman campaign in 1943, but many returned to the gridiron after the war ended, including Lujack, who would go on to win the Heisman in 1947.

For the players who returned to Notre Dame in 1946, losing a college football game was not to be one of their postwar experiences. From 1946 to 1949, Notre Dame went 36–0–2 and won three national championships in one of the most successful four-year periods in college football history.

The 1946 season started it all.

Halfback Terry Brennan and linemen Bill Walsh, Bill Fischer, and John Mastrangelo were among the group of returnees from the previous season. There were several new faces who came to Notre Dame after Navy hitches had interrupted their respective careers at Holy Cross and Texas A&M. There were also players for whom the war had postponed college football, like end Jim Martin and running back Emil (Red) Sitko, and there were freshmen like Leon Hart. Returning to Notre Dame along with Lujack were veterans such as tackle Zygmont (Ziggy) Czarobski, end Jack Zilly, and fullback Jim Mello. Even Leahy was coming back to Notre Dame after a couple years in the service.

Leahy was a perfectionist and strict disciplinarian, and enduring his practices wasn't much more fun than being a soldier. But it sure produced results. The Irish usually had two separate platoons ready for each game, and often the first string didn't play much more than half the game.

On the football field, the Irish had strength in numbers, and Leahy fought a war of attrition. The season began with the Irish routing their first five opponents—Illinois, which went on to win the Western (now Big Ten) Conference championship, Pittsburgh, Purdue, Iowa, and Navy, before facing top-ranked Army. Coached by the great Earl (Red) Blaik and featuring Doc Blanchard and Glenn Davis in the backfield, Army had won two straight national championships and 25 consecutive games, including two defeats of Notre Dame in the previous two seasons by a combined score of 107–0.

The showdown was set for November 9 in Yankee Stadium, where 74,121 fans turned out to see a 0–0 tie. Notre Dame advanced to the Army 4-yard line in the second quarter for the game's deepest scoring threat, but the Cadets held on downs. Blanchard broke into the clear once and appeared to be headed for a score, but an open-field tackle by Lujack saved the Irish from defeat.

Army retained its top ranking in the Associated Press poll after the game. But the Irish walloped their final three opponents by a combined score of 94–6 and were named national champions in the final poll of the season.

When the smoke cleared, the Irish found themselves the nation's statistical leaders in total offense (441.3 yards per game), rushing offense (340.1 yards per game), total defense (141.7 yards per game), and scoring defense (2.7 points per game), and had allowed only Illinois, Purdue, Iowa, and USC to score points against them.

For the season, Notre Dame outscored its opponents 271–24 in nine games.

Irish in Their Own Words

BOB LIVINGSTONE

There was great competition on the Notre Dame team in 1946. Young guys like Terry Brennan, Ernie Zalejski, and Coy McGee were battling the older players like [Gerry] Cowhig and me. And, of course, we had John Lujack back. He had been a freshman in 1942, and I knew he would be good. He finished out the 1943 season after Bertelli was called into service.

We had a good season in 1946 [8–0–1]. The 0–0 tie against Army rankled us, but we did finish as national champions again.

Irish in Their Own Words

JOHN LUJACK

[Notre Dame] had assembled a great squad in the spring of 1946. We had former Irish players from as far back as 1941, and Leahy had persuaded some veterans to transfer to Notre Dame. That meant we had players like George Connor, who had been an All-American at Holy Cross, and George Strohmeyer from Texas A&M.

After that 0–0 tie [against Army], we went undefeated and were No. 1 ahead of the Cadets and Michigan. With most of our players coming back, we were favored to repeat as national champions in 1947.

Irish in Their Own Words

BILL FISCHER

In 1946 the veterans were back at Notre Dame, and I got a chance to play for Coach Leahy. He was tough and he was demanding, and I'm sure some wondered whether all those freshmen that played in 1945 would be able to compete with those guys coming back from the war. But several of us were able to make a contribution.

I lined up at left guard next to the great George Connor, a fellow Chicagoan [who had transferred from Holy Cross]. We also had Terry Brennan and John Mastrangelo from the 1945 team, and some veterans who were freshmen, like Jim Martin and Emil Sitko.

Of course, during those years, Navy and Army were powerhouses. In 1945, with all those freshmen playing, we tied Navy [6–6] and were a foot away from the winning touchdown when the game ended. I remember Rip Miller, a Navy assistant athletics director and former Notre Dame player, saying, "Those little freshies from Notre Dame were tough!"

Irish in Their Own Words

JOHN PANELLI

On good college teams there always is a lot of camaraderie and kidding. We were playing Iowa [in 1946], and the line opened a hole big enough for an elephant to run through. When Lujack went to give me the handoff, he dropped the ball but picked it up and ran behind me for an easy touchdown. I used to razz him about taking a touchdown away from me.

1947

In any discussion of college football's greatest teams, one team that always comes to mind is the 1947 Notre Dame squad. The Irish never trailed in any game that year and compiled a 9–0 record, their first unblemished mark in 17 years.

Notre Dame held its opponents to under six points a game while averaging over 32 points. Only one team—Northwestern—scored more than one touchdown against the Irish that year. But maybe the most impressive note about the squad is that it sent 42 players on to professional football.

The mainstays on that team included consensus All-Americans George Connor, Bill Fischer, and John Lujack, who won the Heisman Trophy that year. The team also included future Heisman winner Leon Hart and the man who later succeeded Leahy as head coach of the Irish, Terry Brennan.

The Irish began the season with six turnovers against Pittsburgh, but Lujack scored three times to lead Notre Dame to an easy 40–6 win. Leahy's squad stumbled a little bit in the next game, too, but came out ahead of Purdue 22–7.

Notre Dame then exploded for three consecutive shutouts over Nebraska (31–0), Iowa (21–0), and Navy (27–0). The win over the Cornhuskers avenged a 17–0 loss that Knute Rockne's 1925 squad suffered to Nebraska the last time the two schools had met.

Following three impressive shutouts, the Irish faced Army, a team that had become such a fierce rival in previous years that the series was discontinued for 10 years after the 1947 game. The two teams had battled to a 0–0 tie in 1946 in one of the most famous games in Notre Dame history.

Notre Dame entered the game as the top-ranked team in the country while Army was rated eighth. The Irish struck first when Brennan broke loose for a 97-yard kickoff return. Notre Dame built a 20–0 lead before Army finally scored. The Irish won 27–7 before a record crowd of 59,171 at Notre Dame Stadium.

The next week was the only close game of the year. Northwestern became the only team in 1947 to come within two touchdowns of the Irish as Notre Dame won 26–19. The Irish ended the season with a 59–6 thrashing of Tulane and an impressive 38–7 win over third-ranked USC.

When the final national polls came out, Notre Dame was No. 1 for the second straight year.

Just how good was this 1947 team?

Well, consider that several of the first-string players that year (such as Brennan) didn't even try out for professional football but opted to coach, instead.

The great 1947 squad also included six players who were elected into the National Football Foundation College Hall of Fame— Lujack, Connor, Hart, Fischer, Sitko, and Ziggy Czarobski. And to top that off, their coach, Frank Leahy, wound up the coach with the second-highest winning percentage in major-college football history just behind his mentor, Knute Rockne.

The *Boston Herald* called the 1947 Irish team, "the greatest Notre Dame squad of all time. Its third string could whip most varsities."

The immortal sportswriter Grantland Rice added after the final game of the season, "There no longer is any doubt as to the best team in college football, it happens to be Notre Dame. College football never before has known a team so big, so fast, and so experienced."

His words may still hold true today.

Irish in Their Own Words

JERRY GROOM

I loved Notre Dame from the start, but the football was pretty tough when you had to live up to the expectations of Frank Leahy. Leahy and his coaches meant business, and the freshmen of 1947 scrimmaged almost daily against the varsity teams that were headed for another national championship.

We even scrimmaged against the No. 1 team on Friday afternoon before the climactic Army game [a 27–7 victory] in 1947.

I guess Leahy thought his top team wasn't ready for Army the next day. Believe me, they were ready, and I had the bruises to prove it. They ran all over us in the scrimmage.

Irish in Their Own Words

JOHN LUJACK

Purdue had a new coach, Stu Holcomb, who had been an Army assistant, and he had a good team ready for our second game after we opened with a [40–6] victory over Pittsburgh. I had one of my best games that day, running for a touchdown and passing for another, and we won [22–7].

Our big game was to be at home against Army. The Cadets decided to end the long series with Notre Dame and would play the final game at Notre Dame. There was almost as much hype for the game as [there had been] a year earlier, but after Terry Brennan ran the opening kickoff back, there wasn't as much fight in the Cadets. We won 27–7, and it could have been a bigger score.

We ended the season with a 9–0 record by walloping Southern California in Los Angeles [38–7] and we were again national champs.

I went to New York for the Heisman Trophy, but it wasn't such a big televised deal as it is today. There was the dinner and the presentation, that's all.

1949

November 15, 1945, ranks as one of the most important dates in Notre Dame football history.

Check the record books, though, and you won't find one of the greatest games in Irish history played on that day.

November 15, 1945, was a Thursday, not a Saturday, and that was the day Lieutenant Frank Leahy was discharged from the Navy. He returned to Notre Dame campus, signed a 10-year contract, and began what was to be one of the most successful four-year runs in college football history.

The 1946 and 1947 seasons brought national championships to Notre Dame. The 9–0–1 1948 team was runner-up to Michigan. But a national championship in 1949 would allow Notre Dame to close the decade in magnificent style.

That's exactly what happened.

Notre Dame went 10–0—which made for a four-year mark of 36–0–2. End Leon Hart won the Heisman Trophy, and Leahy had his fourth championship and the school's seventh. Before the season, however, nobody expected a championship team to emerge from the South Bend campus. The Irish needed somebody to emerge as a leader and attention was focused on Hart, already recognized as the finest end in the college game, along with Emil Sitko, Larry Coutre, and co-captain Jim Martin.

But most observers agreed that the Fighting Irish would need more than that. Soon enough, they got it. In the sixth game of the season, against Michigan State on November 5, quarterback Bob Williams stepped to the fore. He led the top-ranked Irish to a 34–21 victory over the 10th-ranked Spartans in a game at East Lansing that the press thought would knock Notre Dame from its lofty perch atop collegiate football.

Williams continued to shine in subsequent games. He was at his daring best the following week in a game versus North Carolina played at Yankee Stadium. Leahy had given Williams instructions that he was never to pass the football on the fourth-down situation on their own 19-yard line, with the score tied 6–6 in the second quarter.

He couldn't help himself. Knowing that if he failed he'd have to head to the nearest exit to avoid Leahy, the self-assured Williams completed an 18-yard pass to Coutre for an Irish first down. Notre Dame went on to a 42–6 win, and Williams soon became recognized as the nation's best quarterback.

The Irish eased through their final two home games, rolling over Iowa 28–7 and 17th-ranked USC 32–0. All that remained was what was sure to be an easy win over Southern Methodist in Dallas. SMU would be without its top player, 1948 Heisman winner Doak Walker, and the nation had virtually conceded the national championship to Notre Dame.

Notre Dame jumped to an early lead before Mustangs running back Kyle Rote came to life in the steady afternoon drizzle. Running at will, he scored two quick touchdowns, and thanks to a missed extra point by SMU, the score was tied at 20 with seven minutes to go. Notre Dame's back was to the wall for the first time all season, and the offense rose to the occasion.

In blitzkrieg fashion, the Irish simply pushed SMU straight back into its own end zone with 10 determined rushes that covered 54 yards and put Notre Dame up by a touchdown, 27–20. The drive was so quick, however, that SMU still had time to score.

But in the shadow of the Notre Dame goal post, when Rote tried to pass for the tying touchdown, Notre Dame's Jerry Groom made a game-saving interception.

It was the final play of the game and of a dominating decade that saw Frank Leahy lead the Fighting Irish to three national championships in four years.

1966

Coach Ara Parseghian, in his third year at Notre Dame, made a difficult decision at the start of the 1966 season, picking sophomore

Terry Hanratty as his starting quarterback over classmate Coley O'Brien. Yet the decision proved without a doubt to be the correct one, as Hanratty and sophomore split end Jim Seymour turned out to be one of the best passing combinations Notre Dame fans have ever seen.

The two had begun working together during the previous winter, developing their timing, moves, and patterns so they would know each other's habits inside out when the 1966 season began. Seymour was a good bet to take over one of the end positions that was being vacated after the 1965 season, but Hanratty had no such assurances of whether or not he would be the No. 1 quarterback.

Fortunately for Hanratty, Parseghian decided to balance an already steady running game, manned by Nick Eddy, Larry Conjar, and Rocky Bleier, with the passing talent of Hanratty. The decision bore fruit in the first game of the season, as Hanratty and Seymour hooked up 13 times for 276 yards—Notre Dame records for receptions and yards—and three touchdowns, which tied a school record. The Irish defeated Rose Bowl–bound Purdue that day, 26–14 in South Bend.

Notre Dame traveled to Northwestern for the second game of the season and won 35–7. The Irish defense gave up its last points for the next three games and showed the kind of stiffness that ensured Notre Dame would never be out of any contest. Notre Dame returned home for the next two games and defeated Army and North Carolina by a combined score of 67–0, setting the stage for a showdown with 10th-ranked Oklahoma.

Notre Dame traveled to Norman for what was supposed to be anybody's ballgame. The game was billed as a matchup between the small, quick, strong Sooners and the big, slow Irish. Although the Irish lost Seymour to an ankle injury that would cost him two games, the Fighting Irish rolled to a 38–0 victory and their third straight shutout of the young season.

Notre Dame pounded its next three opponents—Navy, Pittsburgh, and Duke, giving up only one score, a touchdown to Navy. Meanwhile, the offense was hitting on all cylinders, racking up 31 points versus the Midshipmen, 40 against Pitt, and a whopping 64 against the Blue Devils.

The game of the century took place on November 19 when No. 1–ranked Notre Dame traveled to East Lansing, Michigan, to play second-ranked Michigan State for all the marbles. Notre Dame fell behind 10–0 in the second quarter, but O'Brien, who had been diagnosed with diabetes only a few weeks earlier and was still adjusting, brought the Irish back to a tie in the second half. The Spartans offense was unable to net a single yard running the ball in the second half, and when Notre Dame intercepted a pass and returned it to the Spartans 18-yard line in the fourth quarter, it looked like Notre Dame's chance to win. But three plays and minus-six yards later left the Irish with a 41-yard field goal attempt, which sailed wide to the right.

Notre Dame had the ball again on its own 30 with 1:24 left in the game. But rather than gamble with passes deep in their own territory, the Irish attempted to run the ball out of danger. The game ended in a 10–10 tie.

The Irish held on to their top ranking and traveled to Los Angeles to play Rose Bowl–bound USC. The Irish tore the Trojans apart, 51–0, posting the team's sixth shutout in 10 games and ensuring another unanimous No. 1 selection for the national championship.

In the recent book *Fifty Years of College Football*, the 1966 Notre Dame squad was rated the ninth-greatest team in college football since 1955.

Irish in Their Own Words

JOE AZZARO

Before the 1966 season started we all knew how good of a team we were going to have. That team was an example of everything coming together. We had a great class and the group behind us was very solid, too. All we lacked was a quarterback. When Terry Hanratty and Coley O'Brien came in and started throwing the ball to Jim Seymour, who was something special, and Curt Heneghan, who was pretty darn good, too, until he got hurt, we were able to get it all together.

We never had any question about whether or not we were going to win; it was just a matter of by how much. I think that was everybody's attitude, and it wasn't that we were cocky; we just had a pretty good team. That defense was so good that I don't know that I've seen one on that level since. And on offense, even though we had the great breakaway passing game, the running backs always seemed to come out on the other side of the pile. They weren't flashy, but they just beat you with Larry Conjar, Rocky Bleier, and Nick Eddy. That group was about as good as it got. There was never any doubt that everyone was going to do his job. Everybody knew how good everybody else was on that team, so you knew people were going to make plays.

Irish in Their Own Words

KEVIN HARDY

By the time 1966 rolled around, I was ready to go. We knew we were going to be really good with my class coming back for its senior year. That defense had a ton of talent, and the offensive line had been there for two years. It's incredible how much talent was on that team. But no one could have expected the effect that [quarterback] Terry Hanratty and [receiver] Jim Seymour would have. We basically had the same team as 1965, but we were able to throw the ball.

We beat some good teams that season and shut out a lot of people. It never surprised me that we blew out USC [51–0] the very next week. The surprise of the season to me was that we didn't score more against Michigan State. With Hanratty and [Nick] Eddy out, there were physical reasons for us not scoring more, but I really believe we should have won that game. And yet we were still the national champions and deserved to be.

Irish in Their Own Words

TERRY HANRATTY

You look at that team, and the offensive line was fantastic, the defense was fabulous, and the running game was great. That 1966 team had everything. Jim [Seymour] and I were just the missing links.

1973

Every college football season seems to have its own game of the century, but the 1973 matchup between Notre Dame and Alabama was special. It came in the Sugar Bowl, and it was to be a dream game.

Two undefeated, highly ranked teams with long and storied gridiron traditions were set to battle for the national championship. The prognosticators' predictions rang true as the Fighting

Irish emerged 24–23 victors over the Crimson Tide of Alabama in a thriller that saw the lead change hands six times.

Bob Thomas, who had missed two earlier attempts in the game, kicked a 19-yard field goal with 4:26 remaining to give the Irish and coach Ara Parseghian the one-point triumph over top-rated Alabama. The win clinched Notre Dame's sixth wire-service national championship and ninth overall as the Irish finished the season with a perfect 11–0 record.

The balanced Irish attack was keyed by four backs who gained more than 300 yards apiece that season: fullback Wayne Bullock (752), halfback Art Best (700), halfback Eric Penick (586), and quarterback Tom Clements (360). It was one of the fastest back-fields Notre Dame had ever assembled, as Penick had 9.5 speed in the 100-yard dash, while Best checked in at 9.7.

The Irish were ranked in the eighth spot in the polls with wins over Rice and Army, setting the stage for what everyone considered to be Notre Dame's first real test of the year, a home battle with sixth-ranked USC.

The Trojans came to town riding a 23-game unbeaten streak, and Notre Dame was full of memories of the previous season's clash, which saw running back Anthony Davis romp for six touchdowns in a 45–23 Trojans win. Squib kicks were the solution to the problem of Davis returning kicks, and a fired up defense held him to just 55 yards on 19 carries.

Quite simply, the day belonged to Notre Dame, as Penick ran for 118 yards, 50 more than the entire USC squad. The Irish pulled off a 23–14 win and jumped to fifth in the polls.

Notre Dame cruised through the remainder of the schedule. Navy was an easy victim, 44–7, and 20th-ranked Pittsburgh played the docile host to the Irish and fell 31–10. The Irish finished off Parseghian's first perfect regular season with a 48–15 win over Air Force and a 44–0 whitewashing of Miami at the Orange Bowl.

The stage was set for the contest between No. 1 Alabama and third-ranked Notre Dame that seemed to deserve every phrase of its high-powered buildup. It marked the first-ever meeting between the Irish and the Crimson Tide—and ESPN college football expert Beano Cook still considers it the best bowl game he's seen. The Irish opened the contest with a superb defensive effort that held the Tide without a yard in the first period, as Notre Dame took a 6–0 lead. Alabama's thoroughbred backs made it out of the starting gate in the second period, however. They produced three long drives that resulted in a pair of touchdowns, the first of which put the Tide up 7–6.

Early in the fourth quarter, the game took a wild turn with three turnovers in 90 seconds. Alabama took charge and put in its own version of the razzle-dazzle.

With the ball on the Notre Dame 25, quarterback Richard Todd handed off to halfback Mike Stock (he was from Elkhart, Indiana, maybe 15 miles from the Notre Dame campus), then raced to the sideline where he took a return pass from Stock and went in for the score. But Alabama missed the conversion try, and the Tide had only a slim two-point lead.

Notre Dame then marched 79 yards in 11 plays. Strong runs by Hunter, Penick, and Clements, and a 30-yard pass from Clements to Dave Casper carried the drive to the Alabama 15-yard line. The Irish got to the 3 but couldn't get any closer before the call went to Thomas.

His kick was true, the game belonged to the Irish, and so did the national championship.

Irish in Their Own Words

FRANK POMARICO

That year, Ara [Parseghian] had broken precedent by making three of us captains. I think it was very close in the voting between me and David Casper as the offensive captain. So Dave was the team captain, I was the offensive captain, and Mike Townsend was the defensive captain, so to speak. We all had different roles. I was more of a quiet leader. I tried to lead by example through hard work during the off-season and tried to do the right thing.

Ara concentrated on ball control and always gave us an advantage as far as blocking rules were concerned. Tom Clements was Ara on the field. He was the fulcrum of the offense because he understood what Ara was talking about, and you could recognize it on the field.

I think the closest we could get to what Ara did was having Tom out there. He had such a command of Ara's offense, and it was a very complicated offense. We had guards pulling one way, backs going the other way; we were always screwing up the defense.

1977

Who could forget the cover of *Sports Illustrated* the week after Notre Dame had defeated top-rated Texas 38–10 in the 1978 Cotton Bowl? A fierce Terry Eurick was pictured fighting through a hole in the offensive line, the caption reading, "The Irish Wake the Echoes."

On the inside, "Shakin' Down the Thunder" was the title of an article about how Notre Dame's victory over the previously unbeaten Longhorns was enough to vault the Irish from fifth to first in the wire-service polls and give the University its seventh wire-service national championship and 10th overall.

The theme for that January 2 matchup in Dallas could have been "and then there were none," for there was not one unbeaten team remaining after the Irish had knocked Texas from its No. 1 ranking. Third-year Irish coach Dan Devine made sure his charges were ready to take care of America's last undefeated team.

An unrelenting defense was the reason why. The defense featured 1976 Outland Trophy winner Ross Browner at one end and Willie Fry at the other, supported by a tough, mobile group of linebackers headed by All-American Bob Golic.

The Irish forced six Texas turnovers in the Cotton Bowl, and an opportunistic offense capitalized on five of them. Notre Dame's devastating strength in the trenches roped up Texas' Heisman Trophy winner Earl Campbell. He managed a tough 116 yards on 29 carries.

Notre Dame's defensive strength came as no surprise in 1977, and it was the primary reason the Irish were near the top of the polls in the preseason rankings. But it was an unexpected boost from the offense that gave Notre Dame the national championship in 1977.

Quarterback Joe Montana and running back Jerome Heavens both rebounded on offense, teaming with All-America tight end Ken MacAfee, who led the team in receiving for the third straight year.

The offense came on strong in 1977 as Montana threw for over 1,600 yards and 11 touchdowns and Heavens led the team with 994 rushing yards. Montana earned a reputation as "The Comeback Kid" with performances like the one he had in the third game of the season when, in his first appearance in more than a year, he engineered the Irish to 17 fourth-quarter points in Notre Dame's come-from-behind 31–24 win at Purdue.

Later in the season, the Irish traveled to Death Valley to play the 15th-ranked Clemson Tigers, and Montana scored two fourth-quarter touchdowns to bring the Irish to a 21–17 win.

Heavens proved himself with 136 yards against Michigan State and followed his outburst against the Spartans with a Notre Dame–record 200 yards rushing versus Army. Two weeks later he went for 100 against Navy.

But the key regular season win came in a mid-season 49–19 thrashing of fifth-ranked USC in Notre Dame Stadium. In that one, the Irish warmed up in their usual blue jerseys, only to emerge in green just prior to kickoff. That triumph helped wipe out the memory of Notre Dame's second-game road loss, a 20–13 defeat at Ole Miss that proved its sole 1977 blemish.

The Irish ran out to a 24–10 halftime lead in the Cotton Bowl and then added touchdowns in each of the final quarters for an overwhelming 28-point victory. Few questioned who was No. 1.

"I don't like to say it was easy, but...well, the way we played today, we could have dominated any line in the country," said Irish offensive tackle Tim Foley on the Irish win over Texas.

"At least the team that beat us was a good one. Everyone can't say that," said Texas coach Fred Akers.

Notre Dame leapfrogged over the four teams ranked ahead of it to grab the nation's top position. Only one time in history (Wisconsin from No. 8 to No. 1 in 1952) did a team make a bigger AP jump into the top slot. The Irish did, indeed, wake the echoes and shake down the thunder.

The Irish that season ranked in the national top 10 in three statistical categories—fifth in total offense (440.0 yards per game), seventh in scoring (34.7), and third in rushing defense (89.2).

Irish in Their Own Words

DAVE REEVE

I think you can sum up the 1977 season with a show we saw during the Cotton Bowl week in Dallas. We went to a restaurant during the week, and Frank Gorshin, who played the Riddler on *Batman*, the television series, came out and did a song and dance that included a tune called, "It's Not Where You Start, It's Where You Finish." We took that song to heart, and before the Texas game, I went up and wrote those words on the chalkboard.

We used that thought as motivation because it didn't matter where we were ranked in September; it was where we could finish after the bowls. We kept believing from the Mississippi game on because we had the schedule on our side, including the USC game, which obviously stands out as the green jersey game.

Irish in Their Own Words

LUTHER BRADLEY

We weren't tight at the start of the 1977 season. We just didn't gel, particularly offensively. We knew we would be real good on defense, and that's the main reason most everyone picked us No. 1 in the preseason. It always takes about two or three weeks for the offense to catch up with the defense. We carried the offense the first two or three weeks but still lost at Ole Miss [20–13]. By the middle of the year, the offense finally caught up and became a machine.

Joe Montana lining up as the third-team quarterback in practice was something we talked about all the time as a first-team defense. We had to go against this guy on the scout team, and he made us look bad. But he wasn't playing, so we knew it was more of a political thing than the fact that he didn't have the talent to play. Eventually, the cream rises to the top, and he did.

Irish in Their Own Words

JOE MONTANA

For me, it was being in the right spot at the right time and having the right things fall into place to be able to get into a game. The one thing I try to tell guys today is that if you're not starting, you've got to practice like you're starting because you may get thrown into a game, and if you're not prepared, you may only get one chance. That chance will blow by you quickly, and you won't get another chance if you're not ready.

I probably wasn't a very good practice player, especially when I was a freshman. I was overwhelmed once I got to Notre Dame, academically and on the football field. When I got here, there were 11 quarterbacks. There were two *Parade* All-Americans, and there were seven freshman quarterbacks. You start to think, *Oh my God, what did I get into?* Coupled with being away from home, as much as I wanted to be here, I really wasn't prepared those first years for what I was embarking on.

So that probably made me a bad practice player. Getting into Ara's offense was difficult for me to learn. I came from a pure numbering system into a pure word system. Some of that stuff is still Greek to me right now.

1988

It wasn't long after Lou Holtz's arrival as head football coach at Notre Dame that he opined that the Irish couldn't expect to be a great team until they were great on defense.

That prophecy came true for Holtz and the Irish in 1988— ironically, just a year after Notre Dame's Tim Brown had captured the Heisman Trophy. But with his departure came a revitalization of the defense, led by senior defensive end Frank Stams, junior linebacker Michael Stonebreaker, sophomore defensive tackle Chris Zorich, and senior linebacker Wes Pritchett, all of whom merited some sort of All-America honors (as did offensive tackle and captain Andy Heck). They were supported by cornerback Todd Lyght, linebacker Ned Bolcar, and defensive tackle Jeff Alm, who went on to earn that same All-America acclaim a year later.

The end result was a consensus national championship for the Irish in 1988, a fitting reward for a perfect 12–0 campaign. The title came in Holtz's third season as Irish head coach, much as Frank Leahy, Ara Parseghian, and Dan Devine before him had claimed national crowns in their respective third seasons as Irish head coach. It came thanks to riveting regular season triumphs over Michigan, Miami, and USC—and it ultimately featured wins over teams ranked first, second, and third in the polls when they faced Notre Dame.

When the 13th-ranked Irish debuted against ninth-rated Michigan in Notre Dame Stadium, Holtz knew his youthful offense would be tested, particularly with a green group of receivers featuring Ricky Watters at flanker in a switch from tailback, plus rookies Derek Brown and Raghib Ismail. His concern appeared legit when Notre Dame did not score a touchdown from scrimmage.

But Watters returned a Michigan punt 81 yards for a touchdown, and unheralded walk-on kicker Reggie Ho knocked through

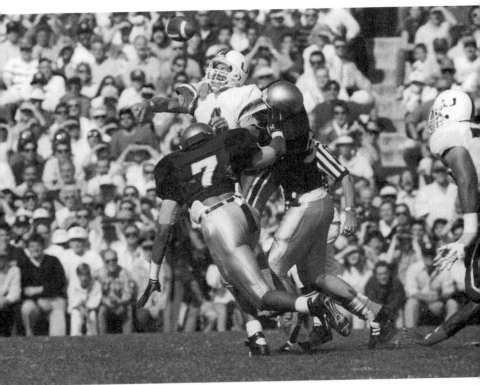

Notre Dame's midseason win in 1988 over top-rated Miami put the Irish in position to bid for the national title. *Photo courtesy of Mike Bennett/Lighthouse Imaging*

four field goals, twice bringing the Irish from behind—including the game-winner with 1:13 remaining. A field-goal miss from 48 yards as time expired by the Wolverines earned Notre Dame a 19–17 opening victory.

Four wins later, the fourth-rated Irish welcomed top-ranked Miami and its 36-game regular season unbeaten streak to Notre Dame Stadium. The streak bit the dust that day by a 31–30 count, as Notre Dame forced seven Hurricanes turnovers and made use of a bevy of heroes, lastly Pat Terrell, who knocked down Miami quarterback Steve Walsh's two-point conversion pass with 45 seconds remaining.

Terrell previously ran an interception back 60 yards for a score; Stams forced two Walsh fumbles, recovered another, and tipped the pass Terrell intercepted; and quarterback Tony Rice threw for a then–career-high 195 yards. The Irish took the lead for good midway through the third period after thwarting a fake punt by Miami and then held on down the stretch. Though Walsh threw for 424 yards, the stingy Irish front line limited the 'Canes to 57 rushing yards.

The season finale found the 10–0 and top-ranked Irish underdogs against second-rated and also unbeaten USC in the Los Angeles Coliseum. Again, it was defense that dominated for Notre Dame in a 27–10 victory. Stams had nine tackles, two and a half sacks, a fumble recovery—and he made life miserable for Trojans standout Rodney Peete. Cornerback Stan Smagala ran an interception back 64 yards for a 20–7 halftime lead after Rice had skirted left end for 65 yards for the first points of the game.

The Irish prevailed despite going 29 minutes in the second and third periods combined without a first down—and in spite of the fact leading rusher Tony Brooks and leading receiver Watters, both sophomores, were suspended the day before the game.

Notre Dame met third-ranked and unbeaten West Virginia in the Fiesta Bowl in hopes of claiming the championship—and the Irish rode early leads of 16–0 and 23–3 to an eventual 34–21 victory, banking on another staunch defensive effort.

Rice ran for 75 yards and completed seven throws for 213 more yards. Meanwhile, Stams had two sacks on his way to the Defensive MVP award, and the Irish dominated a heralded

Mountaineers offensive line that had been one of the main reasons West Virginia had never trailed in a game all season.

Just as it had beat up USC's Peete, the more physical Notre Dame team knocked quarterback Major Harris out of the contest early due to a bruised shoulder and limited the potent Mountaineers ground game to 108 yards.

The Irish finished third nationally in scoring defense (12.3 points per game)—and 22 of the 24 starters eventually were drafted by NFL squads.

Holtz's final pronouncement: "This team will go down as a great football team because nobody proved otherwise. If we are No. 1, I don't care who is No. 2."

Irish in Their Own Words

SCOTT KOWALKOWSKI

We had some great teams. The biggest thing that turned us around the national championship year in 1988 happened in August, right before the season started. We had a scrimmage, and the coaches were pulling us back, kind of pulling back the reins because the hitting was so intense. That was kind of a turning point that year.

We had a good mix of young guys and older guys, good leaders, and that was what put us over the edge. It was our little moment of clarity where we realized, "Hey, we're pretty good!"

Offensively we had Andy Heck, Mike Brennan, Tim Grunhard—all strong personalities. Mark Green, Anthony Johnson…A.J. was one of my favorites. I used to hate going against that guy in practice. He was great. He did everything right all the time. I don't ever remember him messing up. Tim Ryan was my roommate, and he made the transition from linebacker to offensive guard.

Irish in Their Own Words

Frank Stams

There was a great mix between the young and the old on that team. To me, the personalities that were on that defense were so unique. Like [Wes] Pritchett that one day when he took the cigar and went back out on the field. He was smoking it in his helmet. Barry [Alvarez] looked at him like he was out of his mind, and then he cracked up laughing. It was that loose attitude, and it just seemed like the chemistry was really there defensively. The chemistry was there offensively, too; it was just a different mind-set.

I tell people with some seriousness that part of our motivation to be good as a defense was to keep Holtz off our side of the field during the week. If the defense had a bad game, there would be times when he would come down and coach the defense for a couple of days, and it was just miserable, miserable!

Irish in Their Own Words

Wes Pritchett

A lot of things have to happen to win a national championship. You've got to get lucky, you've got to have the right players, the chemistry.... After we beat Miami, there was absolutely no doubt in anybody's mind that we were going to win the national championship. We knew we weren't going to lose.

chapter 10
THE IRISH TEAMS THAT WALKED WITH CHAMPIONS

1919 AND 1920

Knute Rockne's second Notre Dame team in 1919, led by all-purpose standout George Gipp, finished a perfect 9–0—with only one opponent scoring more than nine points against the Irish defense. Many of the Notre Dame players had recently returned from World War I duty. Rockne's team earned championship recognition from the Parke Davis Ratings, but a 9–0–1 Harvard team generally was considered the top team. The start of the 1919 season marked the beginning of a 38-game streak in which Notre Dame would lose only one time (a 10–7 1921 defeat at Iowa).

The 1920 campaign produced the exact same 9–0 record, with Gipp earning first-team All-America honors across the board in his final season in South Bend. The Notre Dame defense again excelled, permitting only 44 points all season and shutting out four opponents. A key midseason 27–17 win over unbeaten Army at West Point featured 150 rushing yards by Gipp plus 207 kick-return yards and 123 passing yards. Notre Dame played its first homecoming game in a 28–0 win over Purdue. Three weeks after Gipp's final game appearance at Northwestern, he died in a South

Bend hospital. Notre Dame tied with 6–0–1 Princeton in the final Parke Davis Ratings—and 9–0 California and 8–0–1 Harvard also received title notice.

1926 AND 1927

Knute Rockne's 1926 defense proved superb in shutting out an amazing seven of 10 opponents. But a stunning 19–0 loss in Pittsburgh to Carnegie Tech spoiled the 9–1 Notre Dame season. Notable was the first-ever meeting with USC, a 13–12 Notre Dame win in the season finale in Los Angeles.

In 1927 the Irish ended up 7–1–1—with a tie against Minnesota and Bronko Nagurski, a tough 18–0 loss to Army at Yankee Stadium, and a narrow 7–6 win over USC in front of 120,000 fans at Soldier Field in Chicago.

1938

This one qualified as a near-miss after Notre Dame won eight straight games to open the season and never allowed more than a touchdown. That propelled the Irish into the No. 1 spot in the Associated Press poll heading into their final two games against No. 16 Northwestern (a 9–7 victory for Notre Dame in Evanston) and No. 8 USC. But the Trojans pulled out a 13–0 win in Los Angeles in great part due to five Notre Dame turnovers. That kept the Irish from beating out unbeaten Tennessee and TCU squads.

1941

Frank Leahy's first team at Notre Dame featured a sophomore quarterback in Angelo Bertelli on a unit that defeated sixth-rated Navy in Baltimore (20–13) and eighth-rated and unbeaten Northwestern in Evanston (7–6). The Irish ranked fourth in the AP poll heading into the regular season home finale against USC. The Irish finished 8–0–1, with the only blemish a 0–0 tie with 14th-rated Army at Yankee Stadium. Notre Dame ended up behind only Minnesota and Duke in the final rankings.

1948

Frank Leahy had to deal with the graduation losses of John Lujack, George Connor, and Ziggy Czarobski—but Notre Dame nonetheless began the year ranked No. 1 in the AP poll and never stood lower than second all season. The Irish offense averaged 32 points per game, and guard Bill Fischer claimed the Outland Trophy. A 9–0–1 record featured nine straight wins, then a 14–14 tie at USC in a contest in which the Irish lost six fumbles.

Irish in Their Own Words

JOHN PANELLI

One of my best games was against Purdue as a senior in 1948. We were in a tough battle, but late in the third period we were behind by a point, and Jim Martin blocked a Purdue punt. The ball bounced around off of several helmets and finally popped out to the side. I grabbed it and took off for the end zone, 70 yards away.

A bit later, Steve Oracko, who had missed two extra points, came through with a 33-yard field goal, and Al Zmijewski intercepted a Purdue pass in the end zone for a one-point win [28–27].

1953

Frank Leahy's final season as Notre Dame head coach produced a marvelous 9–0–1 mark, with only a 14–14 home-field tie against No. 20 Iowa keeping the Irish from a consensus title. With John Lattner winning the Heisman Trophy and contributing in all sorts of ways, Notre Dame opened the campaign ranked No. 1 and held the spot for eight consecutive weeks. Along the way Notre Dame vanquished No. 6 Oklahoma in Norman, No. 15 Pittsburgh, No. 4 Georgia Tech (ending a 31-game Tech win streak), and No. 20 Navy. A 10–1 Maryland team finished first in both the AP and UPI polls, and Leahy resigned on January 31, 1954.

Irish in Their Own Words

RALPH GUGLIELMI

In 1953 the rules makers limited substitutions, which meant that I had to play defense, too. I liked it and led the team in interceptions the next two years. We won every game but one that year, and that was a [14–14] tie with Iowa.

That was the final season for Coach Leahy, and no one admired the coach more than I did. No one worked harder with us to make us better. He was very disciplined and he expected you to be the same. The practices were so tough that the games on Saturday seemed to be easier.

Irish in Their Own Words

DAN SHANNON

The next year [1953] we were battling Iowa in a home game and I was playing both ways, at end on offense and linebacker on defense. Late in the first half, Iowa was leading 7–0, but we were driving. The clock was winding down and tackle Frank Varrichione suddenly collapsed. Naturally, the officials called timeout. One second remained on the clock, and Ralph Guglielmi threw me the game-tying touchdown pass. We did it again in the fourth quarter, and Don Schaefer kicked the extra point for a 14–14 tie. We dropped in the polls to No. 2 because of that tie, and that's where we finished, No. 2 behind Maryland with a 9–0–1 record.

Irish in Their Own Words

JOHN LATTNER

Our 1953 season was remarkable. We defeated Oklahoma in Norman [28–21] in the opening game, which was another time that we had to play in searing heat. We won the first seven games against some top teams.

The Georgia Tech game was played on my birthday that year. We were ranked No. 1 and Tech was No. 4. They had a 31-game undefeated streak. But we grabbed an early lead and were ahead at halftime, 14–7, when Coach Leahy suffered a fainting spell. We didn't know much about it, but Coach [Joe] McArdle handled the team in the second half. They came back to tie, but I remember scoring the final touchdown while the student body was saluting me with their rendition of "Happy Birthday."

Coach Leahy was gone the next couple of games, but we kept on winning and were 7–0 when Iowa came to town. Coach was back, but not looking very good. We played our worst game of the season and tied them [14–14]. We managed to tie 7–7 at halftime when Guglielmi threw a short pass to Dan Shannon. They repeated it late in the game for a 14–14 tie. That knocked us out of No. 1, but we romped over Southern California [48–14] and Southern Methodist [40–14] for Notre Dame's first undefeated season in four years. It turned out that it was Coach Leahy's final game when he retired in late January.

It was a great off-season for me. When I went to New York for the Heisman Trophy dinner, I took my mother along. She had never been on an airplane, and it was her first visit to New York. She had a ball. Having my mother along really made it a memorable trip. She had more fun than I did.

I did receive the Heisman in December of 1953, but not everyone knows that I have had three of them. When I opened a restaurant in the Chicago Loop, we had been there only a few years when we had a devastating fire. I had put the Heisman Trophy on display in the foyer, and it was destroyed in the fire. They were able to cast another one, and I had that on display for a few years in another restaurant. Some time later, Notre Dame wanted to put all seven Heismans on display at the university. So I, along with Angelo Bertelli, John Lujack, Leon Hart, Paul Hornung, John Huarte, and Tim Brown, took our trophies "home" to Notre Dame for this display.

Shortly after that, the Heisman committee decided to cast two trophies each year, one for the player and the other for his school. So that made it my third Heisman Trophy.

When I was a senior, I was featured on the cover story of *Time* magazine. I use the reproduction of that cover for autograph sessions. That green uniform and that leather helmet look a little funny, but that's what we wore in those days.

Irish in Their Own Words

JIM MORSE

On the field that year [1953], when freshmen were ineligible, it was a great season, undefeated with a late tie against Iowa. I don't believe I ever saw a better team, and Coach Leahy called it the best college-aged team he had ever coached. Leahy collapsed at halftime in a game at midseason, and in late January he made the decision to retire. It was mostly because of his illness. He put such a demand on himself to develop a team that he was burnt out, and yet he was only 45.

1964

Ara Parseghian's first season at Notre Dame was perfect—until the final two minutes of the final game of the season. The Irish won their first nine outings, as quarterback John Huarte emerged from obscurity to pair with split end Jack Snow to make up one of the great pass-and-catch pairings in Irish history. With a title in their grasp, the Irish worked to a 17–0 halftime lead in the finale at USC, only to lose 20–17 on a Trojans TD pass at the 1:33 mark. A controversial holding penalty negated a second-half Joe Kantor TD run for the Irish. Notre Dame doubled its offensive yardage total from the previous year, Huarte claimed the Heisman Trophy, and Parseghian was the national coach of the year. The National Football Foundation awarded Notre Dame the MacArthur Bowl.

Irish in Their Own Words

JOHN HUARTE

We were starved for leadership in 1964. But keep in mind that we had the talent to win and that Joe Kuharich brought in talent. You look at that team in 1964, and there were about 20 guys who played in the pros. Maybe a lot of them didn't play more than a year or two, but that shows how much talent we had on that squad. We won most of our games that year going away. Other than Pittsburgh [a 17–15 victory] and USC [a 20–17 loss], we pretty much dominated.

I don't know if we surprised ourselves as much as we were just doing what we were told to do and listening to the instructions of a maestro. We weren't strategists; we were just young kids blocking and tackling. At the time you're just playing football—you're not thinking about grand strategy.

We treated the USC game just like another game. We knew we could move the ball on them and we did. We got them down 17–0 at halftime, but they came back in the second half and played like a hang-loose outfit. They had some players, and a few things happened that got them believing they could win after catching a ball here and a ball there. Then all of a sudden they passed us up and nipped us, and we finished the season 9–1.

The pep rally when we returned home had a phenomenal turnout. To see that kind of appreciation was remarkable. It capped a very dramatic year for everyone. It was an emotional reception that really marked a return to prominence. It was unbelievably uplifting to see how excited the student body was for us to have such a strong team. Maybe because we got nipped in the last game, maybe they felt like they wanted to show us that we were the team.

Winning the Heisman Trophy that year—it's hard for a young kid to realize the power of that award. My parents were treated so well, flown in and shown the red carpet. I was excited that my folks were treated so well.

It was an unbelievable moment, and coming from being an unknown at the beginning of the year made it special. There's a lot of luck and a lot of fate in sports. There are a lot of guys who struggled, but I experienced a Cinderella story my senior year.

Irish in Their Own Words

BOB MEEKER

Once the 1964 season started with a guy like John Huarte at quarterback, I think if you asked most guys, they thought Tom Longo should have been the quarterback because he was such a great athlete. But Ara [Parseghian] saw some magic in Huarte, who of course went on to win the Heisman Trophy.

Then there's the story of Jack Snow, who went from a 230-pound running back to an All-America wide receiver and had a wonderful senior year. Ara had a way of finding talent in guys across the board, plus developing a lot of young guys who helped out in a big way on that 1964 team.

As much as I'll remember that 1964 season as one where guys came off the depth chart to play huge roles, the year, to me, was about how strongly we believed in Ara Parseghian. It was a total commitment to him.

Irish in Their Own Words

ARA PARSEGHIAN

When I went to Notre Dame, the talent was already there. It was a matter of putting people in the right positions, motivating them, and giving them direction. At Northwestern, the talent wasn't near what Notre Dame had, and we didn't have the tradition, facilities, or exposure, either. Add in the incredible spirit at Notre Dame with its history, and we felt we could have something special.

Maybe it sounds strange or you might say it was exorbitant overconfidence, but I really believed it. After our first year when we started 9–0 and won the MacArthur Bowl, Father Joyce wanted me to sign a five-year contract. I said fine, but not because I thought it was necessary. I've always felt if things aren't going well and you aren't doing the job, you shouldn't be there. After the five years expired (in 1969), I did not have another contract that went beyond one year. I did not ask for a lengthy contract or an extension. I respected Father Joyce and Father Hesburgh, and they respected me.

The 1964 season was special because there is a euphoria that comes with turning around a program. You can't duplicate it; you don't want to duplicate it. What I mean is you don't ever want to be 2–7 again and have to try to do it all over. That's something you can—and want to—experience only once.

I would agree with the statement that 1964 was my most fun season as a coach because of the unknown variables heading into the year. When you come into a program that hasn't had success, you have everything to gain and nothing to lose. Once you win, then you become a victim of your own success and you can't ever recapture that renewed invigoration. Climbing the mountain is easier and more fun than staying on top of it.

1970

Ara Parseghian helped convince the Notre Dame administration that the Irish needed to consider playing in postseason bowl games if Notre Dame wanted to seriously contend for the national title— and the 1970 season proved why he was right. With Joe Theismann at the helm, Parseghian's squad won its first nine games and rose to No. 1 in the polls by mid-November. From there the Irish squeezed out 10–7 and 3–0 wins over Georgia Tech and No. 7 LSU, respectively. Then, Notre Dame fell 38–28 in the rain at USC to end the regular season despite a record 526 passing yards from Theismann. Against top-rated Texas in the Cotton Bowl, the Irish prevailed 24–11 and ended the AP runner-up.

1989

A year after winning the national title, the Irish put the finishing touches on their 23-game winning streak by winning their first 11 games of the season, all while ranked No. 1 in the nation. Included in that sequence was a 24–19 win over No. 2 Michigan (on two kickoff returns for TDs by Raghib Ismail), plus victories over No. 17 Air Force, No. 9 USC, No. 7 Pittsburgh, and No. 17 Penn State. Miami handed the Irish a 27–10 loss in the regular season finale in Miami—but Notre Dame bounced back with an impressive 21–6 win over top-rated Colorado in the Orange Bowl. That left the Irish second in the final AP voting.

1993

Quarterback Kevin McDougal was architect of a nifty 27–23 Week 2 win at No. 3 Michigan—and the Irish were off to the races. That victory pushed Notre Dame to No. 4 in the polls, and they stayed at least that high by winning 10 straight games to open the campaign. The 10th of those was far and away the most impressive—a 31–24 triumph over No. 1 Florida State in maybe the most-hyped game ever played at Notre Dame Stadium. In solid position to win a title, the Irish fell 41–39 to Boston College the very next Saturday—and even a 24–21 Cotton Bowl win over No. 7 Texas A&M was not enough to keep the Seminoles from winning the poll vote.

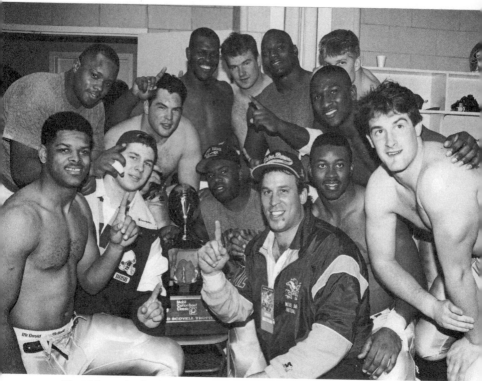

The Irish put the finishing touches on the 1993 season with a Cotton Bowl victory against Texas A&M. *Photo courtesy of Mike Bennett/Lighthouse Imaging*

Irish in Their Own Words

AARON TAYLOR

Before the start of the 1993 season, I think there were a lot of questions surrounding Kevin McDougal following the departure of Rick Mirer. What a job Kevin did! I still, to this day, do not know how he didn't make it in the NFL and did not get drafted. He was unbelievable—not only what he did physically throwing the ball and running the ball and making the plays, but that guy was a winner and he was a leader. We believed in Kevin and we would bust our asses for him, and he would lead us down the field and make plays. We looked at him as our guy.

The loss to Boston College that year was devastating. It was an absolute 180-degree, seven-day period from November 13 against Florida State [a 31–24 victory] to the Boston College loss [41–39] on November 20. I have never been as emotionally high and then so emotionally low.

We didn't sense a letdown against Boston College, but the coaches sure did. We certainly talked about it as players, that we couldn't have a letdown and that we needed to do certain things. But I didn't think we would go out there and play that poorly against Boston College, and the opportunities for us to win that ballgame were so numerous it's ridiculous.

I have never been in a quarter of football like that fourth quarter when we scored those three touchdowns to take the lead. I knew that God loved Notre Dame when I saw Derrick Mayes make that catch. It was a shame that we let it slip away.

We knew coming in they were talking and they were cocky. Joe Moore said up front that these guys were very good on defense. He said, "They run around and they fly to the ball and they are by far faster than any defense we've faced, and we will probably not be able to run outside on these guys, which is okay because we're going to run it right up their ass!"

BIBLIOGRAPHY

Bonifer, Michael, and L.G. Weaver. *Out of Bounds*. Blue Earth, MN: Piper Publishing, Inc., 1978.

Cohen, Richard M., Jordan A. Deutsch, and David S. Neft. *The Notre Dame Football Scrapbook*. Indianapolis/New York: Bobbs-Merrill Company, Inc., 1977.

Doyle, Joseph. *Fighting Irish: A Century of Notre Dame Football*. Charlottesville, VA: Howell Press, 1987.

Heisler, John. *Greatest Moments in Notre Dame Football History*. Chicago: Triumph Books, 2008.

Heisler, John. *100 Things Notre Dame Fans Should Know & Do Before They Die*. Chicago: Triumph Books, 2009.

Layden, Joe. *Notre Dame Football A to Z*. Dallas, TX: Taylor Publishing Company, 1997.

Marder, Keith, Mark Spellen, and Jim Donovan. *Notre Dame Football Encyclopedia*. New York: Citadel Press, 2001.

Notre Dame Football Media Guide. Notre Dame, IN: Ave Maria Press, 2004 and 2011.

Prister, Tim. *What It Means To Be Fighting Irish*. Chicago: Triumph Books, 2004.

Rappoport, Ken. *Wake Up the Echoes*. Huntsville, AL: Strode Publishers, 1975.

Steele, Michael R. *The Fighting Irish Football Encyclopedia*. Champaign, IL: Sagamore Publishing, 1996.

Walters, John. *Notre Dame Golden Moments*. Nashville, TN: Rutledge Hill Press, 2004.

ACKNOWLEDGMENTS

No book of this magnitude, containing the multitude of facts and figures you'll find in these pages, comes together without all sorts of contributors and cooperation. So, here's who we appreciate:

—*Always Fighting Irish* represents the ultimate collaboration. In 2004 University of Notre Dame graduate and longtime Irish athletics chronicler Tim Prister authored *What It Means to Be Fighting Irish*. The book consisted of a series of interviews with former Notre Dame football greats, from Bob Saggau in 1938 to Courtney Watson in 2003. Fast forward to 2012 and you now have *Always Fighting Irish*, a compendium of information about the most noteworthy traditions, games, seasons, people, rivalries, firsts, and championships in Notre Dame football history. Meanwhile, we've cut and pasted Tim's original work, dropping the comments of those players next to material about them or the games and seasons they played. You end up with the ultimate combination of the best of Notre Dame's 125 years of football—with running commentary by those who created that history. Tim has been around Notre Dame football on a day-in, day-out basis for multiple decades—and there aren't many if any Irish players and coaches he hasn't come to know well. That makes his contributions particularly credible.

—I had just turned nine years old in 1963 when Ara Parseghian was named the new Notre Dame head football coach. So I began attending Irish home football games regularly the following fall—and that turned out to be a Camelot-like period in Notre Dame football annals. I came to Notre Dame to work in 1978 and, beginning with that first Joe Montana–led team that season (capped by one of the most amazing comebacks in postseason history in the Cotton Bowl), I've had the opportunity to work with and meet a long list of Irish players and coaches who have made their own contributions to the 125 years' worth of Irish gridiron memories.

—You can't do justice to 125 years worth of football without understanding the roles of all those who have helped to chronicle that century and a quarter at Notre Dame. Start with Knute Rockne, maybe the most talented football marketing guru Notre Dame has even seen. In his day, the sportswriters who covered the college football games also officiated them—and the head coaches did the hiring. Joe Petritz started as the sports information director at Notre Dame in 1929—and he was followed by Walter Kennedy, later to become NBA commissioner. Next came Charlie Callahan and Roger Valdiserri (he hired me to come to Notre Dame), both legends in the media relations business. A long list of other media relations staffers includes Ted Haracz, Dave Kempton, Bob Best, Karen Croake, Eddie White, Jim Daves, Mike Enright, Rose Pietrzak, Doug Walker, plus current employees Bernie Cafarelli, Chris Masters, Michael Bertsch and Brian Hardin—and their efforts have been supplemented by many more interns and student assistants who have been involved in football in one way or another.

—Steve Boda has been retired from the NCAA for some time now, but he played a unique role in recording the accomplishments of Notre Dame football. While serving as the longtime associate director of statistics for the NCAA, Boda (who was born in South Bend) kept arguably the most extensive records anywhere on Irish football. In fact, for years he updated the records section of the annual Notre Dame football media guide. That publication used to include Boda's home phone number (with the numbers listed in reverse), just in case there was a need to call Boda to ask about a record or statistic from a press box somewhere in America.

—I'm sure there are a few people in America who have witnessed more Notre Dame football games than Joe Doyle—but there can't be many. The longtime *South Bend Tribune* sports editor for years qualified as the media authority on what was going on with Irish football—dating all the way back to his days when Doyle and Irish coach Ara Parseghian shared early-morning breakfasts regularly at Milt's Grill in downtown South Bend. When you needed an answer or opinion on Irish football, Joe's was the number to call.

—When I first came to work at Notre Dame, we didn't have a huge staff. It was Roger Valdiserri and I on a full-time basis, with administrative assistants Jeanne Neely and Kim Moses. But we also had an extremely talented group of student assistants on board. Tim Bourret, Ted Robinson, Monte Towle, Craig Chval, Paul Mullaney, Chip Scanlon, Tom Desmond, Brian Beglane, and Leo Latz are among those who quickly showed me what being dedicated to Notre Dame football really meant.

—Photos at Notre Dame come from a variety of sources. Charles Lamb oversees the University Archives and knows all things historical. Carol

Copley understands the Portfolio storage system in media relations. Mike Bennett has been shooting Irish football games home and away for all of three decades. They are responsible for the images on these pages.

—I'll forever be indebted to the late Bill Callahan, longtime sports information director at the University of Missouri. With no full-time assistant on his staff, he put plenty of sports information responsibility in the hands of his student assistants. He took a chance on a young college freshman from Indiana who didn't know much about Mizzou athletics and—despite great intentions—barely knew his way around a manual typewriter. He taught me how to write a news release, how to write a feature story, and what media relations were all about. I'll also forever be indebted to Roger Valdiserri, who opted to hire me at the ripe age of 23—knowing that I'd have to find my way around while working with a football program coming off a national championship and a men's basketball program coming off an NCAA Final Four appearance. He never once looked over my shoulder and he was always there when you had a question—and that's all you can ever ask.

—Most of us who think we can write are our own worst editors and proofreaders. In this case, it's because sometimes you've read the biographies of people like George Gipp and Knute Rockne and the stories of games against Alabama and Texas and USC so many times, you can view the passages in your sleep. That's why I've benefitted immensely from the assistance of my wife, Karen, a proficient writer and author in her own right. She reads my "stuff," she isn't afraid to tell me when it's boring—and she wields a mean red pencil that helps make what follows in this effort better for her contributions.

—Thanks to Beth Hunter, executive director of the Notre Dame Monogram Club, for her exhaustive research on the 1887 Notre Dame–Michigan football game.

—Thanks to former Irish tight end Robin Weber for his amazingly detailed recollections of the Tom Clements pass from the end zone that clinched Notre Dame's win and national championship in the 1973 Sugar Bowl against Alabama in Tulane Stadium.

—To anyone who ever crafted so much as a single sentence about Notre Dame football, thank you. Irish fans everywhere are in your debt.